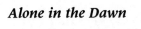

Alone in the Dawn

Karen Alkalay-Gut

Alone in the Dawn

The Life of Adelaide Crapsey

The University of Georgia Press
Athens and London

© 1988 by the University of Georgia Press
Athens, Georgia 30602
All rights reserved
Set in 10 on 14 Meridian
The paper in this book meets the guidelines for
permanence and durability of the Committee on
Production Guidelines for Book Longevity of the
Council on Library Resources.

Printed in the United States of America

92 91 90 89 88   5 4 3 2 1

Library of Congress Cataloging in Publication Data

Alkalay-Gut, Karen.
   Alone in the dawn.
   Bibliography: p.
   Includes Index.
   1. Crapsey, Adelaide, 1878–1914—Biography.
2. Poets, American—20th century—Biography.
I. Title.
PS3505.R277Z54   1988   811'.52 [B]   87-25575
ISBN 0-8203-1016-6 (alk. paper)

British Library Cataloging in Publication Data available

In memory of my parents,

LOUIS AND DORIS ROSENSTEIN

Contents

Acknowledgments

It was because of the work of Susan Smith that I became interested in this project in the first place, because of her encouragement, help and willingness to meet me halfway (Vassar College is midpoint between Cooperstown and Long Island, New York, where I stayed while writing this book) that I felt the work was possible at all.

Without the warm cooperation of Arthur and Jean Crapsey, this book would have been much shorter.

Thanks are due to Robert Walker, who led me on with promises; Hugh and Marilyn Nissenson, who gave me the initial push and a great deal of inspiration; the late Bernard Beckerman and Ann Douglas, who sponsored me as a visiting scholar at Columbia University from 1984 to 1987; Natalie Robins and Chris, for the title and that final burst of confidence; Anne Birstein, for kind, continuous, and much-needed encouragement; and Bandi Gut, for relief from the tedious and arduous tasks of printing and correction. Deborah Guth and Linda Landau proved more than helpful, especially at the finish line.

Thanks also to Edward Butscher, Stanley Barkan, Cyrus Hoy, Aileen Ward, and the entire biography seminar at New York University (1985–1987).

For aid in research, I am grateful to Jim Armstrong, University of Rochester Alumni Association; Barbara Sheiritt, Historic Saranac Lake;

Mrs. Dagmar (Schmidt) Wright and Mr. Oliver Wright; Marinna Morbiducci; Maureen Cobb Mabbott; Edith Martin; Maurice Soanes Gardner; Frances Carpenter, Kemper Hall Alumnae Association; and Alan and Mary Simpson.

In addition to the librarians of Columbia University and Syosset Library, who responded with alacrity and kindness to the most erratic and eccentric of questions, the following librarians and archivists deserve particular note: Mary M. Huth, Special Collections, University of Rochester; Nancy Mackechnie, Rare Books and Manuscripts, Vassar College; Maida Goodwin, College Archives, Smith College; Frank Paluka, Special Collections, University of Iowa; Birthe Cipriani, Library, American Academy in Rome; Kathleen Jacklin, Archives, Cornell University Libraries; Wayne Arnold, Local History, Rochester Public Library; Luella Vines, University Archives, Parkside Library, University of Wisconsin; Geoffrey Wexler, State Historical Society of Wisconsin; Arthur Breton, Curator of Manuscripts, Archives of American Art; Lois Stein, Kenosha County Historical Society and Museum; Marlene Parks, Kemper Center; Raymond Beecher, Volunteer Librarian, Green County Historical Society; and Russell Bastedo, Stamford Historical Society.

The most basic acknowledgments must go to my immediate family, especially to Ezi, Orit, and Oren, who spent their vacations visiting cemeteries, dating tombstones, photographing old houses, and listening to stories of Adelaide—again and again.

An earlier version of the final chapter appeared in *American Literature,* and an article on the last years of Crapsey's life appeared in the *Journal of Modern Literature.*

There may still be errors and inaccuracies. They were made by me despite all this help.

Alone in the Dawn

Introduction: The Return

It is, almost, as though you had not spoke,
but existed merely
as some certain
function of the spring,
and shall return with the primroses.[1]

Adelaide Crapsey did not believe in spiritualism. She laughed at theosophy, joked about ghosts, and—an ex-minister's daughter—was even suspicious of heaven. Yet had it not been for her visit to the house of a friend, months after her death, her poems might never have been published and all her work would have remained forever lost.

The facts concerning her return are simple, clear-cut, and well documented. At 6:45 A.M., July 18, 1915, Eugenie Bragdon awoke from a dream to ask her husband, "Who's Adelaide?" Someone had called, "Adelaide, Adelaide," and Eugenie was certain the message came from beyond the grave.

Eugenie Bragdon, despite what her husband called her "cloistered soul,"[2] had already demonstrated her capacity for attracting unquiet spirits hungering for fulfillment or communication. The ghost of Eu-

1

genie's previous husband was an annual visitor, and the wraith of a mystic black box purchased by the couple to store spiritual messages had told them its long and tortured biography. But these incidents were very different, and Bragdon—an architect and amateur mathematician—was careful to make the distinction. This visitor was the only one who was known to Bragdon but not to his wife. As such, he could verify the information she was presenting to him, information otherwise unavailable to her.[3]

Although the Bragdons were living in Rochester, New York, the visitors did not appear in the sensational manner for which Rochester had become known. There were none of the eerie rappings or mysterious moving tables of the infamous Fox sisters, who had started the national fad of spirit knockings over fifty years before. Messages had come to Eugenie through automatic writing, a medium which was quickly becoming the latest spiritualist fashion.

Eugenie sensed the possibility of an impending message and prepared herself ritually to become a passive agent. She washed her hands, cleared her desk, burned incense to rid the air of influences and distracting aromas, made "the sign of the cross," and meditated "with closed eyes and the lifting up of the head to the Most High" in passive anticipation of a sign. Her right hand was held loose, free of the desk, as it grasped a crow-quill pen lightly between first and second fingers. Then the arm moved, like a lever, from the shoulder, and the pen began to write a delicate wavering script. "It was done effortlessly," Bragdon emphasized, "*automatically,* sometimes in darkness: the eyes saw not, and the mind knew not what was written until afterwards."[4]

The Bragdons lived at 3 Castle Park, a street named after the small castle that fronted it. Their house behind the castle, remote, isolated, intentionally mysterious, was near the picturesque local cemetery of Mount Hope, and Bragdon often found occasion to pride himself on the magnificence of the view and the privacy resulting from such a fortunate choice of neighbors.

In that cemetery an urn containing the ashes of Adelaide Crapsey had been buried nine months before.

Claude Bragdon explained the name to his wife. There were actually two Adelaides. Adelaide Trowbridge Crapsey was a friend, an attractive and dignified woman, married to a well-known leader in the Rochester community. She had had a daughter, Adelaide, who had been an even closer friend but had died of tuberculosis nine months before, just after her thirty-sixth birthday. Bragdon had often exchanged visits with the family of the departed Adelaide in the many years he had lived in Rochester and had even been present at her deathbed. For years he had been friendly with the older woman and fascinated by the younger one. Bragdon had entertained the daughter often at small dinner parties and had accompanied her to her father's trial for heresy at Batavia, amused and relieved by her *sotto voce* commentary. He had recorded in his diaries her arrivals and departures, her injuries, and her illnesses and was obviously attracted to her. Bragdon, who considered himself a man "never long out of love," rhapsodized that Adelaide was a "true daughter of Astarte."[5]

During one of the hardest times for Bragdon, when his first wife, Charlotte, died in childbirth, leaving him with a small son and a newborn baby boy, the Crapsey family attended to him. Adelaide's father, the Reverend Algernon Crapsey, had spoken the only words to console Bragdon over the grave of his first wife, and Bragdon remembered them. "Standing there beside her flower-covered coffin, in our light-drenched living-room, amid the small, hushed company of mourners, the kind wise old man declared that sudden death is only a seeming; that no life ends here until it has reached its appointed term."[6]

While Bragdon was undergoing the trauma of widowerhood, Adelaide came with her brother to comfort him. Although a powerful man in the community and a noted architect (the designer of some of the major edifices in the city, including the local Grand Central Station and the Chamber of Commerce, and the author of a number of books on architecture as well as theosophy), Bragdon was feeling helpless, in great need of spiritual comfort, and his interest in theosophy intensified. Adelaide was wise enough to keep her scepticism to herself at such a delicate moment and was rewarded with reciprocal sympathy when she herself was in need. When Adelaide was dying of tuberculosis at Saranac Lake, Bragdon sent his latest books, a pamphlet on the fourth dimension and *A Primer of*

Higher Space "hot from the press,"[7] to comfort her with his philosophy of theosophy. Doubtless this was his thought as well during his visits when she came home to Rochester to spend her last days in uncontrollable fits of coughing.

Now Eugenie, who had been married to Bragdon for two years, was anxious to discover why this unknown name had invaded her sleep and began the careful ritual that preceded her automatic writing. The response came at once. In a shaky and spiderlike hand, an explanation appeared: "It was an attempt to reach you she is sad for her mother."[8] This first sentence seemed to come from Eugenie's mediator, the intervening spirit who spoke for the silent Adelaide from the other world; the message was clear and Mrs. Bragdon immediately perceived her own responsibility in the world of the living. "Take me to see Mrs. Crapsey," Eugenie said.[9]

Recalling their close relationship, which he had neglected a bit since his recent second marriage, Bragdon brought his wife to see the bereaved family on the same day. The visit was intended to comfort the Crapseys with news from their daughter. It appeared to the Bragdons that it succeeded, since on their return Eugenie sat down once again at her desk and wrote out a message that came from a relieved Adelaide herself: "Know that I am grateful. It is full of terror that I came, but I am glad I doffed the body. Life has been so full here, and I have known things impossible to the flesh. I am going now."[10]

Messages began coming with frequency, inspired either by the dead or by the Bragdons' conversations about the Crapseys. Mrs. Bragdon, who had come to town as a bride in July 1912, had been busy with her stepsons, her new husband, and a younger, more lively set of friends and did not know the Crapsey family. Now they had reason to discuss the subject, and further writings followed.

The next day their discussion continued. "Claude commented on the difference between mother and daughter," Eugenie noted in her regular handwriting on the page of the automatic message, as if putting the spider passage in context.[11] Bragdon remembered the conversation as having a more positive emphasis, but both agreed that the love shared by mother and daughter was great. The two Adelaides had very different temperaments and lifestyles: the mother, wed at seventeen, was preoccupied with her children, her husband's encompassing and demanding way of life, and later her own burgeoning children's clothing factory, and the unmarried daughter was, like her father, independent, scholarly, idealistic, and travelled. Yet they sympathized with one another, accepted their differences, and admired their mutual accomplishments.

As if to reinforce the Bragdons' agreement on the Crapsey family closeness, another message followed: "Great grief purifies and the terror of coming brought us together. It is not remorse, but love for her and for him. My father is in sad need of faith. SSS It will perhaps be possible later. Let it rest for now."[12] Eugenie was in a position to be appreciative of this kind of relationship. Her own mother, with whom she returned to live when her first husband died, "had a Frenchwoman's ideas about filial devotion,"[13] and when Bragdon's courtship was successful despite her objections, refused to attend her daughter's wedding. Eugenie Bragdon was consequently even more impressed, as others had been, by this strange, caring, and nonpossessive love.

Adelaide's need to reassure her parents was repeated in succeeding messages, and Bragdon conveyed these telegrams reiterating the joy of the dead and the comfort the living might reap from this knowledge: "Let me tell you again my story. I died in terror but I found here a strange new beginning   It was a work full of anguish, but so blessed to do   The life that follows death is all so different but so full of thought."[14] Bragdon asked the spirit what he and his wife could tell her father and mother, and this was the reply: "You are good to try and I want them to know that I am glad I died Glad I died   I do not want life; this is so rich in experience."[15] "My wife affirmed," Bragdon recalled, "that as her hand wrote this message she was inundated, so to speak, with a strange gladness, that she felt an unaccountable exultation of spirit, different from anything she had ever known."[16]

Eugenie Bragdon and Adelaide Crapsey were very different. Eugenie Bragdon was a gentle but exotic beauty, with olive skin, sloe-black eyes, and crow-black hair.[17] The woman who made of her a medium was, according to Claude Bragdon, tiny, fair, and bewitching. "Her eyes," he wrote, "were blue grey; her hair was ashen blond; her mouth was large and mobile, and her teeth extraordinarily regular and white."[18] Eugenie was intuitive and dependent, and Adelaide believed in logic and individuality. Despite these differences, the identification of Eugenie Bragdon with Adelaide Crapsey grew so great that messages eventually came literally from the grave. A startling image on July 21 at 6:20 P.M. concludes this series of communications:

> Let me try to be patient SSSS
> from the earth I took a light flower It was on my breast
> father put it there
>
> he was alone SSSS
>
> SSS
> from adelaide
>
> from Adelaide
>
> Goodbye
> SS[19]

The fact that Adelaide was cremated may lessen the possibility of the actual truth of this message but not the strength of the identification.

Dr. and Mrs. Crapsey, both people whose concerns were primarily with the social realities of this world, could not have taken these messages from Bragdon as truth, although they may well have wished to believe them. It had long been Algernon Crapsey's contention that faith in miracles prevents the believer from creating his own miracles, from improving the quality of the world God created, and it was in part for this belief that his authority as an Episcopal minister had been challenged.

Yet one miracle was created by these strange messages from the dead. In the visits that followed it emerged that Adelaide had left behind some poems with the expressed wish that they be published. These were poems of which her parents had known nothing. Only hours after her death her friends handed Adelaide's mother a sheaf of papers and she was apprised of her daughter's talent and her tormented confrontation with death.

Adelaide, otherwise close to her parents, had not kept the knowledge of this poetry to herself out of modesty or shyness. These were not "letters to the world" that never wrote to her. Had all else been equal she would have enjoyed giving her family a mark of her success, a reassurance that this child, upon whom they had pinned so many hopes, had not disappointed them. But the subject matter would have been terrifying, for she had written many of her poems and arranged others for publication in a sanatorium for tuberculosis at Saranac Lake as part of her efforts to comprehend the terrifying fate that awaited her. To permit her parents to experience her struggles and confrontations with death while she was still alive would have been to compound their pain needlessly, and so the "Presentation Piece" was offered only when the struggle had ended. "It was terrible," her mother confessed, "to hold in our hands those poems which reveal what her thoughts had really been through those long months at Saranac; to know that we had been powerless to help her and could only know of her battle when it was ended."[20]

The poems had not been written for her parents, however, but for the world: they were the one chance she had that her existence would not end with her death. She had been unsuccessful with publication while she was alive, and the anticipation of their publication after her death was a small but real comfort. But Crapsey's parents, uncertain about the proper publishers for a manuscript of this nature, had been unsuccessful in finding a place for the poems.

Claude Bragdon had a press which published primarily works on theosophy, and Adelaide had assumed that Bragdon would publish her book,[21] although she neglected to mention this expectation to Bragdon. The family discussions about Crapsey and her poetry, punctuated by the automatic messages transmitted through Eugenie, made this expectation a reality. Within a few months of the spiritual communications, the small gray volume of poetry appeared, and Bragdon's emphatic introduction contributed a great deal to its initial accessibility.

Had Bragdon been less of a connoisseur of the arts he would not have recognized the poems' quality. Had he been married to a less psychic woman he might never have renewed his friendship with the Crapsey family, and the book would not have been published. But perhaps the factor which most determined the bringing of Adelaide Crapsey's verse to the public eye was her own incredible resolution that her story be told after her death.

Despite physical prostration so severe she was forbidden to write more than one letter a day, she had prepared, through two separate friends, copies of manuscripts to be published. Jean Webster, her "literary" friend, circulated one manuscript among publishers in New York and succeeded in getting a poem accepted in *Century Magazine* just before Crapsey's death. Esther Lowenthal, her "academic" friend, arranged for the typing of her poems as well as her complex research on prosody. When the end came, a good portion of the material was ready.

The need to leave behind something eternal was strong in Crapsey. "Dead immortals have passed me by," she wrote in her notebook.

> The ghosts of Gods—who then am I
> to cry aloud for Eternity?
> Yet see them in the farthest sky!
> How when it comes to me to die
> May I be of your company
> Potent wraiths of infinity.

Yet Adelaide Crapsey was not interested in autobiography. Her life, constantly hampered by illness, grief, and impecunity, was nothing like what she had wanted to live, and the discrepancy between what she had anticipated and what she had actually achieved was embarrassing to her. What she wished to record was the struggle with death as a realistic, practical, intelligent young woman experienced it, with no illusions about afterlife and the small hope that her poetry would be a small monument, an insufficient container for her fiery personality, a poor substitute for existence, yet simultaneously an explanation and artistic justification for it.

The form she devised was the cinquain. A five-line poem, it usually followed a specific stress pattern. The first line had one stress, the second two, the third three, the fourth four, and the fifth was shortened to one. Sometimes, however, syllable count was the basis for the structure, and still other poems are based on an interplay between stress and syllabic rules. The basic pattern, however, was maintained in all the cinquains.

There are many possible implications in this form that could be utilized in a poem, but the strongest is that of expanding and curtailed growth, like the life of the poet itself. A cinquain like the following, for example, begins with a sensual expectancy which expands and develops in the subsequent three lines but stops in an inevitable, abbreviated conclusion.

NOVEMBER NIGHT

Listen . .
With faint dry sound,
Like steps of passing ghosts,
The leaves, frost-crisp'd, break from the trees
And fall.[22]

Crapsey's student, Louise Townsend Nicholls, perceived immediately the symbolic significance of this form, "from likeness to her own abbreviated, but perfected life. The five lines, one-stress, two-stress, three-stress, four-stress, and then caught back suddenly again to one-stress, were her life, her young, joyful life, broadening and straining—and then, with a faint gasp of terror at the unfulfillment of promises which life and love and art had made, but still undaunted, caught back again to one."[23]

In this context Crapsey's death could be considered the final line, the proper conclusion completing and fulfilling the poem. It would not have to be the unfair theft of her productive years but a neat consummation of the previous lines. The trick is in perception and structure: like the leaves falling from trees, her entire life, perceived as a cinquain, was not a wasted anticipation of future health and development but an inevitable, artistic arabesque. "Few poets have left," Nicholls noted, "as this one has done, the very outline of their lives stamped into a form which they have made."

But creation and structure were only part of the immortalization of existence. Communication was another aspect, almost as important as the perfect poem itself. Publication, which could not have taken place in her lifetime because of the pain it would inflict on loved ones, could now occur.

Once publication of the book of poems was determined, the tone of the messages became practical and explanatory, recalling another side of this multifaceted woman. During preparation of the poetry manuscript for publication, the spirit seemed to point out the direction of the promotional campaign of the book and to nudge the publishers about the other manuscript that was as yet unattended to: "This immortal residue contains the pearl of a heart sick with terrible despair. It has in it all the poignancy and power of a strong, brave soul doing battle with the Silent Watcher. She left another side of her nature, the work on prosody."[24] The extensive research on prosody, however, was scholarly and incomplete and its conclusion and relevance unclear to the layperson, so this strong suggestion was ignored. How could a person unaware of the necessity for application of scientific methods to poetry, unaware even of the complex infrastructure of each cinquain, be able to appreciate the minute analysis of syllables and syllable-weight upon which Crapsey had labored for years?

The hint was not repeated, and the publication of *A Study of English Metrics* three years later, the result of the individual efforts of Esther Lowenthal, was made on the assumption that the growing interest in Crapsey's poetry would awaken an equal curiosity about its academic basis. So even the publication of *Metrics,* to which Crapsey had devoted so much of her life, was linked to the magical discovery of the manuscript of verse. Adelaide Crapsey, forced by illness and love to be silent when she was alive, was given a voice after her death.

After publication of the poetry, another message was received.

> It is well, I am pleased, accept my gratitude. You have done me a great service; I thank you from the country of the free in thought; so good bye, Adelaide Crapsey.[25]

Bragdon's brief, sympathetic introduction portrayed Crapsey as a romantic ideal, a wraithlike figure even in life: "fair and fragile, in action swift, in repose still, so quick and silent in her movements that she seemed never to enter a room but to appear there, and on the stroke of some invisible clock to vanish as she had come."[26] A ghost called up at night and disappearing at dawn, Crapsey appeared in Bragdon's sketch as quite unreal; and the romanticism of her image was compounded by Bragdon's addition of a second aspect of her character, that fieriness of spirit, destroying the body by the intensity of its spiritual fever. "Although her body spoke of a fastidious and sedulous care in keeping with her essentially aristocratic nature, she was merciless in the demands she made upon it, and this was the direct cause of her loss of health. The keen and shining blade of her spirit too greatly scorned its scabbard the body, and for this she paid the uttermost penalty."[27] This description seemed by many to be an accurate one, and it pleased Mrs. Crapsey so much she wrote Bragdon: "I find myself quite unable to tell you how keenly I feel your deep insight into that lovely personality—I have no criticism to make—I think that you have succeeded in giving to the stranger a most fair picture of the dead—to one who loved her—you have made very vivid—so much that made this a rare person."[28] Mrs. Crapsey must have been reacting to the extremely warm and human lines in the introduction that followed: "Of her passionate revolt against the mandate of her destiny she spared her family and friends even a sigh. When they came to cheer and comfort her it was she who brought them cheer and comfort." She was unaware that despite the literal accuracy, the description had cast her daughter as a contemporary literary stereotype, that of the tubercular writer whose soul burns away the flesh in the intensity of its artistic experience.

But apparently Bragdon and his wife were troubled by the possibility that the portrait was not complete, for after the book was published, on December 12, 1915, the hand of Eugenie Bragdon wrote:

> Eugenie have no contrition
> the book is all that I desire
> I would not a book more [sic]
> choice for it is of the verse that
> I would have them think. Too
> grand apparel too often covers lightness
> of thought ss[29]

Bragdon, who wrote over forty books in his lifetime, many of them weighty, may not have comprehended Crapsey's obsession with spareness, and he felt it necessary to add one long poem of hers to the "Presentation Piece," the manuscript prepared by Crapsey for publication. Even with this poem, "To the Dead in the Graveyard by My Window," the volume remained an extremely spare one, characteristic of Crapsey's closeness and concision. This was a conscious effort on Bragdon's part to represent Crapsey as he knew her and as he thought she would have wanted to be known.

Bragdon tended to believe he had been led into publication by authentic visits from the dead not only because he had implicit faith in his second wife and had long been involved in the occult, but also because he recognized an emphasis and concern in the messages that very much reminded him of Crapsey. "I am quite aware," he wrote, "that all this is of small evidential value as establishing the survival of the personal consciousness after death, yet from my knowledge of Adelaide's character, the circumstances surrounding her death, and her relation to her parents, the messages seem strangely apposite. . . . The messages seem to me to have her own strange 'soul-color,' and this at least is certain; the last unexpressed wish on the near side of the grave—to comfort her parent—was the first to which the oracle gave utterance. Surely, if a liberated spirit such as hers must have been should consent to return to the place of its purgation, would it not be for that?"[30]

But Bragdon's credulity was also influenced by his sense of the dramatic. A book published from beyond the grave by a beautiful, frail, tragic creature was far more exciting a notion than the simple release of brief enigmatic poems by an unknown author. It was this sense of the dramatic that caused Bragdon to omit the information concerning his close acquaintance with Crapsey when he related the story of the publication in two of his books. Psychologically and dramatically he was right. The idea of a passionate voice from the dead was perfectly in tune with Crapsey's poems, and when the book was reviewed it was with the same approach. Harriet Monroe wrote of the "song-impassioned [woman] of this century [who] used her art like a sword to defend herself bitterly against the threatening enemy. . . . And so, 'mistily radiant', she was led off by the conqueror—but not to utter silence and darkness, for the shadowed fire of her spirit burns on with singular intensity in her small book of tragic but exultant song."[31]

As with Sylvia Plath, readers of the posthumous work reacted initially to the person, acknowledging an inability to separate the poems from the tragic death. Herself recovering from tuberculosis, Alice Corbin Henderson admitted her difficulty in separating "Adelaide Crapsey's poems from the circumstances of her death, as recorded in the brief preface written by a friend."[32] Carl Sandburg's response to his discovery of her book also illustrates that paradox of intimacy with a distant, departed stranger.

ADELAIDE CRAPSEY

Among the bumblebees in red-top hay, a freckled field of brown-eyed
  Susans dripping yellow leaves in July,
    I read your heart in a book.

And your mouth of blue pansy—I know somewhere I have seen it rain-
  shattered.

And I have seen a woman with her head flung between her naked knees,
  and her head held there listening to the sea, the great naked sea
  shouldering a load of salt.

And the blue pansy mouth sang to the sea:
    Mother of God, I'm so little a thing,
    Let me sing longer,
    Only a little longer.

And the sea shouldered its salt in long gray combers hauling new shapes on
  the beach sand.[33]

Sandburg's poem is a record of the introductory experience of Crapsey in her poems. The contrast between the vital experience of the living reader and what he elsewhere called the "irreducible glimmer"[34] he encounters in a book, the remote, "reticent,"[35] plaintive voice of the unknown bodyless poet, begging to sing "only a little longer," is the immediate image received of her in her work. Sandburg's emphasis on the violence of the emotion and ephemerality of Crapsey's actual existence with her "blue pansy mouth" is the emphasis Crapsey herself would have warmed to had she indeed been a spirit fluttering about Eugenie Bragdon's elbow.

It is not strange that those who encountered Crapsey or her work reacted with such force to a departed woman. The character and attitude of Adelaide Crapsey were at least in part responsible for it. In the last year of her life, as she obeyed the orders of her doctors and nurse to remain immobile so that she might have some chance of recovering from the tuberculosis that wracked her whole body, she wrote "To the Dead in the Graveyard Under My Window." Her anger at the passivity of death, mercifully masked in her relations with loved ones, screams out here: "How can you lie so still?" she shouted to her neighbors in their graves. "Have you no rebellion in your bones?" She herself would never accept the abject passivity of death:

> And if the many sayings of the wise
> Teach of submission I will not submit
> But with a spirit all unreconciled
> Flash an unquenched defiance to the stars.
> . . . .
> And I will clamour it through weary days
> Keeping the edge of deprivation sharp,
> Nor with the pliant speaking on my lips
> Of resignation, sister to defeat.
> I'll not be patient. I will not lie still.

The poem is a passionate paean to life, to the activity and creativity of life, and it is not surprising that her friends and readers perceived a woman with such personality as attempting to return to the life she loved. Nor is it surprising that the lessons of her return are such benevolent ones—the comfort of friends and the reminder to the living of the beauty and value of life.

The person in this poem, however, is very different from the wraith-like poetess described by Claude Bragdon. Here is a logical woman who knows that her argument with the dead will do no good. She will be dead and no amount of struggling will negate that truth. Death cannot even be made into art, into eternal life, this poem says, and no matter how beautiful and dramatic the legend is, life would have been better. It is this clear-sightedness that is so striking. "Can anyone doubt that the attitude of these poems is one of victory?" Alice Corbin Henderson asks, " 'Keeping the edge of deprivation sharp,' she tasted experience to the full, and as the thought of death could not numb her will, she perhaps experienced death to the full."

While she was experiencing "death to the full" she was also aware of the ultimate insignificance of her experience, and while she fashioned the poems into a volume which she called her "funeral urn" she wrote a "warning to the mighty": "When the pomp is passed away, / 'Here's a King,' the worms shall say."[36]

This is the paradoxical voice of Crapsey, the spirit who returns from the dead through her poetry, reminding the reader that this art is really but a poor substitute for life. And yet, through the voice, she does return, like the primroses with the spring.

Part One

Blossoming plum and cherry,
Flowering apple and quince,
In springtime I was merry
I've learned weeping since,
Bitter weeping since.

Adelaide Crapsey

The Choice to Serve

The surroundings were propitious for a productive, successful, and happy life. When Adelaide Crapsey was born on September 9, 1878, her father, at thirty-one the junior assistant minister of Trinity Church in New York City, was at the beginning of what promised to be an extremely bright career, and the status and economic security his position afforded, and would continue to afford in years to come, would have been such that his children would lack neither social connections nor financial security for the rest of their lives, conditions which would have been ideal for either scholar or writer.

The brownstone house on 28 Orange Street in Brooklyn Heights in which Adelaide was born was situated, moreover, to provide two of the most important characteristics of a neighborhood for the Crapsey family: a rural atmosphere, with water and green areas, and proximity to the excitement and society of New York City. The apartment the newlyweds had first occupied on Van Dam Street when they married on June 2, 1875 was in the city and even closer to the Reverend Mr. Crapsey's church, but it was shared with someone else, and though it was abandoned for a more suburban dwelling as the family began to grow, a social context remained important. From Brooklyn Heights the city was just a short ferry trip away and the church a short walk from the dock. Algernon Crapsey worked long hours at Trinity, both at fulfilling his religious duties and initiating philanthropic projects. And there were many friends, as important and influential as Seth Low and as modest and self-effacing as Sarah Thorne, with whom ideas and plans could be shared for the future of the church, the city, and the society.

For Algernon Crapsey and his twenty-year-old bride Adelaide Trowbridge, society and stimulation were of the essence, but for the three children who lived in that house in the first three years of the Crapseys' marriage the benefits of fresh air were also significant. Since both Algernon and Adelaide had come from small towns—Algernon from Fairmont, Ohio and Adelaide from Catskill, New York—this was an important consideration. Adelaide Crapsey's first outing on October 1, three weeks after her birth, was an event recorded in her mother's diary.[1]

Certainly the first years of their marriage were too crowded for the couple to reap all the joys of marriage and parenthood. Their first child, Philip Trowbridge, was born on March 7, exactly nine months after the marriage, and named after the junior minister with whom the apartment was shared, Phillip Brown. Emily, born one year later, on March 4, 1877, was welcome but must have added to the tumult of the newlyweds' establishment. The third child, Adelaide, who arrived a year and a half after her sister, "strong and healthy" and weighing eight pounds,[2] could not have made much of a difference as far as household management was concerned and might have been received with the indifference and reconciliation with which children are welcomed by experienced parents, an indifference that allows for a more relaxed attitude and the possibility of relationships less charged with parental expectations. But Adelaide did not permit indifference. "She's a strange little bundle," Mrs. Crapsey wrote in her journal, "and needs much nice tender care."[3]

Mrs. Crapsey was happy with her status and her neighborhood, especially since, confined a great deal to her home with her children, she could find things of interest just outside. Since they lived down the street from the Plymouth Church, they frequently saw its minister, Henry Ward Beecher, as he passed by their windows on his way back and forth from "Beecher's Church," as Philip "disrespectfully" called it. "As he went by he always waved to Philip and Emily, who were old enough to wave back."[4] For advice about housekeeping there was a friendly neighbor, Sophonsiba, who was always available and informed. And for in-formation about etiquette she could consult Mrs. Morgan Dix. ("To meet the Bishop? Just wear your wedding dress, my dear.")[5] It was as if by just staying still, everything interesting and good would come to their doorstep.

Years later Mrs. Crapsey was to recall her daughter's baptism on All Souls' Day as one of the more significant moments in that past that au-gured an auspicious future. "I well remember that gray November day we carried her through the old graveyard in Trinity and into the histor-ical church so full of memories. A fitting place for her to be baptized."[6] Dr. Morgan Dix of Trinity Church, minister to the wealthy and well known, performed the ceremony on November 1, insisting the little girl be named Adelaide, and the young Mrs. Crapsey basked in the honor of the event. Her first two children, Philip and Emily, may have had the status of coming first, but they did not come at quite this time of fulfill-ment and security.

Yet these outward forms of status were not foremost on Algernon Crapsey's mind. In the first year of Adelaide's life he was beginning to weigh the possibilities and limitations of his career. He could, he rea-soned, go far in New York City, but buried under the hierarchy of the church he would never be free to perform the kind of social experiments and reforms he longed for. Never would he be in possession of the kind of power he needed in order to provoke change.

Commitment to change was a family tradition. Forty-five years later, as he began his autobiography, *The Last of the Heretics*, which was to be an apologia for his seeming decline from respected minister to ardent socialist, Algernon Crapsey felt it incumbent upon himself to mention his heritage. His grandfather had been a U.S. senator, his career directed by moral convictions. Thomas Morris, the grandson emphasized, moved on his own from Virginia to Ohio when he was still a boy because the latter was a free state and slavery was morally abhorrent to him. He became a lawyer there, then a justice, and finally a senator. "The whole life of Thomas Morris was mastered by a deep-seated, passionate hatred of human slavery as practised in his native State of Virginia. To escape it he exiled himself into the wilderness; to fight it he forfeited his political career."[7] Crapsey then delineated the social decline and moral apogee of his grandfather, which took place, significantly, about the time that Morris's daughter Rachel married Jacob Tompkins Crapsey. Morris's refusal to compromise on the issue of slavery, his absolute belief in the necessity of freedom for all, was the cause of this social decline:

> The political exile, the social ostracism, the religious excommunication of my grandfather was the consequence of a speech made by him in the Senate in the session of 1836. This speech was made in answer to one of Henry Clay in which the Senator advocated one of his many compromises between freedom and slavery. Morris attacked the whole scheme of Clay, root and branch; he would permit no compromise with slavery; he not only defended the right of petition against it; he not only called for its abolition in the District of Columbia, he denounced the whole institution as a foul thing, cruel to the blacks, degrading to the whites, a violation of human rights; a contradiction of the fundamental principles of the American Republic, and repugnant to the Word and will of God. This speech had in it the sublimity of a biblical prophecy—it laid bare the hideous social ulcer and called down upon the sins of the nation the wrath of God. Occupying the attention of the Senate for the better part of two days, this speech closed with these fateful words: "The Negro shall yet be free!"[8]

Crapsey emphasized this particular member of his family and this particular action of morally motivated defiance, although he might have told the story differently or emphasized other characteristics of his noble patriarch. Not content, for example, with the political system as it stood, Thomas Morris joined the Liberty party, and in the last months of his life ran for vice-president of the United States with James Gillespie Birney in 1844. Surely this continued effort in the same direction of political achievement was also worthy of imitation.

There were also other Morrises to whom Crapsey could have pointed to show the significance of his background and others upon whom he could have patterned himself. One uncle, Benjamin Franklin Morris, a minister in the New-School Presbyterian Church, was stricken from the list of heroes for his dullness. This sentence was unjustifiable, for Benjamin Franklin Morris, believing in the principles for which his father had been persecuted, chose to write his father's biography in 1856, "in the humble hope that it will add an additional momentum to the resistless power of a growing public sentiment, that will overthrow the system of American slavery, and give freedom a complete and perpetual triumph over the American continent."[9] Morris's idea—that plodding truth, laid bare before the people, would eventually accomplish as much as the self-destructive defiance of his father—may not have been justified, but there was another book, by Harriet Beecher Stowe, that had an even greater effect on the freedom of the slaves than the speech of Thomas Morris.

Careful to point out that the history of the family was one of freedom fighters, the author became one himself: "Some fell among the martyrs in the reign of 'Bloody Mary,' and others have a place in the history of the Parliamentary struggles with Charles the First, and in the campaigns of Cromwell. Uniformly they were found on the side of freedom, and the name is extant with numerous and honorable representatives in England, Wales, Scotland, Ireland and America."[10] This family tradition even helped make Benjamin Franklin Morris a freedom fighter, despite his lack of dash and sparkle.

But Algernon Crapsey did not perceive the relation between his uncle and himself, although he too wrote numerous books of various degrees of social and religious reform as well as one exemplary biography. The Reverend Mr. Crapsey had other alternatives: he might have modeled himself after any of his other maternal uncles, two of whom also served in the U.S. Congress. The eldest uncle, Jonathan David Morris, "after filling with ability for nearly twenty years the clerkship of the Supreme Court,"[11] lived a successful but relatively uneventful life, serving two terms in Congress. Dying in 1875 at the age of seventy, he was certainly well known to his nephew, both as child and adult, but "dullness" too must have disqualified Jonathan David Morris.

Isaac Newton Morris, however, was a more exciting and practical role model for an ambitious young man. A lawyer at the age of twenty-three, he practiced first in Warsaw, Illinois and then expanded by moving to Quincy, Illinois. Declining the appointment as secretary of the state of Illinois at the age of twenty-eight, he waited another year to become president of the Illinois and Michigan Canal Company and began to promote the construction of the Northern Cross Railroad. Beginning in the state House of Representatives in 1846, he moved to Congress and served in the 35th and 36th Congresses, then stepped out of politics, retaining his post as commissioner for the Union Pacific Railroad until he died, at the age of sixty-seven, in 1879. It was Isaac Newton Morris who gave Algernon Crapsey the first bit of significant advice he received when he was an aimless boy, sent to work in the Dead Letter Office in Washington, D.C., while his Uncle Franklin took off six months to complete the biography of his father. "Uncle Isaac" told the uneducated sixteen-year-old boy to press forward to New York City and make his career there rather than return to Ohio, and this eye for opportunity was one that Algernon appreciated. Only after Isaac's death did Algernon Crapsey consider leaving New York City.

But, although proud of his uncle's business acumen and his own organizational abilities, Algernon chose to form his own image on the risky model of the idealistic and humanistic pioneer. "Thomas Morris was not a politician, not even a statesman in the popular sense; he was a seer and a prophet, a hero and a martyr."[12]

Algernon Crapsey barely acknowledged the existence of his father, a lawyer, "a Calvinist Baptist in religion—in politics a Democrat,"[13] whose dreams of benefiting his community resulted in the failure of his family's fortunes and the conclusion of formal education for Algernon at the age of eleven. The story is told briefly and matter-of-factly, and no responsibility or blame is assigned. "When I was about eight years old my father removed from the town of Fairmont to the village of College Hill where we resided for four years. During this period I learned by letter and mastered the rudiments of what is called education. . . . while we were living in College Hill, my father gave the most of his time to create a pleasure park for the benefit of the people of Cincinnati, this to the neglect of his business. The scheme was a failure."[14] That the Reverend Mr. Crapsey, while recalling his father's failure and the "ghost of want" that "sits at table,"[15] nevertheless chose to ally himself with the idealistic pioneer of the family is a true mark of both his strength and his weakness, the characteristics that would affect the lives of his children as dramatically and completely as his own had been affected.

Now, in New York City, the frustration of being a mere figure in the religious hierarchy was not caused by a desire for power but a vital need for freedom. His autobiography reveals a man trapped:

> When I reached my thirtieth year I awakened to the fact that I was drifting with the currents of life. So far my ministerial career had been a series of seemingly fortunate accidents. I had not shaped my destiny from within; it was the result of the play of external forces. As matters stood, my way lay plain before me. I would hold my job as junior assistant minister of Trinity parish until the senior assistant died or was retired on a pension; that he should resign was not within the range of possibilities. I could look forward to at least twenty years of subordination, when my waning energies would unfit me for new and constructive work. My relations with my immediate superior were becoming more and more difficult with each succeeding day. If I consulted him he was sure to frustrate any plan that I had in mind; if I did not consult him he was naturally offended.[16]

The hunger for freedom of operation and for the power to do good in the independent manner that characterized both his father and grandfather was to motivate his career moves as well as his politics throughout his life and to influence the financial, emotional, and social situation of all those he loved.

But there was another hunger as well. Algernon Crapsey needed, more than almost anything else, to speak and be heard. "It was the call to preach that determined my entrance into the ministry of the Church," he noted and then described the circumscription of the sermon opportunities of the junior minister, who could be called on to preach only twice a month and then at different churches in the parish. "This circumstance forbade his exercising any intellectual or spiritual influence over the minds and souls of the people and it bred in the man, himself, intellectual and spiritual sloth."[17]

If his unconscious motivations were egocentric, he was not at all aware of this but perceived himself, with a great deal of idealization, as the "simple pastor of a simple folk."[18] When Rochester, New York became a possibility, he felt that here was a chance for him to do all the good he had been meant for.

The Reverend Mr. Crapsey might have chosen more solid ground, might have returned home to Ohio or found a small community to lead that was nearer his wife's family and closer to security. Had he waited until a position became available in the neighborhood of Catskill, he would have had the backing of his father-in-law's newspaper, the *Catskill Examiner*, a relatively powerful voice in the peaceful area. At this time, the *Catskill Examiner* was occupied with two major local issues: the preservation and acknowledgment of the superiority of the historic Catskill Mountain Home, a rustic hotel preserving the ideals of the natural life popular a generation before, and the persuasion of the antagonized resident community to accept Jewish summer vacationers into the hotels. In the months that the Reverend Mr. Crapsey was casting about for a community, Trowbridge was writing, "In the limits of our village we have a number of these descendants of Solomon and if we have observed rightly a better class of visitors could not be desired."[19] Despite a number of outbursts of anti-Semitism, from the terrorizing of the guests of a small Jewish hotel to the refusal of the Grand Union Hotel to accept the Jewish banker Joseph Seligman, the calm and reasonable opinion of Trowbridge was winning out.

The Reverend Mr. Crapsey would have found a people willing to learn and a progressive congregation inspired by the vastness and beauty of their environment to a simple respect for nature and religion. But to choose Catskill, despite his familiarity with the area (he had studied for the ministry at nearby St. Stevens College and met Adelaide Trowbridge there) and despite the ease and comfort for his wife of her relatives during his long hours of pastoral duty, would once again be to accept a lesser position, one controlled by his in-laws. He preferred to brave the unknown, going off alone, like his grandfather, into the wilderness.

At the age of thirty-two, the Reverend Mr. Crapsey travelled to Rochester with his friend from the seminary, William Bradley Douglas, to visit the new parish Mr. Douglas's father had organized in place of the failed St. Clement's. He was impressed with Mr. Douglas, drawn to the challenge of the small new parish, St. Andrews, and took the job. "I did not do what any sane person ought to have done," Mr. Crapsey later perceived. "I did not go out into the city, visit the clergy and make any inquiries as to the reason for the failure of St. Clement's and the general prospects of the church in that neighborhood."[20] He did not inquire further because the less there appeared to be finished and settled the more there was for him to do. Because so little was established, Mr. Crapsey would be able to start from scratch, to build a community out of the materials of his imagination. His plan was a perfect one for the nurturing of his soul and his imagination. It was not at all founded on personal practicality.

His action was indeed rash but characteristic of the impulsive idealism of which he was secretly proud. "I resigned my position as a junior assistant minister of Trinity parish at a salary of four thousand dollars a year, paid the first of every month by check on the Chemical National Bank, and accepted the rectorship of St. Andrew's Church, Rochester, at a salary of fifteen hundred a year, which, when paid at all, was in the pennies of the collection."[21] His statement rings with the acknowledgment of the financial sacrifice he was to make and, in retrospect, of the ultimate sacrifice to his career and his own and his family's happiness. For had Mr. Crapsey remained in New York City it is quite possible that the radicalization of his ideas might have been accommodated within the relatively liberal and sophisticated structure of the local church. His move to Rochester at once allowed him the freedom of isolation to develop his own ideas and ultimately prevented the fulfillment of these ideas. Like his daughter years later he would be placed in the position of Moses, with the knowledge of the sufficiency of his own potential, the rightness of his goals, the yearning to enter the promised land, and the overwhelming, painful, external ban.

Rochester

Moving a large and still growing family to another city was not a simple task, and to provide the reverend with sufficient time to transport their belongings and prepare a suitable environment for them, Mrs. Crapsey took her children to her parents for a while. Adelaide was six months old when her father left for Rochester and she was brought to visit the Trowbridges in Catskill-on-the-Hudson, where Mrs. Crapsey had grown up.

Marcus Henry Trowbridge and his wife, Harriet Gunn, were very close to their grandchildren, particularly the rambunctious Adelaide. The only grandparents the children knew well, the Trowbridges were perfectly suited to their role. Living in a resort town that had both the benefits of small-town country life all winter and the excitement and controversy of the growing tourist class in the summer, they were people who did not feel the need to leave their beloved home: the world came to them. Unlike the Crapseys, they were secure and placidly settled people, and despite the fact that he was a learned man, particularly in the area of English and German politics, Marcus Trowbridge of the *Catskill Examiner* was fondly described as "wedded to his home and office."[1]

The Catskill Mountains were still a focus of attention as a result of the current emphasis upon raw and beautiful nature. John Burroughs, considered a literary figure as major as Emerson, wrote many books about

28

the profound pastorality of this area where he lived. The Hudson River School of Painting glorified the unspoiled magnificent beauty of the Catskills, and visitors and residents alike believed in the restorative powers of the healthy mountain air and the simple food and conditions. The belief in the healthy and simple life was not ignorance or fear of the grimy industrial world: it was a philosophy, part of the transcendental movement. And the newspaper reflected this philosophical yet practical and basic attitude toward life.

One result of this was the concern in the *Examiner* with the moral education of youth. A young man who died (probably of choking) while visiting the big cities became an example to the editor of youth foolish enough to desert home, dying therefore "without the ministering hands of loving parents,"[2] and a seventeen-year-old girl who eloped with a "separated" man was held up to the town as proof of what can happen when parents do not keep their children in hand. This philosophy of moral intervention differed from that of Adelaide's parents, but the tone of sympathy was the same, and the *Examiner* was proud to point out the virtues of children and to print the list of children who had not missed school each semester. While the Crapsey children were visiting their grandfather, Trowbridge's paper covered "Children's Day" on June 8 at the Methodist church, reporting with favor that the singing was done by the children and the sermon was on "the Child Jesus."[3]

Although Adelaide's maternal grandparents had very different attitudes from her parents, and the character of Marcus Trowbridge, "a brave follower, not a leader,"[4] contrasted to that of Thomas Morris, their politics were the same. Marcus Trowbridge was one of the few new Republicans in Greene County in the 1850s, and his staunchly antislavery party was opposed by the proslavery Democratic majority. When the times changed and Trowbridge's issues became popular, his newspaper, which had been, when he and his brother-in-law purchased it in 1840, an organ of the Whig party, prospered.

The concerns of the editor were literary as well as political. He "took great interest in literature and liked nothing as well as to talk upon literary topics."[5] While Trowbridge was editor, the *Examiner* regularly published three or four poems and another poem or story in the "children's corner" on the front page. These were the areas belonging to Harriet Gunn, who, with two adult children, had time to pursue her poetic and editorial interests. Yet her tastes were channeled to the fashions of the times, and Mrs. Trowbridge was as likely as her husband to chuckle a bit over the visiting Walt Whitman, "who possesses about the wildest imagination of American poets."[6] Mrs. Crapsey's brother also wrote verse, of which one example survives:

> If you or I today shall die
>> The birds would sing the same tomorrow
> The vernal spring her flowers would bring
>> And few would think of us with sorrow.[7]

But the stable, conventional life of the Trowbridges was tangential to the main event at this point. The focus was upon Algernon Crapsey's new position and his excitement over its potential. He took five weeks to organize himself in Rochester before he began his duties on June 1, and he used this time to become better acquainted with the town and its people. "I made my home in the rectory," he recalled, "taking my meals with Mr. William Dove, who happened to be my twin, born the same day of the year."[8]

Through Dove and the others he met at this time he began to understand some of the possibilities for initiating change in this rapidly altering city. Many new people had come to the town in recent years as a result of growing factory industries and were in need of an anchor, a direction. Even among the population of peoples from the area who had come to the city to find work, this need was not only religious but practical, a substitute for the wholeness and direction of small-town life. And there was a growing number of German and Italian immigrants whose language and skills limited their adaptation to the New World. With his innovative experience with vagrants in New York City, the Reverend Mr. Crapsey felt he knew just what kind of establishment to create and was anxious to begin his work.

His enthusiasm for his new position and his new friends, however, was not matched by a concern for his immediate charges. On the first of July his wife and children disembarked from the canal boat to Rochester[9] and were taken to the rectory at 18 Ashland Street, anticipating, no doubt, a home similar to the one they had left on Orange Street. Her husband had been living there for well over a month, and it was assumed that any alterations or improvements that had to be made were already completed. "When my wife joined me . . . she was utterly cast down; the conditions seemed hopeless. The rectory had been neglected; there was no bath, nor proper sanitary provisions; in nothing was my stupidity more manifest than in the fact that I had not seen this state of affairs and made its remedy a condition of my coming. If retreat had been possible, our stay in that parish would not have lasted a year or a month, or a day."[10] The fact that he had not noticed the condition of the rectory until Mrs. Crapsey arrived was characteristic. His concern for fulfilling the ideal of leading a flock "of a free and open church in a working class district"[11] blinded him to practical considerations, and he was fortunate that his marital partner was of both an understanding and a more practical cast, for she, although eight years his junior, at least opened his eyes to what was needed and forgave his absorption in his work.

Nevertheless, a general depression followed their move. It was rumored in New York City that no one would leave a position like the one Mr. Crapsey had left had he not been sent away, and despite letters of praise by his former superior, Dr. Morgan Dix, and the spontaneous decision of Trinity Parish to continue to pay his salary until September, Algernon Crapsey felt a redoubled need to prove that he was indeed motivated by the highest, and not provoked by the lowest, goals.

Contributing to this need to prove himself was the welcome the new minister received in Rochester. "I had a vision of the people crowding to see and hear the distinguished man who had condescended to undertake the task of enlightening the dark places of the little city of Rochester, bringing to it the wisdom which he had acquired in the largest parish of the largest city in America. I was cast down when I saw my little chapel with only twoscore sheep to wait on the ministration of the newly arrived shepherd."[12] There was simply little anticipation in the community for one such as Mr. Crapsey, no knowledge of the existence of a gap Algernon Crapsey was to fill, and, although the Crapseys were duly welcomed with a "delicious breakfast," "spring chickens, butter, cream, milk, cake, vegetables," and "fresh flowers planted in the garden,"[13] it was clear to him that both he and his family would have to work as if they had no previous status or credentials to make their presence needed and known.

One of the reasons so little attention was paid to Mr. Crapsey and his family was that no one expected him to remain. Two ministers before him, Mr. Flack and Mr. Bonar, had arrived preparing to ignite the community, and both had left within a year. There were other reasons, however, that encouraged Mr. Flack and Mr. Bonar to depart so rapidly. St. Andrews, in this time when parishioners walked to their centrally positioned neighborhood church, was planted in a Catholic community. The Maloney, Daugherty, and Kehoe families who lived around the rectory belonged to a different church and could welcome Mr. Crapsey only as a neighbor, not as a minister. The few parishioners nearby were working-class people, fully occupied with their employment and not immediately available to throw themselves into church activities. Mr. Crapsey perceived all this as an added challenge—until he was joined by his wife and children and the daily reality became more apparent.

The street was dirty and dismal to the new rector's wife, and the rectory very different from what she had supposed. Used to the busy social and cultural life of New York City, the Crapseys found Rochester provincial. Mr. Crapsey had also failed to notice that Ashland Street was not the most active and interesting of neighborhoods. "The rectory is very different than I supposed," the young wife confided to her diary. "The passage of a wagon was an event."[14] Algernon Crapsey noted and sympathized greatly with his wife's pained reaction to this isolation. Her youngest child, Adelaide, was less than ten months old, her eldest still too young for nursery or school, and she was confined to her home and the silent neighborhood by her maternal duties.

But it was the daily duties of the housewife that helped Adelaide Trowbridge Crapsey to overcome her shock. "The children must be cared for; breakfast, dinner and supper must be prepared and eaten; tables laid and cleared away; beds made; rooms set in order,"[15] and within months Mrs. Crapsey was again pregnant. Paul Bontecou was born on August 24, 1880, and added to the activity. As a child of a small family herself, now left to herself by a busy husband, Mrs. Crapsey found her children good company as well as hard, distracting work.

There were visits from the Trowbridges and Crapseys and other family celebrations to maintain a sense of continuity in change. For her first birthday Adelaide was given a tea party with a large cake. On this occasion her mother noted the development of her personality: "A year ago today our little daughter came to me and she was a tiny bundle of humanity and now she is running all around laughing and making us laugh at her funny ways."

Algernon and Adelaide Crapsey also found other solutions to their isolation. By allowing themselves to become entirely available to others and making themselves as useful as possible, they found within a few years they had moved the community to their door. "This loneliness," wrote Mr. Crapsey, "had been our salvation. If we had entered at once the social life of the city, going here and there and everywhere, we should never have entered into the lives of our people and made ourselves their servants as we were compelled to do in order to escape from the loneliness of our situation."[16]

There were plenty of people to help. The growing industrialism of Rochester was resulting in the common tragedies of poverty, families without breadwinners, unemployment, and injuries, and for people who had left their families and their native countries there was no insurance but the mercy of the church. The Reverend Mr. Crapsey had little money but was anxious to help—to actively seek employment for a new widow with children, to help a young mother cope with the problems of managing a household and children, to assist a young man who had fallen into crime because he had no trade. Mrs. Crapsey helped as well, particularly with the problem with which she had the most personal experience—clothing for infants and home economics training for young mothers.

Scarcely two years after the arrival of Paul, Rachel Morris (August 14, 1882) was born and was followed by Algernon Sidney (September 29, 1884), Ruth Elizabeth (August 12, 1887), Marie Louise (November 21, 1891), and Arthur Hunt (February 19, 1896). By the time Adelaide was eight, she had four younger siblings. No one child could expect too much personal attention, and, predictably, Mrs. Crapsey found herself often overworked. Although she often had a cook and someone to help her, Mrs. Crapsey was frequently in need of rest during her children's early years. Nevertheless she continued to enjoy the uniqueness of each child.

At less than a year and a half old, little Adelaide exhibited amazing verbal skills and a poetic bent. "Adelaide is quite wonderful. She learns so quickly and we delight in hearing her say her different rhymes. I almost thought she learns too much. I try to stop them when they figure long lists of things she knows." Her pronunciation and memory were exhibited when she repeated the last word of each line:

Say in the early *morning*
When the air is *cool*
Look at little *Adelaide*
Going off to *school.*[17]

One result of this outward directedness and the size of the family was that the children were allowed to grow up, as much as possible, on their own. This was a policy of the family, even though Mrs. Crapsey found it hard to let go of them. Before she was nine, Adelaide went off to the Catskills with her older sister and brother and another child "a little older than themselves." Their mother "watched them go away with a heavy heart and they left with high spirits filled with plans for the summer. It is always hard for me to see them go."

Difficult though it might have been, Mrs. Crapsey kept to her policy. "To her," the biographer Mary Osborn wrote, obviously paraphrasing Mrs. Crapsey's remarks, "a family was a collection of personalities, to each of whom courtesy was a duty and reserve was a right."[18] The effects of this philosophy were in evidence throughout the lives of her children. Mary Delia Lewis, who knew Adelaide Crapsey well, underlined "her strong belief in the essential right of every individual, however intimate a friend, to unexplained acts and motives,"[19] an evaluation that was repeated by many who knew her. The paradox of a situation of constant companionship together with value placed on privacy and individuality permeated the lives of the children as well as the parents, and Adelaide learned to be extremely sociable while containing her secret thoughts.

"In a large family," Algernon Crapsey noted, "the children always run in pairs."[20] Since they were the only consecutive children of the same sex for a long period, Adelaide and her older sister Emily became constant companions and were frequently paired. They played together and were sent together to their grandparents for the summer, usually accompanied by their father, who continued to be more mobile than his wife throughout his life. "Older inhabitants of Catskill, New York," wrote Sister Mary Edwardine, who had interviewed and corresponded with numerous people acquainted with Adelaide, "still remember the two little girls. . . . Together [they] roamed the low hills near the village."[21] Their older brother Philip remained more attached to their mother and could sway her more than all of her children.

The kind of drive and sense of leadership Algernon Crapsey exhibited was early evident in his daughter Adelaide. Though the younger of the two sisters, Adelaide was the leader, and, with her boisterous sense of imagination and humor, led her serious, sensitive sister into experiences she might not otherwise have had.

Perhaps it was during this difficult period when they were left so often to their own devices that they grew inseparable, acutely sensitive to each other's feelings and needs. Even before Adelaide was two, there was evidence of this closeness. As they played together at the building site of the new church, Emily noticed a stained glass window and asked the workman who the person in the window was. "Saint Philip," she was told, and, aware that both her sister *and* her brother were named after special characters, she began to cry. "And where," she demanded, "is Saint Emily? I want Saint Emily!" She burst into tears, and her wailing was soon amplified by her sympathetic sister, until Mrs. Crapsey came out to explain that there was no Saint Emily. There was no Saint Adelaide either, for that matter, the mother added, not realizing that Emily's protest was more general.[22] Though not at the age where she could speak easily, Adelaide, with no reason of her own to cry, joined her sister and continued throughout her childhood and adult life to identify with her. She pleaded Emily's causes to her parents, adding her own needs in parenthesis, and sometimes could get her way with a subtle version of the reminder, "Emily did the same thing last year."

As the younger child, Adelaide was shielded by Emily and used her sister as a role model. Yet she also "strongly dominated her,"[23] encouraging her sister to follow along a path Adelaide had forged and then returning the title and responsibilities of leadership to the elder.

Both girls were treated alike and performed similarly well in the same schools. But there was really no competition. Emily was far more of a traditional, beautiful, domestic, and submissive girl, and for Adelaide to capture her share of the attention it was clear that she would have to forge her own way. She consequently turned from the traditional concept of the perfect young lady and became perfect in other things—wit, her studies, swimming. She could compete with and even beat her older sister in school, but in beauty, sympathy, and ministrations Emily was special.

As the conditions at St. Andrews improved, the Reverend Mr. Crapsey began seeing reason for pride in his situation. The new church, which had not been built when he came to Rochester, was completed in the spring and summer following his arrival by the architect son of the man who had designed Trinity in New York City. Made curious by the praise for his sermons and his enthusiasm for his work, people began trickling in and Algernon Crapsey began to believe that there might be a chance to fulfill the dream of creating his own Trinity. His wife planted an English garden around the church and the rectory, adding to its dignity and the family's sense of significance. "Standing at gaze, one might imagine oneself in Surrey and think of English parsons and squires, ladies of quality and dames of high degree."[24]

Mr. Crapsey was justified in his growing feeling of accomplishment. Not only had he succeeded where others had failed, but he succeeded well beyond the expectations of his critics. The new church, which would seat five hundred, was built when Mr. Crapsey had a congregation of sixty, which he had built up within months from forty. It did not take him long to fill it up completely.

Mrs. Crapsey considered this period one in which the children grew up "under the shadow of the church, and closely bound to a father who stood for all that was highest in the spiritual world."[25] The Reverend Mr. Crapsey took his calling very seriously and invested every aspect of his life with the holiness he felt emanating from his religion, and his wife was in awe of his power. When she was left alone in Brooklyn while the future rector surveyed the situation in Rochester, she was required to conduct prayers herself for the children and the servants, and she trembled at the magnitude of the task of replacing her husband.

His dramatization of the dogma of the church encouraged the involvement of his family and his parish. Good Friday, for example, offered "the opportunity for the exercise of my peculiar gift of meditation."[26] This day demanded for Mr. Crapsey not only special prayers but an immersion in the last days of Jesus. To feel the emotional charge of the days of the "arrest, trial, conviction and death" of Christ, the knowledge of the inevitability of the crucifixion and the impotence in its face, was the goal of the ritual, and Algernon Crapsey made his entire household participate completely in this event. "On that day we set our house in order as if there were someone dead in the house. The closed shutters shut out the light of day. The children were confined to the nursery; no food was cooked that day. The lights on the altar were taken away and the Cross on the altar was veiled in black. We had what is called the dry communion, no bread was broken, no wine was blessed. When Death himself was present we needed no symbol of death. We looked forward to it with eagerness. On every Good Friday we indulged ourselves in the luxury of grief. . . . As soon as the sun set on Good Friday, we were as people coming home from a funeral: The shutters were opened to the light of day; the children were released from the nursery; the table was laid for dinner and life went on as usual."[27] Religion was vital, immediate, alive, personal. Like Caravaggio, Mr. Crapsey set a place for a spectator at his table of the Last Supper, inviting him to become involved, encouraging him to see his own significance in history.

The immediacy of religion strongly affected Adelaide, who grew up with such a familiarity of the Bible and the church service that they were neither remote nor awesome but a part of daily life. She did not grow up to tremble before her God but discussed, chuckled, questioned, and criticized. Her individuality and pluck were well appreciated by her parents. Adelaide's mother recounted to Mary Osborn that she found the young Adelaide in the rectory one day as the family was anticipating a visit from some ministers trying to open the shutters which had been closed in order to achieve the proper dim light for a dignified meeting.

"What are you doing?" asked Mrs. Crapsey.

"I am trying," Adelaide explained gravely, "to let some light in on the clergy."[28]

Children often make remarks that seem to the parents to be wiser than the children understand. By encouraging these remarks, parents urge a direction on their children, and in the case of Adelaide, this direction was one of the innocent prophet, the child who sees through the stuffiness and hypocrisy of society and does her best, by humorous remarks and harmless comments, to awaken this acknowledgment in others. She was early encouraged to help her father keep a perspective on the seriousness of his position, a perspective which, given the slight tendency to pomposity exhibited in his autobiography and his love of honesty, he knew he needed.

Adelaide became a gentle nonconformist. Although she loved the church and its rituals as her father did, she was also able to laugh at an early age, not at the divine but at the human pretension. "Douglas is saved," she wrote of a friend of Emily's. "I wonder wheather [sic] he intends to be any 'gooder' than he was before. . . . I don't believe I ever laughed so much about anything in my life."[29]

Kemper Hall

When I was about six years old I suffered what seemed to me a
shameful wrong. I was seized by violent hands, and, in spite of
screams and kickings, I was dragged away to what was to me a
prison house and a torture chamber. I was sent to school, literally
sent. No healthy child of six ever went to school of his own accord;
he had to be dragged or driven there.[1]

Mark Twain could have written this description, but in
this case it is the Reverend Algernon Crapsey voicing his disgust at the
school system. It was common of him to portray the concept of education in such extreme and liberal terms and he continually pointed out
with pride the independent direction of his own education, noting that
he had left school at an early age and only returned as an adult when an
internal goal made education reasonable. This individuality of spirit also
made it possible for him to continue learning even after school and to
change his intellectual ideal from Cardinal Newman to Charles Darwin
to Karl Marx.

Algernon Crapsey believed that true education could only take place
if it conformed to the desires and will of the individual. "The present
writer," he writes in *The Rise of the Working Class*, "was once possessed of

a dog, which he desired to teach obedience. The dog had a habit of going under the bed to lie down. Every time his master commanded him to come from under the bed he disobeyed, and the master was compelled, if he would have obedience, to command the dog to go under the bed or to stay under the bed. So it is in our modern family. The will of the child is paramount, and the will of the parent must conform to that if there is to be peace at home."[2]

The Reverend Mr. Crapsey attempted to give his own children and the children of his parish the tools and background with which they could learn to further themselves. When the family moved to Rochester, the children met with him on Saturday afternoons for lessons in which he would illustrate the basic principles of nature. "I taught them the function of the root and the leaf and the power of the seed; we went out into the fields and gathered the various plants and studied their structure."[3] He geared the level of his lessons to his pupils. Complaining of the foolishness of teaching abstractions (such as the concept of faith) to children, he taught fractions by dividing an apple among them.

He did not neglect his duties as educator, but saw at least part of his parental responsibilities as providing the kind of freedom which would allow for discovery and self-education, associating this kind of education with nonconformity; the individual, in seeking his own way, must rebel against traditions. "From my tenth year I have been master of myself. I was, in fact, heretical by nature."[4] Of his daughters, Adelaide was the one to follow his example, and the independent spirit she was born with developed as her schooling progressed, due in measure to the lack of intervention on the part of her parents.

Despite his devotion, Algernon Crapsey's attention to his children was sporadic, partly due to the size of his family, his philosophy of freedom, and his desire to involve himself in more significant issues. Because he was both a busy man and one who concentrated entirely on the task immediately before him, his attentions to his children were available when he was free, not necessarily when they were needed. His neglect to prepare a home at the rectory for his wife and three children, given over a month for this purpose, was typical. But Mr. Crapsey was aware of his shortcomings, acknowledged and regretted them, and was forgiven.

At an early age, Adelaide learned to idealize this absentmindedness. Her father was engaged in what both of them considered extremely significant activities, and it was entirely understandable to her that the children would accommodate themselves. Some of them felt themselves obliged as well to devote themselves to more significant matters than mundane day-to-day tasks. Adelaide idealized and imitated, laughing off household chores and claiming she was just no good at them: her sister Emily was so much more useful. "I cant bear . . . to think of you all alone when you are ill and wish we could both be there," she wrote her mother from school before her youngest brother was born. "But if only one of us can be I suppose Emily would be lots more help than I. You know by sad experience that I'm pretty much of a good for nothing."[5] Her own destiny, when she thought of it, was greater.

Had her mother been an indifferent and undemanding mistress of her household, or had there been unlimited servants, perhaps Adelaide's attention to practical matters would have been unimportant. But her mother was a perfectionist, whose neatness and style in housekeeping were becoming legendary. Yet she was often helpless, weak before the enormous task of managing the lives of nine children and the daily duties of a minister's wife. She expected everything to be perfect but did not effect the kind of authority then popular in families, and she treated Adelaide in particular like a friend and confidante. "Love to everybody," the teenage daughter signed her letter, "and lots for yourself 'Adelaide' dear."[6] Adelaide's assistance in the family resulted from her sympathy, her loyalty, and her desire to participate in any way she could, not from a fear of punishment or a blind sense of duty. The house was simply not an authoritarian one: patriarchy was outmoded and was described by the reverend as an ancient primitive institution. "In the ancient family the father was prophet, priest and king. It was the duty of the father before each meal to offer libations to the gods of the house; it was his function year by year to walk the bounds of his lands and, by the sacrifice of the lamb or the he-goat, to propitiate the gods of the land; when he entered the bridal chamber he, as the high priest of the house, called down the blessings of the gods on the bridal bed."[7] In a democratic household like this, the children often become more independent and yet retain their ties to their family from a heightened sense of love and participation. "The children," Mr. Crapsey wrote, "are not bound to their parents for the simple fact of their existence. The parents did not have the children in mind when they were indulging themselves in the pleasures of marriage."[8] Within the family at least, Adelaide Crapsey was given to feel that she was an independent person, bound to her parents only by love, friendship, and concern and not by obligation. She was responsible for her own destiny and had the freedom to shape it.

There were many advantages to this relationship with her parents. The Crapsey home was considered by other children "the happiest they had ever known."[9] Adelaide spoke and argued from a very early age like an adult. She discussed intellectual and psychological matters with her parents and her teachers to the surprise of her friends and classmates. She felt confident in behaving in ways that shocked her neighbors and contemporaries. She dressed as she pleased. She was to be remembered with some disapprobation by her contemporary adolescents for being so free as to kiss boys.[10] At fourteen she received a poem from a young man, P. H. Savage, "What are the eyes of Adelaide," apparently in response to her flirtatious encouragement. This letter she shared with her mother as she shared the humorous evaluation of the young man who was wooing her sister. On the family's summer vacations in Massachusetts, the Catskills, and Canandaigua, New York, she and her siblings ran free and were encouraged to develop their imaginations and their own activities. The summer before Adelaide's tenth year, for example, was spent on a farm in Spenser, Massachusetts, where the Reverend Mr. Crapsey was leading a mission. There the seven children were allowed total freedom and fed the cattle and chickens. Paul tried to ride a cow, and Emily and Adelaide would put their heads against the head of one special cow, Tamasia. Then, when the parents had to return to Rochester for a funeral, the children travelled to Albany on their own, where they were met by their grandfather's foreman, who took them to Catskill. Certainly this freedom in a sophisticated and cultured family was rare and contributed to Adelaide's creative development.

There was an inherent paradox in this relationship of freedom, however. A parent, releasing his child from accepted social obligations to him, may well cause the child to internalize the obligations. Thus, although Adelaide was not forced to pay obeisance to her elders, she worshipped them for the freedom they gave her and felt even more of an obligation to love and respect them for their liberated affections. By asking only for deserved love, Algernon Crapsey caused an undying adoration in his daughter's heart. This idealization extended to her mother, who never had cause to raise her voice. A low word was usually sufficient to send the children, who felt she was due enormous respect, scurrying.

Mrs. Crapsey was also considered an extraordinarily capable woman who devoted her talents to the aid of others as a minister's wife who went beyond the call of duty. She organized aid for other women—new immigrants, young mothers, widows—and children. Constantly admired by the congregation for her abilities and her devotion, she was a model mother, one who was to be loved by her children not only because she was a parent but also because she contributed to the improvement of society.

Not only was she greatly respectful of her mother, Adelaide Crapsey was in awe of her mother's beauty, her strong personality, and her success with men. With the same names, they were also similar in some ways. Both had magnetic eyes, strong opinions, and the quality of suddenly appearing in a room, their silent entrance having gone unnoticed. The similarities caused endless comparisons, particularly on the part of the daughter. From boarding school Adelaide wrote her mother about her friend from Princeton. "I had a letter from Hawlely [sic] the other day directed to Mrs. Adelaide Crapsey. Guess he was thinking of you."[11] Another time she wrote, "I have stopped curling my hair and wear it parted in the middle just as straight as yours. Marjorie says I look exactly like you. Everyone here likes it much better straight."[12] For the rest of her life Adelaide was the magic mirror to her mother, reminding her of her beauty as others saw it. "Tell mother," she wrote twenty years later, "[Mr. Kershner] says she is the most beautiful woman he has ever seen."[13]

Adelaide's extreme ambition to succeed, already evident in her childhood competition with her sister Emily, was related to this need to prove worth in order to gain love. For if parents were to be loved because they had earned their child's love, children could not be loved if they did not earn their parents' love. And yet how could she hope to be worthy of two such powerful parents? Her successes were always wrapped in a great blanket of modesty when presented to her parents, but the throbbing hope underneath was for unqualified approval.

Another result of the partnership between parent and child was the unmitigated exposure to the hard truths of life. Adelaide was kept from nothing and early in her life was introduced to the agonies of childbirth, the pains of economic hardship, and the difficulties of the careers of her parents. It was part of being daughter of a minister to whom people came in times of crisis. She also had encounters with illness and death most children do not have to suffer. When she was ten her father became very ill, hospitalized with pneumonia, "hovering between life and death." He recovered but was too weak to resume his duties and was sent by his parishioners to England for a few months of recuperation. Less than two years later, in 1891, Adelaide was taken out of school in January to visit her grandfather on his deathbed in Catskill. She sat calmly by his bedside, as though accepting the inevitable and accepting as well her responsibility in alleviating the sorrow. She played a quiet game with her grandfather and stayed with him during the day until evening. "When he died, she was with him, gentle, but intense."[14]

Although Marcus was in his eighties and was survived by his father, James Trowbridge, the shock of witnessing her grandfather's death must have been great and the funeral at St. Luke's Episcopal Church traumatic. The Trowbridges had sold the paper a few years before but kept their position in the community. Now her grandmother, bereft of both home and occupation, left Catskill to live nearer her son, and the lives of the grandchildren were irrevocably altered.

The next year Adelaide herself returned ill from a visit to her grandmother and had a special nurse, Mrs. Hawkes, to take care of her for four months. The nature of her illness is not clear, but her mother noted that Adelaide was "wonderfully sweet and patient,"[15] perhaps preparing herself for her own end. But by September of the next year she was well enough to be sent away to school and full of high spirits. Except for a missed year, leaving her behind her sister and companion, her own brush with death left no visible scars.

Her first school was the one run by the church. The Crapseys had established a kindergarten, a new idea in Rochester, and the teacher, Katherine Whitehead, was also an instructor to other prospective teachers in this field. Doubtless the children of the innovators were involved in this project.

In addition to the kindergarten, classes with professional teachers were held in the evenings. These classes, held in the parish house only a few doors away from the rectory, attracted many children from other faiths. The sexual division of courses was maintained (girls were taught sewing, knitting, and embroidery, while boys learned wood carving, carpentry, and brass engraving), but this was a practical division, a preparation for the real world, and, as the reverend noted amusedly, this division disappeared when the classes were dismissed and the children met outside.

The intention of these classes was the fulfillment of the idea of the "institutional church," the kind of center that could incorporate all aspects of the life of the individual. The idea was to make the church all-encompassing, as it had been in medieval times. Unlike the medieval church, however, the purpose was not to draw people away from the world, but to bring the church into the world. This concept was announced formally by the Reverend Mr. Crapsey only in 1892, but he had been preparing for it since he arrived in Rochester. [16] Certainly in his own life and in the lives of the children the church was the overwhelming organizational power. Their lives were formed around the festivals and fasts, the christenings and burials, the philanthropy and the needs of the parishioners.

But even this expanded church had its educational limitations, and at the age of eight Adelaide accompanied Emily to a Mrs. Doolittle's school. It was a long walk from home, but it had been offered to the children tuition-free, and the Reverend Mr. Crapsey encouraged his wife to develop independence. Next year they were in more nearby public schools.

At the age of fifteen and sixteen Adelaide and Emily were sent off to Kemper Hall, an Episcopal boarding school for girls in Kenosha, Wisconsin. With so much of their education so close to home this change was a drastic and almost unprecedented one; there were no other pupils from Rochester at Kemper. The considerations were not entirely academic ones. Most of Adelaide's friends were content with local private schools, even those who went on later to achieve higher degrees at institutions as prestigious as Columbia University. The quality of the education, then, was not the criteria for sending the girls away.

The Crapseys were interested in promoting the school since Algernon Crapsey was among the fourteen distinguished citizens, primarily from the Midwest, who formed the board. There were also family ties to the school; the foundress, Mother Harriet, was related to Mrs. Crapsey. Together with the sisters of the Community of St. Mary, Mother Harriet had come from Peekskill a few years back in order to restore solvency to the ailing Episcopal school. At Kemper Hall the girls would be well sheltered in the bosom of the church and family and would have opportunities for excitement, individuality, and change.[17]

Nevertheless, the distance proved somewhat difficult for the girls. Adelaide adjusted easily and seemed to fulfill her father's ideas of the individualistic child, but Emily suffered from homesickness and took a longer time to feel comfortable. Both exhibited a longing for home, a longing that was increased by the distance and the extreme difficulty of financing visits home. Vacations and other standard visits home had to be curtailed. In an early letter home (1895) Crapsey wrote her mother of her excitement and anticipation about coming home for Christmas, adding, "I suppose it is about time to talk about the money for my ticket. Papa knows how much that is doesn't he? O dear! I feel as if it were awfully selfish to take all that money for travelling expensis [sic]. If you think I had better I will stay here this vacation too. Doesn't Papa know some railroad man he can get a pass from?"[18] A child remaining at Kemper Hall during short vacations paid six dollars board, and reduced train fares were offered for the pupils. And yet these incentives were not sufficient to finance the trip home. On this particular occasion, Emily was planning to spend her vacation with friends. Adelaide would have stayed alone at Kemper Hall while her friends and family celebrated the most important Christian holiday without her. Her offer to remain may have been just a ploy to speed up family sympathy and therefore the money for the trip, but even the fact that she might perceive it necessary suggests a faint fear of her superfluousness in the family festivities, particularly since she had evidently passed previous vacations alone at school.

As another vacation drew near, her sighs became louder: "the thought of staying here makes me pretty blue. The number of girls who are to stay here has greatly diminished and you can think how dismal this big place will be with eight or nine of us floating round in it . . . O dear! it makes me so home sick to think we have got to be hear [*sic*] Easter. I dont think June will ever come. Why don't you come out here and spend the vacation? Really I don't think I shall survive if you don't."[19]

The family had not planned for this enforced separation, and could not have taken into account the fact that the panic and depression of 1893 would considerably lessen the reverend's income from the weekly offerings and limit the possibility of expensive train rides home. Mrs. Crapsey would have preferred them by her side and always had a foreboding of doom when they left for school, noting in her diary: "Each time as they go down the garden walk I stand and watch them and think and wonder when it will be when they come back and much can happen to them and to us." Yet they did not consider moving the girls to a closer school.

Because the school was so inaccessible, Adelaide's letters continually refer to home as a kind of Eden. It is not necessary to go away for the summer, she remarks, even though the humidity of Rochester summers is, indeed, unbearable. "As long as we are home we will not ask for anything else."[20] Elsewhere she writes, "How is everything at the Rectory? In two weeks we will be there, houpla!!!"[21]

Her involvement in the economic difficulties of the family is everywhere evident, since even at this busy time, when her father was not only fulfilling his duties as rector but also participating in seminars, giving lectures, and publishing books, there was no cash. "We are having a lovely time with money aren't we?" she writes her mother in her junior year of school. "Do you think we will ever get out. I am no end sorry but I'm afraid I'll have to ask for some. I haven't had any since before Easter you know and I'm dead broke. I have some class expenses which I shall have to meets [*sic*]. I think that with a 5 [?] I can get throug[h] till June."[22]

"Emily has told you of our hardupedness I think," Adelaide wrote elsewhere. "Our sole possessions are two cents. It is all becaus[e] of that beastly bill I told you of. Of course we will have to make an Easter offering next Sunday; so if we could have the money before then we would like it very much."[23]

Adelaide seems to have perceived herself as a financial intrusion and an emotional imposition and rarely wrote about her own needs without including her sister's. Consequently her attention in her letters is focussed on her mother's activities—her health, her photographs, her pleasures, and her responsibilities. Adelaide's high school letters refer frequently to the domestic arrangements-the cook, the help, the burden of children. "How are you and the baby and the cook getting on," the fifteen-year-old Adelaide wrote her mother. "Those are the only three members of the family that I worry about."[24] Her concern was with Arthur Hunt, born on February 19, 1896. Adelaide's repeated inquiries as to her mother's health and her reminders that her mother take care of herself seem a bit ridiculous in retrospect since her mother outlived her by thirty-six years, but lying in at the age of forty-one with eight other charges was not an easy matter.

Adelaide maintained an ambiguous relationship with her home and family. Home may have been an Eden, a place to long for and worry about, but it was never a place to be for very long or to turn to when she was in need of help or in trouble. Any anxieties or concerns she might have had in Kenosha she kept to herself, lifting up her strong chin and turning her gaze inward. When she came home for summer vacation she left within days with her siblings for one of the cottages at Sodus or Hemlock Lake or Cook's Point they had hired for the summer, to be joined later by Mrs. Crapsey and to be visited by their father.

Her mother's attentions to her she received with profuse thanks and great understanding of the burden she imposed upon her. When her mother sent Adelaide some clothes left behind, she wrote thanks, adding, "It was awfully good of you to bother about it when you are so tired and busy."[25]

Both parents *were* tired and busy, and her father's preoccupation was often evident. The two sisters, having agreed to embark on a college preparatory program at Kemper Hall, required a letter of consent. "Will you ask Papa to write soon as we want to start as soon as possible," Adelaide wrote a few days after their arrival in September. On October 15 she wrote again: "*Has* Papa written to Sister M. C. [Margaret Clare]? Fraulein is getting very impatient and I don't know what she will do if we don't hear this week. You see we have lost three weeks already and that is quite a good deal. Will you ask him if he wont write *soon*."[26] Perhaps the twenty-dollar difference in the fees was a factor in Mr. Crapsey's delay, but neglect was a greater one.

It was a benign neglect that elsewhere allowed Adelaide to get away with all kinds of antics. And the reverend was happy to come to Kemper Hall for Emily's valedictory award, to give the commencement address when she graduated, and to return home with his daughters and their awards.

Adelaide, on her part, was not at all neglectful of her father's activities and displayed a mature interest in his many and varied achievements. While she denied any ability in the standard female accomplishments, such as domestic duties, she professed great interest in the activities that concerned her father and mother in other spheres. She was interested in the parishioners, in charitable work, in helping others, and in the organizations—religious and political—that were concerned with these activities.

These projects were interesting and provocative and could well engage the imagination of an idealistic young person. During his daughter's stay at Kemper Hall, for example, the Reverend Mr. Crapsey organized a men's club, the Brotherhood, to provide a community center for working-class men. He thought of the Brotherhood as an alternative to the saloons, but the kind of community thinking he encouraged shaped the behavior of a number of businessmen in Rochester for a generation. One instance of the practical focus was the introduction of the insurance pool, based on the idea that self-interest could best be served by communal efforts.

The Reverend Mr. Crapsey was also beginning to become involved in the religious aspects of politics, and even before the sinking of the *Maine* he was discussing such issues as "The Growth of Imperial Power in

America" in a series on the modern applications of the Ten Command-ments.[27] Adelaide was extremely proud of his endeavors and proud to be associated with such a dedicated prelate, and she attended his ser-mons and lectures whenever possible as she grew older. She displayed the same concern for politics, saw the moral responsibility of the indi-vidual in his political attitudes, and believed with him in the necessity of communal efforts on a personal as well as a political level.

Her father was also a cause for great concern; his altruism made him think nothing of taking chances other fathers would have avoided. Hav-ing been chosen to participate in the great Mission of the Episcopalian Church of 1892 in order to revive interest in religion, he and Mrs. Crapsey were sent to Bermuda, where he met with great success. Their voyage in the summer of 1894, however, was an extremely difficult one and caused Adelaide and the rest of the family a great deal of consterna-tion. Algernon Crapsey described the return:

> Our voyage home was disastrous; we encountered the greatest storm in the experience of the captain; at least, that is what he told us. We were blown two hundred miles and more out of our course. My wife, who was subject to seasickness in the calmest weather, suffered extremely in this terrific storm. Our friend, Mr. Rochester, came one morning to visit us in our cabin, to which both Mrs. Crapsey and myself were confined, and on his return, as he entered the saloon, the ship lurched and he was thrown clear across the room against the wainscoting and suffered a severe wound over the eye from which he never fully recovered. For the rest of the voyage he was in great distress and danger, and we began to fear that we shouldn't get him home alive.[28]

Perhaps initially the daughter perceived the resemblance to *The Tempest* and saw herself as Miranda, but the long painful period afterward would have put any fantastic comparisons into perspective. It took the Crapseys many months to recover from this journey—Mr. Rochester never recovered entirely—and Adelaide's concern continued to be felt throughout her sophomore year. They spent the remainder of the sum-mer at the cottage they usually hired at Canandaigua, Vine Cottage, the mother resting, the children swimming and clowning.

Her mother travelled very little after that. Months after her parents' return from Bermuda, the daughter wrote, congratulating Mrs. Crapsey on the improvement in her health: "Rachel wrote me the other day that you would be downstairs soon. We were awfully glad to hear that, you have been having an awfully hard time ever since you came back, hav'ent [*sic*] you? I hope everybody will get well and stay well. All the girls are beginning to count the days to the Easter hollidays [*sic*]. O if we were only going to go to be home for the hollidays."[29]

The regularity and order of the school provided a contrast, a stable, secure, and pleasant framework for Adelaide and Emily. The day began at 6:30 A.M. The seniors "were awakened by a maid who also closed the window and turned on the steam." The others took care of this invigorating duty themselves. "Then chapel, breakfast, chapel again, and to the classrooms." In the afternoons there was exercise, gymnastics, or walks, "two by two, with a Sister at the head and a Senior at the foot." The regular afternoon study hour was followed by supper and, often, by dancing in the old Armitage Hall, which then served as the gym. The minutes between half past eight and a quarter to nine were devoted to prayers and Bible reading and set aside as "quiet hours." All lights went out at nine.

The schedule was altered on weekends, but the rigidity remained. Classes ended at noon on Saturdays, and after lunch the girls mended their clothes and blacked their boots. Regular Sunday night receptions were held in the drawing room where the girls curtseyed to the sister superior, made polite conversation, and sang hymns. All of Monday until evening study hour was free.[30] It was little wonder that Adelaide wrote her mother: "Ev[e]rything here is the same as usual. Indeed it always is the 'same as usual.' "[31] Despite this disavowal Adelaide preferred regular patterns on a day-to-day basis with a few explosions of the order on occasion. She had been accustomed to a regulated life in the church and enjoyed both the regularity and the tiny subversions at school.

At Kemper there were also clear-cut rules for behavior and the girls were expected to follow Mother Margaret Clare's "list of KEMPER HALL DON'TS," which guided the girls into the world of young ladies:

Refinement consists less in what one does and says than in what one leaves undone and unsaid.

Don't talk about yourself or your family affairs. It is a sign of verdancy.

Don't be inquisitive with either tongue or fingers, because curiosity is wholly vulgar and common.

Don't begin sentences with "Say!" Leave that to gum-chewing girls.

Don't make a display of ruffles and ankles while sitting on the porch; don't sit on your spine.

Don't be ungracious. If you do a favor, do it in a whole-souled way; if you receive one, accept it with honest thanks and acknowledgements. If you beat a game or excel in a lesson, don't exult.

Don't be afraid to say upon occasion, "I don't know," or "I was mistaken."[32]

The emphasis here is upon consideration for others and the establishment of values. Sexual modesty and vulgarity are minor issues.

Adelaide was not alone in respecting these values. Many of the girls grew so attached to Kemper Hall that their relationships with it continued throughout their lives. A number were married in the chapel at Kemper and many continued to participate in the activities of the hall in some way whenever they could, attending commencement ceremonies, corresponding with the sisters, and simply remembering it fondly.[33] But most of the girls could easily keep up their acquaintance because they lived nearby.

As one of the only girls in a school of ninety who was far from home, Adelaide was frequently invited for holidays to the more proximate homes of schoolmates. She spent a week with a classmate, Louise Ferguson, and another girl at 559 Marshall Street in Milwaukee, and Louise, though busy with her fiancé, gave a luncheon for Adelaide, entertaining her to the point where Adelaide wrote her mother that her vacation was "quite out of sight."[34] Milwaukee was made more pleasant by the fact that she had other acquaintances there, including Margaret Bloodgood, who lived on the same street as the Fergusons. On another occasion she went to Chicago as the guest of a classmate and had "a jolly good time."[35] Operating on the Crapsey principles of independence, she asked afterward, "It was all right for me to go wasn't it?"

These trips were proper but quite daring for a non-Crapsey. Perhaps she inherited her disposition from her great-great-grandmother Rachel Davis, who, in 1796, travelled with her sister on horseback to Washington, Kentucky, from Columbia, Ohio, through "unbroken wilderness, unmarked, except by a horse-path. The Indians were roaming in the forests, and travelers were in constant danger."[36] But wherever it came from, this spirit was growing in her, and Adelaide planned to travel forever. A later poem expresses this hunger to see and possess as much as possible:

ADVENTURE

Sun and wind and beat of sea,
Great lands stretching endlessly . . .
Where be bonds to bind the free?
All the world was made for me!
(*CP*, p. 80)

The vacations she passed at Kemper Hall offered far less freedom. "During the Easter vacation we can go *down town* alone the girls say. Did you ever hear of anything so shocking?" she laughed conspiratorially with her mother.[37] The candy pulls and fudge and popcorn making which the sisters contrived to keep the girls busy seemed to leave Adelaide with energy left over that could be released only with mildly mischievous behavior. She faked ghosts for Emily and gave one of her teachers, Mrs. Jemmison, a "caniption" [*sic*] by laughing during grace. But her joking was always within proper bounds and she remained on the right side of both students and teachers.

When not on vacation she was an eager and happy student, taking as many electives and participating in as many school activities as she could and basking in the adoration of her teachers. Fräulein Schwartz "loved her very dearly"[38] and Sister Flora Therese found her unforgettable. Mother Margaret Clare, who was in charge of the school, believed in an atmosphere of encouragement, that "we are here not just to teach but to inspire,"[39] and there was a spirit of enthusiasm about all the work at Kemper. In this congenial environment Adelaide's energy found appropriate and appreciative outlets.

There was a great deal to be enthusiastic about. The physical surroundings were idyllic—an elegant, relatively new building at 6501 Third Avenue, neighboring other lovely mansions and overlooking Lake Michigan. The facilities were far more advanced than other schools of that period. For many girls' schools, athletics consisted of weekend walks in the country, but at Kemper there were gymnastics, military drill, bowling, and basketball.

Adelaide was very much involved in the various kinds of athletics offered at Kemper Hall and participated in a demonstration put on by the students for the townspeople of Kenosha with "vaulting and swinging and barbell exercises."[40] She was also lieutenant of the military drill, an activity intended to encourage carriage and poise.

When the new game of basketball was introduced at Kemper Hall, Emily became the first president of the Kemper Hall Basketball League, and the school was divided into "reds" and "blues." There were twenty to twenty-five "of the athletically inclined girls" participating.[41] Adelaide was captain of the blues in her sophomore year, while Emily was umpire and president of the league. When Emily left, Adelaide, as a senior, captained the reds.

The newness of the game made a great deal of coaching necessary. "The point," Adelaide explained to her classmates, "is to throw the ball, which is the size and shape of a foot ball, into the basket."[42] The girls played four times a week, and Adelaide, in a story called "The First Game," describes with humor the difficulty of teaching a new game to new athletes.[43] "You mustn't kick the ball," the umpire tells the new player, "or run with it, or hug it; you mustn't talk." "Would you mind telling us what we *can* do?" a player asks.

Four times a week gave Adelaide needed experience for basketball at Vassar. Her diminished height (She was about 5'2" as an adult) made it difficult for her to compete with the taller girls. Before she resolved this problem entirely by becoming manager, she probably devised the system her friend Jean Webster was later to describe—using her minimal height to advantage: "I'm little of course, but terribly quick and wiry and tough. While the others are hopping about in the air, I can dodge under their feet and grab the ball."[44]

In literary activities, as in basketball, Adelaide followed Emily. In her junior year, Emily was the assistant editor of the recently founded monthly *Kemper Hall Kodak* and became editor-in-chief in her senior year. Adelaide took the position of junior editor while her sister was editor and stepped into her shoes once again as editor-in-chief a year later. There was great pressure, both of editorial deadlines and of quality of content, for the girls wrote much of the material. But there was also a feeling of responsibility to a family tradition—Marcus Trowbridge had meant much to the girls. Adelaide succeeded so well that the editor who followed her apologized in advance for her inability to maintain the high standards Adelaide's *Kodak* had set. In addition to providing the school news, Adelaide wrote stories, translated stories from the French, reviewed books, and collected famous poems for reprinting. Emily Dickinson and Robert Louis Stevenson were her favorites at a time when Stevenson was a popular poet but Dickinson almost unknown. "I never saw a moor" and "He ate and drank the precious words" were re-produced in their regularized manner, with commas instead of dashes, but even so the poems must have struck the Kemper girls as radical and new.[45]

Adelaide's job was a difficult one technically as well as intellectually and often kept her at school after her friends had left for vacation. "School closes on the elevent[h]," she complained, "but I have to stay a week later to get out that wretched Kodak."[46] It was this devotion and professionalism that made her *Kodak* such a good one. The material by her contemporaries was no better that year than other years.

Her own work was exceptional. The stories she wrote were full of the psychological depths of adolescents and characterized by surprise endings. One story, "Three Solitaires," analyzes and exposes the nature of self-love masquerading as romantic love for another. The young man, trying to decide which of two women he loves, discovers both of them wearing diamond engagement rings. His long considerations become irrelevant as he becomes the third of the "solitaires." Another story, "The Blue Stocking," concerns the apparent remoteness of an intellectual girl who turns out to be as frightened of intellectual confrontation as the young man forced to talk with her.

To some extent Adelaide herself was a bluestocking. Books were very important to her, but they were not sacred as sources of knowledge so much as they were inspiration for mental activity. She could find value in almost any book because she was able to extract interest and use from almost anything. Charlotte Yonge's novels, for example, were the object of derision among sophisticated young women because of their overt High Church didacticism. Influenced by Cardinal Newman's reform movement, Mrs. Yonge tried to teach the new ideas of the Oxford Movement to youthful readers. In an evaluation of Yonge's "goody, goody stories"[47] Adelaide praised her because "her heroes and heroines are real people and not animated sermons" and, finding Yonge a kind of feminine literary ideal, she entitled her article "An Interesting Woman": "How effectual her work has been is hard to realize, for it has been done in such a quiet, unpretending way. There is no sparkle or glitter about it, nothing to create a sensation. It is merely that one good woman has gone quietly about the work she seemed fitted for, and has done her best to make the world a better and a sweeter place. That and nothing more, but could anything be greater?"[48] What Crapsey derived from the evaluation of an overlooked literature is an ideal for womanhood. "One good woman" goes "quietly about the work she seems fitted for" and does "her best to make the world a better and a sweeter place." Whatever the lessons to be learned from Yonge's books, there was a great deal to be learned from Yonge herself. This was a lesson Adelaide would not forget.

A bad book was good too. "We have just finished reading a highly exciting (?) book by Maxwell Grey which we invoked[?] from the town. By we I mean Miss French, Emily, and I. We got the book (a costly freak) under the impression that it was something wildly exciting and though it has turned out to be just the opposite we have had no end of fun over it. It would be almost impossible to read the book to yourself but read aloud it is awfully funny. Just full of padding. Outside scenery always accords with the emotions of the people or forms a picturesque contrast. The clock always ticks on and the /cinders/embers/ tinkle on the hearth under all circumstances. The fire dies down at exactly the right moment. The hero has a voice like the roll of an Atlantic breaker."[49] The literary sophistication in identifying the pathetic fallacy is amplified by her good-humored acceptance of "bad literature."

Lack of experience with the world outside Kemper was no barrier to her. As in basketball she worked with what was available in the literature. But she was also reading Balzac on the sly, and Daudet, and numerous other sophisticated and significant authors and could use them as touchstones as well.

Actresses—their ability to cover their true emotions without negating them and express other, equally true emotions—fascinated her, and she found in the book *Peg Wolffington*, about the eighteenth-century actress, much to be praised because of its character, dialogues, and because "the story beneath this sparkling exterior comes dangerously near being a tragedy. Gay and bright on the outside but with much of sadness underneath. It is like Peg herself who passes off with a laugh and a jest that which has broken her heart. And still we are inclined to forgive Mr. Vane all the misery he causes her, because without it we would never known [*sic*] quite all of the strength and depth and sweetness of her character."[50]

Even battle songs received her critical interest and attention because of their power to induce emotions. Of the value of songs for stirring up courage, she wrote, "If I had been a French general and had had to choose between another regiment and the Marseillaise, I should have chosen the latter without hesitation. . . . For the men with the words of Marseillaise on the lips, the sound of it in their ears, and the ring of it in their hearts, would more than equal the larger body marching cold blooded into battle. This French 'Chant de Guerre' is perhaps the most perfect war song that we have. There is the crash and roar of battle in it, and the triumphant note of victory."[51] But it was politics and the mores of society that most stirred up Adelaide's feelings and inspired her editorials. The invasion of Crete by Turkey, American patriotism, the shocking illiteracy of college-bound boys, and the political naiveté of the teenager were inspired subjects of her essays. These were subjects she chose herself, subjects unlike previous editorials of the *Kodak* and unlike anything that would be written in coming years. There is a sense in these essays that this position and this paper were only a preparation for something greater. A concern with justice and individual responsibility in questions of moral justice prevails and suggests that these essays were not written for Kemper but a greater world outside.

> Crete belongs to Greece by every tie of position, history, race-sympathy, and religion, but she asks not so much for annexation or for self-government, as for the poor right to exist. Centuries of oppression and warfare have done their work, and the population of the island to-day is only one-third of what it was at the dawn of the Christian era. The Turks, although they are in the minority, are feared by the Christians, for they have the whole Musselman power at their backs, and what that power is capable of, when unchecked, has been shown in the persecution of the Armenians.[52]

Who of her classmates was even aware of the massacre of the Armenians or the struggle for Crete? Certainly none of them felt their opinions need be put into words or that their words mattered.

But while Adelaide was alone in her political concerns, dramatics was important to both the Crapsey sisters. In Kemper Hall, Emily was the more extroverted of the two, took more risks at dramatic parts, and received more compliments. She took the part of Mr. Campbell in *The Albany Depot*, and, although the taking of a man's role only meant masculine attire from the waist up, together with long skirts, women's roles were considered more conventional. Adelaide, more intellectual, was more committed to dramatic readings of papers and closed one celebration of Washington's birthday with the reading of the Declaration of Independence, but also managed to star as Mrs. Roberts in Howell's *The Sleeping Car* and was remembered for her acting proficiency.

There were other aspects of life in which Adelaide was more daring and independent than her sister, and the domestic orientation and painful fidelity to home and feminine temerity exhibited by Emily was treated with more than a hint of ridicule by Adelaide. Coming from a city where the Fox sisters had caused a national epidemic of "spirit rappings," it is not surprising that Emily, even at the age of eighteen, was frightened by ghosts. Her sister's exorcism of her fear, however, demanded less conventional responses. Knowing her mother would agree with her skepticism, Adelaide wrote: "Emily Washburn and I are racking our brains to get up a ghost for Emilys benefit. You see she has ghosts on the brain and last night dragged me over in her bed, declaring that she heard noises. We are going to give her some first class ghosts tonight."[53]

Self-confident and secure, Adelaide had one visible failing, a laughable approach to spelling. She would dash into the room of a friend to complain that a word wasn't in the dictionary. Upon examination, it would emerge that her struggles with the dictionary were based on a complete misconception of the spelling.[54] "I used to read her themes," a classmate volunteered, "and make the necessary corrections."[55] Her roommate in college, Jean Webster, also had the same difficulty in spelling and when asked for an authority for her strange choice of letters would answer "Webster." But Webster's unconcern about details and strong individuality formed the basis for this failing. Adelaide, it appears, was listening to the words, unable to follow the logic of spelling rules in the face of the aural discrepancy—"committee" easily became "comity." This difficulty with spelling may well be linked to her later experiments with the sounds of Cherokee Indian chants as well as the reading of the vowel sounds only in her own poems.[56]

A learning disability might also have been the cause. Her confusion with letters and number order, more salient in times of stress and weariness, is a hint. "I have just been writing the date of my last vaccination. I wrote it in a hurry and first put down that I was vaccinated in 1789 and then changed that to 1897. Finally I managed to get it 1879 the correct date."[57] Other instances of the inability to write, usually blamed on weariness, occur in her letters, but the tendency was covered up in formal writing as Adelaide grew up and reappeared only when illness began to take its toll.

Adelaide's clothing was also unconventional—her aversion to confining garments began in school and continued throughout her life. She was never to wear a corset, standard dress for the woman of the period. In school she adopted very short waisted "Kate Greenaway" dresses, shirred on the bosom and free flowing. Not only did this style disguise her youthful plumpness,[58] but her dresses also seemed to make a political statement. Schoolmates assumed that the Crapsey family followed the dress reform movement, which advocated clothes for women that facilitated motion, encouraging athletics and self-expression.[59] The dress worn at Kemper, at least for portraits, was a white shirtwaist, black skirt, and black bow tie. Even way out on a tree limb for a rather unusual class portrait, Adelaide was dressed this way.

When not in shirtwaists she was known for wearing neutral colors. Gray was her favorite color, and brown was also common, and even at Kemper Hall her monochromatic wardrobe was noticed. Perhaps the loose-fitting dresses gave her a more childish look, a respite from the impending physical responsibilities womanhood might entail. Her hair, which had been worn curled until her sophomore year in high school, was put into long braids for the remaining three years until college, a style which on the one hand imitated her mother's severe hairstyle and on the other certainly contributed to a more childlike appearance, one that was not common to her classmates.

Why should she not wish to flee from impending womanhood? Her mother, who had six children after Adelaide was born, was forced by overwork and ill health to share her burden with her daughters, and Adelaide's high school letters are spotted with concerned questions and conciliatory remarks about her mother's "illness," her impending confinement with her youngest child, Arthur. Years later, Adelaide's friend, Adelaide Draper Gardner, who had become a psychologist, wrote Mary Osborn that "her attitude toward childbirth was abnormal."[60]

However, a negative attitude to childbirth, a reluctance to commit one's body to so prolonged a responsibility as parenthood, cannot be seen as abnormal in itself at a time when women had to choose so definitely between parenthood and career. In the case of her mother in particular, who was left alone so often with her nine children while the Reverend Mr. Crapsey performed his duties as lecturer, missionary, author, and religious politician in addition to prelate, the burden of motherhood was particularly great. It was also not uncommon for some women of this period to look upon childbirth with a certain repugnance as a coarse, immodest, unrefined, and therefore unfeminine activity.

Certainly women schooled in the Victorian principles would find the abject lack of control in childbirth in itself reprehensible. One might add that the incidence of death from childbed fever was considerable. Adelaide's best friend was later to die in childbirth, and there was only one certain way of avoiding it.

A Kemper sketch written from the point of view of the turkey being fattened for Thanksgiving is significant here. Discovering his master's purpose, the turkey says, "I'll beat him this time. I'm not to be killed for a mere man's whim" and starves himself until he is indistinguishable from the other turkeys.[61] This is more than an explanation of the reluctance of the adolescent to develop a woman's body, it is also an understanding of the female self as victim. If the girl fulfills herself in traditional terms, she will be swallowed.

One story from her youth affirms an early, albeit flippant, communal knowledge of the facts of life. On July 2, 1889, Mrs. Crapsey wrote: "After breakfast this morning Algernon said 'Shall I go abroad?' We all said by all means. Lily and I urged all we dared and Phil settled the matter by saying " 'Pappa, if you do not go this year we will probably have another baby by another year and then you cannot go.' "

Adelaide's interest in sports, in editorship, in loose-fitting dresses, her reluctance to take on the traditional roles of women, and her ambition to have a good education and successful career would today be boring in its normality, but for her time it could only have been developed with the aid of the peculiar family and school in which she found herself. For if her father expressed his independence as a child by rebelling against school and institution, a female in the same position at the time would have to rebel in the opposite way. Education was forced upon men but kept from women, so an independent woman would easily opt to struggle for an education, to be allowed to participate in many activities acceptable and confining to men but considered unladylike or questionable for women. And in the fortunate isolation from competition with men afforded her at school, Adelaide was given the opportunity to participate in activities and perfect many skills, an opportunity unavailable in the world outside.

Her drive to excel in education became stronger as she approached graduation. In the last two years of high school she moved into high gear, compressing a number of academic achievements into a very short period of time, spending all her vacations at school during her senior year. Although it was Emily who received the greatest family honors at her graduation, with her respected father chosen to be commencement speaker, it was Adelaide who that year had been lobbying for appropriate courses in preparation for college and who received the highest grade point average. The girls had not entered Kemper Hall to prepare themselves for further education, but as soon as Adelaide decided that college was her goal she roped her sister into the preparatory courses. Emily would not have had sufficient time to make up all the courses she needed in order to enter college the next fall, but she was not terribly interested in any case. The speech given at Emily's commencement by her father characterized Emily's nature: "Athena, the Companion of Heroes and the Keeper of Homes."[62]

Adelaide, however, was very serious about college and crammed four years of Latin into her junior and senior years. The certificate of the "Classical Course" she had taken in the Collegiate Department admitted her automatically to "Vassar, to Wellesley, and to Smith,"[63] and she wasted no time in taking off for Vassar after she had graduated first in her class of sixteen.

Her valedictory address, "The Open Road," made her goals in attempting higher education more salient. They were not academic but individualistic, and she encouraged her fellow graduates to continue the tradition of the "wandering spirit" of man, in the name of science, humanity, and adventure. It was a romantic vision of the exciting world before her, and her enthusiasm was contagious. "The road stretches out before us and our feet are set therein. The wind of the morning blows against our foreheads, and with buoyant steps we renew the journey. Deep into our hearts has sunk the image of the land we are leaving, in all its serenity and beauty. Deeply loved voices still float up to us calling 'God Speed,' and full of their inspiration we press on, bravely, cheerfully, hopefully."[64]

At the age of nineteen she knew what she wanted—the excitement of pursuing knowledge and adventure—and was on her way to achieving it.

Part Two

We want to be, that we may do.

Vassar Miscellany

The Decision for Education

Going to college was not a conventional step. Even her father had thought long and hard about entering St. Stephen's College and was only ordained at the age of twenty-five. Philip was at military school, and Adelaide was the first in her family to take this step. She was one of a very small minority of women, and, conscious of her revolutionary position, she felt the responsibility, the excitement of exploring a new world.

Even though higher education for women was available at the end of the nineteenth century, there were strong arguments that prevailed against it. Scientists still averred that the size of the female brain—smaller and lighter than that of man—indicated its inferior capacity. Dr. William Hammond wrote in *Popular Science Monthly*: "No great idea, no great invention, no great discovery in science and art, no great poetical, dramatic or music composition, has ever yet emanated from a woman's brain. There have been two or three second-rate female painters, and perhaps one first-rate female novelist,—and when that is said, all is said."[1]

Higher education became in this context at best a frivolity, at worst a dangerous diversion from the natural life of women. Education spoiled a woman, both mentally and physically, for her primary duty as wife and mother, and it ruined her general health. The controversy continued through the early decades of the twentieth century, and as late as 1913 Dr. Edith Lowry, who was considered progressive in matters of sex education, warned that pubescent women should be guarded from too much exertion by removing them from school to learn housekeeping at home. This, she noted, may well prevent life-long invalidism.[2] The girl who persisted in her quest for education ran the risk of rendering herself physically unfit for childbirth, shrinking her uterus, and permanently weakening her resistance to disease.

The psychologist G. Stanley Hall summed up both arguments in 1908 by admitting that woman's "academic achievements have forced conservative minds to admit that her intellect is not inferior to that of man," yet concluding "from the available data it seems, however, that the more scholastic the education of women, the fewer children and the harder, more dangerous and more dreaded is parturition, and the less the ability to nurse children. Not intelligence but education by present manmade ways is related inversely to fecundity. The sooner and the more clearly this is recognized as a universal rule, not, of course, without many notable and much vaunted exceptions, the better for our civilization."[3]

Women who wished to be educated, then, had to overcome the very real social objection of their intellectual inferiority and the potential physical damage they would do to themselves as women. They also had to accept the statistical truth that their education gave them fewer chances for marriage: only 50 percent of college women in the late part of the nineteenth century married. The percentage for the general population of women was 90.

After college they would have to choose again, this time between careers and marriage. Few of the women of Adelaide's time had both. By the end of the nineteenth century marriage for college women reached its all-time low at Vassar. Only half the graduating class could be expected to wed, and very few would wed before the age of twenty-five. The women Adelaide Crapsey was likely to meet in academic establishments and choose as models were usually spinsters. Married and educated women devoted their time to their families and societies and were externally indistinguishable from those who were not educated.

Marriage was not necessarily an enslavement. On the contrary, the unfranchised woman could often make her own voice heard more clearly once she had found a voice through her husband. Crapsey's college roommate, Jean Webster, traces an unusual development of feminine identity in her epistolary novel, *Daddy Long-Legs*. Through her orphan-protagonist Judy Abbott, who is first brought out of a dead-end life by an anonymous male sponsor, Webster traces the gradual independence and the self-selected interdependence of a maturing woman. Abbott discovers herself as an individual as she takes advantage of the opportunities in college, succeeds as a writer, and then marries the man who has unobtrusively made her success possible. In the sequel, *Dear Enemy*, Abbott is no longer concerned primarily with writing, but goes off on an extended vacation with her husband while her former roommate, still unmarried, takes over the reform of the charitable institution from which Abbott emerged. The reform, of course, is sponsored by her rich husband, "Daddy Long-Legs." The pattern of individual fulfillment for women here is inextricably linked to the benevolent nurturing of the male. In this context marriage was an indispensable step in self-fulfillment.

Furthermore, since a college education cost a great deal of money. it was unlikely that a family of moderate means, thinking of their daughter's economic future, would wish her to be trained for a profession at college. Not only was it expensive but, although a woman could always earn a salary teaching, the doors that college opened were not all that exciting or different: she might be better able to teach at a higher institution, but she did not have any new professions opened to her, with the rare exception of medicine. Her chances of earning a salary comparable to that of a male were minimal, and there were many people who believed that a woman would have better economic opportunities if she saved the investment of tuition for her dowry.

But for Adelaide Crapsey the situation was different. There was a family tradition. In 1828 Thomas Morris had spoken on the subject:

Our government . . . is a beautiful machinery made up not of parts, but of the whole body of the people. It requires, therefore, not the aid of a few, but the aid of all to keep it in motion. To do this, *every citizen* must understand all its parts and all its movements. He must possess knowledge, virtue, and intelligence; because, in the language of our own Constitution, they are essentially necessary to good government and the happiness of the people. . . . The advancement of the female character, and the instruction and cultivation which woman receives, has always been justly viewed as evidence of the improved state of society where it exists. It is, therefore, an indispensable duty to provide for female education; for knowledge is the handmaid of virtue, prudence, and economy; and where female virtue, knowledge, and intelligence abound, man can never be degraded or a slave.[4]

The theoretical and ideological basis for education was shared by later generations of the family, but there were also practical considerations that people like the Crapseys, whose lives were bound up with those of others, could see more clearly than the average population. As a minister, Algernon Crapsey was daily visited by unfortunate women who had nowhere to turn and no means of self-reliance, and as an involved family the Crapseys were used to doing what they could—making clothes and food—for women bereft of support. A married woman, untrained for any employment, who found herself deserted or widowed one day with children to keep, could often do little but throw herself on the mercy of her relatives or the parish. The Reverend Mr. Crapsey described his anguish at trying to help just such a woman:

A woman came to the present writer, telling him that her husband had just died, leaving her with five children under working age. She begged of the writer that he would find her employment. She must work for wages, or she and her children must starve, go naked, and be thrown on the street. The writer, moved by her pitiful tale, went down into the city and found her employment in one of the large office-buildings. The superintendent of the building was very ready; he needed a woman, and he said with considerable satisfaction that it was just the place for her. She would only have to come down at five o'clock in the morning and stay until nine; she would have all the rest of the day to herself in which to care for her children. For this work she would receive the sum of one dollar per day, with which to provide for herself and her children the three primal necessities of food, clothing, and shelter. Out of her abundant leisure she could also give them that essential of child-life, the mother's care and love. But unfortunately at the times when the mother was at home, the children were either asleep or away at school. She and they became strangers. They grew up without fostering care; they became little savages, and the last the writer heard of them they were throwing fire at each other. This is a single case of which there are thousands upon thousands, one might almost say millions, in our modern civilized countries.[5]

This social understanding was communicated to his children. "Emily and I were so surprised to hear of Mr. Parkins death. What will Mrs. Parkins do?" Adelaide wrote her mother from boarding school, carefully shifting the weight of the tragedy of death to the practical concerns of widows.[6] But even if his fear of destitution had not entered into his consideration for his daughter, the Reverend Mr. Crapsey's observations concerning the changes in society that left so much responsibility to the wife and mother necessitated for him independent women, prepared for the future in a rapidly changing society: "We are living as if the family were still intact. . . . We compel the woman to play the parts of both the father and the mother. She must go out of the house and earn a living for her children and at the same time she must keep the house and bring up her children. Never before in any like degree has this been required of the woman by human society."[7]

Even the choice of marriage for him was not diminished by education but enhanced, for it was only the woman educated in logic, psychology, and economics who could make an intelligent, practical choice.

Left free, the woman in the great majority of cases can marry the man she wants to marry. This is her responsibility. She chooses her mate in accordance with her own mental, moral, and spiritual make-up. She never knows the reality of the man whom she marries; she married her own ideal. . . . The teaching of the English-speaking girl for the last century has made her, in a measure, incapable of wise choice. Romanticism has been rampant. Our literature has been based upon sexual selection, and the woman has been supposed to love the man whom she in the exercise of her freedom chooses to love.[8]

"A woman who fails in marriage," the Reverend Mr. Crapsey noted, referring to "mis-mated" women, "fails in life."[9] He urged a broad and open education, in subject ranging from economics to sexuality, to help the woman determine which marital choice to make: "All of those matters which up to this time have been tabooed must now be released and given over to the knowledge of the woman that she may have some security in making her selection. . . . Matters of sex and maternity must be spoken of with the same freedom as other matters germane to the well-being of the human race."[10] When Algernon Crapsey was writing these words in 1914 he had already witnessed the effects on two of his daughters of the lack of education and practical directions. Rachel had been married to a man whose mother ruled their lives and was doomed to economic dependency upon a grudging and disdainful mother-in-law, and Marie-Louise had suffered an emotional collapse as the result of an unhappy love affair. Certainly these two incidents influenced the vehemence of his argument, for his elder daughters, educated and sophisticated, had not suffered so blatantly, had not made these romantic mistakes, or at least had not seemed to suffer from them. But these were not only the opinions of the father of the family; these were subjects which he had discussed with his elder daughters endlessly, and their decisions were their own. "Parents to-day persuade their children, they do not command them, and where there is a difference of opinion between the parent and the child in three cases out of five it is the parent that yields and not the child. The best mode of ruling the young of the house is for the head of the house, if it have one, to ascertain if he can what the younger elements desire to do and then request those elements to do that thing."[11]

In 1897 there were two daughters in the Crapsey residence who were ready for college—Emily and Adelaide. Emily, with considerable organizational skills as well as literary talent, chose to remain in Rochester. She was engaged to the handsome Channing Moore. She also balanced her position at Remington, Gifford and Willey, attorneys at law, with her family responsibilities. She continued to help her mother with the household and her many charitable activities and to assist her father in his literary endeavors. Emily had never been enthusiastic about college and was only persuaded by her sister to take the college preparatory course when it would be too late for her to complete it. But she was enthusiastic about being useful to others and about writing, and her father was about to begin a novel about social injustice, a novel to which she would contribute no small effort.

The valedictory speeches of the two girls exemplify the distinction. Emily began her speech with a description of the statue of the Victory of Samothrace, a copy of which was to be found at Kemper. "We feel that such a conception of victory means first of all self-mastery, self-control. The figure leaves on our minds the single impression of power and aspiration."[12] The strength and values embodied in the statue provided contrast to those of modern times: "Everywhere in art, in literature, in life, we find the same impatience of restraint, the same scorn of tradition and custom, the same lack of moderation in all things," complained Emily. This abandon awakened in her a confusion, a fear of the future and the multitude of alternatives. "As we stand today looking out upon this eager, restless, modern life, we are bewildered by its problems, thrilled by its possibilities. How shall we meet it?" The world outside with its uncertainties and possibilities was shocking to her, and Kemper, which she was now leaving, was the last bastion of a structured, happy society, the final place of adolescence and security. "It will be to us always a quiet home, to which we may turn for rest and sympathy and encouragement." She took great care to thank Kemper in detail, turning to each of the people responsible for the protective supportive atmosphere: "We have come into contact here with lives that have inspired in us a desire for what is fine, and pure and true, that have shown us the beauty of self-control and self-consecration." What Emily wanted, then, was the comfort of certainty, comfort that could be found in the consecration of the self. She did not wish to pursue goals of her own but to submit to those of a higher being.

Adelaide, on the other hand, took for her opening image the Scholar Gypsy, the legendary Oxford student who "closed his book and went forth into the open. . . . On he roamed, until by chance, he met a band of Gypsies. And by the love of wandering in his heart and the quickening of the blood in his veins he knew them to be his brothers; and he stayed with them and came no more to Oxford." With a rather unique twist to the old story, she connects the Scholar Gypsy with all hunger for the unknown: "It is in the name of science and of humanity that modern wanderers penetrate the frozen lands of the poles or the burning heart of the tropics." Her focus was on the call of the unknown, the beckoning of unknown places. She saw with love the school from which she was about to depart: "Life has been sheltered there, and yet not straitened,—surrounded by gracious influences, wise restraints, and gentle guardianships. And there is holy ministration and reverend counsel there; wisdom, also, leading unto knowledge, and all the dear joys of companionship. . . . Surely, it is a fair land to dwell in! The call of the open road sounds fainter in our ears, and we would abide there. But it cannot be."[13] Like Ulysses, whose adventuring spirit Emily had warned against but Adelaide had praised, the younger sister wanted to strike out alone.

Adelaide Crapsey chose Vassar College. The University of Rochester opened its doors to women only three years later, but even if that option had been available to her she would have preferred a college for women. The protected atmosphere, one in which there was no competition with men and in which women could take on otherwise exclusively masculine activities, was just what she needed to really blossom, and the opportunities for freedom within this sheltered environment were truly unique and fascinating.

A contributing factor was the geographical location. Having lived for four years in Kenosha, a place so remote that her mother was never able to visit (later remembering it to be on Lake Superior rather than Lake Michigan) and so expensively distant that she was forced to spend her holidays there, Crapsey was relieved to be positioned closer to Rochester. She was also near her grandmother, who lived just across the river in Clintondale. Her brother Philip was nearby, and she was not far from New York City and could visit her father during some of his many lectures and meetings there.

But acquaintance with the leaders of the college probably also influenced the decision, as with Kemper Hall. James Monroe Tyler, president of Vassar since 1886, was a graduate of the Rochester Theological Seminary, and James Orton, a former pastor of a nearby church, was a professor of natural history.[14] There were teachers from Vassar at Kemper too who encouraged her, and Elizabeth Kemper Adams, who was an instructor at Kemper when Adelaide was a student, was now teaching English at the college. Also, the situation at Vassar was not unlike Kemper Hall. A large percentage of the girls were Episcopal, chapel was compulsory, and Crapsey would be continuing her training in a congenial sheltered environment.

Two other factors which must have made life much easier for Crapsey even if they were not considerations in her selection were economical and social. The freshman pamphlets reiterated a "democratic" spirit, a deemphasis on financial background and expensive clothes and a higher concern with intellectual matters. Although Crapsey loved clothes, she was always too uncomfortable to spend her parents' money and was extremely frugal unless the money came from her own earnings or gifts from benefactors. When Jean Webster used Adelaide as her model for *Daddy Long-Legs,* she made her heroine into an orphan who was unaccustomed to all the finery of the middle class.

Crapsey became, for Webster, a female version of the two popular characters created by her great-uncle, Mark Twain: Tom Sawyer and Huck Finn. A combination of innocence, rebellion, and sharpsighted ability to cut through false pretensions while maintaining individually derived ethical standards, the ideal of the new woman of the 1900s that Crapsey seemed to embody, was one that was expected to revitalize the jaded world of learning, religion, and ethics.

Perhaps there were other reasons for Webster to perceive of Crapsey as a kind of Huck Finn. It is doubtful that Crapsey was able to attend Vassar under the same circumstances as the other girls. She may have received a scholarship or was sponsored by an individual. There is even the possibility that, like Judy Abbott of *Daddy Long-Legs,* a trustee of a charitable institution underwrote her education. Mr. William Rossiter Seward, who in later years provided a home for the Crapseys and money for Adelaide to continue her travels abroad, certainly fitted the superficial description of the fictional philanthropist, Jervis Pendleton; William Seward was a member of the board of the Society for the Organization of Charity and, in 1893, became the treasurer of the Immediate Relief Fund to provide for the charitable emergencies that occurred during the depression.[15] The romantic denouement in Webster's epistolary novel was a pure figment of her imagination (Mr. Seward was more than thirty-five years Crapsey's senior and it was Webster who displayed a penchant for father figures in her love life), but the idea of a young woman whose independence was brought about by a freedom from financial and filial obligations was one that complemented the image of the new woman.

Vassar

When Adelaide Crapsey entered Vassar she was socially equal to the other girls. Although most of the students came from upper-middle-class families and the income of her family was decidedly inferior, her own academic achievements recommended her and her father's growing reputation was a claim to fame. Even the status of the visitors that had filled the rectory that summer was enough for a freshman trying to make an impression to brag of.

But Adelaide was not particularly interested in impressions among the six hundred students at Vassar, neither the impression she might make on others nor the impression others might try to make on her. That summer Adelaide had walked out of a room full of dignitaries to chuckle more freely when a guest exclaimed, "Three times have I looked on Royalty!"[1] Even in high school she had turned down an opportunity to meet the famous teenage actress Maude Adams when the opportunity for a pleasure jaunt with a friend in Chicago presented itself. The whole concept of fame and pretension was amusing to her, and she was careful to make friends—on the basis of her pleasant personality and the variety and depth of her interests—with those people whose concerns and pleasures were mutual.

She was sure of herself and happy—her family healthy and secure at home, all supportive and excited by this great opportunity, and all certain of their faith and their purpose in the community. Philip's concerns were military and business-oriented, Emily's were domestic, and Rachel's were romantic. Adelaide may well have felt herself to be the educated representative to the world from her family, the one Crapsey with a chance to succeed in the academic world.

Her enthusiasm manifested itself in numerous activities. She began with the Drama Club and the Athletic Association in order to continue the activities in which she had first found success at Kemper Hall. She wrote stories for the *Vassar Miscellany* within months of her arrival, and by November her first college story, "A Maid to Love," was already out.

This story—about four Harvard men who fall in love with a photograph of a girl and use her as a source for inspirational flights, only to discover that the photograph was taken of their classmate dressed up for the Hasty Pudding—is concerned with sexual ambiguity and the imposition of romantic ideals on real people. As a story it is naive, but as an examination of the psychology of sexual identity and of relations between men and women it is extremely revealing. For by dressing the part, one may become an even more exemplary "maid to love" than a real maid could be. This examination of sexual appearances and reality continued to interest Crapsey throughout her college literary endeavors, emerging in her poetry when she began to evaluate the literary stereotypes of women in classical, Victorian, and Decadent poetry.

It was the beginning of the fall, this assertion of the discrepancy between being and seeming, between sexual identity and social assertions. Previous humorous criticisms of men were linked to failures to understand the self and consequent failures to understand others. The *group* misapprehension of sex indicated a *social* weakness, a basic misunderstanding of the opposite sex, and a social ignorance of the nature of love. But Crapsey was neither bitter nor jaded, although her interest in men, sexual identity, and relations between sexes was neither theoretical nor new. Her opportunities to meet men at Vassar were only slightly greater than in Rochester or Kemper, but there was a measure of anticipation and excitement over the prospect mixed with a great deal of mature caution about the dangers of idealization, of romantic courting, of partial knowledge.

The college was far more strict about allowing men and women to be together than the Crapsey household. When "Uncle Jervis" comes to visit the girls at Vassar in *Daddy Long-Legs,* the students encounter great difficulties in obtaining permission to invite him for tea in their study. "It's hard enough entertaining fathers and grandfathers, but uncles are a step worse; and as for brothers and cousins, they are next to impossible. Julia had to swear that he was her uncle before a notary public and then have the county clerk's certificate attached."[2] The tricks of men to approach innocent women were many and the college was always on guard. President Taylor himself was known to chase trespassing men off the campus.[3]

At Kemper Crapsey had corresponded with a young man named Hawley as well as with her uncle Charles Crapsey, a successful architect, and she shared the correspondence as well as evaluations with her mother. As editor of the *Kodak* she found a few of her subjects for editorials in the activities at Harvard, such as plagiarism and insufficient high school preparation for college, which indicate correspondence with a Harvard man. From her plays, poems, and stories as well it is clear that her knowledge of courting was instinctive and considerable and was accepted as a matter of course in the family. Her father wrote: "The man is supposed to choose the woman; but in reality, according to the law of sex, the woman lures the man. Nature has pruned her for this purpose. It has given her beauty, and grace, and ways that are wise, and tricks that are vain, whereby she may lay hold of her mate and compel him to her embraces. The girl of twelve or even younger unconsciously exercises these powers of coquetry. As she grows older she becomes conscious of her sex-power, and she plays it against the stupid strength of the male."[4] Crapsey was aware of her powers and aware of the way in which men could be captured by a mysterious look, a secret sigh, a dramatic phrase. The men who would write about her in later years— professors, travelling acquaintances, doctors, friends—would all acknowledge a mysterious charm that held their attention. But she preferred the direct approach, at least initially, and usually wasted little time with subterfuges. Her story, "A Maid to Love," was a warning against the "perfect picture," the external ideal, and a plea for honesty and understanding.

By her second semester, however, Crapsey was no longer able to devote her entire extracurricular attentions to these concerns of the maturing woman. The Spanish-American War broke out, and her older brother Philip, who was not yet settled in a job or marriage, enlisted. Soon after her younger brother Paul disappeared from home to join the army.

Despite the unmitigated emphasis on patriotism in the entire family, the war was a pivotal political issue for her. Both she and her father perceived this war as an imperialistic one, one which could damage the ideals and the character of the nation. The Reverend Mr. Crapsey described it as "a war in which the decadent Spain brought about the decadence of the Republic of the United States, changing the character of the democratic Republic of Washington and Lincoln to the imperial republic of McKinley and Roosevelt" and saw this mentality as one of the causes of the World War.[5] Perhaps the ideal of American government was not so real after all. Perhaps it too was like the "maid" in the photograph, an attractive deception. Crapsey joined the Current Topics Club and began to explore politics and economics.

She continued to write for the *Miscellany*. Her interest in society is reflected in her reading, and in May she published a review of *In Old Narragansett* by Alice Morse Earle. Concerned primarily with "domestic" history, or history as lived by women and men, Earle did not reach a large or respected audience. These issues were outside history, and only the most independent historians took them seriously. But Crapsey did not approach the book with the superciliousness of the indoctrinated historian. As with Charlotte Yonge, she championed the women writers who were considered minor by the literary and academic establishment because their readers had been educated in a society which trained them to trivialize the very values these women writers espoused and exemplified. The proper approach, the proper language, the proper understanding of motivations would allow the author to be understood, and with this in mind Crapsey wrote her reviews.

There may have been a personal interest in her concern with women writers. It is possible that she knew some of them personally, that Alice Morse Earle had been an acquaintance of her mother's when they lived in Brooklyn Heights together, just as it is possible that Algernon Crapsey had known Charlotte Yonge, whose writing Crapsey championed. It was not personal acquaintance, however, but issues which were the basis of their work and her interest.

The same issue of the *Miscellany* contains a short story, "The Knowledge He Gained," written, as was "A Maid to Love," on a level appropriate for a college journal (Jean Webster shrewdly commented, "Any student who could write a story for *Harper's* would not be writing it for the *Vassar Miscellany*."[6] However, there is once again a promise of further talent and an insight into the developments of Crapsey's mind. "The Knowledge He Gained" is about a writer who is seeking an ending for his story, a way to reveal the secret that would tie together the threads of the plot. Told that young women while combing their hair reveal their secrets, he finds himself eavesdropping on two girls performing this very task. But they tell each other nothing, and, recalling the old legend that women pour out their private thoughts at times like this, they laugh derisively. They go off, and the protagonist, having gained "insight," burns his story. This lesson is not only one of appearances and reality but has far more metaphysical overtones. For not only does it attempt to scrape away at the mystery of the unknown opposite sex, it also tears at the very notion of an inner, hidden truth at all. The intimate secret, the truth, the perfect ending, the one fact that will pull everything together may not exist at all.

About this time, Crapsey lost her faith.

That summer, Algernon Crapsey had the chair of dogmatic theology in a summer school in Canada. His own education, erratic and individualistic, had not really prepared him for pedantic pedagogy and he cheerfully explained the doctrines with lively metaphors. The Trinity was like an interrelated family, and Grace could be understood by comparing it to the lungs and air: "Thus, before a man can appropriate the air, the air must be there to breathe; [*sic*] The air is always there waiting on life, but before a man can appropriate the air, he must have a breathing apparatus."[7] The Reverend Mr. Crapsey did not even know that his discussions of the rational logic of the Trinity, the doctrine of Grace and the Incarnation, would be difficult to accept for anyone trained in dogmatic theology, which assumes the unrationalizable infallibility of the church. Because he was a rationalist and a humanist, he often failed to understand how anyone else could be otherwise and was shocked when a distinguished member of the clergy objected to his scientific method. But his basic conviction of a universal order and universal benevolence made it possible for all the unclear details to be incorporated in his religious practice and daily life. Even the objections of the clergy could be incorporated. He simply saw the interruption as a disagreeable moment and forgot about it.

Adelaide Crapsey, however, was gaining a more complete education in rational thinking and scientific method and was discovering that many questions could not be answered even by her father's generous, modern methods. A family tragedy was the catalyst.

On the fourth of June, Crapsey came home from Vassar to discover her youngest sister, Ruth, ill with undulant fever. Guilford Farm on Lake Ontario had been arranged for the summer in order to provide a better climate for her recovery. But recovery was impossible. Ruth's condition worsened, and, after calling Philip home from army camp and surrounding herself with her mother and siblings, she died on June 24. Crapsey went with her father to choose a family burial plot, aware that if the most cherubic and intense of the children could fall, the fate of the others was in question.

There was no fairness here, no logic, no justice. Ruth was not the sinful, the doubting one—Adelaide was. Ruth, in fact, could provide an ideal contrast to her sister. She too wrote poems, dictating them that summer to her nurse, but her poems were of the complete and utter acceptance of her faith.

A little wildflower by the wall
    Looked over at some poppies tall
And roses sweet and daffodils
    She thought they were so beautiful

II
But out of the house came a little maid.
    She carried scissors in her hand,
And she cut the beautiful flower
    Down, down to the ground

III
The little wildflower by the wall
  shuddered at the thought
But then it smiled and said,
  "I grow for God."[8]

As she lay on her deathbed at Guilford Farm, Ruth ordered candles for her feet and head, while her elder brothers and sisters (the poppies in the poem?) refused to accept her fate and played outside the house like children.

Crapsey returned to Vassar in the fall to publish the following poem, "Loneliness," in the November *Miscellany*:

The earth's all wrapped in gray shroud-mist,
  Dull gray are sea and sky,
And where the water laps the land
  On gray sand-dunes stand I.
Oh, if God there be, his face from me
  The rolling gray mists hide;
And if God there be, his voice from me
  Is kept by the moan of the tide.[9]

This was her first published poem at Vassar, and her father began laughingly calling her an atheist, certain that this stage in her religious development would soon be followed by a more mature one.[10] Her background with her family and with the Episcopal boarding school and the continuing discipline of compulsory chapel attendance at Vassar would probably bring her back to a more mellow approach. But this phase was not to be overcome, and, although she lost the sense of guilt, loneliness, and pain and made efforts at self-conversion, she could never again take the church quite so single-heartedly.

She was fortunate to have an alternative environment to her home to which to return after the tragic summer. Ruth could eventually be forgotten in the joy of Vassar.

Her roommates in her sophomore year were Margaret Pinkney Jackson and Jean Webster, a prospective author herself. Webster and Crapsey shared many basic similarities in their backgrounds, and the differences were complementary. Although Crapsey was somewhat more sophisticated, Webster was two years older and had experienced a great deal more. Her father, Charles Webster, who had managed the Charles Webster Publishing Company for his uncle Mark Twain and had experienced the sudden rise and fall in his career as the company first succeeded and then went bankrupt, had died a failure in 1891. He left his heirs with sufficient means to continue in their upper-middle-class life-style, but he also left them with a feeling of shame, a shame that was only mitigated by their knowledge of Webster's suffering from Twain's impossible demands.

It was a sudden death, a self-administered overdose of drugs, and at fifteen Jean was too old to have had this secret kept from her. Her reaction to this tragedy was blurred by her departure for boarding school in Binghamton, but there were also two clear attempts to dissociate herself from her past—she changed her name and her religion, becoming Jean instead of Alice and Episcopalian instead of Presbyterian. Obviously Webster's relationship to her famed great-uncle was not a particularly close one, for, like Hamlet's uncle, his crime precluded the possibility of his becoming a substitute for her father.

Although Webster spent much of her childhood in New York City and Far Rockaway, New York, from the time of her early adolescence she lived in Fredonia, New York, the small town where Twain had moved his family years before. This mixed background gave Webster the same mixture of sophistication and provincialism that characterized Crapsey. At Vassar this proximity meant that Webster and Crapsey could take the train home together on vacations, and, since the towns were only fifty miles away, could visit frequently when they were home.

Both girls were short and wiry and loved literature, justice, and a good time. But Webster was less of a dedicated student, willing to work only at what interested and pleased her, and Crapsey worked hard at everything, interested in all and longing to please the teachers she respected so much.

Webster had spent a year at the Fredonia Normal School before she enrolled in Vassar and perhaps for this reason was more practical in reaching out for actual goals than was Crapsey. She earned money from her writing, planned a junior-year semester in Rome to examine social institutions for a thesis on poverty in Italy, and attempted to publish in commercial magazines. Crapsey confined her activities to Vassar, accepted the last-minute failure of her plans to accompany Webster to Rome, and planned an evaluative thesis on the Socialist Democratic party in America.

The irrepressible Jean did much to raise Adelaide's spirits, and the finding of a kindred spirit helped Crapsey overcome her depression at her sister's death. They rode horses and bicycles together, co-wrote plays and operettas, travelled back and forth from Poughkeepsie to Rochester and Fredonia, and planned wonderful, fun-filled, and productive lives.

For many of the literary and dramatic activities, Margaret Jackson also contributed to the diversion that year. She too had literary inclinations and was loved by all. Elected class president in her sophomore year, she was more of a public figure than her roommates, but they were influenced by the activities of their successful roommate nevertheless. In *Daddy Long-Legs* the atmosphere is recounted. "Sally is running for class president, and unless all signs fail, she is going to be elected. Such an atmosphere of intrigue—you should see what politicians we are! Oh, I tell you, Daddy, when we women get our rights, you men will have to look alive in order to keep yours." Later, after the election, she writes: "We're very important persons now in '258.' Julia and I come in for a great deal of reflected glory. It's quite a social strain to be living in the same house with a president."[11]

The school encouraged independent thinking and original research. The use of original source materials and independent investigation was part of every course, and many courses were augmented by projects that encouraged participation in the world outside. One of the many projects Webster was to become involved in was a weekly column for the *Poughkeepsie Sunday Chronicle*, credited by the English Department. Webster described the job as a kind of lark, interviewing the maids who made butter curls, misunderstanding the astronomers, getting her first piece accepted. The gruff editor read her proposed column as she stood waiting and then growled, "How much do you want for it?"

I gasped. I had not the remotest idea what the price of a column might be; but I remembered that in the village where I was living a perfectly green servant girl who did not know anything received three dollars a week. So I said three dollars. He opened his cash register and handed it out. I went out to my two room mates [Crapsey and Jackson], who were waiting with their bicycles on the sidewalk, with the money clasped in my hand.

"Where did you get that?" they asked.

"I earned it."

"Good!" they said. "We'll go into Smith Brothers and have dinner."[12]

At Smith Brothers, next door to the newspaper office, lobster dinners cost thirty-five cents, a small fortune for Crapsey but not for the wealthy Jackson and the wage-earning Webster.

Webster claimed to have kept up the column for three years, but the semester she spent in Rome made a substitute imperative, and her roommates must have helped to continue it under her name and in her style. How Crapsey maintained solvency and stayed at Vassar remains a mystery.

The prize-winning sophomore play she wrote with her two room-mates was another event that helped raise Crapsey's spirits. *A Belated Feud* was chosen by a committee of faculty judges as the best play, the one to be produced the next year by Philalethetis, the dramatic society. The play was decidedly a happy one. A classic comedy in which the young members of two feuding families patch up an old insult to honor and tradition with love and inspiration, it followed all the rules for successful organization and dialogue. Guy Cotesworth, last of a family whose young uncle insulted the honor of Rosamund Ludleigh and caused her suicide, makes up for the ancient curse by loving and honoring Helen Ludleigh two generations later. The villain, Alan Ludleigh, whose love for his fair cousin Helen causes him to force a duel between himself and Guy Cotesworth and fake a serious wound, is found out when a scientific invention is tested by the young people, lighting up the woods and revealing the uninjured Ludleigh. Realizing that not all Ludleighs are good and therefore not all Cotesworths are bad, the old Colonel determines to accept the wedding and all is well.[13]

The team was presented with the prize cup for the play. Jean Webster exulted: "We are so happy we don't know what to do. Omega [the sophomore chapter] hasn't gotten it for years. All three of us on the committee were sophs, too, and the whole class is rejoicing. The girls on the other committees were seniors, etc. and the brightest persons in college, and we are, therefore, perfectly stunned. Three of the faculty judged it. One of them, Dr. Woodbridge, has just written a book on 'The Technique of the Drama,' and said in her letter to the President that our play was far ahead of the others in literary merit, in possibility for acting and in technical construction. Isn't it grand? Its [*sic*] going to be given for the first hall play next year."[14]

Crapsey had individual successes as a playwright as well. The *Vassarion* of 1899 contains her farce *An Insane Episode*, which, like so much of her work, questions basic concepts of perception in society. Once again, as with her first story, the opaque relations between men and women are used to illustrate a problem in definition and distinction. Two young men, on their way to visit some girls at Vassar, mistake the "Hudson River State Hospital" for the college and type the patients as typical Vassar girls. Like the focus on the questionable distinctions between men and women of "A Maid to Love'" this farce lightly bases itself on the arbitrary distinctions between sane and mad, fashionably eccentric and seriously ill. And, as in "A Maid to Love," sexual stereotypes prevent accurate assessments of reality.

The farce, which makes fun of the pretensions of Vassar women as much as the pretended *savoir faire* of the youthful would-be suitors, shows Crapsey at least as talented an author as her best friend and invokes curiosity about all those works Crapsey felt insufficiently significant to be preserved. "Adelaide could write finished verse in her early college days," wrote Webster, "with the ease and readiness that the majority of people reserve only for the most commonplace prose. I have actually known her to produce a book of an acceptable operetta over the weekend."[15]

Writing was not Crapsey's only connection with the stage. On February 11 in her sophomore year, she took the part of Lucy in *The Rivals* for the Second Hall Play. In contrast to the previous year, when a blood-and-thunder tragedy had been produced, *The Rivals* was light and gay, suited to Crapsey's mood as well as the tastes of her classmates. The *Chronicle* reported: "The cast was well chosen and the acting as a whole compared very favorably with that of former hall plays. . . . The costumes and wigs were made in New York and were exceedingly effective. . . . Lucy, the little maid, was dressed in a lavender satin petticoat with big flounces and looked quite like one of Watteau's shepherdesses."[16] It was only a college play, but the attention and professional quality of everything to do with it must have contributed in no small way to Crapsey's feeling that all the options in the world were being set before her.

Crapsey was not going to close out any of these options and continued her involvement with sports. She joined the recently formed Athletics Association and took on the job of managing the basketball team. Basketball had only been introduced to Vassar three years before her arrival, and so her talents were in demand. The players wore bloomers, which could not, of course, be worn in public or photographed, but as manager she might have avoided them.[17] For team pictures at least she wore dresses or shirtwaists. Small, with a round, serious, and gentle face, Adelaide sits in the center of the team photograph among a group of broad-shouldered, healthy women, altogether out of place. But she was not out of place, and her friendship with her team members was as genuine as her friendship with her literary acquaintances.

The games at the gym in Philosophy Hall were well attended and much discussed, and as manager Crapsey's decisions affected her team and the college. Webster reported one event in the *Chronicle*:

Some of the "subs" in basket ball who have never played against any regular team have been heard to say that they did not think there was much skill in the game, the only thing required being "natural quickness." On Wednesday afternoon, however, certain sub-players found that they were mistaken. The Seniors were to have played the Sophomores, but the manager of the latter could not collect the regular team, so she put in substitutes instead, who bravely faced the Seniors secure in their "natural quickness." But twenty minutes later when "time" was called an astonished and gasping group of "subs" dropped limply on the floor and marvelled inwardly over the "passes" and "signals" and various other kinds of basket ball lore that those seniors had picked up in their four years of practice. After the game was over that night when one of the crest-fallen subs dragged herself home, her room-mate exclaimed in astonishment with a glance at her dishevelled person, "What have you been doing?"

"Oh, I have not been doing anything myself," she replied sadly, "but the Seniors have been mopping up Phil. Hall with me. I've decided one thing though, and this is that I'm never going to play basket ball any more against people who know how."[18]

Crapsey's literary ambitions were twofold. Influenced very seriously by the scientific atmosphere in literature at Vassar, an atmosphere which countered the sentimental attitude popular particularly among women at the time, she worked at becoming a literary scholar. And it was for this that she was remembered. Edith Rickert, who taught Crapsey Anglo-Saxon and whose scientific approach to literature was to have a deep and abiding influence on Crapsey, remembered "both her scholarship and her charming face and personality. But her excellent work notwithstanding, no one then suspected that she would develop into an exquisite poet. Suffering was needed to develop that quality."[19] Rickert, who used some particularly painful poems by Crapsey as illustrations of various techniques in sound in her anthology of American literature, was careful to point out what many others noted about Crapsey's boarding school and college personality: she was totally lacking in self-pity and had a remarkably happy disposition. Crapsey was, in the romantic stereotypes of literary biography, too unlike the image of the poet. Her poetry, furthermore, did not imitate the *Sturm und Drang* of the popular adolescent Marie Bashkirseff or the romantic agony of the Pre-Raphaelites but advocated practical, sometimes hedonistic solutions to the romantic problems that beset college women. With such an unfashionable attitude to writing poetry, it was not surprising that she was persuaded of its trivial significance for her.

With happy college experiences and good friends to bolster her spirits, she tried to adopt a more hedonistic approach to life. After all, if nothing had any meaning, then any meaning was permissible. Elected class poet, she had license to express her dilemmas in print. She published "Time Flies" in the same *Miscellany*[20] as "Loneliness," and imitative *carpe diem* piece necessary to her well-being.

Yesterday in the garden-close
Budded and blossomed and blew a rose,
Faded and fallen its petals gay;

The rose lies dead in the garden to-day.
But, sweet, I pray you do not sorrow,
As fair a rose will bloom to-morrow.

Yesterday, dearest, you and I,
Swore that our love would never die.
Our vows were frail as all vows be.
To-day love's fled from you and me.
But, sweet, I pray you do not sorrow,
New love will come to us to-morrow.

Thus the hours swiftly by us go;
Well, I e'en wist it must be so.
Do not weep now for what is past,
Love and roses will never last.
Then gaily speed past what is over,
And gladly greet new rose and lover.

Perhaps love had come and gone, for despite the imitative character of the poem, Crapsey rarely fabricated experiences and rarely went further than metaphorizing her emotional states, but the sense is that her own experience was transformed into a "standard" poem.

In another sense the poem is not imitative at all. For although this genre was common to male poets, it is not at all characteristic of women of this period. Edna St. Vincent Millay (Vassar '17) still managed to shock her readers over fifteen years later with a similar message. The lesson was simple—that women should be as modern and irreverent about love as men are, that women too may now add up their lovers as part of their new experiences. The automatic equation of love with marriage, so basic to the education of women of the nineteenth century, was really passé. Had the language been as modern as the thought, this boldness might not have passed muster and would not have been published, particularly at a conservative place like Vassar.

The next poem, published a month later, is far more mocking of the lover who takes her experience, so romantic and remote from reality and feeling, seriously. "The Heart of a Maid," which changes as the daisy predicts first success and then failure, careens between ecstatic indifference and romantic agony.

> "Loveth?" laughs she gaily,
>   "Let him sigh!
> For all the love he offers,
>   What care I?"

Here the overblown language is strangely suited to the overblown sentiments. The maid pretends the indifference of the woman in Marlowe's
"To His Coy Mistress," but, under pressure, reveals the truth, that love is
central to her existence.

> "Loves not?" weeps she sorely,
>   "Let me die!
> For life without his love,
>   What care I?"[21]

Both sentiments are inappropriate, extreme, romantic, and worthy of
the irony Crapsey bestows on them. The romantic ideals of love, in
which the individual identity is fulfilled only through the admiration of
the other, deserve the kind of public mockery Crapsey chooses to
shower on them. If the poem is lacking, it is not for want of sophistication of sentiment.

Two months later an adaptation from old French, "Repentance,"
mocks the old roué who considers salvation only when he can no longer
enjoy his hedonistic life.

> My boon companion's been the devil.
> But now, alack! gay youth is spent;
> I'm getting old—I'd best repent![22]

These kinds of self-mockery may have been necessary steps for her in a
self-cure or public efforts to cure her friends, and, given the intimacy of
the format (a poem written to be read by all those who are acquainted
with the poet), it is doubtful Crapsey would confess to anything that
affected her immediately or deeply. Had she really been crossed in love,
or in pain, she would have kept it out of the *Miscellany*. Poetry, for her,
was becoming of necessity a public medium.

A strange little piece published in the *Miscellany* of December 1898,
urging fellow students to notice the collection of classic reprints always
hanging in a much-travelled corridor, suggests a continued effort on her

part to focus on the present and the richness of experience available to the observant. Entitled "Eyes that See Not," the essay indicates the effort Crapsey was making in her life to concentrate on the present, the living, and the available and to ignore some unpleasant memory. Her need and her ability to focus away from the ugly unalterable truth onto something of beauty, or to laugh, was to serve her and comfort her later in life.

While Crapsey was dealing with grief and loss of faith by concentrating on the present and by involving herself in the light-hearted, sheltered world of college, Crapsey's father too was feeling a great disappointment with his situation, but he was in a position to do more than she could. He was becoming disillusioned with the church, and in 1899 published a sermon entitled "The Disappointment of Jesus Christ" affirming his will to inspire the various churches to work together. "To-day the Christian religion seems to be the one disintegrating force in the world."[23] He was a significant enough figure in the church to escape unscathed with that kind of criticism, and his goals of uniting the different Christian faiths seemed to him achievable. Voicing his questions and aspirations made him even more popular than before. In May of Crapsey's sophomore year, he was invited to conduct services at the chapel in Vassar, an invitation which proved his acceptance in society and the solidity of his reputation.[24]

Crapsey was forced into a more passive position than her father, isolated from the power to change an imperfect world; it is probably at this time that she began to while away the time in lectures copying out nursery rhymes and writing her own.[25] One can never be certain to what extent Crapsey was herself aware that her lighthearted writings were examining certain fundamental tenets of society. Certainly her classmates and friends were not conscious of this, and perhaps Crapsey buried her doubts about the absoluteness of anything in her own subconscious. Yet the irreverence with which she treated the pompous members of her father's ministry, the dissatisfaction she voiced about basic principles of contemporary education (such as grades), and her refusal to accept almost anything as absolute truth without painstaking examination seem to indicate the kind of personality that had discovered the relativity of existence and found nothing—not love, not

God, not friendship—eternal. And yet she could not, as another might, forget the questions entirely. Her concerns were theological and philosophical, and her lapsed expectations for the universe continued to trouble her for the rest of her life.

There were more exposures to Emily Dickinson that would have struck a corresponding chord in the theologically troubled Crapsey. A scene in *Daddy Long-Legs* recreates the naiveté of the students in the face of the bold Dickinson:

> In English class this afternoon we had an unexpected written lesson. This was it:
>
> I asked no other thing,
> No other was denied.
> I offered Being for it;
> The mighty merchant smiled.
>
> Brazil? He twirled a button
> Without a glance my way:
> But, madam, is there nothing else
> That we can show today?
>
> That is a poem. I don't know who wrote it or what it means. It was simply printed out on the blackboard when we arrived and we were ordered to comment upon it. When I read the first verse I thought I had an idea—The Mighty Merchant was a divinity who distributes blessings in return for virtuous deeds—but when I got to the second verse and found him twirling a button, it seemed a blasphemous supposition, and I hastily changed my mind. The rest of the class was in the same predicament; and there we sat for three-quarters of an hour with blank paper and equally blank minds.[26]

Webster took this episode and these verses from her English class and expressed the attitude of most of the students. But it is almost impossible to believe that Crapsey, having read and published Dickinson and having experienced the same emotions and attitudes toward the divinity in recent months, would not have reacted with intense recognition to what was on the board before her.[27]

Perhaps because she had strayed so far from the domestic into the realms of intellectual speculation, she spent the summer at home, subdued, doing all the marketing for her mother. She had written a review of the latest book of poems by Martha Gilbert Dickinson, Emily Dickinson's niece, focussing on the characteristics to which she herself aspired, "epigrammatic brevity with a subtlety and suggestiveness astonishing in the narrow limits she allows herself."[28] A review of the niece allowed her to ignore, for the time being, the metaphysical implications in the poetry of the aunt while studying the style Martha Gilbert Dickinson imitated. That conventional spirit continued for the summer.

Even after she returned to school, she remained close with her family, and a week after her birthday celebrated her Uncle Charles's and her mother's appearance in New York City with dinner at the Grand Central. Her spirits were good. Possibly over dinners like these she wrote the joyful poem "Champagne."

Yellow-pale and bubbling-bright,
Effervescence of delight,
Froth of laughter, foam of song,
Rain of rose leaves blown along;
Pretty women dressed in pink,
Kisses swift as glasses' clink:—
Over brim of lifted light,
Yellow-pale and bubbling-bright,
Life, a laugh's length old is he,
Tips alluring wink at me!

Although temperance was obviously not a concern for her or her family,[29] other aspects of politics did concern her, and that year she plunged wholeheartedly into that world. Crapsey's concern for society and politics was untypical of her contemporaries in American society, who generally equated women's suffrage with temperance, and of her classmates at Vassar, who were primarily passive and hereditarily Republican. She continued her membership in the Current Topics Club and the Marshall Club and joined the T & M (Tempus et Mores) debating society to take part for the first time in official political debates. Perhaps as a result of the recent informal lecture of Sidney and Beatrice Webb, visitors of Herbert Mills's, on "The Scope of Democracy in England," the formal debates that year focussed on England's policy in the Transvaal. Twice Adelaide joined in formal debates on this subject. On January 20, her team divided in two to argue the issue, and Adelaide was on the side of the opposition, protesting England's policies. "The house resolved itself into a committee of the whole and the debate proceeded with unusual fervor,"[30] but Crapsey's side lost. A month and a half later her team of juniors battled with Qui Vive, the senior team, an annual event of central concern to the school because of its identification with class interests. "It is amusing," commented the *Chronicle*, "to see young women, otherwise apparently sane and sensible, behaving as though the winning of a debate were a matter of life and death." One can imagine the ensuing description Webster gave in the *Chronicle* as a debate between herself and Crapsey: "If you tell them soothingly that it will be all the same a hundred years hence they will return savagely that it will make a heap of difference now and that is what they are about. An attitude which after all it is easy to understand." To a packed auditorium each leader spoke for twelve minutes and then the assistants, of which Crapsey was one, spoke for eight minutes each. But, despite enthusiasm and sincerity, the juniors lost. "The victorious class rose in a body, stopped a minute to seize its debaters, and then rushed out to the class tree to give vent to its feelings. Any place inside of the house was a little too small for them. The defeated class made a sorry attempt to console itself and then went sadly home while outsiders laughed again and said: 'All this fuss about a debate; isn't it absurd.' "[31]

Despite the cavalier attitude Webster was attempting to impose on the situation, the political feelings were genuine. Crapsey's argument was an unpopular one and not nearly as remote and academic as it would seem. The dominating public opinion was for the "white man's burden," particularly since the United States was beginning to see the economic advantages in taking up the yoke of its own "white man's burden" in Cuba. The undemocratic nature of England's policy was not then clear to anyone but the Socialists, who pointed out in their obscure journals to an unheeding public:

The great English nation, boastful of her civilization, cannot much longer escape the odium of her frightful inhumanity.

The direful physical condition of the 3,000 Boer captives in the prison pens at Bermuda has induced a local community on the island to send an appeal to Americans for aid for the poor wretches. . . .

Among the prisoners are over 100 boys under 16 years of age, while the oldest is a man of 80. If this is civilization, what, then, is savagery? Why does not this "liberty loving" America say the word to England that she said to Spain? It is because the English capitalists will not let her. Capitalism is one. It knows no country. It knows no pity. It is Capitalism which sent the Czar to France: poor puppet of a class exploitation. It is Capitalism which is starving these noble and heroic burgers [*sic*] in Bermuda, on our very shores. It is Capitalism which is slaying American boys and Tagalong [*sic*] boys for its ends in the Phillipines [*sic*]. Human life is nowhere sacred placed against the dollar.[32]

Crapsey criticized the use of this kind of overblown rhetoric but applauded the ideas.

The return of Lucy Maynard Salmon, who chaired the History Department, after a two-year absence in Europe, was another impetus for Crapsey's public involvement in politics. "You have a mind, use it!" Salmon urged her students,[33] and encouraged them—sometimes against the will of the college—to participate in politics and to become involved in their studies in active political issues, although she herself knew the limits of its success.[34] While in Europe she wrote a book which included a severe criticism of the United States for its growing imperialism and found that publication was impossible. "Nobody cares a straw what a woman has to say on a public question (unless she writes to the newspapers on the horrors of war and signs the letter 'A Mother')," Salmon wrote,[35] but she continued her efforts, despite personal depression and pessimism, because, as she wrote, "the Transvaal has stirred me up even more than the Philipines [*sic*] and I can't bear to leave stone unturned."[36]

But few of her students took her specific political views seriously, except Crapsey, who could see both the moral need for involvement and the impossibility of change. At Kemper she had written a story about a mayor who, to get an important bill passed, held his city council at gunpoint all night, certain they would be too embarrassed to admit the coercion, the failure of the system of democracy. A story Crapsey published in the October *Miscellany* of her junior year, "Mr. Percival Poynton and a Pig," also illustrates the beginnings of social awareness. Although farcical, it is concerned with the intervention of the upper and middle classes in the reforms of the working classes. Poynton, a stereotypical dandy, moves into a small town in an effort to run against Finnegan the barkeeper in a local election. But when he is made to win the weight-guessing contest for a pig and is presented the pig in the middle of his condescending political speech, he gives up on the election and leaves the town to Finnegan.

There is much of a gentle imitation of Mark Twain here, as well as a rationalization for staying out of politics. What good would it do anyway? Poyntons, like women, come into the world of the common man with good intentions and an inflated sense of their own morality, but they have no connection to the real world. What can they accomplish? "Mr. Percival Poynton and a Pig" is a gentle, veiled look at the contemporary economic and political situation for Crapsey.

The three courses she took in economics, "Principles of Economics," "The Labor Problem," and "Economic Seminar," together with three elected courses in history, "General European History," "The Revolutionary Era in Europe, 1763–1815," and "Europe in the 19th Century," reveal that although her major was English her academic concerns were not limited to language. Certainly the environment created by Herbert E. Mills (Millsie), professor of economics, made involvement in economics essential to any thinking woman. In the winter of 1899, for example, a group of graduates lectured the students on the economic position of women.[37] Adelaide became friendly with Mills, a University of Rochester graduate with a doctorate from Cornell, whose courses consisted primarily of the examination of social institutions such as orphanages and prisons. When Sister Edwardine wrote him over twenty years later, asking him to describe Adelaide's personality, Mills was happy to respond with a warm letter. "I knew Miss Crapsey well. She was a lovely soul, combining scholarship and aesthetic appreciation in an unusual way. There was a dainty, whimsical quality about her which

---

quite defies description. She was possessed of a keen, alert mind, a great sense of humor, and contempt for sham. It is impossible to convey in words any idea of her personality. She was dainty, appealing, charming. It was a great joy to have her in my classes, especially in a small intimate one of six unusual minds."[38] Adelaide's character so delighted and mystified him that Mills emphasized only her mind and personal appearance. He did not note those aspects of his students which he characterized as typical in later years.

> In that last decade of the nineteenth century, and with increasing vigor and momentum in the first decade of the twentieth, students were displaying that awakened social compunction and were filled with that intense sense of social obligation which characterized so many of the finer men and women of that period. . . . Seniors asked: "What can I do? Where can I be useful after leaving college?" . . . Willingly they accepted small incomes, sacrificed careers the world would have applauded, proudly marched in militant processions, joyfully they accepted arrest and imprisonment for the sake of "Votes for Women," for free speech, and to help a strike.[39]

The delicacy with which Millsie described Crapsey—and his silence on her political and social opinions—is not only a result of his awareness of what his religious correspondent wished to hear. Crapsey, although concerned with social reform, was rendered almost immobile by the conflict that still welled in her—the desire to be accepted by society and to be a part of the religious world warred with the desire to do great things, to turn the world around. Her hunger to influence major changes was countered by the image of the ideal woman with which she grew up and the feeling of impotence which suffused so many of the famous women she knew. A poem, published as late as December 1899, "Hail, Mary!,"[40] reveals the extent to which Crapsey even now longed for the certainty and wholeness with which she had been brought up. The sense of responsibility she must have felt as class poet to set a sincere but conventionally virtuous example is extremely evident here.

> In loveliness and purity,
> In faith and grace and piety,
> In love and in humility,

God give me grace to be like thee,
That in my poor and low degree
I, like thyself, may blessed be.
       Hail, Mary!

This poem, written when her father had already become certain that Jesus had not been born of a virgin and the Lord, when her ties to religion were at best weak, reveals a last-ditch attempt to relinquish the divided self, the rebellious personality, to give in to greater forces and become the ideal of womanhood as well as religion. But, despite its fervent desire, this is a poem that might have been written by Oscar Wilde, so caught up in sin and guilt that only the most pure attracts.

Had she been born ten years later and gone to school with the ardent socialists Mills would soon encounter in his classes, her tentativeness about social reform would have been less pronounced; had she been born twenty years before, the incipient voices of reform might not have shattered that sense of wholeness and completeness for her or her father. Perhaps a difference in time might not have erased the desire for change, the desire to tear down established traditions or the longing for traditions that could not be pulled down, that would withstand examination. Yet this uncertainty, shared secretly by many women reformers of this period, paralyzed her activity.

A story published in the *Miscellany* of January 1900 offers a clue to one of the reasons Adelaide stayed behind as Jean Webster began to test her limits by seeking adventure, taking a semester in Italy. "Milord and Milady" is ostensibly about the tragedy of the lack of communication in marriage, but the artifice of the situation and characters makes the sincerity of the author's desire for realism questionable. Having taken a lover after years of loneliness and unhappiness in her marriage, the duchess of Glastongate is about to leave her husband. After a discussion with him in which it is plain that he loves her, she goes out for a short ride, promising not to depart until the next day. The duke, convinced she has ceased to love him, decides to sacrifice himself for her happiness and commits suicide. Returning home to find him, she admits she would not have left and concludes with the judgment: "Both of us dead."[41]

The story is about choice, choice made halfheartedly and without clear guidelines, choice which leads to tragedy, not only for the other party, but also for that part of the individual which has incorporated the other. Cutting oneself off from one portion of one's life, one destroys a portion of the self, and yet the possibility to be whole cannot exist after a major crisis of division. The woman's husband and lover may have allegorized for Crapsey her own conflict between her love of knowledge and independence and her longing for security.

Her longing for freedom was beginning to receive some institutional supports in her junior year. By the system recently copied from Harvard, students in their junior year were able to elect all of their courses. With very limited electives in their sophomore year, the students were brought to their freedom gradually, but it is certain that Crapsey appreciated the new choices available to her.

That semester, Adelaide took the part of Fanny Hadden in *Captain Letterblair* in the first hall play. She posed charmingly in the photograph, a delicately small-waisted girl with a figure very much in fashion. Her co-star, Margaret Jackson, who played the male lead, wore the customary skirts, cunningly hidden behind Crapsey's. "Almost every part was well done, and some were remarkably well done," their objective roommate at the *Chronicle* reported. "Miss Margaret Jackson in the title role, and Miss Adelaide Crapsey as Fanny Hadden, were especially worthy of mention."[42]

During the second semester, Crapsey was probably kept more busy than usual by Webster's absence, for Webster's column about Vassar life in the *Poughkeepsie Chronicle* continued to be written, and Crapsey must have written some of these pieces. However, she also found time to combine her love of literature with her growing sense of political awareness in a "Grand Opera" for Washington's Birthday Colonial Ball, *Der verlorene Vater*, which no longer exists. This opera, which was written by a committee of six girls, may be assumed to be concerned with lost political and moral values.[43] An opportunity for her humor was also employed, for this was a comic opera, featuring the family of George, America, and Columbia Neverlie posed against British officers such as Lieutenant Digan-Grind.

Her growing emphasis on realistic political considerations is manifested in a review of Tolstoy's *Resurrection*. In Crapsey's analysis Tolstoy's idealistic attempt to replace the violence of human law with religious love and understanding is minimized. "Most of us will find it hard to accept and most of us will not remember the social doctrines as the vital part of *Resurrection*. When we think of the book we will think first and foremost of the story of Demitri Nekhlúdoff and Katúsha Maslova." Her criticism was basically that literature cannot be used to teach a lesson, that it must first follow aesthetic criteria. A few months before, in reviewing Kipling's *Stalky & Co.* for the *Miscellany*,[44] she had taken critics of Kipling to task for their extraliterary criteria. "The stories are good examples of Kipling's heaven-sent gift for narration. In the simple telling of a story, the working out of it from start to finish, Kipling has few tales much superior to these." Back in Rochester, her father and sister were working on a novel about social injustice and attempting to follow this very advice.

Crapsey spent part of the summer of 1900 visiting her grandmother.[45] Harriet Gunn Trowbridge had always been the one to whom she had shown her poems, since her mother's busyness and practical nature must have made passionate discussions of literature impossible. Her grandmother was aging and would have few years left to share with Crapsey. And, too, Adelaide was lonely. With all her friends on the basketball team and in dramatic societies there would never be anyone like Jean Webster to share her literary life and discuss those aspirations with. When Jean returned in August, Crapsey went directly to Fredonia to visit her.

Crapsey's senior year began with great success. She played the title role in *Kitty Clive,* a Restoration period piece, to exuberant praise by her roommate, now back at her reporter's typewriter. "The character of the fascinating little actress, Kitty Clive, was admirably fitted to [Crapsey's] . . . style, and she has never done better work even in a hall play."[46] With her New York City costume she was certainly dressed the part, and "made her entrance in a huge black velvet hat and a long black redingote. Her gown was red silk with a white over dress having a watteau pleat in the back and trimmed with black velvet bows. She wore her hair powdered, patches on her face and carried a stick with a ribbon bow." The play itself was a serious one and earned serious praise.

Kitty Clive was the Drury Lane comic actress and rival of Peg Wolffington who so inspired the admiration of the great literary figures for her wit. This was the kind of life Adelaide could live—to be in the center of dramatic and literary activity, to have intelligent men swarming about her, to dress up and act, to be independent, to influence the opinions of powerful men. Even Dr. Johnson had told Boswell that "in the sprightliness of her humour he had never see her equalled."

But this was becoming a new world, where women did not have to use such art to be influential. The return of Jean doubled the membership of the Socialist party at Vassar and Crapsey and Webster threw themselves into the national elections. Sam, Webster's brother, recalled the family reaction to Adelaide and Jean's brand of politics. "We read in the papers that the Vassar girls had held a political rally, and two girls carried the Socialist banner reading 'Vote for Debs.' My mother commented, 'That shows what kind of homes they came from.' But the next day Jean wrote enthusiastically, 'We had a wonderful rally, and Adelaide Crapsey and I carried the Socialist banner.'"[47] Jean's version of it was even lighter:

> 510 votes were cast, 441 for McKinley and 61 for Bryan, 2 on the Independent ticket, 2 on the Socialist and 4 on the Prohibition ticket. A bulletin board was placed in the main corridor the even of election day and the returns were telephoned out from Poughkeepsie. A large and excited crowd gathered before the bulletin and remained during the entire evening, somewhat to the detriment of the next day's recitations. Between messages the two parties formed into impromptu processions and marched up and down the corridors beating pans, blowing horns and trying to drown each other's yells. The two forlorn people who had voted the Socialistic ticket marched around by themselves with a banner labelled "Debs" and were very much disappointed when they heard that he was not elected.[48]

That sense of humor was sorely needed then, but it must have given Webster and Crapsey a great deal of satisfaction to note that socialism made deep inroads at Vassar only a few years after their departure. The socialist demonstration of Inez Millholland (Vassar '09) on May 9, 1909, made the *New York Times*.[49] Partly because of Millholland's personal attractiveness and partly because of the social awareness of her class-mates, radical politics would soon begin to be associated with Crapsey's alma mater.

That year Crapsey concentrated on her senior thesis, which was con-cerned with the history, composition, and future of the Socialist party. Although a sincere adherent to the party, she was also able to use some of the perspective of her humor in analyzing its flaws and revealed her objectivity in her awareness of its limitations. Her thesis points out, for example, the extent to which socialism concentrated on criticism of the present and ignored future plans, as if they were doomed to remain a minor, powerless group of gadflies. Her own vision was further-reach-ing, and she noted "that very little is said of fresh evils to which so-cialism might give rise, as for instance, political corruption." There were insufficient leaders in the party, the party had a tendency to "a glib use of catch words, a meaningless array of statistics and an hysterical de-nunciation of everything in existance [*sic*]" and it had a propensity to-ward vulgarity which was "a particularly grave [fault] when it can be brought against a party whose avowed aim is to exert an uplifting and educated influence on those with whom it comes into contact."[50]

These faults were forgivable in a youthful party and could be out-grown. Their consequence, however, was that Crapsey could not im-merse herself wholeheartedly in the Socialist party and kept at an aca-demic distance, despite her sympathies. Her ultimate belief was that the Socialist party itself would not change the world, but elements of so-cialism would infiltrate into the public realm of politics in general, so why not concentrate on a more academic, objective, and potentially an ultimately productive analysis of the situation.

Perhaps Millsie helped to influence Adelaide's political opinions, but her father certainly had a greater influence upon her. By her senior year, Crapsey was taking the reverend's ideas a step farther than he himself dared. She was beginning, in fact, to become an influence on him.

In the summer of 1900 he was awarded a degree from Hobart, an honorary doctorate in theology. Dr. Crapsey was happy with his religious position and his nascent thoughts on social reforms did not disturb this position. Despite the popularity of prohibitionist speakers, for example, Dr. Crapsey was vocal that year in deprecating their philosophy, noting the actual ineffectiveness of rallies and violence. Together with William Thurston Brown, the socialist minister of Plymouth Church, he noted that the prohibitionists hadn't solved any of society's problems.

> Indeed, although the hardships of the depression had disappeared by the late nineties, the number of widows and orphans did not diminish and the number of unattached young men and young women actually increased. The problems created by their search for excitement, as well as those involved in their struggle to earn a living, became more insistent. The churches, many argued, had a responsibility here which they could not fully meet through the regular services, which called for united action, for wide support of interdenominational and nondenominational agencies, for a more understanding approach to community and world problems.[51]

The possibilities for the future were great, and as Adelaide gathered success after success in college, she built up hopes for a positive creative future in which society would be improved and she would be fulfilled. "When I knew her," one of her English teachers, Florence Keyes, wrote, "things still had the freshness of the dawning." Keyes saw this optimism as sophistication: "Adelaide Crapsey and Jean Webster belong closest together, and a little apart, in a band of beautiful young beings—I speak inwardly—who remain with me in an aura of Springtime, its fresh fragrance, its lifting skies, its open promise."[52]

Crapsey was growing, and an old classmate from Kemper Hall who came to visit her in Rochester for a weekend was impressed with that growth. But Crapsey did not reciprocate her friend's visit, and, although she returned to Kemper Hall for two years, failed to notify her outgrown schoolmate of her presence.[53] She became more selective of intimate friends, more concerned with people who liked what she did—poetry and politics.

Keyes remembered her student in a haze of glory and recalled that "Adelaide was larger, more interesting, and more varied than her work. . . . That is just the opposite of what one sees in so many students

whose work is the highest part and most concentrated essence of themselves. Adelaide was deliberate in the use to which she put her thinking
and her literary enjoyment and her ethical reflections."[54]

This was indeed a student that one could readily label "most likely to
succeed."

Emily and Patty

The last semester at Vassar seemed as if it would move in a perfect crescendo to the peak of graduation. Crapsey's classmates were finally in the "privileged" class and were becoming involved in the last expressions of their sheltered existence. On Valentine's Day the seniors had center stage as they went through all the traditions allowed only to them. Webster wrote in her column:

> The valentine celebration is a Senior monopoly. The under classes merely look on respectfully and wait their turn. The Seniors all wore white and red to dinner Thursday night, their tables were lighted with candles, and the room rang with their laughter. Two huge baskets had been standing outside the Senior parlor door all day ready to receive valentines, which were distributed just before dinner and placed in the center of the tables. If any members of the lower classes were rash enough to want to write valentines, the missives had to be tamely sent through the mail. . . . The Seniors have been writing poetry this week in honor of the season, and one girl who has composed no less then twenty seven valentines says that verse has become such a habit with her that she can barely refrain from taking her lecture notes in rhyme.[1]

Even in the normally staid German Club excitement reigned. Heinrich Conreid, the director of the Irving Place Theatre, a German institution in

104

New York City, came to lecture at Vassar on "The Stage." An actor decorated by the kaiser before he became a director and an enthusiastic lecturer, he cut a dramatic figure. His lecture—in German—could only
have interested those few fluent students of the club, but they made up
in enthusiasm what they lacked in comprehending numbers.

> In the course of the conversation some of the girls said that the next time
> they were in New York they would attend a German play in his theatre. He
> was immediately enthusiastic and said "Come at once," and then as an
> inspiration struck him, "Come tomorrow, come as my guests. I will tele-
> phone for seats. Lead me to the telephone." He was promptly led to the
> telephone, and he ordered that six boxes and twenty orchestra chairs be
> reserved for the Vassar girls. He beamed upon the astonished German Club,
> and when asked how many girls his invitation included, waved his hand in
> a gesture which took in all the college and all Poughkeepsie, and murmured
> "Je mehr, je besser." The German Club took him at his word and some forty
> went to New York on the 9:35 train yesterday morning and attended Less-
> ing's "Minna von Barnhelm."[2]

Webster knew no German (except, as she once confessed, "Wo is [*sic*]
das Glas Wasser?")[3] and took the story from Crapsey, who had progressed so well in high school German that she was considered the best
student ever by her teacher, Henriette Schwartz.[4] Knowing her interest
in German and in the theater, as well as her boldness it may be assumed
that Crapsey was the one who suggested the jaunt.

Crapsey was elected to Phi Beta Kappa along with Margaret Jackson.
Webster, whose interests were elsewhere, did not make it. Phi Beta
Kappa had a great deal of significance: it was a new organization at
Vassar, only two years old, and Vassar was the first women's college with
a chapter. "It is a virtual acknowledgement that our standard is as high
as that of any men's college" Webster crowed.[5] Equality of opportunity
was not far off, and academic achievement was proof of it.

The feeling was that there was nothing that good spirits, good will, or
scholarly investigation could not accomplish. The world was before
them. The yearbook Crapsey was editing was shaping up to be a more
comic and gently satirical version of previous yearbooks, with sophisticated Beardsleylike drawings from Jean and humorous poetry by Ade-

laide. It would be a pleasant good-bye to childhood and a good experience for a future career.

In the spring of Adelaide's senior year, Emily Crapsey contracted appendicitis. She was rushed down the street to the Homeopathic Hospital but died within hours on Saturday, April 13.

Adelaide's competition was gone. The sister against whom she had constantly measured herself, with whom she had consistently argued and played, the sister she adored and resented, who gave her so many reasons for rebelling and developing, had won the contest with her innocent death. But Crapsey had also lost her best friend, her most cherished intimate from whom she had slowly been growing away in the past years. Both grief and guilt were overwhelming, and escape into school activities was more difficult this time. On June 12, Class Day, she was caught by the camera strolling in her white dress with Jean Webster, her face a study in tragic seriousness.

There was much in her that would not admit to the tragic impact of her sister's death on her own life. She continued to fulfill not only her academic obligations but also the social commitments of a Vassar senior as if nothing had happened. The annual pilgrimage to John Burroughs's country cottage was made in May as if nothing had changed.

John Burroughs, the man who made Whitman known, the author of countless books on nature, was then at the peak of his popularity, and he was visited yearly by admiring Vassar girls at Slabsides, the rustic place at which he could entertain his guests away from his wife's obsessive and forbidding housekeeping. Not all the Vassar girls were treated to his pleasant and garrulous personality. "He does not mix well with every newcomer," Burroughs's friend and biographer wrote of him. "One must either have something of Mr. Burroughs' own cast of mind, or else be of a temperament capable of genuine sympathy with him, in order to find the real man. He withdraws into his shell before persons of uncongenial temperament; to such he can never really speak—they see Slabsides, but they don't see Burroughs."[6]

This was not true in Crapsey's case. Even when she first visited him—with fourteen other girls in October 1899—her group had been particularly successful with the potential hermit. Jean reported:

They were royally received by Mr. Burroughs, who turned them loose among his possessions. He showed them his books and pictures, and ingenious furniture, made of silver birches with the bark still on. The girls dug potatoes in the famous naturalist's garden, and roasted them in his fire place, pronouncing them infinitely superior to the plebian ones grown by an ordinary farmer. They spent the day wandering through the woods and scaling cliffs. On their way back they visited "Riverby," Mr. Burroughs's other home on the Hudson, after which his last book was named. They returned to the college tired and scratched and torn, but affirming that the day had been as good as Mohonk, which is the highest praise a Vassar girl can give.[7]

But this time, though Burroughs was delighted to see Crapsey, she had changed. A friend from Rochester, Florence Van Demark, knowing how highly Burroughs regarded Adelaide, brought her camera along to record the meeting for posterity. Her snapshot captured an amused and delighted Burroughs but a strained and mortified Crapsey. The girl who had looked so directly into the lens on so many previous occasions, who had posed and primped in her costume, who had mugged before the camera with her sister, was now ashamed to be caught at her pleasure, embarrassed to be found with a smile.

It was not that her taste for humor was gone. Crapsey was responsible for "General Execution" of the *Vassar College Exhibition Number 1901* that month. Her title in this "Exhibition" was "professional funny man, Chairman (*ex-officio*)," and she was aided by her comrade in the debating team, "Helen Storke, fellow funny man." The program is full of class jokes: the head of the Economics Department is "one of the mills of the Gods," alluding to Millsie, and the difficult first-year course in English is titled "Freshman Vivisection." The course in philosophy is defined as "the future development of self government. Offered to any one who will take it." The degrees conferred include "P.M. (passed math)," "A.B. (able breakers of precedent and everything else) conferred on Seniors after four years of strenuous effort," and "A.M. (a mistake) to get it at all."

The entire program was a musical, with the teachers, reporters, students, and friendly critics all presenting at least a chorus of their transformation into parody. The faculty, to the music of the "Burgomeister" [*sic*], sang:

> We're the high muckee-mucks of the College V.C.,
> You can tell right away we're the faculty.
> But we've suffered a change that's exceedingly strange,
> Since last we assembled your lot to arrange,
> For now we intend to be broad and progress,
> And exhibit ourselves as we are—we confess
> We've tempered it somewhat but still we'll allow,
> We're Faculty, whoop-la! Unsanctified now.[8]

But the humor is automatic, not ebullient, a necessary stay against the tragedy of life, and her edition of the *Vassarion* was less than her funniest work. The subversive uniqueness of the editor is evident in only a few statements and juxtapositions. Listing the names of the Daughters of the American Revolution, she added a poetic comment loosely adapted from Robert Burns:

> Ye see the daughters set down here
> Wit' pedigrees and a'that,
> They count back full a hundred year—
> But are they mair for a'that?
> For a'that and a'that.
> The man of independent mind
> He looks and laughs at a'that.

Alongside her own senior portrait she placed the caption, "It is a very serious thing to be a funny man." "After great pain," Emily Dickinson had written, "a formal feeling comes," and now humor was an external, social function, not a way of looking at the world, as if Crapsey had taught herself that she must keep up her optimistic exterior, even if the interior joy was gone. Later she wrote a poem to exhibit the confusion that such self-imposed schizophrenia wrought.

> There's a gay girl laughing
>   For pleasure of the sky,
> Oh, laughing low and tenderly
>   In love of soft-breathed sigh

Of wind and greying shadows,
  That incorporeal lie
Across sun-ardent grasses
  Where bird wings poise and fly.

There's a woman very sorrowful
  As empty days go by,
Uncounted hours watch hopelessly
  By heart too hurt to cry;
There's a gay girl laughing
  For joy of earth and sky,
And a woman dumbly sorrowful,
  Who am I . . . Who am I . . .
                    (*CP,* p. 127)

On June 10 Adelaide Crapsey graduated from Vassar College with honors, having achieved the most solid general education a woman of her age could expect. Her future—within the limits of the period—was before her. She could, like some of the other pioneering women of her time, carve a career for herself out of a male stronghold—in editing, in politics, in literature. But that would have required enormous effort, and it seemed that all of her energy was gone.

Certainly the publication of Algernon Crapsey's only novel, an emotional story of the New York City slums, influenced her feelings about what to do with her life. The book, a study in socialist realism, was the joint effort of Algernon and Emily. In style and technique it had the naiveté that Adelaide had learned to detect and avoid at Vassar: the lesson was foremost. And yet the characters and subject matter were interesting. The description of the life of the young female protagonist, Keturah Bain, exhibits extraordinary understanding of the heart of a girl, a deep feeling for social injustice, and a good measure of fictional stylistic control. By reviewers it was described as a "realistic study" even though it was "crude, somewhat wanting in the elegance of polish, but then we defy any one reading it without emotion."

The book dealt with the corruption of the rich and the oppression of the poor in New York City. Its heroine had a drunken father, an opium-eating mother, a crippled brother, and an only sister who, wild and heedless, involved the rector of a rich and fashionable parish in a scandal. A reviewer concluded: "Books written for a purpose are not to be treated lightly, particularly when such familiarity is shown with those who people the slums and their vicissitudes so powerfully described."[9] There were more than social elements here—the exploration of the "guilt of the fathers" reveals the extent to which the Reverend Dr. Crapsey was aware of his own role in the family, his blame and the limitations of his guilt, and his responsibility for the future.

Since *The Greater Love* was written together with his beloved elder daughter, he dedicated it to her memory.

> While this book was in process of preparation for the press, it was subject to the criticism of one to whose judgement the writer constantly deferred. Before the book was completed, this wise critic was suddenly taken away by death. That event, saddening as it did the life of the writer, delayed the completion of the work.
>
> Now that he is about to submit his creation to the colder and impartial judgement of the reading public, the writer wished to say, that, whatever may be the fate of his book, he has already been amply repaid for any labor and anxiety it may have cost him, by the fact that it gave some pleasure and added some interest to the last days on earth of Emily Margaret Crapsey; who was both the loving daughter and the judicious friend of the writer, and to whose blessed memory and pure spirit, as an act of gratitude for all that she was to him and of all that she did for him he now dedicates this book.[10]

Never again was he to exhibit such emotion concerning his children in print. Never again did he dedicate a book to his offspring.

Emily, equally as talented as Adelaide, was the right kind of writer, a person who used her gifts for others. She was first stenographer in a lawyer's office, and her employer, Mr. Harvey Remington, was so impressed with Emily that he spoke of her warmly at every opportunity years after her death, and years later, in charge of the local draft board during the war, turned down the application of Emily's nephew when he recognized the name, sentimentally advising him to go home and study.

Just before she died, Emily was occupied at her office with writing up her employer's journal of his trip to Europe. He wrote in the unfinished journal: "The foregoing journal was dictated to Miss Emily Crapsey, daughter of Rev. Algernon S. Crapsey, D.D. of Rochester, N.Y. and was left by her as partly finished a few days before she left our office in April, 1901. She died Saturday, April 13, 1901 after a brief illness. Her work was most conscientiously, intelligently and carefully prepared and in all the dictations which she took in our office, displayed the existence of those qualifications essential to the work of a successful and useful amanuensis."[11] Adelaide would visit her sister in her office at the Lincoln Alliance Bank Building at 183 East Main Street when she was home on vacations and could see the distinction between Emily's selfless dedication and her own individualistic desires to "do." So that even though Emily's employer perceived her as "of the same cheerful intelligent and buoyant type as her beautiful and accomplished sister," there was a major difference.

Emily was in many ways an ideal woman for her time. Not only was she dedicated to others, to people whose work was clearly significant and productive, but her future life was to have continued this cheerful selflessness. Her long engagement to Channing Moore and her disinclination to continue her studies marked her as a conventional girl.

If the theories about the education of women had been correct, if all the ideas of divine justice had been right, then Adelaide should have died and Emily lived to a ripe old age. Adelaide was the individual, the rebel, the slightly naughty, slightly selfish child who managed to appear proper and to stay alive when the basically more virtuous ones were taken away. She was the one who kept late hours with her books and studies and neglected the accepted physical feminine limitations. She was the one who mocked religion, who doubted and hungered.

The forward impetus of her life stopped. Crapsey was suddenly weak, drawn, having probably used up all her adrenalin getting through those last two months at school, and so she agreed to postpone any career decisions for a year and stay home. It was reminiscent of the year she had stayed home after her father's mortal illness, this respite after great pain. Perhaps her parents convinced her that she was needed to fill the gap left by her sister. Perhaps she perceived this as her immediate duty.

But there seemed to be no struggle, no quarrel, no disagreement with the need for temporary passivity.

She was not well, and two of her sisters had already died. Other graduates were content to stay home and await a husband or an offer for employment, and there was no stigma attached to her idleness. But certainly her own guilt, the guilt of the successful, unworthy survivor, contributed to her decision to postpone her life.

The political scene provided an appropriate backdrop to her conflict of withdrawal. The country was undergoing confusing changes that suggested that perhaps passivity was the proper response. The anarchist Leon Czolgosz had shot and killed President McKinley. On September 6, 1901, seven thousand Rochester citizens who had come to Buffalo for the Pan American Exposition were at the scene of the assassination by a man accused of acquiring "anarchistic views and inspiration from Emma Goldman . . . [and] was reported to be hiding at her parents' home in Rochester."[12] There was a danger in radical politics, an extremism that passivity avoided.

Adelaide wrote her class secretary for the *Vassar Class Bulletin* of June 1902 that she was "studying law in Rochester, St. Andrews Rectory." Evidence of these home studies is apparent in her father's sermons, which became more learned in legal matters that year. On October 17, 1901, for example, Dr. Crapsey gave a very factual sermon on prison methods in compliance with a request of the New York State Prison Association. He suggested three lines of progress: (1) treatment of prisoners with respect (2) employment for prisoners, and (3) professionally trained personnel. The emphasis was upon the responsibility of society for the existence of prisons and the concerns similar to those registered in the economics seminar of Herbert Mills.

Two months later, in December 1901, the Reverend Dr. Crapsey delivered "A Constitutional Defense of the Negro" at St. Luke's Church in Washington, D.C. His concerns with the fate of the black man in the modern world were of course linked to those of his grandfather, although he never mentioned the historical precedent in his speeches or publications. And his recent involvement in the mission for the church underlined to him the discrimination that permeated his society. But rather than appeal to the humanity and the morality of man, Dr.

Crapsey, influenced perhaps by his daughter's new scholarly method, chose to prove the case for the amendment of the Constitution to enfranchise the black man by examining the premises of the Constitution itself and condemning the illegal treatment of blacks in the contemporary South. His plea was for civil disobedience in the tradition of Thoreau, and he asked his audience to go to the polls and vote even if their lives were in danger. "God forbid that you should lift up your hands save in defense of the rights of man and the lives of women and children. Do not kill, but be killed; be killed until your blood becomes as a river defiling all the land, until like the blood of Abel it cries from the ground for vengeance. Be killed until you have lost from your veins the last drop of the blood of the slave and can stand up as free men in a free land."[13] The speech was so successful that he was asked to repeat it at a mass meeting in the Metropolitan Methodist Church in Washington, D.C. the following Sunday, December 15, and the contents of the speech were published in a pamphlet.

This direction her father was taking was particularly suitable to Crapsey, one which continued her own thinking. But there was no place for her in this profession except as an aide to her father, and despite her desire at this point to be a helpmate rather than an independent "doer," she was not formed to be second to anyone.

If she accompanied her father to Washington at this time, as she in all likelihood did, she had the opportunity to renew her friendship with Margaret Jackson, who was teaching English and history at Whitor and Bangs' School there, and to reconsider the profession of teaching.[14] Crapsey needed money and expansion. The emphasis at Vassar had been on considering a career, not sitting at home. From her junior year, Adelaide had been hearing lectures on subjects such as "The Occupation and Education of Women of the Twentieth Century,"[15] and, despite her weakness, she could not accept a vestigial role in society. Now she determined to take a position, one requiring not too much emotional effort or drive. That winter she accepted a teaching job at Kemper Hall, a place that had long meant security and shelter to her. The job would begin in September and she would have plenty of time to recuperate fully without having to undergo the anxiety and anticipation of an unknown future.

It is possible that Adelaide's decision to return to Kemper Hall, where she had imitated and competed with Emily as an adolescent, was linked to her sister's death—a return to a childlike, known world where she was loved and her memories of Emily were intact.

Certainly this could not have been a planned career move. Crapsey had not thought of becoming a teacher. Vassar students about that time were advised "not to teach until they looked into the opportunities in law, medicine, journalism, business, and college settlements."[16] The Teachers' Club at Vassar had invited: "If you aim to be a teacher / When you get your first degree / Just put your name upon the list / Of this society."[17] And Adelaide didn't, joining the Current Topics and Athletic Society instead. But she possessed the required credentials, and teaching was easier than struggling in an unknown world.

She prepared her way for a reunion with Kemper by sending the *Kodak* some of her work in response to a request for literary material. Both the poem and story she sent were geared to a less sophisticated audience than she had been addressing at Vassar, but both reflected her attitude. "Bob White" is a delicate, determinedly optimistic sentimental piece, utterly unlike the ironic verses of the *Miscellany.* Beginning in a time and mood of uncertainty, "On brink of night, / On edge of day," the song of the bird brings the speaker to "sweet of day, / While dawn grows bright."[18]

BOB WHITE

Bob White! Bob White!
On brink of night,
On edge of day,
While dawn is grey
In eastern sky,
I hear your cry,
Bob White! Bob White!

Bob White! Bob White!
As dawn grows bright,
You sing, you sing,
On bough a-swing.

What do you say,

Bob White, Bob White?
That sun is come,
That it's light, light, light,

That it's time to be up,
Up, up, and away,
For day is here,
The glorious day!

All this you say,
Bob White, Bob White,
In sweet of day
While dawn grows bright.

The conventional form and subject of the poem seem to be deliberate—
an attempt to put the lid on her individuality. Adelaide knew too much
about poetry to write unconsciously, had discussed the "sacrifice of
sense to sound" and the avoidance of triteness.[19] The effect is a musical
children's poem.

A more interesting piece is the story "Gustav's Solo," about a little boy
who is ostracized by his nursery school classmates because his speech is
defective and uncommunicative. One day he asks to sing a song in
school, but it ends in mockery, and when he hears a little boy say, "His
mother talk baby talk to him, en she'd oughta know better," he shapes
himself and his mother up and adjusts his language to the real world.

> When he got to the house he slammed the gate behind him and pounded
> viciously on the door. His mother rushed to open it for him. "Did 'oo tum
> back to 'oo mover?" she cried.
>
> But Gustav looked at her frowning. Then he spoke with great sternness
> and much deliberation, unconsciously imitating the little boy's scornful
> voice. "Don't——talk——baby talk——you'd ought'er——know better."
>
> Then he marched into the kitchen. His mother stood speechless but his
> grandmother chuckled. "I told you it was time to stop that, Mamie," she
> observed. "I'm glad some one's learned him to speak like a human being."[20]

Perhaps "Gustav's Solo" was meant as a warning to the Kemper Hall
girls of problems they would be experiencing as teachers and mothers,
but Crapsey also wrote the story for self-therapy. Using the medium of

children's experience as a distancing device, Crapsey was telling herself two things: (1) To succeed, one has to pull oneself up by one's boot-straps. Understanding and coddling were not what got things done. (2) To get anywhere, one had to get out of the house.

As a story it is not successful. The enthusiasm and humor of Crapsey's voice had made up for occasional youthful awkwardness or naiveté in the past, but the voice was now a touch pedantic, dry, prosaic. Crapsey's talent—smooth, easy language and dialogue—seems to have disap-peared, and all the lessons of understatement she had learned from her student years at Kemper and Vassar forgotten. Crapsey had either lost her interest in writing fiction or was aware of the loss of her talent—it was the last story she ever wrote on her own.

Although they seemed far from her heart, the old subjects—of young men and women—were not far from her mind. By February she was forced back into the world of society. A dance for her brother Phillip and his unit was held in Albany on February 2 at the Hotel Van Eyk. The officers, all the right age for the twenty-three-year-old Adelaide, could not help but perk up her spirits.

She may also have become involved in a local monthly journal of eight pages edited by William Thurston Brown, assisted by J. W. Cas-tleman and H. T. Mosher. This socialist journal, entitled *Here and Now,* came out of Rochester and was being edited by Crapsey's friends.[21] But all of her efforts of this period—literary and social—are undramatic and unrecorded.

When the weather cleared a bit, Crapsey went to visit Jean in Fre-donia for a month in March and April. It may have been at this time that they were photographed on the Webster front porch, Jean, her brother Sam, and Adelaide, engaged in meditative conversation. Webster had a great deal to talk about with Crapsey. She was intent on carving out a career for herself as a writer and wanted to work on her first book with Crapsey, since Adelaide had long been her help and inspiration. Webster bought a new typewriter and began hammering out pieces about col-lege. Crapsey took turns typing them.

It was a wonderful opportunity to relive those wonderful experiences at college, and Jean happily dedicated the book to the good times they had all had in their rooms at 234 Main. The title character of *When Patty Went to College* was considered by many to be modeled on Adelaide, and there was good reason for this assumption. Patty had all of the wonderful paradoxical characteristics of Adelaide in college. She was complex and self-examining in the extreme as well as extroverted, social, humorous, and sensitive. But Patty is not always a consistent character and probably had a bit of both friends in her construction.[22]

Some chapters are more reminiscent of Adelaide than Jean. Getting her way in a man's world, for instance, was as little a problem to Patty as it had been to the youthful Adelaide. When the girls make some rather major changes in their room, changes forbidden to students (such as taking up the carpet and painting the floor), Patty finds a way to manipulate the janitor so that he not only approves the changes but also fixes their illegal stove. "You must remember," Patty tells her roommate, "that Peters is not only a janitor; he is also a man."[23]

The convolutions of a minister's daughter were clear. In the chapter "A Question of Ethics," Patty has developed a great reputation for answering questions in class because her psychological and logical gifts enable her to plan for the questions she knows teachers will ask. One day she miscalculates and is forced to resort to bending over so that she will not be seen to be called on. She does not fail, but the others do, and the guilt engendered by her "success" brings her to confess her guilt and ignorance to her professor, who is so charmed by her admission that he offers to teach her the material she should have failed.

The stories are humorous and often based on true experiences. But they were intended to be more than just stories about Vassar girls. Books about Vassar had been written before by other alumnae; this one tried to collate an image of the modern woman, the woman who was not domesticated and even scorned the feminine arts. Patty, for example, defies the ladylike ceremony of tea by picking up the hot kettle with a golf club. Learning had not ruined her, however. Her sense of humor and morality had been developed, and college was enabling her to understand herself and her world, to cast off stereotypes and the intellectual restraint that was limiting society.

Patty is a polite Tom Sawyer. When she escapes from compulsory chapel and the prospect of the bishop's dull sermon by sitting outside on a beautiful Sunday morning, she accidentally encounters the very bishop she was avoiding and they discuss the presence of God in nature. To his inquiry about her notorious rebelliousness, she answers: "You have to have a reputation for something in a place like this or you get overlooked. I can't compete in goodness or in athletics or in anything like that, so there's nothing left for me but to surpass in badness—I have quite a gift for it." One can well imagine a conversation like this taking place between Algernon Crapsey and Jean Webster or even his own daughter.[24]

The image of Webster and Crapsey in Fredonia in the spring of 1902 is a pleasant one: two women who had been successful in all their joint efforts in college are now considering how to expand their horizons. One is exuberant, the other restrained, still shocked by a tragic blow. And the exuberant Webster recreates her changed roommate as she was before the tragedy, before her loss of spirit. As the "Patty" was dying in Adelaide, Jean made that "Patty" eternal.

Webster was full of the optimism she had not lost that year. Crapsey, content to sit back and watch her best friend make the career she herself had lost heart for, kept her fingers crossed.

Webster later claimed ignorance of the existence of carbon paper and the pair banged out three copies before their energies gave out, mailing them to publishers simultaneously. Back home Crapsey waited for good news, but soon it began to seem that the real world was not as accepting a place as Vassar. Webster's mother wrote to her brother Sam Moffett, who was up for the job of senior editor at *Cosmopolitan*, "If you should go on the *Cosmopolitan* staff maybe you could help Alice [Jean], she doesn't seem to have much luck. *Scribners* have held her manuscript for four or five weeks and neither accept or refuse it—very trying."[25]

By the end of summer not only Scribners but a number of other houses had returned the book. "The manuscript came back from all three, also from the next three," Webster reminisced. Particularly trying was a letter from McClure's: "Dear Miss Webster: If you had read our magazine as carefully as we have read this manuscript, you would know that it is not fitted for us."[26]

While Crapsey was getting ready to leave for Kemper, it was beginning to look as if her conservative direction was the better one. But then Century accepted the book and a spring publication was arranged with 10 percent royalties. McClure's soon wrote Webster: "Have you not something to offer us in the line of 'When Patty Went to College?' I have been searching for years for just a manuscript for my magazine."

Public acceptance was soon followed by that of the problematic family. Webster's famous great-uncle, Mark Twain, wrote her mother: "I read the most of Jean Webster's book today; and the most of what I read greatly pleased me—the workmanship, I mean. It is limpid, bright, sometimes brilliant; it is easy, flowing, effortless, and brimming with girlish spirits; it is light, very light, but so is its subject. Therefore its lightness is not a fault; its humor is genuine and not overstrained. There are failures in the book, but that happens with all books."[27]

Webster, with her vision of success first coined with Crapsey in college, was off.

Part Three

*Millions of presumptuous girls,
intelligent or not, daily affront their
destiny, and what is it open to their
destiny to be, at the most, that we
should make ado about it?*

Henry James, *Portrait of a Lady*

The Escape to Kemper

Adelaide had belonged to the Kemper Hall Club during her last year at Vassar and remained in close touch with her alma mater. The sisters took pains to give the girls a continued sense of belonging. One year Sister Florence sent the Vassar girls a "genuine English 'plum-cake' thick set with *American* nuts in the frosting"[1] and the girls—Elizabeth Adams ('89), Emily Wells ('89), Dora Merrill ('97), Mary Spalding ('98), Florence Wells ('98), Helen Whitemore ('98), and Adelaide—met in Elizabeth and Emily's room to eat and reminisce. Each girl was given a "dainty namecard, with its familiar daisy and the girl's name and class written on it. Everything from the cake to the cards was perfect, as only the Sisters, I think, can make things perfect," Elizabeth Adams wrote the nuns.

All this sentimentality did not seem childish or extreme. Despite the development Crapsey had undergone she continued to feel that Kemper had contributed greatly to her life. Adams and Wells were now teaching at Vassar, and their continued interest in their old school showed some of the continuity—the feeling that life was not just a linear thrust forward, but there were emotional and spiritual retreats to times and places of earlier great feeling. In her valedictory address, when she had urged her classmates to press forward, seeking unknown territory, Crapsey warned: "But even as we set out, we feel a rush of tenderness for the

dear home country we are leaving; and on the first slope the eager foot
falters, and we pause with a sudden tightening of the throat for a last
backward look. . . . Surely, it is a fair land to dwell in! The call of the
open road sounds fainter in our ears, and we would abide there. But it
cannot be. The road stretches out before us."[2]

Though Adelaide Crapsey had said a firm goodbye to Kemper when
she left, looking forward to a new and progressive life, she found herself,
in September 1902, back in an environment she had already perceived
as a teenager to be a bit constrained and restricted as a teacher of literature and history—"Ancient, Medieval, and Modern."[3]

But her life there was not as confined as might have been thought.
There were new and interesting people to meet, and her English chairman, Mary Delia Lewis, who had recently arrived at Kemper, became an
immediate and close friend.[4] There were a number of other Vassar graduates on the faculty to whom she could relate. Dora Merrill, the out-
standing athlete who had graduated from Kemper with Crapsey and
Vassar one year after her, was also now back at Kemper teaching physical education. Henriette Schwartz, her beloved German and French
teacher, was still there, and their acquaintance was renewed. And Kemper Hall had not stood still. As the home of a progressive community of
sisters, it had recently been equipped with a new gymnasium, a bowling
alley, and an art studio.[5]

The transportation to Chicago, fifty-one miles south, and Milwaukee,
only thirty-four miles north, was considered convenient, with eight
trains passing through Kenosha daily, and now that Adelaide Crapsey
was an adult and not financially dependent upon her parents she was
able to take advantage of those places she had only glimpsed once or
twice as a pupil.

Teaching became interesting to her, despite her reservations about
some of the aspects of the system. Mother Margaret Clare, still in charge,
told her teachers that their function was to teach their students to use
their minds, and wrote: "It is the desire of the Sisters to maintain a high
standard of scholarship; and as it is believed that the chief aim of education is to teach the pupils to think, every effort is made, especially in the
Preparatory Department, to direct and increase this power."[6] "The

aim . . . is not primarily to fill the memory with facts, but to form such habits of mind and character as shall enable a girl throughout life to grasp and use what she learns." This kind of pedagogy appealed to Crapsey. All the other, unproductive aspects of teaching, such as examinations and preparation for examinations, she could do "tongue in cheek," one of her pupils remarked years afterward.[7]

Her interest was in providing her students with the materials with which they could make up their own minds on issues. As a history teacher she not only supplemented the textbook with topical references to authorities, as was prescribed in the catalog, but she helped Mary Braislin, who was librarian as well as English teacher and also a Vassar alumna, with the remodelling of the new reference library so that both she and her students could be sure to find the necessary material. "Kemper Hall," the catalog enthused, "has a well chosen reference library in constant use by teachers and pupils."[8] "Emphasis is laid upon the continuity of history and upon the close relation between history and literature," the catalog affirmed, but although Adelaide Crapsey taught both, her interest gradually shifted to the latter. Politics now began to seem too far beyond her.

Crapsey taught the principles of composition and how to write. The students were drilled frequently with short themes, which were corrected and discussed in class at length, "in regard to style, thought, and general interest." The scientific method Crapsey had learned at Kemper and perfected at Vassar was once again emphasized, and she found herself teaching the girls "note-taking . . . the making of reports; abstracts, and outlines." The courses in literature were no less serious and stringent. Crapsey taught major English and American authors, "in reference to subject matter, structure, and style. This study is supplemented early in the course by a manual of literary history, which during the rest of the course is used constantly for reference. The great types of prose and poetry are analyzed and compared, and effort is made to train both the imagination and the critical faculty."[9]

As part of an effort to keep up her own interest with creative material and to encourage independent thinking in her students, she began to examine some of the rules of poetry and prosody. Together with her class she explored the question of what constitutes a poem. "There must be something apart from the content of the lines, however beautiful that content might be." She took the first lines of "Lycidas," "Yet once more, O ye laurel, and once more / Ye myrtles brown, with ivy never sere, / I come to pluck your berries harsh and crude, / And with forced fingers rude, / Shatter your leaves before the mellowing year," and asked what made it the pure poetry it was. How did the content of the lines introduce the theme? Couldn't the sounds and sequences of the vowels have something to do with the effect of sonorous grief? She pointed out the " 'syllabic pull,' a term which she used to designate a subtle rhythmic pattern underlying the conventional metrical structure of the line,"[10] and began to realize that meter was not the single measure of rhythm in a line.

Perhaps the agnosticism she felt but couldn't reveal at Kemper caused her to turn her attention to a less dangerous examination of established traditions. The entire concept of hierarchy upon which an Episcopal school was based, with God at the top, had little significance for her by now. And at Kemper religion was a given and prayers were constant and unavoidable. The Book of Common Prayer was the basis for education and in addition to regular services on Sunday there were required daily Evening Prayers in the chapel, "corresponding to family devotions at home," and a short Office at the opening of school.

The examination of poetic principles was not obsessive but distracting. And anything Crapsey attacked she did with "indefatigable industry . . . a fastidious taste which would admit of no standard but perfection, and dominating all, extraordinary intellectual grasp and power."[11] She was at Kemper, after all, for the money, and was beginning to formulate plans for an escape to Europe in the near future. Her critical endeavors were short-term outlets, relief from the tedium and from her hypocrisy of silence.

She was also there for her health. When she had come there as a child she had enjoyed a much better state of health than she had experienced in Rochester. The climate was better at Kemper, much milder than Rochester or even Vassar. "The close proximity of the lake," the catalog pointed out, "serves to temper the extremes of heat and cold, so trying in places further inland, while the Hall is protected from the violence of prairie winds by high evergreen hedges and by magnificent pine and cedar trees. The water supply is from an artesian well of thoroughly tested hygienic value. Epidemic diseases seldom touch houses where it is used. The uniform good health among pupils resident in the town as well as among those of the household is worthy of note as indicating the healthfulness of the climate and other outward conditions."[12]

A stay for her health was certainly needed. She had lost a great deal of weight and seemed weaker, tiring easily and participating less completely in extracurricular activities, although her positive attitude gave color and bravado to her appearance. "She never lost her bright and alert look," one of the nuns said. Crapsey did not rely only on the physical environment to restore her energy and believed in will power and optimism in refusing to relent to a reluctant body. "Her keen and penetrating mind no doubt carried her through many an hour of physical weakness," her fellow teachers observed.[13] Her sense of humor aided as well, and it was her ability to laugh at her failing flesh that helped her go on.

The impression she made on the people she knew at Kemper was strong. It was not only her alertness, intelligence, and wit that struck others but her values as well. "Her unswerving loyalty, her power of understanding, arising from her strong belief in the essential right of every individual, however intimate a friend, to unexplained acts and motives; her instinctive shrinking from any talk which savored of the petty or unkind, and her keen relish for a humorous situation in literature and life"[14] were all appreciated, and there were many students and teachers who wanted to be close to her.

She was in the same position as many of her fellow alumnae at Kemper. Most of the girls who had graduated three years or more before Adelaide were married, but Emily's class had only three married alumnae out of twelve, and all but three of Adelaide's fifteen classmates were still single. Three of the sixteen were at Vassar.

But she had learned to distance herself from others. Perhaps the loss of Emily and Ruth made her suspicious of the pleasures of friendship, perhaps the seriousness with which she continued to approach her life made too many friends an unaffordable luxury. Whatever her reasons she did not renew intimate ties with Kemper alumnae, most of whom were in the neighborhood, single, and occupied in similar professions.

Instead her ties were institutional, organizational. At Kemper Crapsey became vice-president of the alumnae association and her classmate, Dora Merrill, was the corresponding secretary. Since Kemper Hall was always in financial difficulties, the purpose of the organization was promotion. The ministers and trustees, Algernon Crapsey among them, had a great deal of status and education, but their financial resources were not sufficient to keep the school solvent. The president was from a different generation, the class of '83, and with their organizational skills the young Vassar graduates thought to streamline the alumnae association and promote the interests of the school. "A strong effort is now being made toward the closer organization and greater practical efficiency of the Association."

She had returned to Kemper Hall to the same teachers and the same organization she had grown out of when she left for Vassar, and she overcame the pain she must have felt at her lack of progress by remodelling, by controlling the place in which she was once controlled. The library, the alumnae association, the grades could only have been part of what Crapsey tried to revise and rejuvenate in her old school.

Webster, in the meantime, was devoting her efforts to the publication of a series of stories that would be collected as "Much Ado About Peter." Capitalizing on her success with her characterization of Adelaide, she was selling profitably to magazines while Adelaide herself ground away at a less glamorous task. Webster made more money with eight stories than Crapsey could earn in a semester of drudgery. And, as if to prove the contrast, Webster took off in November 1903 for Rome, where she hoped to get more inspiration and make her earnings stretch further.

This second year must have been exceedingly difficult for Crapsey. She had conquered her past, had taken control of Kemper as a teacher, and although she had replenished her pocket had not recovered her health. She was tired after each teaching day, drained, and on weekends had no energy to take advantage of her free time. When she wasn't busy with her duties, she took to her bed.[15] She had had so many plans in college, and now she could barely keep up with the same existence she had mastered and outgrown years before.

From the emptiness of her present existence a plan began to emerge.

The adventures of Jean Webster, travelling in Italy that year, began to influence Crapsey's thoughts. Webster, who had left in November of Crapsey's second year at Kemper, was attending lectures at the American School in Rome in her informal, offhand way and was impressed. The serious, scholarly institution was a perfect place for Crapsey. The climate would be better for her than Kenosha, the expenses would be few, and she would have the opportunity to see the world and study with the great classical scholars of the time.

Furthermore, Crapsey knew that Italy was a good meeting place for writers and artists, and, like the Scholar Gypsy she had idealized in her high school valedictory speech, she wanted to wander among them. She began to feel once again that she was destined for something great— some great discovery, some great exploration, some great writing. She was going to be reborn to do what she had always dreamed. Her family agreed that Crapsey was in need of a rest and she submitted her request for a leave of absence to Kemper Hall.

The plan solidified. Jean was returning to the United States to take care of the publication of a new book but would leave for Italy again with Adelaide in October and help her to settle in for a year in Rome. Crapsey would study at the School for Classical Studies and be allowed the advanced studies for literature that schools for women, with their practical orientation, often did not provide. Her good Latin background would be a great asset.

Excited and anxious for travel but physically weak, Adelaide would probably not have been able to concoct the entire plan by herself. She was used to changing environments, but her long trips had been structured and organized by someone else—her sister or her mother—so that the details of where to sleep, where to eat, and how to get around were usually arranged for her. Jean had learned the ropes from Lena Weinstein and Ethelyn McKinney, two friends she had met on a previous trip, and could give good practical advice to one who had never been abroad.

There may have been some hesitation at this point. There was certainly enough excitement going on at home to keep her busy, and, had she been like Emily, perhaps she would have stayed at the rectory to help out. Her father was beginning to disclose some of his dissatisfactions with the church to his parish. The people of Rochester, immensely satisfied with him as a sincere social reformer and an inspiring public speaker, always received him with good cheer, no matter how unorthodox (and sometimes theologically unwise) his attitudes were. He spoke to a people who wished to be able to relate their religion to their everyday life, to put into practice the ideas of virtue they were taught, and so when Algernon Crapsey, in the fall of 1903, began his series of sermons on "Religion and Politics," which continued for over a year, at first giving the history of the church and then criticizing its remoteness from reality, no parishioner objected.

In fact the Reverend Dr. Crapsey was at the height of his popularity. In honor of his twenty-fifth anniversary at St. Andrews, a week-long, city-wide celebration took place in June 1904. His family was there to reap the glory, and only when it was over did Adelaide leave for Fredonia to discuss her forthcoming trip with Jean.

Webster and Crapsey had not seen each other since Jean's trip to Italy, and she must have been full of stories about her adventures in Rome in the winter and Palestrina and Lake Como in the spring. In Rome she visited the graves of Keats and Shelley, in "the cemetaryist cemetary [*sic*] I know,"[16] and had an audience with the pope, during which Lena Weinstein asked him for a blessing for her friends. "The Pope cocked his head to try and catch the words and then said, 'Si si.' "[17] In Palestrina she had stayed at the Casa Generale, a convent, and was full of typical Webster-Crapsey stories. For Easter at the convent she concentrated on the four orphans, the *poveretti,* in the care of the convent.

> The *poveretti* all have new shawls of blue, the virgin's color, sent out from Rome by the Mother Superior. I gave each a chocolate Easter egg, and they are "molto molto contento!" This is a *festa* all day long and they have nothing to do but play, says the *Madre,* though I notice they are attending masses and services pretty assiduously. They have been learning something to recite the last two or three days. Yesterday *Suor* Prisca had them out for exercise, she with her breviary, they each with their little books. Sabina climbed a knarled olive tree—reciting her verses all the way up—the refrain was in Italian, "The Lord is risen, Hallejuia Hallejuia."
>
> "Come down out of that tree," said Sister Prisca. "The Lord is risen, Hallejuia," said Sabina, affecting not to hear.

"Descend yourself—descend," said Sister Prisca, raising her voice.

"Hallejuia, Hallejuia," chants Sabina, still not hearing.

Sister Prisca caught her by the foot before she could remove it to safer heights and she came down still singing her refrain. I looked out half an hour later and they were all running races in the vineyard—each down a separate row of vines—*Suor* Prisca well to the fore—her head up, her elbows back. I have never seen a racer do it in better form—and Oh! but it was a spectacle, her crucifix and veil streaming out behind—her black draperies catching the wind and ballooning out like sails. Sister Prisca, panting and rosy cheeked, dropped down on the terrace to rest.[18]

These were not the standard stories of the standard European tour for young ladies. They were full of the excitement of new and exciting people and old and staid places to be viewed without awe. The taste for Italy could only be increased by a discussion with Jean Webster.

It was probably in Fredonia that Webster began to fear she would not be able to go with Crapsey. Busy with her publishers and her new book about social conditions in Italy which had just been accepted for publication, she was forced to remain in New York City for revisions. Webster had high hopes for *The Wheat Princess* and, reluctant to leave it, could only promise to join Crapsey at some later, undefined date. And at first it seemed impossible that Crapsey should go by herself, exhausted from teaching and inexperienced in travelling as she was. Crapsey left Webster to join her father at Cook's Point in Canandaigua for the rest of the summer with the thought that the magnificent adventure for which she had been longing for years might escape her again.

There was a hotel at Cook's Point, run by Eleazer Carter, Jr. and his brother George, and a number of notable people had been coming for the past ten summers to enjoy the point, the lake, and the stimulating company.[19] Among the regular visitors at nearby Elm Lodge was the Reverend Dr. Augustus Hopkins Strong, who was a trustee for Vassar, and his wife, Harriet Savage Strong. Strong conducted daily reading-discussion sessions in the works of the world's great poets, tackling a different poet each summer. This effort resulted in the printing of at least two of his many books.[20] But Crapsey was not terribly interested in intellectual company this year and spent most of her days in the hammock, "world weary," another visitor wrote, "and a little desperate."[21]

She was twenty-four that summer, and many women her age were, if not wives and mothers, at least working on careers they respected and loved. Her younger sister Rachel had been married a year before and was now pregnant with her first child. Crapsey's desperation, however, stemmed not from an urgent need for marriage so much as an urgent need for romance and excitement, for a path to fulfillment. The two years at Kemper had suppressed and intensified her anticipations, and now her dreams of Rome were threatened.

Her hunger for romance was apparent. She was brewing the first poem she saw fit to preserve in years, "Birth Moment." Composed, perhaps, as she lay on the hammock, the poem's setting is the beach, and the speaker views a young woman, a newly born Aphrodite, emerging from the sea.

Behold her,
Running through the waves,
Eager to reach the land;
The water laps her,
Sun and wind are on her,
Healthy, brine-drenched and young,
Behold Desire new-born.

"Birth Moment" reflects the anticipation, beneath that "world weariness" Crapsey exhibited, of a union with the world, a mystical joining with nature.

And she who runs shall be
Married to blue of summer skies at noon,
Companion to green fields,
Held bride of subtle fragrance and of all sweet sound,
Beloved of the stars,
And wanton mistress to the veering winds.

The anticipation was sexual as well. Crapsey had never agreed with the puritanical attitude toward young women and sex and was accustomed to being looked at in her girlhood with disapprobation because she kissed boys. Her descriptions of a kiss are graphic, concentrating on the lips and not on the identity and relationship of the lovers. The physical description here is charged with intensity and romantic excitement:

(Ah, keenest personal moment
When mouth unkissed turns eager-slow and tremulous
Toward lover's mouth,
That tremulous and eager-slow
Droops down to it:
But breathless space of breath or two
Lies in between
Before the mouth upturned and mouth down-drooped
Shall meet and make the kiss.)

(CP, p. 64)

The conclusion of the poem makes clear her own desire to become a part of the erotic picture:

O Aphrodite!
O Aphrodite, hear!
Hear my wrung cry flame upward poignant-glad . . .
This is my time for me.
I too am young;
I too am all of love!

She had not been educated to think of sex in Victorian terms. Her father repeatedly lectured on the beauty of love between man and wife. "When the Hebrew prophet would set before men the relation of God to man, he used the figure of marriage of man to woman; and when he would testify to the joy which comes of the union between God and man, he can find no higher symbol of that joy than the joy of the bride-groom over the bride. . . . It is surely grievous to say to the youth and the maiden, as they long for the other, that this, their longing, is a guilty thing that must be concealed lest it should bring upon them the scorn and the contempt of others."[22] If she dreamt of love as she lay in her hammock, she could see possibilities for romantic fulfillment before her eyes.

James Holley Hanford had come to Cook's Point that summer to tutor a young boy. He was externally an appropriate lover for Adelaide Crapsey: a fresh graduate in literature of the University of Rochester on his way to study for a higher degree, a lover of Milton (as was Adelaide), and only two years her junior. But although she was interested enough to initiate a relationship, he could not take up the challenge. He was already engaged to be married and found close communication with her uncomfortable. "We sailed together on the lake. I recall that she wanted me to tie the sheet and otherwise defy the elements. I must have explained to her that the boat carried a lee helm and needed two handed attention every moment to keep it upright." Her request to tie the sheet was, as Hanford clearly understood, an invitation to free his hands for her. Regretfully he wrote, "I found her a very romantic figure but I was engaged at the time and did not accept the invitation I felt (perhaps mistakenly) [added as superscript] she was extending." Crapsey was not crushed by this rejection. When Hanford brought a friend down, she shifted her attentions to him. "They went out in a skiff at night together," Hanford recalls, a bit enviously, and speculated that she might have been a "little desperate."

Edmund Maurice Evans was a classmate of Hanford's described as "charming," good-looking, suave, with beautiful manners, always well groomed and immaculate, smooth-shaven, neat, and debonair. The word used most often to describe him, however, was elegant. And as a teacher of Latin he may have appeared to Crapsey to be even more "elegant." He was a year younger than she, and having just graduated from the University of Rochester was about to take on the position of principal of the boys' department of Geneva High School. Despite his attractiveness, the mundaneness of his biography might not have appealed to her.

She was not desperate for want of attractiveness to men. She may have been the older woman in this little scene, but her appearance was that of a young girl. Her diminished stature, her slender figure, and her wide, gray-violet eyes gave her at times a childlike quality.

More than her appearance, her attractiveness was based upon her poetic nature. "Her conversation was that of a poet," Hanford said. "I remember asking what was the color 'mauve' and having her point to a cloud in the sunset glow and say: 'That's dreaming of mauve.' "[23]

The intense delight with which she enjoyed basic pleasures—swimming in particular—contributed also to her attractiveness. She often attracted attention with the excitement of her expression and could ignite almost any companion with the passion of her enjoyment.

It might have been this knowledge—that she was never by herself for long—that made her decide to go to Rome without Webster. She knew that, even though it was very irregular for a woman her age to be in a foreign land alone, she would find people who would help her and keep her company.

Her decision was a good one. As soon as she boarded the German liner sailing for Naples that October of 1904, Crapsey found friends. Seated at the captain's table that night at dinner, she waited until the captain had made all the necessary introductions and had lapsed into silence, then, turning from the captain on her right to the distinguished man on her left, she commented: "So many souls, so many interests, great and small, delightfully trivial, or terribly important."[24] She seemed like such a small child to him, "a slip of a girl who had undoubtedly been put in [the captain's] special charge by thoughtful parents," but her conversation was so erudite, fascinating. He was immediately enchanted.

Crapsey had chosen an interesting man to charm. He was Nathaniel Schmidt, a professor of Semitic languages at Cornell on his way to Jerusalem to serve as director of the American School of Oriental Study and Research. Alone because his wife and daughter were to meet him in Rome, Schmidt was happy to find any interesting companionship but was particularly fascinated by the contrast of Crapsey's childlike appearance, "so petite, so delicate," with her range and depth of knowledge.

> She obviously was older than she appeared, though her years could not by any means be as many as the maturity of her mind would suggest. We talked of literature. She knew the best; she loved poetry, the form as well as the substance, perhaps even more. Why the form? Because without it it would not have the beauty peculiar to poetry; it would be only prose. We spoke of art. How much she would see in Rome! We turned to science. It was not the results, she thought, that were of the greatest significance, but the experimentation, the trying out of theories. Astronomy appealed to her. In the vast stretches of the universe was there life like ours, or unlike ours? And beyond, in the eternal science, what was the essence of it all?

Her wistful peering into the depths of the inscrutable mystery overwhelmed Schmidt, who found it difficult to believe that her interests could be narrowed down to a single subject. "Could she possibly be interested in theology? . . . Something had made me dubious whether she would ever devote her life to archaeology. Now I began to doubt whether the study of metrics or even poetry would claim her vital interest. In this, of course, I was wrong. But theology seemed really to be the subject on which she dwelt with the greatest enthusiasm. She had an astounding amount of information concerning our little systems that have had their day, yet will not cease to be, and about the struggles of the humble seekers after truth.

Schmidt, sixteen years older than Crapsey and a bit of a heretic, was accustomed to universities and profound thinkers and not easily impressed. Certainly the impact of her personality was heightened by the contrast of her delicate and youthful appearance, but it was the openness and vastness of her mind which remained with him.

This strong positive impression was also a result of her gentle diplomacy. This was election year, and in response to Schmidt's reflection that he would lose his vote, Crapsey arranged a straw vote aboard ship. Everyone was eligible to vote, all passengers and crew as well. "We had torch-light processions, transparencies, watchers, and counters, oratory galore, and soapboxes for our socialist friends, members of the Swiss parliament who were returning from the Congress of the Interparliamentary Peace Union held at Saint Louis. 'Shall we join the comrades?' Adelaide asked. 'Perhaps we ought to do so,'" answered Schmidt. But, despite her cogent arguments and the influence of her status as organizer, the hated Roosevelt won.

The shipboard friendship between the two continued. Together they travelled from Naples to Pompeii to Rome, where they were joined by Mrs. Schmidt and the Schmidts' little daughter Dagmar, and continued as a group to visit the sights. Schmidt noted that Crapsey was more interested in nature than the galleries, however, and wanted to absorb the experiences themselves, not interpretations of them.

Roma Aeterna

Adelaide Crapsey did not know exactly what she was doing in Rome. Webster had apparently made the arrangements and had been her usual imprecise self when passing them on. As a result Crapsey was not even certain of what school she was in or what she would be studying.

She told her mother and Schmidt that she would be studying archaeology, but there were two schools—the School of Archaeology and that of Classical Studies. These two schools united seven years later, but when Crapsey reached them in 1904 they were separate. Once she arrived and the distinction was clarified to her, it was certain that her interest was in Classical Studies, and thence she repaired.

The school, housed in the Villa Borghi, provided a good environment. With its $100,000 endowment it was not lacking in financial possibilities to provide materials for study, and with its large library of books and drawings there was much to be learned.[1] The School of Classical Studies had twenty-one students in 1904, six of whom had already been there for a year or two. Eligibility was attained with a "satisfactory certificate from the University or College," and, although attempts were just beginning to make these criteria more stringent, it was noted that the students of that year were better than previous years.

One professor divided the students into two classes: "those who have

received more special training and have distinctly scholarly qualifications, and those who have come here to pass a year which shall enable
them to teach Latin and Roman history in our schools and smaller col-
leges with a greater sense of reality."[2] Crapsey's plans were not yet determined, but her sense of excitement at the open-ended studies, with no
specific goal and no specific time limit, was manifest.

Although there were many distinguished professors at the School of
Classical Studies and Crapsey studied with Professor Richard Norton,
the director of the school, Jesse Benedict Carter, professor of Latin language and literature, Herbert Fletcher de Cou, who taught Greek archaeology, Professor August Mau in Pompeian archaeology, and Professor Arthur Mahler in Greek and Roman sculpture, there was a far
more significant influence than all the teachers. As Professor Carter
pointed out, "By far the most effective teacher connected with the
American School in Rome is the City of Rome itself. Our courses are
valuable just in proportion as they take their keynote from here, and our
best courses are those which supplement the perpetual instruction
which 'Roma Aeterna' is forever giving."[3] The dashing Carter, who at
thirty-two knew Rome well and was well known by the Romans for his
reputation of making ladies swoon, warmly encouraged his women students and taught his lesson of the city to Crapsey well, as evinced in one
of her first cinquains:[4]

Roma Aeterna

The sun
Is warm to-day,
O Romulus, and on
Thine olden Palatine the birds
Still sing.

This was the feeling of the eternality of Rome that Carter and the school
had attempted to instill. It was not so much a respect for the ancient as a
wonder at the continuance of life, the layering of existence.

Despite her saturation in architecture and statuary, Crapsey's Rome
did not consist of monuments but of birds and sun. Perhaps this too was
encouraged by Carter, who also believed in adjusting the studies to the
character of the student's interests. Crapsey's emphasis might be some-

what attributed to the effects of growing up in "Rainchester," but it was to beauty and warmth that Crapsey always reacted, her face glowing in sunny gardens.

Crapsey might have originally intended to achieve greater qualification for teaching Latin and Roman history, but the proximity to scholarship provoked her interest. She became friendly with an Englishwoman, Alice Mary Edith Pritchard, who had come that year to the academy with specific and distinctly scholarly goals. Pritchard was at the beginning of a long-term academic project, and although Crapsey admired her commitment to scholarship, her own interests could not be channelled by a specific school or a specific project. It was typical of Crapsey to learn the rules for one discipline and apply them to a completely different field. Just as she had analyzed the Socialist party at college using literary criteria, focussing on language and effect, through the reading of classical literature she was developing her own scientific interest in the rules of English poetry.

Despite the difference in their background and approach, the two women became close friends. Crapsey was obviously in need of orientation and Pritchard seemed very capable in that department. First of all there was the orientation to Rome. Crapsey may have taken great pride in her management of practical matters, particularly monetary ones, but she was easily lost once outside her focus of concentration, and her friends were so concerned about her lack of orientation that they made it their business to fetch her from school so that she would not wander lost about Rome on her way home to the hotel.

It is not hard to get lost in Rome. The Corso Romano, the north-south axis, by which one might orient oneself, is oblique, and the Tiber slithers through the city in such curves that it is sometimes impossible to know if one is near the river. And for a young woman accustomed to travelling with other, more knowing guides, Rome affords none of the certainties of New York City. But it was her friends who seemed concerned, not Crapsey, who did not appear to mind wandering about and finding herself in forbidden neighborhoods. She looked like a child, tiny and innocent, and her appearance ensured her safety.

The possibility that her poor sense of direction was the cause of her wandering about Rome is a bit questionable when set against the fact that Crapsey became a part-time tour guide herself in the Eternal City, lecturing American visitors on the places she learned of at school. She "looked rather like a precocious little girl reciting a lesson," Alice Pritchard thought, but she knew her lessons well.

The course at the academy really left her little time for the job of guide. There were numerous lectures, class trips to museums and churches, explorations of ruins, and field trips to out-of-the-way places.[5] There was so much tourism, in fact, that Crapsey was content to leave unvisited this time places as significant and awe-inspiring as Keats's tomb.

Crapsey was not there to be a tourist. The determination to turn her life around which seems to have motivated the trip to Italy channelled her energies in two directions. The study of classical poetry increased her growing suspicions that the basis for theories on prosody had never really been examined and would not hold. She had studied government and religion scientifically and discovered that the assumed truths at their core did not always stand up to examination. The same might be true for literature. Many of the rules about what succeeds in literature and how and why it succeeds were simply based on unexamined reverence and critical fashion. Swinburne, for example, who had captured the hearts, imaginations and respect of so many contemporary scholars and poets, was, she suspected, using primitive techniques for cheap effects. (In this she may have been influenced by the same criteria as John Burroughs, who expressed nausea at Swinburne's verse.) Milton, however, seemed to have based his theories of writing on more solid principles. Even if she were wrong, the quest itself was exciting. But, hampered by an ignorance of Greek and Greek meters, she approached the subject with extreme caution.

Crapsey was also beginning again to write verse seriously. Her religious background and her sensibility demanded unity and honesty, a poetry that emerged from the unified truth of the self and whose every aspect and technique were parts of this projected whole. This kind of poetry could only be written when the most significant aspects of her life could be faced. Now she was facing them and beginning to articulate them in the direct way she had long respected. Emily Dickinson's "Tell the truth but tell it slant" was foreign to Crapsey even from the onset not only because it was foreign to her concept of prosody but because it was alien to her personality and sense of the obligation of communication. Writing had to be straightforward and honest. Something secret could be hidden in the drawer after it was written fairly. But she had nothing to hide. In fact, the theological examinations she was making were a source of great happiness to her, and her desire to share them with her friends was great.

Together with "Birth Moment," that amazing burst of excitement, she placed "The Mother Exultant," a ripe image of maternity and fruition influenced by Renaissance Italian painting—particularly Raphael and Leonardo—and messianic visions from Isaiah and other biblical sources. The poem begins with the sense of excessiveness, the drunkenness of harvest:

> Joy! Joy! Joy!
> The hills are glad,
> The valleys re-echo with merriment,
> In my heart is the sound of laughter,
> And my feet dance to the time of it;
> Oh, little son, carried light on my shoulder,
> Let us go laughing and dancing through the live days,
> For this is the hour of the vintage,
> When man gathereth for himself the fruits of the vineyard.
>
> Look, little son, look:
> The grapes are translucent and ripe,
> They are heavy and fragrant with juice,
> They wait for the hands of the vintagers.

The excitement seems overdone, but the lines following explain the great rejoicing.

> For a long time the grapes were not,
> And were in the womb of the earth,
>
> . . . .
>
> At the touch of life, life stirred,
> And the earth brought forth her fruits in due season.

The birth is not only sensual but spiritual as well. It is the Madonna who speaks, who cries out the story of the Annunciation, although the language is not that of the ideal remote Mary, holy and pure, to whom Adelaide Crapsey had prayed while at Vassar.

> I was a maid and alone,
> When, behold, there came to me a vision;
> My heart cried out within me,
> And the voice was the voice of God.
> Yea, a virgin I dreamed of love,
> And I was troubled and sore afraid,
> I wept and was glad,
> For the word of my heart named me blessèd,
> My soul exalted the might of creation.

If she had asked, in her "Hail, Mary!," to become "blessed" like the Virgin, she was now reversing the prayer, transforming the Virgin into her own image. For the God from whom she conceived was the God of her heart, and the spiritual conception is followed by a real one:

> I was a maid and alone,
> When, behold, my lover came to me,
> My belovèd held me in his arms.

> Joy! Joy! Joy!
> Now is the vision fulfilled;
> I have conceived,
> I have carried in my womb,
> I have brought forth
> The life of the world;
> Out of my joy and my pain,
> Out of the fulness of my living
> Hath my son gained his life.

Human and divine lover weave in and out of the poem as in the Song of Songs and messianic texts. And Virgin and Earth Mother become equally interchangeable.

Look, little son, look:
The earth, your mother,
And the touch of life who is your father,
They have provided food for you
That you also may live.

   The vineyards are planted on the hillside,
   They are the vineyards of my belovèd,
   He chose a favorable spot,
   His hands prepared the soil for the planting;
   He set out the young vines
   And cared for them till the time of their bearing.

   . . . .

   Out of the heart of the living grape
   Hath the hand of my belovèd
   Wrung the wine of the dream of life.
                              (*CP,* pp. 65–68)

The initial excessiveness of the poem now becomes clear: it is only
through the madness of excess can the borders—of holy and profane, of
divine and human—be broken down.

    This was heresy. By any standards of the Episcopalian church in
which she had been brought up, the pagan marriage she had described
could not be acceptable. Crapsey, immersed in the overwhelming Ca-
tholicism and classicism of Rome, could not help but find religion again,
but this time it was in her own personal, humanly comforting form.

    There were other poems as well. Crapsey enjoyed an enormous re-
birth of energy and creativeness in the congenial climate of Italy. She
showed the poems to Alice Pritchard, but Pritchard, with her academic
proclivity, let them slip through her memory, and Crapsey made no
efforts at publication.[6]

    If Crapsey found a mortal lover in Rome, it must have been a man
who introduced her to the pagan, who helped her to find that which she
had come to Rome to seek, who reminded her of a reason for living.

    In the spring Crapsey journeyed to Germany, expecting to return to

Italy for the summer, linking up at last with Jean in "a most desirable little village I know of on Lake Maggiore."[7] Although Pritchard was staying on at the academy, Crapsey wasn't sure as yet what she would do and was fishing for a place to study and live for the next year. A great deal depended upon her family's financial situation and their ability to contribute to her maintenance.

The Heresy

While Adelaide Crapsey was developing her experimental form of religion and poetry in the comparative safety of the poetry drawer, her father was coming to similar conclusions in the pulpit of his church.

Although Algernon Crapsey had given himself to the church, having studied theology at St. Stephen's College and the General Theological Seminary of the Episcopal Church, his mind, like his daughter's, had always remained his own. For the first two decades of his career he was immeasurably content with the ritual of the church and enjoyed the comfort of its drama, its predictability, and its direction for human life. But his eyes remained open, and when he perceived the indifference in his church to the poverty and discontent of the human race he began to question seriously the place and function of religion in such a world. A rational and practical man when it came to eschatological thinking, he noted that questions of man's relations to God were ultimately of no significance in the daily economic world. In fact, when religion emphasized the omnipotence and grandeur of the Deity, it relieved itself of power and responsibility in the actions of man. Marx's observation concerning religion as the opiate of the masses must have struck an amazing note of recognition in Dr. Crapsey when, at this point in his life, he began reading *Das Kapital*.

145

Algernon Crapsey had always focused his concentration on humankind. The rituals and imperatives of the church had been for him educational dramas, involving people in the historical events and awakening
them to their own responsibilities as God's creatures. His method of organizing his parish was to provide ways in which his flock could be
active participants by practicing charity, by learning, by teaching. Religion was a means by which people could develop a moral imperative.

Precisely because of his rational approach to phenomena, when Dr.
Crapsey began to perceive indications that the world was not function-
ing according to God's will and that one of the reasons was the church
itself, Dr. Crapsey shifted his emphasis to man. He charted his first disillusion from the time he visited England's great churches and perceived
the disparity between the grandeur and luxury of the churches and the
poverty of the parishioners.

> When I came at last to London, then my indignation passed the boiling-
> point. I visited the great cathedral of St. Paul's and the Chapel, so called, of
> Westminster, and was present at their magnificent offices of worship; and
> then went out into the regions of Shoreditch and Mile End Road and saw
> thousands of idle men leaning against the wall, hungry and hopeless; saw
> bedraggled women nursing children at empty breasts, the children them-
> selves playing in the streets, having the faces of angels, which I knew would
> soon be transformed into the faces of these degraded men and women who
> had brought them into the world. At night I went out and saw other
> thousands sleeping in the parks and under the arches of the bridges, and I
> despaired of Christianity.[1]

In his historical studies Dr. Crapsey found corresponding conclusions
that Christianity had artificially distanced itself from humankind. He
had come upon no evidence that Jesus was the Son of God. This startling idea for a man of the church seemed not at all destructive or revolutionary to him, because it allowed human beings and churches to shift
the responsibility for the situation of the world to themselves. If Jesus
was only a man, albeit a great one, then all men could aspire to the same
holiness, the same attempt at reform.

Dr. Crapsey acted on his revelation in a clerically acceptable manner:
his disillusion with the church resulted in a redoubling of his efforts to

make the church useful and in focussing on the alleviation of poverty, war, inequality, and their related evils. Social inequality began to be important to him—the rights of women, the needs of workers, the obligations of society. The economic-imperalistic basis for war had surfaced for Dr. Crapsey in the invasion of Cuba, a war which had left his son Philip with chronic malaria and had proved to him the necessity of working for world peace, with the church as peacemaker. All these ideas were clearly not acceptable to a church primarily composed of the upper classes. But it was the substitution of social concerns with orthodox religion that brought Dr. Crapsey to the attention of his superiors.

Perhaps because the Right Reverend William David Walker, bishop of the Diocese of Western New York, perceived the relation between the charitable works and eschatological disillusion, he became dissatified with Dr. Crapsey. But Dr. Crapsey's efforts to democratize the church had long made him a personal enemy of Walker's. In 1890 Dr. Crapsey proposed to break down the diocese into smaller dioceses: his purpose was to allow decisions to be made on the basis of personal contact, which would *de facto* have democratized the church. But its effect would also have been to undermine the hierarchy and substantially diminish the power of Bishop Walker. Not surprisingly, Walker perceived Dr. Crapsey as an opponent, a man whose popularity and character were a threat to his own power and perhaps to the church as well.

Bishop Walker did not favor the proposed division, but the clergy did, and the proposal was only defeated by a narrow vote of the laity.[2] Dr. Crapsey had not only voted for the proposition but had also declared that he was opposed to the election of Walker until the division of the diocese had been effected, a declaration that could not have helped Dr. Crapsey's reputation with the bishop.[3]

None of this would have interfered with his successful career; Dr. Crapsey was just too industrious. From a new and doomed community Dr. Crapsey had created a thriving, variegated parish in only twenty-five years. There were 20 teachers and 150 students in the parochial school Dr. Crapsey had established. A successful industrial school was being maintained. And the membership was impressive, with "342 families and 614 communicants."[4] Furthermore, the parishioners came from every strata of society, and while the wealthy members added to his status, the membership of the working class proved him in the eyes of all a true humanist, a man of the progressive church.

Success made him bold. In the community he could do nothing wrong, and any innovation, any departure from standard church procedures was welcomed by his parish and the town in general as an enlightenment. When Adelaide Crapsey was on her way to Rome, Algernon Crapsey was involved in a series of twelve lectures on religion and politics in which he pointed out the need for the churches to become "scientific, democratic, and socialistic."[5] Although innovative, these lectures were not really radical until the final one, "The Present State of the Churches." During his discourse on the ills and the responsibilities of the contemporary ecclesiastical establishment, Dr. Crapsey mentioned some of his theories that had been clear to him for years and he assumed would be perfectly acceptable to all his congregation. His description of Jesus as the son of a carpenter, a son of simple middle-class parents, coupled with his insistence on the fact that the theory of Virgin Birth was only a hindrance to religion were part and parcel of his general attitude, and he so little expected a reaction that he had no objection to the publication of the lecture in a local newspaper two days later.

But the effect was enormous. The written word left no possibility of misinterpretation, and by April the standing committee of the diocese had "received a formal protest signed by ten Presbyters, complaining in particular of one alleged sermon and demanding that an investigation be had of the conduct of the defendant. The Standing Committee referred the communication to the Bishop, and later advised that he appoint a Committee of Investigation unless the alleged utterance should be explained or retracted on or before June 1, 1905. . . . At the Diocesan Council held in May, 1905, an Ecclesiastical Court of five Presbyters was elected, Dr. Crapsey being present. After waiting until July 17, 1905, the Bishop named an investigating Committee of five Presbyters."[6]

Had Dr. Crapsey been a little less radical or a little more private, there would have been no incident or, at worst, the disagreement would have been settled between Dr. Crapsey and his bishop. But for Dr. Crapsey the idea of freedom of conscience in religion was a family tradition as well

as a personal preference. His grandfather had said, "The right of conscience is an unalienable right, for the exercise of which man is not
accountable to man: he is accountable to no power short of that of his
Creator. It is a religious right with which human laws have nothing to
do."[7] A public announcement of this was now necessary.

But a public announcement forced a public reaction. The *Church Standard*, the *Churchman*, and the *Living Church*, all Episcopal journals, discussed Dr. Crapsey's views. The bishop felt impelled to demand a retraction; instead, Dr. Crapsey published the entire lecture series as a book
entitled *Religion and Politics*.

Throughout the summer the accusation of heresy hung over the public discussion. It was not a desirable subject for most of the general High
Church community. On July 8, the *Churchman*, an Episcopal weekly,
treated the subject with great delicacy, noting that although the ideas of
a priest might be wrong, "there must be as much of poetry as arithmetic
in an expression of religious faith." A too literal interpretation of doctrine is not Episcopalian, they concluded, but Catholic, and imagination
is needed.

As proof that imagination and progressive thinking need not be destructive to religion, the editor imitated Dr. Crapsey's wonderment at
modern science. Dr. Crapsey, having employed historical and scientific
means to demystify the Virgin Birth, nevertheless affirmed the value of
modern discoveries to religion: "The man of science knows his God as
God has never been known before. He is face to face with his God every
moment of his life."[8] Employing the same argument, the editor showed
his own poetic inclinations by proving what Dr. Crapsey had disavowed:
"Modern science, by suggesting the continuity, and yet the lack of continuity, of all things from the beginning, reads a new and profound significance into our ordinary thought of the Virgin Birth, which gives the
doctrine underlying the expression of the Creed a wonderfully far-
reaching significance."[9] The point of this was to prove that Dr. Crapsey
was not a dangerous thinker and that imaginative and progressive
thinking might in the long run be good for the church.

Despite these kind warnings and defenses, momentum for a trial was
building up, and on July 19 the committee of five men chosen by the

bishop began investigations. A month later the *Churchman* began its editorial with a warning: "Speaking generally, heresy trials have been unprofitable, a scandal to the Church, and unfruitful in results."

> It is a wise plan to have confidence in the honesty and integrity of Christian teachers. If a man can with honesty to his own conscience accept the formularies of the Church, and conform to them, it is best as a general principle to accept his statement that what he holds and teaches is permissible under those formulas. . . . We have ourselves heard honored and entirely orthodox clergymen preach from the pulpit the baldest tritheism, sabellianism, or docetism, heresies long since condemned by councils of the Church. Technically, they were guilty of heresy, but no one brought them to trial, nor would it have been wise to do so.[10]

This attitude met with some opposition, and readers wrote in to criticize its liberality:

> [You] practically condemn the Church of God for requiring that her ministers shall keep faith with her, to teach what they have sworn to teach, her faith, not their own ratiocinations. . . . Do you, can you really mean to say that it is wholly right, just and profitable for every corporation, other than the Church, to require obedience and fidelity to its principles and laws, at the cost of punishment, and, in the last extremity of expulsion; but it is altogether unprofitable and unfruitful for the Church to try, or to punish anyone for flouting her principles, or for flinging from him with contempt, the vows he voluntarily assumed in the full strength of his manhood.[11]

To this force the editors felt obliged to defend themselves, and they did with such gentleness and gentlemanliness that Dr. Crapsey reading it must have scoffed. "We laid down no infallible or inflexible law, but . . . we did venture the opinion that in general it is bad practice to prosecute or persecute men for their opinions and theories so long as they are loyal to the Faith."

Bishop Walker had ordered a retraction, and Dr. Crapsey had refused, and the press did not have sufficient power to keep the two men, who were apparently hungering for a confrontation, apart. The more provocative step, however, was taken by Dr. Crapsey. On September 2 he published an article in the *Outlook* asserting his right to controversy.

"Honor Among Clergymen" was Dr. Crapsey's reaction to a recent pastoral letter by the bishop which stated: "If . . . one finds, whatever his office or place in the church, that he has lost hold upon her fundamental verities, then, in the name of common honesty, let him be silent or withdraw."[12] Dr. Crapsey had not withdrawn and now he would not be silent.

The first two reasons Dr. Crapsey gave for his outspokenness were integrity and honesty. "The price [the silent one] pays for his safety is the arrest of mental and spiritual development," Dr. Crapsey pointed out,[13] and added that duty compelled the individual to "make his conviction known to the Church."[14] These were reasonable and logical arguments, and had Dr. Crapsey stopped there perhaps his appeal would have been more successful. The continuation of the argument, however, begged for further confrontation:

A prophet is one who interprets the will of God to his own time and his own people. . . . By withdrawing from his place he loses his power. It would have been easy for Jesus to have escaped from the Cross by withdrawing from the land of Israel. He could have been a wandering wise man, and have preached his doctrine to eager ears in Egypt and the islands of the sea. But from the first Jesus felt instinctively that he was not sent but unto the lost sheep of the House of Israel. It was Israel that was in darkness and needed enlightenment and until Israel either accepted or rejected the light he would not offer it to the Gentiles. In fulfillment of this conception he went to the very center of Jewish life; in the temple itself he arraigned and condemned the whole prevailing system at the base of his prophetic offices. Had Jesus followed the advice of the pastoral letter of the Bishops of the Episcopalian Church, and, when he discovered errors in the prevailing creed of his people, had quietly withdrawn and gone to the Gentiles, he would have saved the priesthood of Jerusalem the trouble of condemning him, he would have saved his own earthly life, but he would not have saved the world.[15]

Dr. Crapsey foresaw his chosen future and was about to create it, for if the bishop and the church were the Jews, history had proven that the bishop, like the Jews, would reject the truth, and it would be only the Gentiles who would understand his new doctrines.

If nothing else, the tone of this statement must have infuriated the bishop: Dr. Crapsey's comparison of himself to Christ and the bishop to the Jews was not indicative of contrition or compromise. The editorial in the *Outlook* noted: "It may sometimes be the duty of a Christian minister to submit uncomplainingly to execution; it is never his duty to perform hara-kiri."[16]

The article was the cause of a great deal of public discussion of the Crapsey case. The *Church Standard* warned that if the diocesan authorities did not take action against Dr. Crapsey, they would be guilty of encouraging heresy themselves.[17] At the same time, the *Churchman* was giving Dr. Crapsey a kind of tentative support, suggesting that he was indeed a kind of prophet and reformer: "What many Christian teachers are attempting now is a problem not unlike in character to that which faced an earlier generation of Christian thinkers in a society whose religious thought was saturated with Gnosticism. At that time the Church did not content itself with the reaffirmation of the old. It boldly transformed the old—absorbed within itself the best elements of Gnosticism, established the faith and enriched its inheritance—a notable example for our own time and generation."[18] Perhaps Dr. Crapsey believed that the more public the controversy, the more popular he would become and the less it would be possible for him to be humiliated by Bishop Walker. But the bishop was given no alternative by all the publicity: he felt obliged to set up an investigative committee to evaluate if sufficient evidence existed for trial.

Once the seriousness of the situation became apparent, it became necessary for Adelaide Crapsey to return home to comfort her mother and assist her father. Her studies were not completed and she would not be able to receive an advanced degree in classical studies as her friend Alice Pritchard would, or vacation luxuriously with the sophisticated Webster, but she could not have stayed in Rome with the economic, social, and psychological situation of the family the way it was, and she returned home for the winter.

The precise attitude of Adelaide to the trials of her father and mother when she returned can be perceived in an anecdote told by Mrs. Crapsey. The committee of five men appointed by Bishop Walker to determine sufficient grounds for trial came to call at the rectory, but the Reverend Dr. Crapsey was not at home. His wife, who should have received them, was too nervous and worn out from the long months in the public eye. Adelaide, however, with renewed strength and perspective from her sojourn in Rome, volunteered to play the role of Distinguished-Lady-of-the-Minister. "I'll see them," she told her mother. "I'll serve tea."

The emotions that motivated her pleasant behavior were complex, but those following the afternoon were pure. She spent the afternoon playing the minister's daughter, entertaining her father's inquiring colleagues. But she spiked the tea with rum, and though their moods were good when they left the rectory, hers was better. "They enjoyed their tea, mother. . . . Oh, they enjoyed their tea *very* much."[19] The mischievous pleasure she must have felt in her sabotage of the sanctimonious ministers may well have been akin to her joyful identification with the biblical Judith.

THE DEATH OF HOLOFERNES

Israel!
Wake! Be gay!
Thine enemy is brought low—
Thy foe slain—by the hand, by the hand
Of a woman!

(*CP*, p. 77)

The entire investigation was, for Adelaide Crapsey, one of petty spite on the part of the bishop and jealous churchmen. Her cinquain of Susanna, although written later, reflects the emotions that filled her in these months.

SUSANNA AND THE ELDERS

"Why do
You thus devise
Evil against her?" "For that
She is beautiful, delicate:
Therefore."

(*CP*, p. 72)

Algernon Crapsey, in standing firm in his denial of the divinity of Jesus, was created as Jesus in his daughter's eyes. The great and natural man, surrounded by corrupt, jealous, repressed, ignorant, and supercilious priests and made to bear his cross, not down the Via Dolorosa but through all the newspapers in which he had longed for recognition, was to be deprived of his only desire, to do good in the world.

That the latter cinquain also refers to the God who sapped Crapsey's strength when her mind was so active is also significant. For just as she saw her father as a martyr she saw herself as the gratuitous victim, the individual whose great potential is stifled precisely because of its greatness. Her own recurring weakness, returning to her like a punishment just when she seemed to take off into a new and exciting future, was not very different from her father's professional persecution.

The cards were stacked against Dr. Crapsey. The bishop's authority was greater and his influence far more widespread. And he did not hesitate to use that influence to blacken Dr. Crapsey's name and even to influence the decision of the committee. A week before the committee's decision was reached and announced, the bishop visited Rochester to lay the cornerstone for Christ Church. There he took the opportunity to preach against the accused heretic. "I am here in this city to stand up for the faith of the Catholic Church as it is taught in the Gospel, as it is taught in the Creed. I cannot sympathize with the man who teaches anything contrary to that which he has promised to teach. God be thanked that there is a Church still, and that the faith still abides."[20] There was another, more serious intervention. "By a vote of three to two, it was determined to acquit the defendant; and a bishop, not a member of the court, went to one member of the acquitting majority, and communicated his view that the welfare of the church required a different judgement."[21]

These attempts to influence the decision may have been partially successful, for although in the final report on November 11, "a majority of three found that there was 'not sufficient evidence to secure conviction in case of a trial for heresy' in the book *Religion and Politics*, a minority of two found that the book did contain 'sufficient grounds for the presentment [of] the author.' " All the committee agreed that the Rev. Dr. Crapsey impresses us as being a man who easily surrenders himself to intellectual vagaries, and the thing which for the time being appears to him to be true he advocates with remarkable eloquence. . . . His writings indicate that while he recites and affirms his belief in the Creeds of the Church he virtually sets aside the historical sense in which their Articles have been and are received by this Church, and for it he substitutes a "spiritual interpretation," claiming to retain the spiritual reality for which Christianity stands while dismissing as indifferent the historical facts asserted in the Creeds. Your committee is unanimous in its condemnation of the Rev. Dr. Crapsey's position in this matter.[22]

If Dr. Crapsey had nothing else on his side at that time, his moral character had been unquestioned. Now he was being condemned for "intellectual vagaries" and a fixed loyalty to erroneous and changing beliefs. It was as if the committee had decided not to condemn him because it was not good for the church, but their respect for his quest for progress and understanding was minimal.

He was not accused of a crime but was guilty—a Kafkaesque situation—and the journals were quick to note the inconsistency. The *Church Standard* found that the report made the "scandal one degree more scandalous than it was" and criticized the committee's condemnation of Dr. Crapsey as "wholly gratuitous and impertinent" since the committee had no judicial function; yet the decision left the papers suspicious and the *Standard* condemned the committee for not presenting Crapsey for trial.[23]

Despite the aspersions cast on Algernon Crapsey's character there was a sense of relief in the Crapsey home, a feeling that the incident was now over, and Dr. Crapsey could now meditate at leisure over his future plans. His mood was not tranquil, however, and a letter to the editor of the *Churchman* was enough to set him off. On November 25, J. Lewis Parks of New York City asked the editor of the *Churchman* if Dr. Crapsey would clarify his views now that he was no longer in danger of prosecution: "Will . . . that honesty now enable Dr. Crapsey to relieve the situation by telling the Church in direct and simple English whether or no he believes that our Lord was conceived of the Holy Ghost and born of the Virgin Mary, having no human father; and whether or no he believes that our Lord arose from the dead in the body which was crucified? Or is Dr. Crapsey content to write and teach with an ambiguity which shelters opinions which could not possibly escape condemnation if only they were plainly and boldly stated?"[24] Dr. Crapsey's immediate reply revealed his now hairtrigger temper:

> For nearly a year I have been under the most searching investigation, and yet nothing has been found to warrant even my accusation, much less my conviction, for any error in doctrine or viciousness of life. If there is any other clergyman who has undergone such scrutiny and yet remains a presbyter in good standing I do not know who such clergyman is.
>
> Dr. Parks asks me to answer categorically whether I believe thus and so. Now before submitting to this inquisition I would like my friend to tell me if he wishes to know my inward convictions on the points he mentions for his own personal satisfaction, or if it is his purpose to secure some declaration from me that will enable him or others to revive proceedings against me in heresy. . . .
>
> I must, therefore, before answering the questions of Dr. Parks, wait for the declaration of his purpose. Meantime I wish to assure him that our friendship of old days is one of my cherished spiritual possessions, and that now, as then, I am . . .

The necessity for self-defense against his friends and acquaintances arose only weeks after in the pages of the *Churchman* when he felt obliged to clear himself of the charges of thinking bad thoughts to Dr. Van Allen. His remarks continue to be testy and showed more than a trace of superciliousness:

> I have always supposed that a man was to be held responsible to the public only for his public utterances. His private thoughts and opinions, which, because they are private, are held subject to change and revision, are the sacred property of the man himself which he is not obliged to reveal to any chance inquisition. . . .
>
> After dwelling on the enormity of my crime (of which I have been acquitted) and saying that it affects the honor of this and that order of men and this and that institution, he closes by saying that it "concerns the honor of God's Mother and Her Son." This imports an entirely new element into the

matter at bar, and I wish to say that if I am guilty in this regard my guilt is the result of my ignorance, for until I read the letter of that gentleman I did not know that God had a mother.[25]

His attitude was plainly degenerating in respectfulness to his colleagues and patience to tolerate their foibles and vindictiveness.

The justifiable paranoia, the suspicion toward old friends, coupled with a fear that all his utterances were being examined and judged, was certainly the result of the nine-month-long inquiry. Yet his undiminished love of others remained, perhaps because he was now aware of the necessity for friends. For although the journals thought they were burying the case, Dr. Crapsey and the bishop knew better. It was true that the committee had "declined . . . to recommend presentment," but the bishop took no action on the report. This was a predictable tactical move, allowing him to reserve the prerogative to do with Dr. Crapsey as he wished at a later date.[26]

Despite an encouraging editorial from the *Churchman* reminding the readers that "it is not what men believe but what they do that counts" and that "anyone who desires to follow Christ, no matter how imperfectly, in conception or service, should be accepted as His disciple," which encouraged the acceptance of Dr. Crapsey's opinion,[27] the bishop spoke up two weeks later. Preaching at the consecration of Christ Church in Rochester on December 29, he reaffirmed the intractability of his stance: "Creeds are as technical and exact as any of the sciences. . . . The Creeds have not changed, nor have their forms, either. Those gathered Articles of Belief are a group of quartz crystals, clear and pure as the limpid spring water that wells forth from lofty mountain's heart."[28]

The *Churchman* continued to try to make peace and recommended in its pages that "since both Bishop Walker and his priest, in spite of their peculiar opinions and speculations, declare that they are loyal to the Christ of the Gospel and the Creeds, we must believe, as we have no reason to doubt their sincerity, that each is entitled to a place in the Church's ministry."[29] But the placations of the *Churchman* could do no good, for Dr. Crapsey would not remain silent and on December 31 preached another provocative sermon. Being only a minister and not a bishop, the likelihood of his sermon's publication was small, and it may be that the thought of privacy encouraged his freedom, but Dr. Crapsey had made an enemy within his church, and it was this enemy who took care to broadcast the sermon. The Reverend Mr. Frederick James Kerr Alexander, who was Dr. Crapsey's assistant, had recently been refused a raise and thought that replacing Dr. Crapsey would simplify his professional progress. He recorded the sermon in notes and passed it on to the bishop, together with a suggestion that perhaps Mr. Alexander could take over for Dr. Crapsey when he was deposed.

A month later rumors were rife about a new heresy trial. The *Churchman* quoted a correspondent who wrote responding to a report of a retrial in the *Church Standard,* protesting and complaining that "to hound him with committee after committee until one is bound to convict him is an evidence of inhumanity that is repugnant to a civilized state and ought to be impossible in the Christian Church." The argument focussed on proper punishment. Is deposition the penalty for publishing heretical statements? "The Roman Church in passing upon a book may condemn it as dangerous and put it upon the Index. It does not for that condemn or cast out the man."[30]

The *Living Church* also argued in favor of Dr. Crapsey's case and published a "Declaration of New Testament Criticism and Other Subjects" signed by a number of leading clergymen and laymen, pleading for "an earnest effort to solve the problems posed by the critical study of the *New Testament,*" asking for "authoritative encouragement to face the critical problems of the *New Testament* with the candor, reverence for God and His truth, and loyalty to the Church of Christ." There was clearly a danger that qualified men might not enter the ministry unless the door remained open to critical historical scholarship questioning the historical validity of the New Testament narratives.[31] Among the names of distinguished leaders was that of the Reverend Mr. Alexander Viets Griswold Allen, professor of church history at the Episcopal Theological School. Although his interests were not personal, not primarily with Dr. Crapsey himself, his intervention would later be of great significance.

With this strong backing Dr. Crapsey was encouraged, but on February 23 the standing committee recommended presenting Dr. Crapsey for trial, and almost all the Episcopal church papers agreed with the recommendation. On March 3, 1906, the presentment and a citation from the bishop, directing him to appear for trial on April 17, was delivered to Dr. Crapsey. The standing committee charged that Dr. Crapsey "did openly, advisedly, publicly and privately utter, avow, declare and teach doctrines contrary to those held and received by the Protestant Episcopal Church in the United States of America."[32] Fifteen passages in *Religion and Politics* were cited as potentially heretical. Most of them had little relevance, but the fourteenth passage was a challenge:

> In the light of scientific research, the Founder of Christianity no longer stands apart from the common destiny of man in life and death, but He is in all things physical like as we are, born as we are born, dying as we died, and both in life and death in the keeping of that same Divine Power, that heavenly Fatherhood, which delivers us from the womb and carries us down to the grave. When we come to know Jesus in His historical relations, we see that miracle is not a help, it is a hindrance, to an intelligent comprehension of His person, His character, and His mission. We are not alarmed, we are relieved when scientific history proves to us that the fact of His miraculous birth was unknown to Himself, unknown to his mother, and unknown to the whole Christian community of the first generation.[33]

Dr. Crapsey also had footnotes with biblical references proving the foundation of his statements, but these were not included in the accusation.

The accusations were far more wide ranging than before. Dr. Crapsey was not only accused of denying the Virgin Birth but also that Jesus is God, that he was conceived by the Holy Ghost, that he was resurrected, and that the Blessed Trinity exists. Using the notes of the Reverend Mr. Alexander, the accusation specified that in the sermon of December 31, 1905, Dr. Crapsey had made the following statements: (1) "Jesus was born of parents belonging to the middle class." (2) "He was born of a simple father and mother." (3) "He was the son of a carpenter." (4) "The fact that the early Christians predicted a miraculous birth of Jesus was to be regarded as one of the greatest misfortunes that had ever befallen mankind."[34] Even though the charges were accurate, the trial was destined to be an unfair one. Dr. Crapsey asked for an adjournment until

May, when the newly elected members of the standing committee would take office, so that the same court that had accused him would not sit in judgment on him. He was also under great pressure of time to prepare his case, because he was still working full time as the rector, it was now Lent, and he was without an assistant.

A petition dated April 6 appeared in the *Churchman* on April 21 asking for postponement or adjournment until May so that a fair trial could be insured. It had been signed by many important people, including the Reverend Mr. Edward M. Duff and the Reverend Dr. Edwin Hoffman, who had been on the special investigating committee a few months before. (Duff had reported that the facts warranted trial and Hoffman had gone with the majority.) The editorial in that same issue added: "Thus the powers of designating members of the court is lodged in officials who have prejudged the case, a situation which outrages every notion of justice and fair deal."[35] The *Churchman* was quoting from a letter by the ex-mayor of Rochester, published in the Rochester *Democrat and Chronicle,* asking for "A Square Deal for Dr. Crapsey." It had appeared on April 6, and on the same day Dr. Crapsey was defended in the pages of *Harper's Weekly.*

On April 18, 1906, Adelaide accompanied the Reverend Dr. Crapsey and his counsel, James Breck Perkins, to Batavia, New York for the heresy trial.[36] The bishop could not have held it in Rochester if a conviction was the desire of the court because of the immense popular appeal of the minister and the sophistication and involvement of the citizens. So it was removed to a sleepy town, where the members of the court "were country clergymen, far removed from the influences that were disturbing the intellectual life of the Church in the greater centers."[37] A place more sophisticated than Batavia would have been inappropriate.

Dr. Crapsey, expecting publicity, must have been surprised to discover that no one was waiting for them at the station—no reporters, curious onlookers, none of the massive crowd who usually came to hear him speak. But it was not for the sake of publicity that Dr. Crapsey was allowing the trial. "If he had the vanity of authorship," Edward Shepard told the court, "what could better please him than a prosecution which has made his book to be read perhaps a hundred times more than it would have been if the standing committee had seen fit to follow a different course. If he were vain, what could gratify him more than to be for the moment one of the shining marks of public interest and widespread admiration? But that is not his temper. He loves his church. He would abide in it, and work in it and for it."[38] The quaintness of the situation was striking. Claude Bragdon, with his eye for the absurd, came along just to watch the strange medieval trial that could only be humorous to a modern individual. It was the quaintness that was endangering Dr. Crapsey, that very remoteness from his own, progressive terms.

At first they were taken to the parish house of St. James Church for the proceedings, and the participants met there. The counsel for the prosecution was John Lord O'Brian, a Buffalo lawyer, assisted by the Honorable John H. Stiness, former chief justice of Rhode Island, and the Reverend Dr. Francis J. Hall, professor of dogmatic theology at the Western Theological Seminary. Dr. Crapsey's counsels were the Honorable James Breck Perkins, a congressman from Rochester, assisted by Edward M. Shepard, a prominent New York City lawyer, whose devotion to his client would continue for the rest of his life, and Samuel McCombs, a professor of theology.

The defense submitted a request for postponement, it was denied. A postponement would have taken the trial past the election for a new counsel and would have had the trial presented to different men from those who had accused Dr. Crapsey. It would have made the case less prejudiced. This denial of sufficient time to prepare a defense was a sign to the Crapseys that there would be no logic or justice to this trial. Accordingly, both father and daughter removed themselves emotionally from the proceedings and behaved like spectators in a provincial pageant.

But the facilities were not satisfactory and some changes were necessary. The court reconvened on April 25 in the local courthouse to make room for all the "clergymen who desired to follow the proceedings, or who had been summoned to give testimony."[39] And the courtroom was filled. The many witnesses brought by the defense to attest the character of Dr. Crapsey and the general acceptability of his teachings were enough to fill the room. Those who had come to see Dr. Crapsey condemned were also there, although in much fewer numbers. There was the Reverend Dr. Van Allen, rector of the Church of the Advent, Boston, whom Dr. Crapsey had answered so sharply in the pages of the *Churchman,* and Dr. Crapsey's friend, Dr. Elwood Worcester, rector of Emmanuel Church in Boston. The two of them, Dr. Crapsey laughed to see, "sat opposite each other and glared their mutual hostility."[40]

Although this had become a public issue of much strong feeling, Dr. Crapsey, estranged from this unreal world, concentrated on the trial room in much greater detail than the trial itself, noting the provinciality of his court and his own feeling of removal: "The courtroom itself was the downstairs front room of the parish-house hall, formerly an old-fashioned double parlor from which the partitions had been torn away. The walls were dull, the floor was bare and gave proof of long use. There was a low railing separating the room in half."[41]

Adelaide Crapsey's role in this trial was once more passive, and she may well have raged against a society that not only presumed to judge her parent but also prevented her from attaining the law degree which would have allowed her to defend him. She was reduced to the role of jester, of returning the situation to its proper proportion in the world outside. Claude Bragdon, who sat with Crapsey, found her comments useful. Because she was learned both in religious literature and legal history, she was capable of understanding more than most about the procedure of the trial, and her "ironic comments on the proceedings helped to make the whole thing appear positively grotesque."[42]

There was much that appeared grotesque. After an adjournment or postponement was again requested and refused, the prosecution opened its case, offering *Religion and Politics* and other documents for examination, and, following a break for lunch, called up its star witness, the Reverend Mr. James Alexander. The impropriety of using Alexander was obvious to all. As a clearly prejudiced witness of questionable character, he could not have been taken seriously in any real court.

Frederick James Kerr Alexander, thirty-four years old, stumbled his way through the examination and cross-examination. Asked by the prosecuting attorney to recollect the sermon, hedged, claimed to be unable to recall it, and then, under prodding, proceeded with a detailed outline:

The first statement that I remember is, he said Jesus was born of parents belonging to the middle class. The second statement, He was born of a simple father and mother; He was the son of a carpenter. He was born right. Then in the latter part of his sermon he criticized the position or attitude the church had taken on what he would call the first birth. He said the church paid all her attention practically to the second birth, rather than the first birth. And then I should say the climax came when he said the fact that the early christians predicated the miraculous birth of Jesus must be regarded as one of the greatest misfortunes that had ever befallen mankind. I should call that the climax of his discourse.[43]

Under cross-examination, when it became obvious that Alexander's memory was sharp because he had taken careful notes, Alexander attempted to explain this apparent set-up with the excuse that he had planned to discuss the matter with Dr. Crapsey. "It pained me very much to hear the statements, especially at Christmas time, when I think that the church teaches some other doctrine."

Q. Did you mean to say that when you took down this evidence, you had no thought that at some time you might now state to others than Dr. Crapsey what he had uttered? Did you not think of that?
A. I am not prepared to go into that, I have not—
Q. You are not prepared to go into it, but what I ask you is to go into it, and I have a perfect right to ask you.
A. I decline to answer any such question.
Q. You decline to state?
A. Unless the Court shall say that I shall go into it. I am not here to prove a case for you, or for anybody, or especially to be used by the defense, if that is your object; I don't wish to make—
Q. In other words, you don't propose to furnish any evidence that would be of benefit to the defense, that is your position, is it?
A. I am willing to give you whatever information I have.
Q. I thought you said you were not willing, you would furnish no evidence that would benefit the defense?
A. I didn't mean that.

The question is asked again
A. I have no recollection of having made the statement for that purpose.
Q. What do you mean by making the statement?

A. The written statement, you refer to.
Q. You have no recollection?
A. No, no recollection.[44]

Perkins then asked Alexander when he had been refused a raise, and after much hedging received the answer of autumn 1905. Then Perkins asked Alexander why, even though Dr. Crapsey had begun giving his "heretical" sermons in the fall of 1904, Alexander had been willing enough to remain to ask for a raise and only when refused a raise decided to quit.

Q. What we would particularly like to know is the state of your mind with reference to Dr. Crapsey's sermons at the time you asked to stay at his church if you could receive an increase of salary; that is the point to which I am directing my question.
A. At that time I couldn't tell which way Dr. Crapsey would go.
Q. You were willing to stay there if you received an increase of salary, were you, whichever way he went?
A. Not indefinitely, no. I wouldn't say I would have remained indefinitely.
Q. You were willing to listen to heretical statements if it was remembered in the wages?
A. I don't know as I was willing; I might be obliged to.
Q. You were willing to stay if they gave you more pay, and you asked for more pay?
A. For the time being; I thought I should have more pay. I believe it was promised in Dr. Crapsey's letter, before I came to St. Andrews. I can produce those letters. If they had raised my salary, they should have raised it on the first day of July, when my time expired.
Q. At various times in the autumn and winter you spoke to members of the vestry and said that if Dr. Crapsey was removed you would like to have his position as rector of St. Andrews?
A. I wouldn't say so.
Q. Will you state if you didn't?
A. Will you please state that again?
Q. I ask you whether last autumn or winter you did not speak to vestrymen of the church of St. Andrews, stating the possibility that Dr. Crapsey might be removed, and asking if you could not have their support as rector of that church, if he were removed?

A. I wouldn't put it that way.

Q. Tell us what way you would put it, then? Give us your memory? . . .

[after much hedging]

Q. Now, I will have to ask you that question again, and certainly, Mr. Alexander, as a truthful and intelligent witness you can answer a plain question. Did you or did you not to any vestryman of St. Andrews Church, state, if Dr. Crapsey were removed you would like to have their support for the position as rector of the church, did you or didn't you?

A. I wouldn't answer such a question; I have stated all I can say in regard to that. I was called by the vestry, and it was a matter I wished to consult with the vestry about, whether I should remain or resign.

Q. And are you willing in the presence of this Court and of this audience to deny that you made such statements and requests to the vestry of St. Andrews Church?

A. The way I will put it, Dr. Crapsey frequently spoke of resigning, and on several occasions asked me to remain; and one day he sent for me and requested me to take charge of the parish.

The same kind of answers were given when Perkins asked him if Dr. Crapsey had asked him to retire.[45]

The *Times* noted that "the witness does not cut an attractive figure,"[46] and Shepard said that it would be "a sad day for the influence of the church in this community, if a man with the standard of life of Dr. Crapsey must be thrown out, and a man with standards of Dr. Alexander shall stay in."[47] The remainder of the day was taken up with comparing Dr. Crapsey's statements with the Book of Common Prayer.

How the contrast of her father with that familiar, homey book must have jarred Adelaide, despite her distance and sophistication. The reassuring repeated prayers were now set up as witnesses for the prosecution, as if two parts of her were pitted in battle. Her smiles and easy manner must have seemed just a bit strained. But the certainty in her father's rightness gave her strength for the pain as well as the tedium.

The next day was no more exciting and no less absurd. The prosecution continued to submit "documents," tried unsuccessfully to introduce a witness, the Reverend Mr. Frances Woodward, of St. Paul's in Rochester, who had spoken once with Dr. Crapsey and claimed that Dr. Crapsey had made libelous statements about Jesus. It was clear that heresy was too tentative a charge, but the prosecution had no further case, and when the defense's objection was sustained, rested. The defense opened with the Reverend Mr. Joseph A. Leighton, professor of theology and chaplain at Hobart College. Leighton, whose college had granted Dr. Crapsey an honorary S.T.D. (doctor of sacred theology) degree only six years before, was anxious to show that Dr. Crapsey's opinions were not outside the acceptable limits of interpretation, and to this end tried to introduce a number of books which were known to and accepted by the church and made statements not unlike those made by Dr. Crapsey. But the court declined to accept such evidence, since, as Judge Stiness had said: "Courts could not determine questions of doctrine; that would produce chaos instead of unity; they had only to ask themselves if Dr. Crapsey uttered the words alleged and if they violated the doctrine of the Church."[48]

This absurdity was clear only to the prosecution, and the defense replied: "We admit the publication, we deny the innuendo. We say we published these things, but we say in them we proclaim no disbelief in the creed."[49] "It is not a question whether this doctrine is true or not true, it is a question whether the utterances are in accordance with the doctrine of this church as it hath received the same."[50] There was no defense that could be made against that: the defense was based on a democratic concept of religion and the church was not democratic. Therefore Dr. Crapsey could only be guilty in this court. But until that court he had not realized the extent to which he had drifted from the church.

Following the morning adjournment, the defense tried a different tack, calling character witnesses instead of documentary evidence. Although there were many important people, including Elwood Worcester and Edwin S. Hoffman, the court declined to accept character witnesses at all, and the defense was left with no case.

Friday morning was the last day of the trial. Mrs. Crapsey came up to Batavia for the occasion with a whole party of supporters. "He seems to gain in cheerfulness the nearer he approaches the great crisis of his career as priest of the Episcopal Church," the *Post Express* recorded. "He laughed and chattered gaily." The cameras snapped photographs of Adelaide Crapsey with her family, and one sketch artist drew the reverend and his daughter walking elegantly arm in arm.

Inside the courthouse, the mood was less ebullient. A prominent Buffalo lawyer, Franklin D. Locke, summed up the prosecution. Perkins answered with an equally lengthy argument, one which included a statement by Dr. Crapsey that endeavored to explain the potential validity of a metaphorical interpretation of the texts. "When I say that on the third day he rose again from the dead, I do not necessarily imply that the body in which He had lived was dematerialized, so that He assumed it and walked through doors. But I do believe that He rose again and revealed His spiritual body to the keen spiritual vision of His disciples, and I believe that in the strength of that Resurrection they went forward to conquer the world. I believe that His personality was virgin born, because to me it is the personification of all that is pure and holy."

Perkins's speech was followed by another for the defense by Dr. Elwood Worcester, who attacked the attitude of the prosecution to the church "as if it were a political club or a voluntary society of persons who met together in Philadelphia in the year 1785, and who by the simple means of adopting a constitution and passing by-laws closed all the great questions of religious truth forever."[51]

Francis J. Hall then began to speak for the prosecution. He related the history of the jurisdiction of the English Judicial Committee of the Privy Council in ecclesiastical matters to the defendant. "It is reported that one of our great statesman said: 'You can fool some of the people all of the time, you can fool all of the people some of the time; but you cannot fool all of the people all of the time.' So it is in matters of this kind. There are some things which are greatly in evidence. We have had a formidable array of gentlemen of learning who have come here to testify to their private opinions. (Holding up his ear trumpet) My ear is greatly in evidence, but it is not evidence of the soundness of my hearing."[53]

At this point Dr. Crapsey, worn out and uninvolved, reacted to the triviality and irrelevance of the trial by falling asleep. Adelaide Crapsey, outraged that her father was the subject of such malice, touched a reporter. "Will you please wake up my father?" she whispered, and her words went down on the reporters' pads. "I couldn't let him sleep, you know," she told her mother afterward, "while they were all abusing him so!"[53]

The soporific speech was followed by a lighter one. McComb replied to Hall's speech by inviting those questioning Dr. Crapsey's beliefs to debate with him. "The only true way in which these great problems can ever be solved is not by an ecclesiastical trial, which never settles anything, but by frank and free discussion, by testing theories and doctrines at the bar of reason and history. What is needed is that one who disagrees with Dr. Crapsey's views should come forth and grapple with them, and overthrow them if he can."[54] This was an invitation Adelaide Crapsey must have applauded, taking her back as it did to her own days of debate and her belief in the quest for truth. Surely her father could not lose! And everyone, even the prosecution, constantly reiterated their respect for his character. In the summary of the defense Shepard reminded the court of this on the next day: "There is something of veneration toward him on Mr. Locke's part, as there must be on the part of any one who knows him or knows of him."

The final argument had been prepared by the Reverend Mr. Alexander Viets Griswold Allen, professor of church history at the Episcopal Theological School, and was revised and expanded to form the basis of Allen's book, *Freedom in the Church*.[55] Its argument is simple. "The real question is this: A clergyman, having taken his ordination vows, devotes himself to the study of Holy Scripture and is driven to the conclusion that the Creed has such a meaning. Is it his right and duty to preach that, or is it not? That is the whole question."[56]

This might have been the whole question to Allen and Shepard, but the judge saw no connection between Shepard's impassioned speech and the issue. "Their addresses reminded me of a little incident that happened once in my practice. A good old Irish woman came in and wanted a warranty deed drawn and the practice in our State being to use the old English form, with all the covenants against easements, etc., and all the warranties against jointures, etc., and I read, as was my custom, the whole deed over from beginning to end; and when I had closed she put her hands together and said: 'Oh, that is beautiful.' I have felt that way as to the speeches that have been given here today and yesterday, and I must say that I have failed to see any real connection between these arguments and the point which this Court has to decide."[57]

John Lord O'Brian was given the final word, and he used it to vilify Dr. Crapsey.

> The points of evidence at issue in this matter are at last clear. They were not clear on the return day, because the defendant in his answer denied the delivery of the second sermon specified in the presentment; and I hope the Court in considering our side of this case will remember that we have been met with no ordinary situation of clearness or frankness, and that the burden was put upon us of proving beyond a doubt that all the statements alleged had actually been made. And now that all those utterances have been proved, all the argument of the defense is a plea of confession and avoidance, a plea of justification on the grounds of toleration.[58]

And with thanks and compliments on both sides, the court was adjourned.

Dr. Crapsey, whose greatest joy was to give sermons, to teach, to speak, had not said a word.

The Verdict

As if to make up for his enforced silence, he went with his daughter to Ithaca that day and the next morning preached twice at Sage Chapel at Cornell, repeating his views on the Virgin Birth and the Resurrection and expanding on their ramifications. "If we wait for some far-off Saviour," he told the students, and the newspaper reporters who had come from far and wide recorded it assiduously, "if we wait for a curtain of blue to open and for some mighty being to come and achieve our salvation, we shall wait forever. The day will never come. It is not necessary. It is a degrading idea that perfection exists the like of which we cannot attain, albeit it be predicated on one hanging on a cross."[1]

It seemed that the Reverend Dr. Crapsey was out to shock the congregation on as many fronts as possible. The morning's text was Hebrews 11:39–40, which he attributed to an "unknown writer, possibly a woman."

He succeeded.

But the basis for his statement was more than nose-thumbing. Crapsey's asserting a female writer was not heretical; it was antipatriarchal. Perhaps it was done with Adelaide in mind, for Algernon must have realized by now that his own career was doomed and was beginning to see that his daughter had learned more in Rome in one winter than most clergymen learn in a lifetime. And she had sensitivity and wisdom to complement her logic.

170

The Reverend Dr. Crapsey had certainly come far in his views of women. When Emily graduated from Kemper, he had spoken at her commencement on "Athena, the Companion of Heroes and the Keeper of Homes."[2] No longer did he perceive the role of women as supportive but was moving to his later belief of women as the only hope in leadership for the future.

There was also a personal message in the text. The message of Hebrews is faith, and faith was the subject of the trial. But the faith of Hebrews is the courage to endure trials because of the knowledge of a higher goal, "God having provided something better for us." Of this provision the Reverend Dr. Crapsey was secure.

Although the sermons might have released Dr. Crapsey's pent-up emotions and explained his situation to those who were ready to follow him, they did more to harm him than the trial itself. His attitude was not compliant, and it was clear to the church that he would not fade back into anonymity in Rochester if the court agreed to forgive him. Algernon Crapsey would continue in this direction, giving more and more embarrassing sermons and publishing more and more provocative books.

Even his allies in the *Churchman* turned from him now. A week before the *Churchman* had argued: "False teaching is not to be passively endured, but the false teacher is, if possible, to be enlightened and saved."[3] After the news of Crapsey's exhibition at Cornell, they wrote: "The Brooklyn Standard Union voices a very generally expressed opinion when it says that 'Dr. Crapsey convicted himself' and made his conviction doubly sure by his sermons on the Sunday following his trial. 'He has not made himself a martyr. He has only made himself an object lesson to other clergymen.' "[4]

On May 9 the *New York Times* announced that a decision in the trial had been reached and that the judgment would be forthcoming from the bishop shortly. They noted that whatever the court had determined, it was the bishop's decision that was crucial. "He has the power to modify the sentence if the verdict is against Dr. Crapsey, although he is without power to increase it."[5]

The verdict took six more days to be delivered. With only one man on the committee averring, Dr. Crapsey was judged guilty. "The lengthy decision convicted Crapsey of impugning and denying, in his book, the

Virgin Birth and the Resurrection; in his sermon the Virgin Birth; and in the book and the sermon of impugning the doctrines 'That our Lord Jesus Christ is God' and the Trinity."[6]

> In accordance with section 18 of the ordinances of the Ecclesiastical Court of this diocese, we state that in our opinion sentence should be pronounced as follows: That the respondent be suspended from exercising the functions of a minister of this Church until such time as he shall satisfy the ecclesiastical authority of the diocese that his belief and teaching conform to the doctrines of the Apostle's Creed and the Nicene Creed as this Church had received the same. However, we express the earnest hope and desire that the respondent may see his way clear, during the thirty days which, under the canons of the Church, must intervene before sentence can be pronounced, to fully satisfy the ecclesiastical authority of such conformity on his part.[7]

Repentance was still an honorable release, but the Reverend Dr. Crapsey could not take up that option, even if he perceived no financial alternative. He could not be a hypocrite, finding it impossible to leave the subject alone once he had been accused of it, and he could not trust the church to accept his apology once he had humiliated himself by giving in on what he believed. He had to fully satisfy them; how could that be done? Furthermore, as Shepard pointed out in the appeal, "It was a pathetically fatuous suggestion of the Diocesan Court that within thirty days after he should learn what was the opinion of a majority of them, Dr. Crapsey should reverse—and acquaint the Bishop or Standing Committee that he had done so—not only his preaching, but also his inner belief, which whatever its expression to men, he holds to the Almighty God who sees and knows, spite of declarations to bishops or lesser men."[8]

If no retraction was possible, an appeal was inevitable. Even rigid church scholars like Dr. Allen, who thought "that when a man *denies* the Virgin Birth, it has become a case in pathology rather than in theology,"[9] disagreed with the sentence, noting the large numbers of clergymen who feared that they too, by these definitions, may well be heretics as well.

The appeal, filed on June 6, was necessary, not only for Dr. Crapsey but for the church thrown into confusion. Dr. Allen wrote:

We are in the beginning of a controversy, which it may take another generation to bring to its conclusion. We must be patient and willing to wait, with
an open mind, listening to what can be said on both sides, and especially on
the conservative side, where there is much to be said, which has not yet
been said. . . . The English are not going to follow the Germans, but will
determine this issue in their own way; they have a great historic Church to
carry with them, and the Germans have no baggage, lightly equipped for
movement in the world of religious speculation. The English have a worship
and a religion to look after and maintain, as well as a Church. With the
Germans religion consists in thinking.[10]

In order to be available to her father during this hard time, Adelaide
Crapsey remained in Rochester. The family had considered their argument with the church as inevitably victorious, and the only thing that
had been needed was Adelaide's support, comfort, and good humor
through the crisis. But now over a year had gone by, the crisis was still
not over, and the situation was beginning to look more grim every day.
The questions were no longer mere questions of support and comfort
but of Adelaide Crapsey's academic and literary future, kept in sus-
pended animation for eighteen months, and, equally important, her financial situation.

To develop as a writer she needed to be far from home, able to reach
her source for poetry. Her mother and father were overwhelming influences, and when she taught she was usually too bound up with her
responsibilities to allow that flow of imagination. Yet with her mother so
upset by the possible outcome of the trial and her father dependent
upon her for support, she could not consider going back to Europe or
even to Kemper.

To add to her complications, her economic future was bleak. Her father, who could usually be called upon to bail her out of a really serious
financial crisis, was now clearly in danger of losing his livelihood. She
needed a job, then, and one that rendered her relatively accessible to her
family.

The crisis was ameliorated by the offer of a position at Miss Low's School in Stamford, Connecticut, not unlike that she had filled at Kemper but closer to New York City and Rochester. The offer was probably obtained for her through the intervention of Mary Delia Lewis, who had been head of the English Department at Kemper when Crapsey taught there and had taught at Miss Low's School when Adelaide was a student at Kemper. It was a fortunate offer, for it began in Stamford in September, just after the appeal was scheduled to be heard in New York City.

This time both Philip and Rachel joined Adelaide in the audience in the Diocesan House on Lafayette Street in Manhattan on September 4 when her father faced the court of appeal for the first time. Rachel had come in from New Jersey, where she was living with her husband and baby daughter, and Adelaide had probably already unpacked at Stamford and taken the short train ride to New York City. But Philip, who was becoming a successful businessman, having formed a company to challenge the Gas & Electric monopoly in Rochester, accompanied his father from home.

Because the seriousness of the situation had been so often reiterated, the family apparently anticipated an immediate trial and a speedy decision, but the presiding judge, the bishop of Scarborough, New Jersey, had not had an opportunity to study the trial record and adjourned until October 19. So Adelaide returned to Miss Low's School at Stamford even more unsure and uncertain about the future of those she loved than before. The bishop of Scarborough was not a wholly reliable or sympathetic man and in his convention address at the end of the month openly discussed the case "upon which he was to pass as a judge."[11] In a civil court this transgression would have been grounds for removal from the case, but in the ecclesiastical court only the reporters objected.

Shepard was optimistic about the appeal. Like the Crapsey family he still wanted to believe that progress and the quest for truth would have to win out, but he appealed on the basis of the numerous technical irregularities in the Batavia court, adding: "Dr. Crapsey is here, we rejoice to believe, in the protection of a true court of justice."[12]

It was an extremely hot day, and although Shepard spoke for three hours, "the members of the court . . . urged him to continue after the usual time for adjournment arrived."[13] They knew the extent to which the public eye was on them and the dire predictions of the results of conviction. The *Times* headlined: "Schism is predicted if Crapsey is Dismissed,"[14] taking a few lines out of Shepard's speech and putting the court even more on its toes.

Luckily for Adelaide Crapsey her friend Jean was in New York City to give her the support she was giving to her father.[15] Jean was now living on Central Park West and, having just finished her new novel, *Jerry Junior,* was preparing to sail in November to Italy and the Far East. But although Webster was fulfilling all that her friend would have wanted to do herself, Crapsey's concentration was on her father and there was no room for envy.

The hearing was short and closed the next day, on October 21, 1906, like a short-lived but many-ringed circus. The *Times* coverage accents the emphasis:

> John Lord O'Brian, Church Advocate, at the hearing in review of the heresy charges against the Rev. Algernon S. Crapsey, completed his argument as prosecutor yesterday. The courtroom in the Diocesan House in Lafayette Place held many interested auditors yesterday. Miss Adelaide Crapsey, a daughter of the clergyman who is fighting to retain his place in the Church, was present. She followed with the closest interest every word of the argument against her father. At the conclusion of Mr. O'Brian's reply to the briefs of Edward M. Shepherd [*sic*] and James Blech [*sic*] Perkins for the appellant, the court went into executive session. At this session it was decided to adjourn for two weeks. The court will convene on Nov. 2, and it is expected that its decision on the appeal will be ready by that time.
>
> The Court of Review cannot pass on the construction of doctrines. It must review the trial given Dr. Crapsey by the lower court and decide whether that trial was fair and properly conducted. It may reverse the decision of the lower court, and the case will then be dropped, with Dr. Crapsey still in the Church. Should it decline to interfere with the decision of the diocesan court at Batavia, the matter will then be taken before the General Council of the Church next year, and a court of appeal will hear the case.
>
> Mr. O'Brian, in his argument in defense of the action of the lower court, did not spare Dr. Crapsey yesterday. He declared that Dr. Crapsey had treated

the immaculate conception and the resurrection as "rude legends." "And yet," he said, "Dr. Crapsey says the Creed daily. His statement is filled with subtlety and evasion. The question is 'Was our Lord Jesus Christ divine or was he not?' Dr. Crapsey seems to hold to a divinity in Jesus that is present in all men. That is nothing but modern Pantheism. It is also nothing but Unitarianism.

"If this defendent is right then the Creed of the Church is all wrong. Perhaps we are all wrong, and perhaps the Lord Jesus Christ is a distorted figure. But all that is outside of the case. This decision is important. If the decision of the lower court is reversed on a technicality, the resulting demoralization will be large."

Mr. Shepherd, in rebuttal, warned the court against the effect of error in treating the alleged heresy of his client. "I ask you to guard carefully against error," he said, "and to take into consideration the fact that it will create a disturbance through the whole of the American Church."

In ending the session of the court Bishop Scarborough said: "Pity the court in the momentous task it has before it. It has been one of the most remarkable facts of this case that there has seemed to be present in pleaders, spectators, and court the feeling that a great question was at stake."[16]

The article essentially begins and ends with the spectators—with Adelaide. For by now the poor diminutive clergyman had become a symbol to the press, and they watched the trial with interest not for the effect on the career of Dr. Crapsey but for the possibility of further repercussions. How would people who witnessed this trial feel about the church now?

How Crapsey and her father must have felt their own self-importance here, and no wonder he could not recant when he had the opportunity. He must have thought he would always be as famous as he was that moment. And she knew that if they were proven right, not only would all the time she had wasted be well worth the while but she would be given a spiritual push forward in her work with the certainty that she and her father were not the outsiders of society but leaders. But when the court reconvened a month later, it upheld the previous decision. "There is a widespread conviction that the conditions of the trial in Western New York did not conform to the ordinary principles of justice,"[17] cried the ecclesiastical papers, but Crapsey's guilt would no longer be contested.

For his return to Rochester that weekend he was accompanied by the now ubiquitous reporters, who knew that any decision the Reverend Dr. Crapsey made at this time would be crucial. He could, at least theoretically, repent; he could also ask his parishioners to follow him out of the Episcopal church, forming instead an independent religious organization; or he could quit. Every word he spoke was not only heard by the massive congregation he had acquired but was also recorded for the media. "CROWD TO HEAR CRAPSEY—He Tells It the Road to the Higher Goal Is Strewn with Martyrs' Bones," the headlines of the *New York Times* proclaimed, following the human drama as if Dr. Crapsey were a publicity-hungry president and not a simple, modest, parish priest.

> St. Andrews Church . . . was crowded this morning with his friends from many denominations to hear the first of his last three sermons before his final withdrawal from the Protestant Episcopal Ministry. As Dr. Crapsey entered with the vester choir those who had expected to see any great change in his appearance were disappointed. The kindly expression of his face was tinged with sadness, but otherwise the sorrows and agitation of the last few months have left him untouched. At no time during the service did his manner betray any change. His sermon was delivered calmly and dispassionately, and its message was free from bitterness.

It was a sermon which pronounced both his character and his direction. Announcing as his text the words of Jesus, "My Father worketh hitherto, and I work" (John 5:17) he delineated his religious work ethic: "We are only in the first day, not in the last day, of creation. The work of God, so far as we can see, will never be finished, and our one aspiration is to be workers together with him, that we may aid him to bring to pass that which he has in mind, and to promote, as we know he desires we should, the betterment of the world."[18] Dr. Crapsey was continuing the direction he had first set out to the public in his sermon at Cornell. No longer troubled by the trials and castigations of the church, he perceived his goal to be beyond the petty questions of doctrines and verbal interpolations. He was on his way to contributing to the inevitable revolution in ecclesiastical and secular thinking, the revolution of Christian Marxism.

He knew he was succeeding. In the same pages that announced the topic of his last sermon, the warden of the Protestant Episcopal church, Spencer Trask, pleaded that the conviction of Dr. Crapsey had perplexed the religious thinking of numerous clerics: "I ask this space in your columns because numbers of young men studying for or thinking of entering the ministry of the Episcopal Church have earnestly affirmed that if this verdict should be given adversely, as it has been, they would seriously consider withdrawing from the Church, and also there are many halting between two opinions, and those who stand outside of the Church, with small knowledge of the life of Christ, looking to the Church as the intepreter of that life." Trask's wish was to announce to the world that there were many within the church who believed as Dr. Crapsey did.[19]

Algernon Crapsey took his letter of resignation to New York City to show Edward Shepard and probably consulted with his daughter as well.[20] The letter reached the front page of the *New York Times*. Regretful of the loss of the position he loved and sorry for the outcome of the trial, the letter was also forgiving and modest, and the *Times* editorial was profuse in praise of his character: "Nobody, we suppose, who has read it, could help being touched by the manly, eloquent, and pathetic letter of DR. CRAPSEY which we printed yesterday. It justifies the attachment of the host of friends he evidently possesses. It explains his pastoral success. It shows that any organization which has lost the services of the writer of it has sustained a grievous loss."[21]

The most recent accusations by the bishop, that Dr. Crapsey was clinging to his office "for a piece of bread,"[22] were obviously belied by the pure goals exhibited in Algernon Crapsey's letter, and his image, for future battles, had been established. "I am about to carry our case," wrote Dr. Crapsey, "to the high court of the free intelligence and the enlightened conscience of the world, and if I win it there, I will win it for every church and every soul in Christendom. If I fail before that court, it will be because I am wrong in my conception of truth; and then I will be glad to fall, for my contention is not for my conception, but for the eternal truth of God. Let my brethren within the Church abide the issue of this trial. For when the Great Tribunal of Free Thought has decided this contention, the men who administer the Church on earth will conform to this decision. It is to this work of showing that God is in man and man is in God that I consecrate the rest of my life."[23]

There were other, less idealistic alternatives. Algernon Crapsey could have taken his church with him and become a religious independent of the Episcopal church, or he could have appealed in civil court. But neither alternative was appropriate to his character.[24] Instead, Dr. Crapsey made his departure with grandeur, "without," as he put it, "the slightest animosity to any that I leave behind, and with love unspeakable to that host of men and women within the Church who have comforted me in my tribulation and most of all, with a gratitude that will never die, to four men who have done for me what men can seldom do for another— to Seth Low and George Foster Peabody, to James Breck Perkins and Edward Morse Shepard."[25] That Wednesday night, the twenty-eighth, Dr. Crapsey bade farewell to his parishioners, who "were moved to tears as they listened to the parting words of their beloved rector." But his departure was operatic in more than an emotional sense. It also continued for two more sermons, sermons in which he explained his decision in detail.

I am sorry to say that our ecclesiastical superiors have as little confidence in your intelligence as in mine; they do not think that you have the capacity to separate the wheat from the chaff in my preaching, nor are you, in the estimation of these gentlemen, able to search the Scriptures and determine for yourselves whether what I say is true or not. Whether this reflection of our superiors upon my intelligence and upon yours is well founded is not for me to say. I know that it is effectual in bringing upon me the greatest sorrow of my life.

I am not only barred from the pulpit, I am also forbidden to stand before the altar and to celebrate the sacred offices of the Church. This, however, though a sorrow to us both, is certainly not a misfortune to me. No one but a minister can know how dangerous to his soul is the constant repetition of the acts of the ritual and the continual rehearsal of the words of the liturgy. Through continual use the words become dulled and the actions mechanical, and I am sure that, however sad it may be, it is better for my soul to leave my place before the high altar and go down and kneel in the midst of the people and receive the sacraments of the Church from worthier hands than mine.

Urging his parishioners to remain in the church despite his departure in order to keep the now unstable church steady, he still justified his position and explained the injustice of the same church toward himself. And with a "touching tribute to his wife, saying that whatever was best in his pastorate was not only owing to her inspiration, but was directly the product of her work," he acknowledged her terrible fate, for which he was responsible. "For a man to break up the home was a comparatively easy matter, he said. For the woman it was the rending of life."[26]

The drastic end was on the second of December when he gave his farewell sermon. "With standard lowered and heads bowed, the members of St. Andrews Episcopal Church choir marched through the chancel this morning in absolute silence at the conclusion of the farewell sermon of the Rev. Algernon S. Crapsey. Grief at the breaking of relations that had existed so long expressed itself in the sober faces of the congregation, and here and there by sobs. . . . Accommodations were far too limited to provide for the people who sought to attend the service. The church was jammed at 10 o'clock, an hour before the time for the exercises to commence."[27]

And with this lengthy and painful farewell to his people, Algernon Crapsey, on December 5, 1906, formally left the church.

Algernon Crapsey, Adelaide's father. (Courtesy of Arthur H. Crapsey)

Adelaide Trowbridge Crapsey, Adelaide's mother. (Courtesy of
Arthur H. Crapsey)

ul up h Adelaide .

Adelaide (left) with her sister Emily. (Courtesy of Arthur H. Crapsey)

Adelaide and her sister Marie, 1895. (Courtesy of Arthur H. Crapsey)

September – 1895

Adelaide Crapsey with her brothers and sisters, 1895. From right to left: Philip, Emily, Adelaide, Paul, Rachel, Algy, Ruth, and Marie. Arthur, born in 1896, is dubbed in at the left corner. (Courtesy of Arthur H. Crapsey)

Adelaide (second row, third from left) and some of her classmates at Kemper Hall, the Episcopal boarding school for girls that she and Emily attended. (Courtesy Kemper Hall)

At Kemper, Adelaide (front right) was expected to follow a list of "Kemper Hall Don'ts" that guided the girls into the world of young ladies and emphasized consideration for others and the establishment of values. (Courtesy Kemper Hall)

The three oldest Crapsey sisters: Rachel (left), Emily (center), and Adelaide (right). (Courtesy of Arthur H. Crapsey)

Adelaide as manager of basketball team at Vassar, 1899. Interested in physical as well as intellectual freedom, Adelaide (center) was a firm believer in nonrestrictive clothing and vigorous physical activities for women. (Courtesy Vassar College Library)

Adelaide Crapsey and Margaret Jackson in *Captain Letterblair,* a drama production at Vassar. Margaret was one of Adelaide's roommates. (Courtesy Vassar College Library)

Vassar students annually visited John Burroughs's country cottage "Slabsides."
Burroughs particularly enjoyed Adelaide's company and is pictured here with Adelaide
in May, just before her graduation. (Courtesy of Arthur H. Crapsey)

Jean Webster and Adelaide Crapsey on Class Day at Vassar College, June 1901. Jean, one of Adelaide's roommates and her best friend at Vassar, later used Crapsey as a model for some of the progressive and spirited female protagonists in her fiction. (Courtesy Vassar College Library)

Adelaide's senior portrait from the *Vassarion*, 1901. (Courtesy Vassar College Library)

Adelaide Crapsey, 1901. (Courtesy Vassar College Library)

Adelaide (left) with Jean Webster and her brother, Sam, in Fredonia, 1902. (Courtesy of Susan Sutton Smith)

Adelaide Crapsey, probably at Miss Low's school, where the students described her as a "thrilling" instructor. This photograph, obviously cut from a group photograph, was glued onto the title page of the copy of Crapsey's *Verse* belonging to Medora Addison, a student with whom Adelaide became friends. (Courtesy University of Rochester, Rare Books and Special Collections)

Too ill to continue teaching, Crapsey traveled to Rome in 1908 for rest and recuperation. (Courtesy of Arthur H. Crapsey)

Lines Addressed To My Left Lung
Inconveniently Enamoured of
Plant-Lirs

It was, my Lune, most strange of you,
    A freak I cannot pardon,
Thus to transform yourself into
    A vegetable - garden.

Though Laking William set ere while
    His seal on rural fashions,
I must deplore, bewail, revile
    Your horticultural passions.

And as your ways I thus lament
    (which, plainly, I call crazy)
For all I know, serene, content,
    You think yourself a daisy!

Her health declining further, Crapsey returned home and went into a
sanatorium at Saranac Lake, where, bedridden, she wrote "Lines Addressed
to My Left Lung" and other poems. (Courtesy University of Rochester, Rare
Books and Special Collections)

With her death from tuberculosis imminent, Adelaide returned to Rochester to spend her last days with her family. (Courtesy of Arthur H. Crapsey)

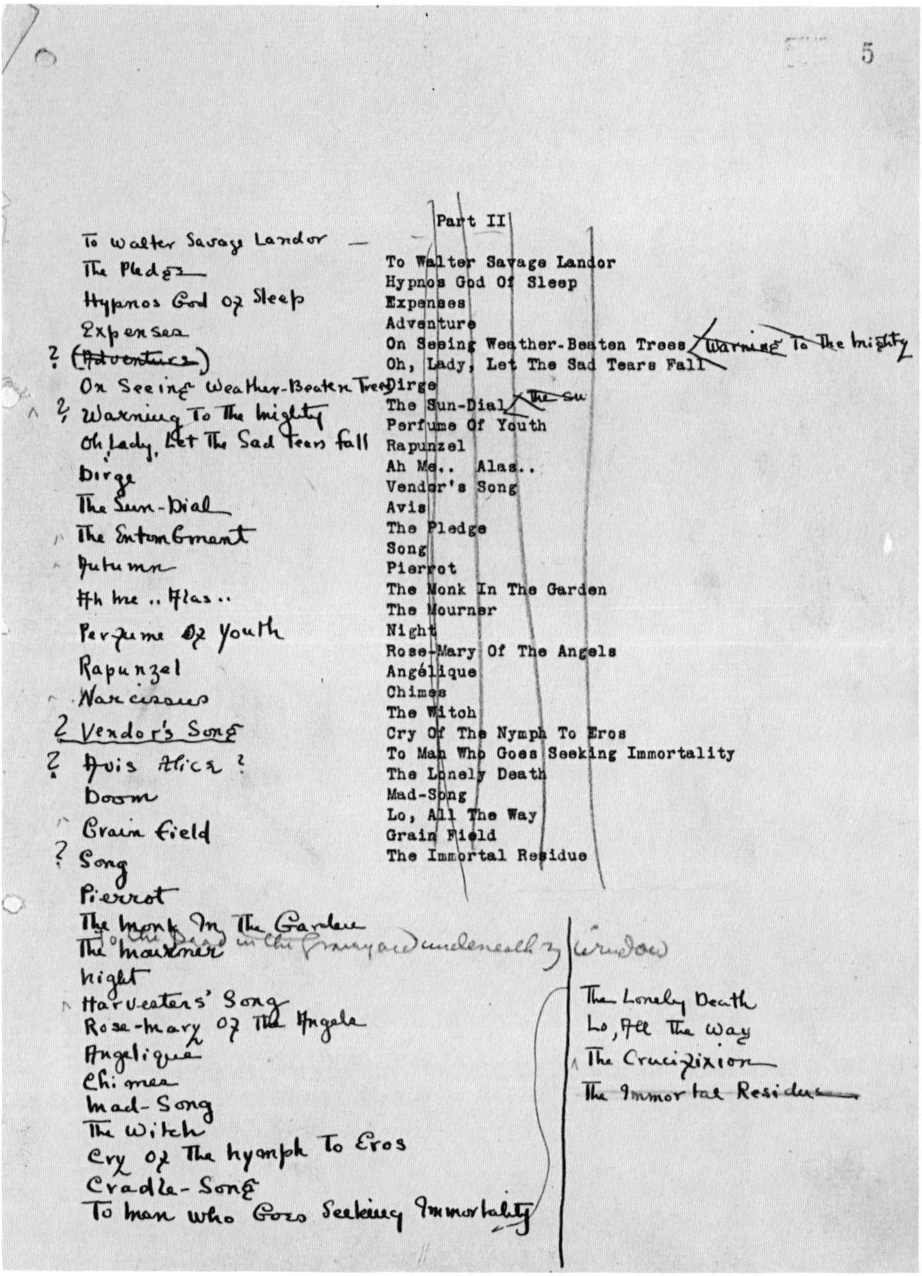

Handwritten left column:

To Walter Savage Landor —
The Pledge
Hypnos God Of Sleep
Expenses
? (Adventure)
On Seeing Weather-Beaten Trees
? Warning To The Mighty
Oh Lady, Let The Sad Tears Fall
Dirge
The Sun-Dial
The Entombment
Autumn
Ah me .. Alas..
Perfume Of Youth
Rapunzel
Narcissus
? Vendor's Song
? Avis Alice ?
Doom
Grain Field
? Song
Pierrot
The Monk In The Garden
The Mourner of the Dead in the Graveyard underneath my window
Night
Harvesters' Song
Rose-Mary Of The Angels
Angelique
Chimes
Mad-Song
The Witch
Cry Of The Nymph To Eros
Cradle-Song
To Man Who Goes Seeking Immortality

Typed middle column:

Part II

To Walter Savage Landor
Hypnos God Of Sleep
Expenses
Adventure
On Seeing Weather-Beaten Trees / Warning To The Mighty
Oh, Lady, Let The Sad Tears Fall
Dirge
The Sun-Dial / The Su
Perfume Of Youth
Rapunzel
Ah Me.. Alas..
Vendor's Song
Avis
The Pledge
Song
Pierrot
The Monk In The Garden
The Mourner
Night
Rose-Mary Of The Angels
Angélique
Chimes
The Witch
Cry Of The Nymph To Eros
To Man Who Goes Seeking Immortality
The Lonely Death
Mad-Song
Lo, All The Way
Grain Field
The Immortal Residue

Handwritten right column:

The Lonely Death
Lo, All The Way
The Crucifixion
The Immortal Residue

Frustrated by not having much to show for all her endeavors and knowing that her work would remain incomplete, Adelaide pushed herself to prepare her poems for publication. This is a worksheet for the order of "The Presentation Piece," a manuscript of poems Adelaide gave to Jean Webster for possible publication after her death. (Courtesy University of Rochester, Rare Books and Special Collections)

Miss Low's School

During all this final controversy, with its emotional publicity and earth-shaking implications, Adelaide Crapsey was tucked away in as sheltered a situation as was possible. Her position at Miss Low's School enabled her to maintain anonymity now that the publicity was not that good, but it was one that was already becoming tiresome to her. For this school had all of the constraints of Kemper and few of the compensations.

Miss Low had named the school after herself when she took it over fifteen years before from a Mrs. Richardson. Her principles and those of her school were clear and stern. "She meant her school to be simple, strong in fundamentals, solid—and that was the type of school she had. Its physical features were simple and unadorned." While Adelaide was enjoying gymnastics, military parade drills, and basketball as a student at Kemper, here "there was no gymnasium; a long glass-enclosed piazza served as a recreation room in stormy weather and as a place for mild and ladylike Delsarte exercises." For exercise the young ladies "walked two by two through Stamford's streets, rejoicing sometimes in going to the South End along the dyke . . . [to] scramble around on the shore and pick flowers in the fields." Occasionally, "as a great event," there would be picnics. The physical accommodations were also spare. There were few students, about sixteen boarders and forty day scholars, and when Crapsey was invited to teach there they all fit into one old building on Willow Street, with only the recent addition of a tennis/basketball court.[1]

The year Crapsey arrived the school moved to newer quarters, renting "the fine old Ferguson place in Atlantic Street." It was aesthetically a considerable improvement, having large and beautiful grounds with "magnificent old trees and wide lawns." The change enabled an increase of pupils, and it was in preparation for this that Crapsey was hired. Resident pupils grew in number to thirty who now could enjoy "space and beauty of outlook."

The expansion caused a change in administration, and Miss Low took on Miss Heywood, who had been a teacher at the school since its inception, as an associate head of the school. With this change in administration, the school remained small and relatively provincial, and it was not with a light heart that Adelaide Crapsey gave her address to the *Vassar Class Bulletin*[2] as 42 Willow Street, Stamford, adding, "I'm teaching this year at Miss Low's school." The principles of the school remained as they had been years ago, and the atmosphere was oppressive to her.[3]

Despite the prestige of this private school (Georges Clemenceau had been the French master there forty years before), Crapsey was not happy about teaching school. Her horizons had expanded, she had become involved in a larger universe, and she could not accept quietly the extreme retreat from reality which characterized the typical small private girls' school. Like the governess Jane Eyre, she must have thought the same kind of restless thoughts in the hours she was free from her duties: "It is in vain to say human beings ought to be satisfied with tranquillity: they must have action; but women feel just as men feel; they need exercise for their faculties, and a field for their efforts as much as their brothers do; they suffer from too rigid a restraint, too absolute a stagnation, precisely as men would suffer; and it is narrow-minded in their more privileged fellow-creatures to say that they ought to confine themselves to making puddings and knitting stockings, to playing on the piano and embroidering bags."[4] It is not surprising, then, that family and friends noted that "a great deal of her earlier vivaciousness was gone."[5]

There was also the problem of unwelcome publicity. The publicity that might have been amusing had she found herself in an artistic or intellectual environment could only embarrass her in the girls' school in which she had now committed herself, and the many exciting things she had learned and was exploring—about religion, about poetry, about the nature of government—could not really be continued in this world of sheltered young women. Instead of flaunting her relationship to the famous heretic, Crapsey avoided mention of her family and consequently avoided all unnecessary contact with her colleagues. "She lived among them as a friendly stranger, by choice very much alone. . . . Yet with all this aloofness," a teacher noted, "she gave no one the impression of unfriendliness, for her spirit was essentially a friendly one. The other teachers liked her, though they never came to know her well."

Crapsey renewed her acquaintance with a former Vassar classmate who was also teaching at Miss Low's, Louise Merritt. Now Mrs. William Dalton, Louise Merritt was less limited than her colleagues at Miss Low's. She neither taught full time nor lived on the school grounds, and her house and garden on Blachley Road provided a much-needed escape for Crapsey from the trials and rigors of boarding school life and the lack of privacy to an aesthetically pleasing, isolated environment.

The escape was extremely important to her, and the aesthetic environment was not a little part of this escape. In the garden, Merritt observed, "her face would be radiant with pleasure. I think she had a sense of companionship with it."[6] Watching her joy in the garden, Merritt would contemplate that incredible aesthetic hunger and wonder why, with Crapsey's "great sensitiveness to, and thirst for beauty [she] could have had so little satisfaction; . . . [why] she, who loved quietness so much, should have had to spend so much of her life under conditions which must have jarred on her."[7]

"I think I have never seen in anyone else such capacity for intense enjoyment. It was in itself a rare and lovely thing."[8] "The things which she enjoyed," Merritt noted, "she enjoyed with an acuteness which was almost painful." It was not only gardens that gave her joy, nor drives in the country. It was also the peace of a secure and stable family. "She loved the quietness of a quiet home, and all the simple everyday happenings therein. In congenial surroundings she relaxed and expanded, and her sense of enjoyment seemed to surround her like a halo."[9] "It always seemed to me that Adelaide had a keener relish of the flavor of living than anyone I knew. . . . when she got away from it all, and back into the country, her sense of enjoyment in living was a revelation"[10]— the same sense that one gets in "Adventure."

> Sun and wind and beat of sea,
> Great lands stretching endlessly . . .
> Where be bonds to bind the free?
> All the world was made for me!

Only with Louise Merritt did she allow herself to be thus known. The other teachers were kept at a distance, and she made special arrangements to keep the students at arm's length. Unlike the other teachers, she arranged to supervise all the study periods of the boarding pupils. It kept her fixed to an even more rigorous schedule, but it allowed her to stay away from the more sociable tasks of the other teachers such as chaperoning and supervising recreation. She went out of her way not to coach basketball or arrange plays for the girls, as if the days of frivolous enjoyment were over.

Outside school hours, then, she had no contact with any of the students and became, therefore, a figure of awe and admiration. There was a great deal of mystery in her monastic existence. Her appearance was extremely striking. She was, it seemed, becoming lovelier all the time. Her slight stature no longer made her appear childlike but fragile, her hair was now definitely blond, and her eyes, growing larger as she became thinner, of such changing shades that gray, blue, and violet were variously suggested as their color. She wore her hair in a net at the base of her neck, complementing the brown Elizabethan dresses she wore every day. Only in the evening did she change the color of her gowns— to a pale blue which accented her eyes. Even her voice was exciting: "There was a thrilling, vibrant tone in her voice," one of her friends commented.[11]

The word "thrilling" was repeated when it came time to describe Crapsey's effect in the classroom. The teenage girls she taught seemed to gravitate toward her subject. Afterward they would wonder if it were the subjects—medieval history and Milton's prosody—that could have inspired them so or the pedagogical genius and the exciting personality of their teacher. "She certainly made those dead subjects vividly alive to me," one student testified, "and quite distinct from the ordinary school courses. And I think this was due to the fact that she made you feel her own enthusiasm and interest in what she was teaching."[12]

With her love of privacy and her extraordinary personal charm, it was inevitable that a few of the "devoted admirers" would make an effort to break through the barrier she had set up. One of these was Medora Addison.

Their friendship began in the classroom. In a discussion of a line from *Paradise Lost,* which described a dragon "swingeing the scaly horror of his tail," Crapsey pronounced it as "swinging," and Medora objected. "Swinge" sounded better to Medora, but Crapsey disagreed. That night, Crapsey looked up the word and greeted Medora the next day with a smile, "It's your gloat, Medora—it *is* swinge!"

Their friendship grew around literature, Crapsey becoming her mentor as Medora read and studied independently. And it was with her students that Crapsey could develop her theories about literature with the independence, caution, and care she loved. Unformed by previous theories of literature, they could help her to prove or disprove her own ideas by comparing them to the texts.

Any teacher of meter paying attention to the difficulties of students soon understands that their ears do not comprehend the application of the rules of meter to poetry. Why is it so difficult to find a simple unarguable line of iambic pentameter? Why do so many lines of iambic pentameter that should be rhythmically identical still sound so different? What effect does assonance or alliteration have on meter? What other factors influence meter? If regular meter is so important wouldn't the best examples be the sing-song of nursery rhymes? What is the difference between the meters of nursery rhymes and, say, Keats or Swinburne? Does the same meter apply for big words and small words? How does meter enhance meaning and why is it important if it doesn't? The questions of students could not easily be brushed away. They were basic, unraised by Crapsey's classmates in English classes at Vassar because they had already been inculcated in rules. Now she began to explore the problems.

Crapsey's initial explorations were probably never entirely scholarly or entirely creative. A question, a sense, would strike her and she would write a line of verse to see what happened, then analyze the verse to see whether it fit a rule or raised a further question.

The leisure granted her by her self-imposed alienation provided her with time to think. She was becoming extremely weary and spent her weekends in bed whenever she could. Emerging from her room only for meals on Sunday, she would conserve her physical strength by releasing her intellectual energies.

The very banality of Crapsey's environment forced in her the need for eccentric behavior and the sense of a higher goal. The research she was beginning set her apart from the other teachers, allowing her to label herself a scholar and incipient writer, not just a teacher, and kept her separate.

And she was so tired. She might logically attribute this weariness to the emotional effects of the trial and the strain of the knowledge of her mother's pain now that they were casting about for a new place to live. But there is also a measure of self-denial and self-sacrifice in her failure to pursue a medical diagnosis and cure for her lassitude. She was not important enough to bother with, and the money could better be spent elsewhere. A cheery disposition would go a long way to making for a "cure."

The proximity of Jean Webster helped the administration of the medicine of cheerfulness. Webster's life as usual was full of adventures which, when not taking place abroad, were happening right under her nose in New York City. When she was with Jean the old mischievous Adelaide returned. Webster's Italian cook, Ugolina, was one source of joy. Her language and manner reminded them of the free and warm Italy, and her provincial views gave them constant opportunities for humor and wisdom. Told an operation was necessary, Ugolina prepared herself for death, exploring the cost of a funeral and composing a will for which she brought in Webster and Crapsey as witnesses. "She provided for a brass band at her funeral, divided her seven fields at Biella among her sisters, left a legacy for the poor, gave her jewels to her mother in a package which included a pictorial button she had found in the street labeled 'Buster Brown Shoes,' and left nothing to her brother because he had kicked her in the stomach. The last thing she said before going into the operating room was, 'It is not that I mind dying, but I had hoped to die in Italy. New York is such a long, long way from Paradise.' "[13]

Rochester was even farther from Paradise, and the results of Dr. Crapsey's resignation were beginning to become apparent there. While Crapsey kept herself in her room at Miss Low's, the rest of the family contemplated being without a home. The rectory no longer belonged to them, and they would have to find another, far more modest place. Bishop Walker had warned Mrs. Crapsey of the dire consequences of her husband's rash actions and told her that he was sorry that "because of her husband's heresy, his wife and her children were to lose their home, to live as best they might, with no certain means of support."[14] There was no reason to believe that he was wrong.

The sad task of dismantling a household of twenty-seven years began immediately after the heresy sentence and continued through the Christmas holidays. When Adelaide left the rectory on January 3, 1907, it was for the last time. Her family moved a few days later into a rented home near the University of Rochester.

Although the Reverend Dr. Crapsey had known that this would be a terrible experience, he could not have known about all the little upsets that would accompany the move; the departure of the maid upon whom Mrs. Crapsey so deeply relied (with the remark that she "couldn't a-bear folks that was a-flittin' ")[15] must have cut deeply into Mrs. Crapsey's nerves and her efficiency. And Adelaide could do so little to help from Connecticut.

When one thing becomes disjointed in a life, others follow. Harriet Gunn Trowbridge died on February 21, half a year before her eightieth birthday. A few days later, the carriage of Mrs. Crapsey was struck by a car, and although she was not hurt, she was considerably shaken. And then her beloved Philip, whose life seemed to be going so well, with his new company and his wonderful fiancée, became ill. It was the malaria that Philip had contracted in the Spanish-American War acting up again.

War—that mindless result of the inability of man to exercise his logic, his humility, and his sympathy. Surely as Philip lay dying his father must have turned away to curse the brutal unwillingness of man to learn from the logic of the Scriptures, to learn that the potential of the peacemaker was within each of us. "The war of the United States against Spain was professedly altruistic," Algernon Crapsey wrote. "When the news of Dewey's victory in Manila Bay swept over the land it carried away all the noble altruism upon which the American people had prided themselves."[16]

It was not that Dr. Crapsey was against war altogether. A month before, when he spoke at the Peace Conference in New York, he infuriated the peace promoter, William Stead, by stating his opposition to disarmament. But that war in which Philip had been taken ill had indeed changed Algernon Crapsey's entire attitude toward the absolute rightness of his government. "I can never think of the betrayal and capture of Aguinaldo without a surge of shameful blood rushing from my heart to my face. . . . By this action the character of the American Government was changed from that of a democratic to an imperial republic, and this evil example of imperialism followed fourteen years later by the German Kaiser has been the ruin of the world."[17] But Philip had always been able to convince his parents that whatever he did was right. He was, after all, the firstborn.

In mid-May 1907, Philip died of complications from malaria.

Adelaide arrived in Rochester for the funeral at daybreak, May 23, having taken a night train from New York City. She reached the strange house near the university where the Crapseys had been living for the past five months and sat on the front steps, waiting patiently for the family to awaken.[18] She was now the eldest child. From the nine there were six alive, and Paul, her closest living sibling, had disappeared years ago. Rachel came in from New Jersey, but the strange house must have seemed painfully empty of those with whom Crapsey had grown up.

She stayed only three days. There were classes to teach, and with the end of the school year coming on there was pressure to complete the work.

But it was impossible to go back to a routine life as if nothing had happened. So much had happened, so much that Crapsey was powerless to control. The world was proving itself so much stronger than she was, yet she was not ready to let that world destroy itself around her.

The Hague

The opportunity to become involved did not take long to present itself. On April 17, when Algernon Crapsey spoke at the widely attended Peace Conference in New York City, another speaker also had a message for Adelaide. Lucia Ames Mead, reviewing the history of the Peace Movement in America, had a special message for women about the upcoming conference that summer: "The Second Hague Conference, which this time includes not merely twenty-six nations, but all the forty-six nations of the globe, offers the greatest opportunity in human history to lessen the world's poverty and misery. Let every teacher tell her pupils of it. Let every woman who believes in prayer pray for it. Let every mother, wife, and daughter speak words of wisdom about it in their households. Let not the women of America be childish and inert when such stupendous issues hang in the balance."[1] Algernon Crapsey was chosen to attend this very conference. Edwin Ginn, the publisher and philanthropist for peace, who had been following Algernon Crapsey's trial and the development of his career, offered to sponsor Dr. Crapsey as his personal representative to this conference, since he—sixty-nine years old—would not make the trip himself.

Adelaide went too. After Philip's death it was decided that she would accompany her father, and on June 1, a week after the funeral, they met in New York and sailed for The Hague.

190

If Crapsey had been influenced by such sentiments as Lucia Mead had voiced, if she believed that she too could influence the movement for peace in the world, these goals had to be subjugated to those of her father, for in this "short trip of almost two months,"[2] which would include a visit to England and some of the European countries, "in the interest of the peace movement,"[3] the primary goal would be to restore to Dr. Crapsey the opportunity and the confidence to continue the direction he had mapped out for himself.

On December 6, 1906, *Life* magazine had published a cartoon encaptioned "EXIT DR. CRAPSEY."[4] The photographic cartoon, showing a heavy dark priest with his back to the viewer, shutting the church door on a man, who with cape and arms outstretched is moving out into the light, is initially highly complimentary: Algernon Crapsey moving toward the sun like Plato's philosopher escaping the cave. But the rest of us remain in the darkness with the priest, implying that Crapsey may be moving forward into the light, but he is beyond the reach of the world in which we live. Whatever his future achievements, they will not be comprehended or appreciated by those of us who remained in darkness.

And the world was in darkness. There was a threat of world war with the proliferation of weapons—the arms of Krupp, the bombs of Nobel—and enmity among so many countries.

Among the members of the peace movements, however, particularly among those influenced, as the Crapseys were, by social Darwinism, there was the feeling that mankind was now civilized and would no longer participate in or sanctify the destruction of wars. Assuming that progress was "a natural force operating automatically in human affairs,"[5] many believed that with education and encouragement people would want to work together to make a happier world, but the tentativeness of their evidence could be seen all about them. Even the trial of Algernon Crapsey for heresy suggested that the world was not all that progressive.

Yet the concept of a conference to stop war was overwhelming in its potential. And once peace was established governments would turn to pressing problems of poverty and injustice. This peace conference could indeed be the beginning of a renaissance in the world. It was not until the official delegates actually arrived and the sessions were under way that it became clear that the purpose of the peace conference was to make rules about war. Although Crapsey had heard a lecture at Vassar in her sophomore year by Mrs. Frederick Halls on the Peace Conference of 1899, knowledge of the previous conference could not have prepared her for the awesome impotence of this one.

First, its structure was so complex as to be almost incomprehensible. "The conference divided into commissions, the commissions into sub-commissions, and subcommissions set up special committees. The sub-commissions held frequent 'meetings,' the commissions occasional 're-unions'; the entire conference came together in less frequent 'plenary sessions.' "[6] And there were so many nations, so many topics, and so much extraneous intrigue. Perhaps all this confusion was an intentional peace ploy. After all, as the German chancellor von Bülow pointed out, "Discussions of war simply make conflicts more likely."[7]

Second, the program of the conference proved its ineffectuality. For the first five weeks of the conference the delegates made proposals. There was only one agreement, and that was concerned with a revision of an agreement made in 1899 concerning the application of the Geneva Rules to the sea. The laws of war were topics of discussion throughout the summer, and only in mid-October did the conference turn to arbitration and international courts. By this time the Crapseys were long gone, as were most of the other citizens who had come to discuss the possibilities of peace.

The expectations with which the visitors had arrived had been great. On July 4, for example, Miss Anna Eckstein of Boston presented President Alexander Nelidov with "a petition, signed by over 2,000,000 Americans, in favor of a general arbitration treaty."[8] There were countless other petitions of this sort presented to Nelidov based on good will and a terrible naiveté concerning the many factors involved.[9] Joseph Choate, the leader of the five official representatives from the United States, was heard to say, "Our delegation has received about a cart load of requests and instructions, and the merely *eloquent* pacifists write us as though it were only necessary for the conference to decree that there should be eternal peace and that then eternal peace would be."[10]

Although the public was not admitted to plenary sessions and commissions,[11] it did not take long for observers to draw conclusions about the character and potential of this organization to promote peace. One woman, Suzanne Wilcox, reported that "this august body" was no better than a women's club, the worst insult possible. "Subtle jealousies, petty ambitions and bickering began early to develop, and the gratification of their smaller vanities seemed of greater importance to some of the delegates than the crucial issues under consideration."[12]

Parallel to the official delegates at the plenary sessions were the myriad peace organizations—"anarchists, nationalists, pacificists, and journalists . . . all hoping for opportunities to press their views."[13] Crapsey and her father were involved with these. These peace promoters were active on many fronts. W. T. Stead, backed by the Baroness von Suttner, an Englishman, a German, and a Frenchman, put out a daily paper in French devoted to the conference. On the first day of the conference, "Diplomats were surprised to find copies of the *Courrier de la Conférence de la Paix* at their doors,"[14] and the paper continued regularly throughout the summer.

The spokesmen for peace set up their headquarters in a building on the Prinsessegracht and called it Le Cercle International. Afternoon tea was served every day to the delegates and peace people where famous and less famous figures were invited to give lectures. The speeches of Stead, the baroness, Senator Henri LaFontaine of Belgium, and Prince Yi of Korea and the debates that followed these speeches led many observers to note that debates at Le Cercle International "were often better organized and more interesting than those of the conference."[15]

But even those earnest representatives of peace who surrounded the conference were ultimately no more successful nor dignified than the official delegates. Suzanne Wilcox wrote home:

> The great body of these pacifists were made up of earnest enthusiasts whose attitude toward the powers and evils that be is fairly patient and rational; but, like all radical movements, the ranks of its advocates contain some extremists and bizarre personalities. So it was not surprising that after the regular programs, when the audience was invited to join in the general discussions, one heard some very extraordinary and diverting discourses.

For example, upon one occasion a woman representing several organizations in the United States took up almost a whole afternoon reading her own original but not irresistible poems on peace. Another American woman who came armed with credentials from at least six high-sounding societies delivered a long dissertation on "Peace from the Point of View of the Higher Thought," and ended with a savage attack upon President Roosevelt.[16]

Although Adelaide Crapsey did not read her poems or deliver dissertations, she could not have remained outside the discussions, the debates, the criticisms, and the parties. So many of her talents developed in school were in demand. French was greatly needed, since the conference was conducted in French,[17] the newspaper was printed in French, and few Americans knew the language. And since she had been translating French since high school and remained fluent in it, Crapsey must have been in great demand as a translator. Her experience with debating, her concern with socialism, her pleasure in society must all have been aroused at the conference.

Yet the role she played was passive. To be active required much more energy than she was capable of, not only to gather enough courage to promote her ideas but also to overcome the obvious negative role of the majority of women at the conference. With the exception of the Baroness von Suttner, no individual woman played any major part. William Stead noted:

The International Council of Women did nobly. It was the only organized body that sent an influential deputation to the Conference to urge that something practical should be done. But excepting for social freedom, one half of the human race might have had no existence so far as the Conference was concerned. . . . Of the ladies who accompanied their husbands to the Hague, the wives of Septuagenarians, were practically nurses who looked after the health of their spouses. Of the others, many were charming society ladies, beautiful to look at in a ballroom or at the dinner table; but however pleasant they may have been as companions, they did not aspire to any political *role*. I only remember one delegate who ever referred in the course of conversation to the opinion of his wife upon any of the subjects that absorbed the attention of her husband. In the realm of international politics woman has most emphatically not yet arrived.[18]

It was not necessary to play an active role in the conference, however, to be affected by it. By the end of the summer it was evident that the system of the conference was hopelessly out of date and entirely incapable of dealing with the new dimensions of aggression of the new imperialism. "The old order of things international is gone and the modern has not yet established itself definitely," one commentator wistfully announced.[19]

"In time . . . many became fatigued with the unending round of formal social affairs and the paucity of formal results, and did not hesitate to speak of the Conference as the World's Political Fair and the World's Vanity Fair. But, as our able minister, Dr. Hill, remarked to a press representative who had expressed his impatience with the proceedings: 'If the world at large only knew the difficulty of managing and persuading a body of more than two hundred men, composed of different races, many jealous and suspicious of one another, and of diametrically opposite opinions, and each fettered by positive instructions from his Government, it would marvel that anything had been accomplished.' "[20] It was now clear that the Germany Crapsey had come to respect through her travels there and her studies of its literature was "pacific . . . in a superlative degree, ready to do anything for peace sake except forgo the advantages of war,"[21] and the power of the individual—particularly the individual, untitled woman—to combat all this was negligible.

W. T. Stead published at the top of the front page of the *Courrier* a picture of a tombstone bearing an epitaph:

Hic Jacet
La Question de la Limitation
des Armements
Née à Saint Petersbourg, le 24, Août, 1899
Etauffée à la Haye, le 18, Août, 1907 [22]

For the later, important matters concerning naval warfare and arbitration pending before The Hague, the Crapseys were absent. They left the conference in midsummer and spent their remaining time in Europe. Having come with great expectations and skills that could have helped promote the cause, they departed—as did everyone else—disillusioned and disappointed. Even the peace movement itself seemed just a bit degenerate and naive.

Instead Dr. Crapsey began his first efforts to spread the word in Europe of the new religion. Adelaide travelled with her father to Wales, where he had been invited to speak at the Summer School of the New Theology in Penmayenwayr. There he delighted his audience by stating: "Sin has already become the stock in trade of Christian pastors and priests and if sin were taken away from them what would they have left?" He concluded amid applause with his new message: "The only God we have to depend upon was the God working through our own intelligence and the intelligence of our social organization and that we have to be for the time being Gods unto ourselves."[23] Sitting by his side, Crapsey must have recalled the peace conference and nodded.

The couple may have gone walking in Wales for a short time. Walking was a great sport for Dr. Crapsey, who did not even tire after a whole day of it, but for Adelaide at this point it must have been a serious strain, beyond her ability. The visits to London and Paris were probably easier to bear, and the fact that Ginn was paying the bills must have made the budget-conscious Adelaide more able to enjoy the trip.

By August 30, Crapsey and her father were reunited with their family at Forest Lawn, in Onondaga County ("our summer cottage," as Mrs. Crapsey called it), leaving Adelaide with a month to recuperate and re-evaluate her own potential and the potential of her ideals before she returned to Stamford.

Despite the lessons of the summer, Algernon Crapsey and his family were optimistic. Some of what he had lost was now being returned to him, and on his own terms. He was already signed up for a series of thirty lectures at the Lyceum Theatre, and on Sunday evening, October 6, he began the "People's Sunday Evening Hour," with a report from his European travels: "The New Theology in England and Its Relation to the Social and Political Life of the Country." His popularity was greater than ever and the audiences that winter large and enthusiastic as he discussed "various aspects of the social and intellectual crisis facing the church."[24]

Influenced by Ginn, he looked to the Brotherhood he had founded and was now running together with the young and radical minister

Walter Rauschenbusch as a potential focal point for social and religious reform and devoted his attention to it. Believing that the Gospel, properly applied, "would remake the world and give us a social order in which everyone would have a 'square deal,' "[25] Dr. Crapsey plunged into his mission, freed from the ritualistic distractions of his former church demands.

They had lost their home, but now another one was being built for the Crapseys. William Rossiter Seward, the vice-president of the Mechanics Savings Bank,[26] had long admired the minister and now saw an opportunity to be of help to him by donating his cornfield on Averill Avenue to the building of a house for the use of the Crapsey family. "This miracle of kindness by which our lives were made intimate," Dr. Crapsey rejoiced, "was the outcome of my deliverer's history and character."[27]

This was to be a new house designed expressly for the Crapsey way of life, a generous house with large rooms for meetings and wide entrances for the many guests. There were many bedrooms for the large family and good grounds for a pleasant garden. Algernon Jr., promising as an architect, designed the house under Claude Bragdon's influence, and it was to have all the grandeur and mystery of a Bragdon creation.

The frame of the house was finished by the fall, when Adelaide Crapsey left for Miss Low's, but it would be at least another four months before the family could move in, and so Adelaide took care to stay out of their way in the cramped rented house, spending her holidays with friends. Thanksgiving was joyfully planned with Jean Webster, who finally had the opportunity of introducing Crapsey to her friend and travelling companion, Lena Weinstein, and the three women discussed the possibility of Jean's lecturing about her travels at Miss Low's.[28] Christmas passed with the Daltons in Stamford. "It was a particularly happy one," Louise Merritt thought, and associated Crapsey with Christmas for years after.[29]

The few months away from her family must have been necessary, not only because her father had so relied on her emotional strength for the past two years, but also because she had had to pretend this strength for so long. And now she would have to pretend an optimism she surely could not wholeheartedly feel about the possibilities for world reform.

In one sense, Crapsey was growing like her father, seeing herself as a subversive independent thinker. But while he was now in a position to act out all of his radical thoughts, Crapsey was becoming more and more closed in. As a schoolteacher she had to be extremely careful of her behavior and her potential influence on the pupils who constantly surrounded her. As a woman who was physically weak and becoming weaker all the time, she could not have the energy to lead a "double life," to turn from her school life on weekends or vacations to a more self-fulfilling existence. She was growing to hate the self-righteousness of the pious Christian, the security of world vision of the average citizen, and yet she was now entirely powerless to show this.

Her isolation continued. "She spent, I believe, practically no time 'visiting' with the other teachers in the school," Louise Merritt noted, and explained this as "her instinct and gift for concentration. She believed in spending herself in pursuits which seemed to her important, and companionship with people who really mattered to her. She had a very definite sense of values, and she was true to them."[30]

Perhaps for this reason her interest in literature intensified. It was harmless to attack the established codes of literature: she could only be viewed as even more orthodox if she examined basic concepts of rhythm, meter, sound. If she criticized Swinburne's poetry and examined Milton's it would only appear that she was following the path of the strict scholar of literature. And yet it was entirely subversive. She was doing for literary theory what her father had done for religion, discovering the logic denied by the public.

In January 1908, the Crapsey family moved into their new home. On March 3, at a reception in the new house for all the builders who had participated in its creation, a poem was read praising each worker by name for his part in the house. And the democracy at its foundation was sound and clear.

When Crapsey came home in the summer, she found many things, including this democratic spirit, to be delighted about. For one, she had a new neighbor and friend, Mary Mosher, the daughter of the family's benefactor, William Seward, who lived with her husband in the house behind that of the Crapseys.

The house was in the country, with all the advantages of the city and a new home, and all its potential excited Crapsey. She helped design the garden so that it would provide beauty, variety, and privacy, with "a hedge of honeysuckle along one side, with the rest of the garden bordered by high evergreen." A cedar walk was also planned that would enable the lover of nature to walk alone in the garden, "invisible and undisturbed, unaware of everything except the warmth of the sun and the scent of the cedar."[31]

But her family's decision to remain in Rochester had not been based on aesthetic grounds or on the thought of convenience. It was to be work, as Dr. Crapsey wrote:

> I care not for His heaven,
>   I do not fear His hell;
> But if to me is given
>   His work, then all is well.[32]

There was indeed a great deal of work to do. The Panic of 1907 had left a lot of unemployment in the city and it was up to the Brotherhood to do relief work, to feed the families of the unemployed, to help to retrain and re-employ workers, and to assist wives and mothers in organizing their households. "My pastoral work did not decrease; it increased after my expulsion from the Church."[33]

The Reverend Dr. Crapsey was of course busy, and Mrs. Crapsey was also actively engaged in this activity. Together with three other women, Mrs. Crapsey arranged for community backing for a Model Housekeeping Center on Davis Street in a neighborhood of new immigrant Italian families and hired an Italian-speaking Rochester girl to live in the center. In addition to instruction in housekeeping and sewing, the center offered babysitting service and general counseling.[34] There was also the sewing. Mrs. Crapsey, as wife of the rector, had made hundreds of layettes for needy families with new babies, and she was continuing her activity even though she had no official responsibility now. The sense of responsibility was internal, and the drive was greater.

But Adelaide Crapsey had no strength for all these benevolent activities. She returned to Rochester that summer in 1908 completely and utterly exhausted, and while her family bustled about in their endeavor to fulfill the order implicit in the house with worthy activities, she took helplessly to her bed.

How guilty she must have felt, lying in bed in the house built to promote activity, the only member of the household minimizing the value of the gift. Her efforts to recuperate must have been gargantuan, but the results were minuscule. As June and July crept along, her recovery could be measured in the smallest of activities. When she brought flowers to the Moshers across the lawn her mother recorded it as a significant event in her diary. A drive was an effort, a goal to be achieved, and visiting someone for tea was a cause for rejoicing. But gradually she began going out more and more. She went to the Lyceum with her father to hear him speak and gloried in the size and enthusiasm of the audience, and she went to hear the famous opera singer Lilian Nordica.

She would not be able to return to Miss Low's; that was decided early in the summer. But what would she do? The question loomed over her sickbed as she thought of the immediate and long-term uncertainty of her life. She was now almost thirty, a time when she really should be settled in some kind of comfortable life. But even if she weren't so inconveniently weak and were capable of returning to teaching, the very thought must have made her shudder. And yet what other possibilities were there? Continuing her studies would have been a wonderful solution, but she was taking control of her intellectual direction and was not terribly interested in learning theories from others. And, of course, there was no money. For the time being she went with Mary Mosher to Linden Lodge on Greene Lake to escape the oppressive humidity of August in Rochester.

Jean Webster fell in love that summer. On July 30, 1908, she joined her good friend's brother Glenn Ford McKinney, on his yacht and then for a hansom cab ride up Fifth Avenue. That date was kept as the anniversary of their love for the rest of her life. McKinney, married to a manic depressive and the father of a young son, was an alcoholic whose wealth allowed the luxury of dissipation but whose character and personality indicated to Jean that the effort to reform him would be worthwhile. For the rest of the summer, the couple, paired with Jean's friends Lena Weinstein and Ethelyn McKinney, Glenn's sister, were inseparable.

At what point Adelaide Crapsey was brought in on the secret is un-known. But it was not like Webster to be secretive, even in a clandestine affair, and if she did not share the details, still something of her joy must have been communicated to her friend.

When someone once inquired of Mrs. Crapsey if there had ever been a romantic episode in Adelaide's life, Mrs. Crapsey, who disliked both the inquirer and the question, said that she thought Adelaide had met a man at Greene Lake. She was being purposefully vague, and it is due to this vagueness resulting from mistrust that no more information is available.[35]

But something did happen to her that summer, that summer of 1908 at Greene Lake, something that she would write about for the entire winter, and something that she would not share freely with others. It is perhaps of this time that she wrote "The Source":

Thou hast
Drawn laughter from
A well of secret tears
And thence so elvish it rings,—mocking
And sweet.

(CP, p. 103)

She also wrote other poems not offered for publication, like the follow-ing "Aubade":

The morning is new and the skies are fresh washed with light,
The day cometh in with the sun and I awake laughing.

Hasten, belovèd!
For see, while you were yet sleeping
The cool and virgin feet of dawn went soundless over grey meadows,
And the earth is requickened under her touch.
The vision that came with gradual steps departeth in an instant;
Hasten, lest it be unbeheld of your eyes.

(CP, p. 114)

When she returned to Rochester, Crapsey was feeling much better, and her English friend Alice Pritchard came to visit her. Playing the proper

Rochester hostess, Crapsey took her friend to see the nearby wonder, Niagara Falls, early in November. "Niagara / Seen on a night in November" was the result.

How frail
Above the bulk
Of crashing water hangs,
Autumnal, evanescent, wan,
The moon.

(*CP*, p. 77)

Examining her own apparent frailty, she may have noticed in herself the truth she was portraying about the moon. It is only in appearance that the heavy inevitable waters are greater than the frail moon. Whatever happened to her that summer, it sharpened her vision and sensitivity to nature and poetry and strengthened her sense of her own potential.

But it had not made her well. By the end of that month she had regressed to her summer languor, with a throat ailment for good measure. A throat specialist warned her away from the cold and damp local winter, and Alice Pritchard, on her way back to Italy for more studies at the School of Classical Studies, suggested that they go together.[36] With the minimum of preparations, in the same brown attire for which she had been known at Miss Low's, she sailed on the *Woltka*, the same kind of German freighter she had boarded when she travelled alone to Italy four years before. She could be reached, she told those interested, through the American School of Classical Studies, at 5 Via Vicenla in Rome.[37]

Part Four

Success is counted sweetest
By those who ne'er succeed.
To comprehend a nectar
Requires sorest need.

Emily Dickinson

The Return to Rome

Crapsey and Pritchard were by now seasoned travellers, and the crossing held no new enchantments. "One voyage is very like another,"[1] Crapsey wrote her mother. Her mind, it seemed, was on what she had left rather than where she was headed. She had no idea how long she would be in Rome and what she would do there, and felt the extravagance of travelling to Rome for medical reasons when it would have been so much better had she been able to go for romance, pleasure, or study. "Ones mind doesn't work well on shipboard—or mine doesnt," she wrote, and put off any plans until the climate would begin to restore her health.

Like Keats travelling to Rome, Crapsey sheltered the hope that she would be cured by the climate and the vitality of the ancient city. And for both there was the same effect. The disadvantages of travel outweighed the benefits of sea air and the climate of Rome. Keats arrived in Rome to his "death house" and when Adelaide reached Rome through Naples she was soon confined in the Anglo-American Hospital.

She was taken to the hospital in February—"She has nothing special the matter," Jean reported to their classmates, apparently at Crapsey's request, "just a tiredness."[2] When she was released after a month, she was weak and depressed. "We are all hoping that a winter of Italian sunshine will set her up again," wrote Webster. A check for $100 from

205

her mother cheered her somewhat, and visits and letters from Rochester friends helped even more.

The guilt of her unproductiveness haunted her. Compared to her mother, who was now setting up a diet kitchen in Rochester for the families of the poor in addition to taking care of her youngest son, thirteen-year-old Arthur, and the strangely sensitive and childlike Marie-Louise, Crapsey's entire existence was one of sinful consumption. Elbert Hubbard, the famous Elmira publisher with whom her father was now working on a project, had not long before written an essay entitled, "The Most Important Thing in the World," in which he had agreed with Dr. Crapsey that the answer was work. He added:

> People unable to Earn a Living are a danger, a menace and an expense— They form the parasitic class—and the members of the parasitic class are not all in the penitentiary.
>
> Dr. Algernon Crapsey of Rochester told me the other day that in his mind doctors, lawyers, preachers and professional writers all belong to the parasitic class.
>
> I wouldn't say a thing so rude as that, and I only quote it here because Dr. Crapsey is a clergyman.[3]

Hubbard, with none of Dr. Crapsey's twinkling sense of humor, may well have misinterpreted his friend, and Adelaide herself had little patience with him. "I hope that I didn't speak disrespectfully of Elbert Hubbard," she wrote her father, "but his books really are pretty awful aren't they?"[4] Nevertheless she continued to exhibit the guilt a serious reading of her father's statement might have engendered.

Her health was a subject for embarrassment rather than a source of self-pity or a means for focussing attention on herself. Reporting vaguely on her improving condition, she adds, "How very futile and selfcentered this must seem to you in the middle of all your work."[5] Her brother Paul had returned, having finished a long stint in the army, so ill as to warrant serious maternal concern. "I feel rather horrid with all this fuss over my health when his is quite twice as bad," Crapsey wrote her mother.[6]

Her guilt manifested itself in an indecisiveness that was extremely apparent. She wanted to stay, to pursue some goal, but feared the expense, the guilt of parasitism. A compromise was reached: "she decided to stay and give lectures to tourists."[7] She moved into a room at the Palazzi Patrizio on the Via Margutta 53B, a fashionably bohemian neighborhood, popular with British, German, and other foreign artists, and wrote her parents that she thought it would be cheaper to go home to the United States for the summer. At the same time she had herself photographed for museum passes so she could pursue her research in London.[8]

Unlike most Americans in Rome, Crapsey took care to avoid her countrymen and to become acquainted with the natives and other foreigners. Her knowledge of Italian, augmented by her strong Latin and French background, allowed her freedom to meet and get to know many kinds of people inaccessible to most Americans. The rooms at the Palazzi Patrizio were managed by a German woman, Fräulein Romer, so Crapsey had the opportunity to practice her German. Other opportunities developed as she began to feel better. The von Heuslin family took Crapsey along for a trip around the countryside.

> Fräü [sic] von Heuslins brother was here and he had arranged a trip to some of the smaller places by carrige [sic] with Herr von Heuslin and his daughter and it quite suddenly and unexpectedly got itself arranged that I was to go too—for a day—instead of which I didn't get back until Thursday night— we started on Sunday. In that time we went to Viterbo and saw the Villa Lante, on Monday drove to Toscanella and saw there two wonderful churches, then Lake Bolsano then to Monte Fiascone where we had lunch at a dear little inn saw another nice church and drove on to Orivieto and then went on intending to get to Assisi by train but the trains in true Italian fashion only ran every other day, and we got landed at a most unheard of station for four hours and then stopped at Perugia—getting there at about six in the evening. We spent the evening and the next morning looking at Perugia and in the afternoon went to Assisi, going by train and returning by carrage [sic]. The next day we drove to Chuisi where I took the train back for Rome. It was great fun. . . . We really had a very entertaining time.[9]

Crapsey is careful to avoid mention of the age, name, or character of "Fräü [sic] von Heuslins brother" to her mother, but from the gaiety of the description one may assume that a certain amount of flirtation was mingled with the joy of recovery and of spring. Perhaps it was to him that poems like the following were written:

I offer my self to you as cool water in cup of crystal,
So, sweetly fulfilling the needs of thy body
For thou must drink water or die.

I offer myself as wine graciously held in golden goblet
A subtle drink of fire—
Thy soul hath need of this to live.

Between us two no thanks save knowledge that the gift is life to both:
Were it not sin and bitter waste that thou should die thirsty—
Or poured wine and water lie undrunk?

But the season, with its wonderful opportunities for the enjoyment of nature, even to a person confined to her bed, had the greatest effect. "The weather has been so lovely. Italy is really at times everything that people say it is; enchanting skies, flowers all coming out and everything fresh and clean and beautiful. As for me I'm feeling better than I have for three straight years and its perfectly joyous."[10]

Earlier in the spring, Crapsey had been joined by Louise Merritt, her husband, and her children, who had helped to give her the sense of "family" in a foreign land. This was particularly important to Crapsey since Alice Pritchard had left for the United States. Merritt, who helped to remind her of her love of literature and to connect it with the city, discovered the newly established Keats-Shelley memorial only a few blocks away, and together they visited it.[11] The memorial was a project begun by eight American writers in 1903 to keep alive the memories of Keats and Shelley in the house where Keats had died. The relics, pictures, and manuscripts contributed by the Shelley and Leigh Hunt families and others[12] comprised the first collection of memorabilia about the writer Crapsey loved, and she doubtless was impressed in the same way as was Lord Rennel of Rodd, who wrote "The Keats-Shelley House" in Rome of that year.

And this was all he knew of that great Rome,
    The deathless mother of immortal men,
Dreamed of in vision in his Northern home,
    And reached at last, and still beyond his ken:
A window world—blue noon and even's glow,

The passing pageant of the Spanish Square,
And blown from baskets on the steps below
    The scent of violets in the air.¹³

She who had spent so many months in bed in Rome, looking out the window and wondering if that view would be all she would ever see of her beloved city, reacted with great force to the rediscovery of Keats. It is possible she knew by now that she was afflicted with the same disease; certainly she knew the potential.

The influence of Keats, his poetry and his fate, was so strong that when she visited his grave with Merritt, she was careful to lead the description to her mother away from the experience itself. Shelley's famous observation in "Adonais," "It might make one in love with death, to think that one should be buried in so sweet a place," must have been in her mind, and to read on the grave that exact sentiment she had felt herself—"Here lies one whose name was writ in water"—could not have failed to stir her. Yet she emphasized to her mother the idea of the "coincidences of life," meeting a man whom she once admired.

One day Louise wanted to go out to the Protestant Cemetary [*sic*] to see Keat's [*sic*] grave. You know I'm not much of a person for doing things like that and I never had been there. When we got out there we went, by mistake, into the new section and after hunting in vain for the grave we went back to the gate and I was just asking the woman who seemed to be in charge of things, where to go when an American came in—a rather lost looking man (I mean he seemed not to know his way) with a big bunch of carnations and while I was talking to the woman I heard him ask Louise if this were the Protestant Cemetary and how could he find the grave of James Lee. Louise offered him my small amount of Italian so when I had finished about Keats he told me over again what he wanted, and I told the portiere and she showed him the book where all the registrations are; and of course all the time I was hunting in my mind for James Lee because the name was so perfectly familiar and then I remembered about Professor Lee so I said to the unknown American—"Is it Professor Lee's grave?" and of course he said yes and then in a brief conversation it came out that I knew the Lees, that I had known them not in Milton [?] but in Rochester—the unknown American had known them in Canandagua [Canandaigua]—why so had I; we had a cottage there—so had he—our cottage was Vine Cottage and (in a sudden burst of information) my name was Crapsey—Oh! then he knew who I was, and I knew who he was—his name was—Sherman Morse.

Wasn't that odd? Do you remember how we used to watch all the grown up people at the "Stone House"—but of course in all the ten summers we were there I never spoke to Sherman Morse. He was much too grown up, just engaged do you remember. And now after some sixteen years I meet him, in a place where I've never been before and where I'll probably never go again—and on one of the two days that he had in Rome. He had come over with Roosevelt and was returning at once.[14]

This is the letter of one who has learned that her individual experience, no matter how emotionally significant, no matter how moving to herself as a poet, could not be of as great interest to her mother as something that connects with their mutual social life. Not that Crapsey really felt the insignificance of her own emotions, but that she learned to keep them to herself and, perhaps, share them with intimate friends. No inner experience could be communicated in letters. After all, the presence of Canandaigua-born and Yale-bred Sherman Morse, who had achieved local fame in his job on the *Buffalo Express*, was a far more communicable surprise than the quiet eternality of the grave.

Of course, the encounter with Morse did have significance, connecting Crapsey's own provincial life with that of the poet whose name was writ on water, the dead with the living, the eternally famous with the unwillingly obscure. But the greater connection was between the memorial she had seen, the haunted letters of Joseph Severn describing Keats's last moments, and the peaceful cemetery nestling in the ancient Rome of which she had learned so much.

She identified with Keats, but when she came to write about this identification she saw herself as an empathic observer and not a doomed poet.

JOHN KEATS
(*February* 1820–*February* 1821)

Meet thou the event
And terrible happening of
Thine end: for thou art come
Upon the remote, cold place

Of ultimate dissolution and
With dumb, wide look
Thou, impotent, dost feel
Impotence creeping on
Thy potent soul. Yea, now, caught in
The aghast and voiceless pain
Of death, thyself doth watch
Thyself becoming naught.

Peace . . Peace . . for at
The last is comfort. Lo, now
Thou hast no pain. Lo, now
The waited presence is
Within the room; the voice
Speaks final-gentle: "Child,
Even thy careful nurse,
I lift thee in my arms
For greater ease and while
Thy heart still beats, place my
Cool fingers of oblivion on
Thine eyes and close them for
Eternity. Thou shalt
Pass sleeping, nor know
When sleeping ceases. Yet still
A little while thy breathing lasts,
Gradual is faint and fainter; I
Must listen close—the end."

Rest. And you others . . All.
Grave-fellows in
Green place. Here grows
Memorial every spring's
Fresh grass and here
Your marking monument
Was built for you long, long
Ago when Caius Cestius died.
                    (*CP*, pp. 68–69)

Perhaps it was visiting Keats's grave that made her immerse herself in
the literature of Keats. Many of her poems show his influence after this

point, not his poetry so much as his letters and biography. One example: Keats had wondered at the medical concept that the materials in our bodies are completely changed every seven years. "Seven years ago it was not this hand that clench'd itself against Hammond," he wrote. "We are like the relict garments of a Saint: the same and not the same: for the careful Monks patch it and patch it; till there's not a thread of the original garment left, and still they show it for St. Anthony's shirt."[15] Crapsey's "Amaze" works with this Heraclitean premise:

> I know
> Not these my hands
> And yet I think there was
> A woman like me once had hands
> Like these.

Except for Keats's memorial she seemed to have no interest in the artifacts of Rome. A seasoned traveller who had simply seen enough and knew that all that really matters is the artifacts that have direct bearing on the immediate emotional existence, she ignored blithely the museums and paintings. Describing to her mother a visit to Orvieto she neglects to mention the ceilings by Fra Angelico and the countless other priceless works that were just becoming very much the fashion in the United States. Henry James did not treat these places as lightly as Crapsey and described the church at Orvieto with great fervor: "Intensely brilliant . . . is the densely carved front; densely covered with the freshest looking mosaics. The old white marble of the sculptured portions is as softly yellow as ancient ivory; the large, exceedingly bright pictures above them flashed and twinkled in the splendid weather."[16] It was Crapsey's sense of concentration and not her ill health or indifference that really seemed to be the cause of her neglect. As a student at Vassar she could urge her classmates to notice the art surrounding them, but at this point in her life she really needed to focus on her own artistic direction, and the art of others was usually a distraction.

While Crapsey may have ignored art, she did not ignore life. Her sense of humor returned with the spring and with her usual condensation she managed to sketch perfect miniatures of Rome:

In the Via Margutta 53B. everything seems to be as usual. Fräúlein Romer, Assunta, Rosina, Maddelena, Luigina and Maria being all here and all at least as well as usual. Assunta has been ill but now she is better and betrothed. She would have preferred a policeman but this one will do.[17]

A young man across the way is tying his tie with as much thought as I spend over a whole getting dressed from the ground up. His mirror is hung square in the middle of the window and of course he is perfectly visible to every one in this house. It takes him a solid three quarters of an hour to part his hair.[18]

With the spring came the climatic necessity of leaving Rome for the summer, and the north was the logical alternative. But it was too difficult for her to travel alone. Her plans for Fiesole were only realized because Louise Merritt made the arrangements and deposited her in the convent of the "Blue Nuns" at San Girolamo on the Vecchia Fiesolana. "Louise came out here and got my room for us and looked after things generally—for which I was most deeply grateful," she wrote Medora. "Left to myself I'm sure I should have been still in Rome."[19] At Fiesole Crapsey met up with another family from her past, Mrs. Draper and her two daughters, Mary and Eliza, with whom she could share her time and thoughts. Mary Draper, the younger sister, had been one of Crapsey's many companions and correspondents at Kemper. It was Mary, in fact, who prevailed upon Crapsey to publish some of her work in the *Kodak* before she returned to her alma mater to teach. And Eliza Adelaide, or Elsie, who sometimes switched names and became Adelaide Eliza, or Adelaide, was in Crapsey's class at Kemper. Both sisters had followed Crapsey to Vassar, but Mary dropped out in 1905, and Adelaide waited six years after Kemper before she began college. The erratic education of the Draper sisters was related to the extensive travelling their widowed mother afforded them. They spent a great deal of time in France and England, even while students at Kemper.

This background in Europe, together with their superior intelligence and the excellent education open to them, made the Draper sisters suitable travelling companions for Crapsey. Mrs. Draper, with her efficiency and extensive knowledge of Europe, was the perfect person upon whom to rely for the technical arrangements of hotels and trains, and Crapsey was relieved to be able to hand her money over to her and ask to be taken care of. It was a relief to be with old, predictable friends. Mary was as independent as always, and Adelaide as intellectual.

Adelaide, who had just recently graduated from Vassar, had stood out in her class to the extent that her yearbook photograph was decorated with the statement: "Ages are equal, but a genius is above his age."[20] And it was with Adelaide Draper that Crapsey, hungry for intellectual companionship, discussed some of the literary problems she had been thinking about for the past few years.[21]

Her first problem was with meter. If meter, as she discovered while teaching, was not a complete theory, then what other factors needed to be taken into consideration? There was the theory of stress, about which Coleridge had written in his introduction to "Christabel": "the meter of Christabel is not, properly speaking, irregular, though it may seem so from its being founded on a new principle: namely, that of counting in each line the accents, not the syllables. Though the latter may vary from seven to twelve, yet in each line the accents will be found to be only four. Nevertheless, this occasional variation in number of syllables is not introduced wantonly, or for the mere ends of convenience, but in correspondence with some transition in the nature of the imagery or passion." But the idea of a four-stress line, as T. S. Omond had pointed out in his recently published *A Study of Metre*, "says nothing about the arrangement of these accents, which is at least as vital as the fact of their occurrence."[22] What about the unaccented syllables? How does one determine the accent?

The theories weren't scientific, and metrics, unlike theology, could be ultimately analyzed and theories finally proved. There were numerous factors to be considered, such as syllables, line lengths, and time. But it was ultimately possible to understand how to create certain effects through rhythms and how the music in poems works. Using monosyllables in nursery rhymes, it is easy to reproduce a regular rhythm, but longer, latinate words are far more complex to incorporate into a smoothly flowing line.

In Fiesole Crapsey continued to ponder these ideas. She read Keats and Francis Thompson and also recalled Walter Savage Landor, his regular balladic verse and the loves of which he wrote in that town. Her thoughts of him and her experiments in rhythm were combined in a poem to him.

> Ah, Walter, where you lived I rue
> These days come all too late for me;
> What matter if her eyes are blue
> Whose rival is Persephone?
>
> (*CP*, p. 79)

Following Landor's own pattern in *Imaginary Conversations,* she addresses Landor familiarly as "Walter" and criticizes a basic "truth" of poetry—the immortalization of the beloved in verse. She had in mind two of Landor's poems: the lament of the daughter in "Mother I Cannot Mind My Wheel," and Landor's own solemn declaration in "Past Ruined Ilion." "No longer could I doubt him true" the daughter cries. "All other men may use deceit; / He always said my eyes were blue / And often swore my lips were sweet." Her citation of the lover's vows in this poem is compared to Landor's own declaration in another: "The tear for fading beauty check, / For passing glory cease to sigh; / One form shall rise above the wreck, / One name, Ianthe, shall not die." Landor's declarations, as futile and false as those of the daughter's lover, express clearly the attitude of Crapsey toward standard vows of immortalization in poetry. In the framework of Landor's vision, the blue of his love's eyes are no contest to the force of death, as emotions and experience cannot be said to be given eternal significance by their transformation into art.[23]

Crapsey was certainly grappling in this poem with a personal romantic conflict, but she was also working through the use of monosyllables and rhythm patterns. The line is regular iambic tetrameter, but the regularity is achieved by the use of monosyllables and the placing of significant words in a stress position. Another quatrain written at this time employs a ten-syllable line but makes numerous alterations in rhythm.

THE PLEDGE

White doves of Cytherea, by your quest
  Across the blue Heaven's bluest highest air.
And by your certain homing to Love's breast,
  Still to be true and ever true—I swear.
                    (*CP*, p. 79)

The lines may be read as four stress lines or iambics varied with frequent trochees and anapests, despite the use of monosyllables which should, theoretically, simplify the complexities of rhythm.

Using the depth of her personal experiences as material for poetic experiments was beginning to become natural to her. She could both express her feelings and ignore them if they were uncomfortable by writing them down as metrical experiments. But in Fiesole, she seemed very much in love and quite secure of the eternality of this relationship. After the title "The Pledge," she copied a line from Shakespeare in her notebook, "Love's not Time's Fool." It is not certain when she wrote the following poem, but the style indicates no earlier a date.

TO AN UNFAITHFUL LOVER

What words
Are left thee then
Who hast squandered on thy
Forgetfulness eternity's
I love?
                    (*CP*, p. 102)

The poem is a cinquain, and the form emphasizes the significance of the last two words, indicating that this is a poem written after the experimentation with form had well begun.

With Draper Crapsey began examining the frequency of polysyllabic occurrence in Milton and Francis Thompson. She would count the syllables of each word, marking whether the word was monosyllabic, disyllabic, or polysyllabic. The scientific approach and the emotional appreciation of literature remained equally strong in her. But the emotional was personal and not a proper subject for discussion. Draper recalled, "Often in the midst of her careful counting of words and syllables she would break off to exclaim, 'Oh! isn't that a heavenly line!' and would discuss poetry with all the animation of her quick response to it. After a few minutes, however, she would exclaim abruptly, 'But see how we're wasting time!' and then she would plunge vigorously into her work."[24]

They were living not far from the place where the popular art collector Bernard Berenson continued to derive some of his greatest inspiration. North of Fiesole, on the way to the Convent of Camaldoli, was an old gnarled tree.

> Its bark has the splintering rasp of flint, but its scarred branches still thrust upward, bearing fruit. Its roots have solidified into rock in their grip on the arid ground. They testify to the blind strength of nature, its lavalike flow, its dark complexities.
>
> Such a tree would not seem a particularly likely illustration of nature's handiwork . . . yet this tree was, for Berenson, the focus of a pilgrimage. . . . Arriving at the tree, Berenson would stand in rapt contemplation, his eye encompassing the lines of its growth, its fixity, its relationship to the nice placement of farmhouses on the rising ground. Then he would bestow on its bark, textured like the gnarled hand of age, his perfect and characteristic caress. . . . he went toward nature with an eye so rapturous and indiscriminating that everything, whether a root, a limb, a piece of bark, or a weed battered by the wind, had its own truth to impart.[25]

Berenson learned most from William James, who taught that aesthetic experience was private and subjective. Berenson was exploring what he considered unexplainable "tactile values," while Crapsey was trying to discover the explanations. Her approach to a tree too was sympathetic, aesthetic, and psychological:

ON SEEING WEATHER-BEATEN TREES

Is it as plainly in our living shown,
By slant and twist, which way the wind hath blown?

(CP, p. 80)

As Crapsey lay under the trees, working or thinking about the significance of things, and visiting with the Drapers in the afternoons, indulging her fondness for tropical fruit with a snack of tea and figs, Gertrude Stein and Alice B. Toklas waited in Fiesole, at the nearby Villa Bardi, for the release of Stein's *Three Lives* on July 30.

The physical proximity of Berenson and Stein with Crapsey at this moment in her life is amazing for its contrast, for at no point in her life had Crapsey been less open to the possibilities of the new aesthetic, impressionistic approach to existence. Rules of art, their discovery and their potential for enabling the writing of transcendent poetry, were becoming more and more important.

Lying under the trees, Crapsey had a perfect view over the Arno Valley to the magnificent city of Florence with its golden domes. The proximity to Florence disturbed her, obliging her despite her lassitude to tick off tourist sights, and although she managed to shrug off this feeling for most of the summer, as the time approached for them to leave she said, "There are some things which I really must see, for the credit of the family." So she and Adelaide Draper took a carriage and driver (the only taxi for hire in Fiesole being taken up by Stein and Toklas) and descended to Florence. Like Stein, who was determined in Florence "not to be pleased except by that which ought to please *me*,"[26] Crapsey was not affected by the city which had impressed so many Americans with its indiscriminate plethora of art.

> "We saw a picture or two," said Elsie Draper, who accompanied her, "but she was too ill to be much impressed."
> "It is all very remote," Adelaide remarked. "It is very beautiful, but it is a world with which I have nothing to do." Only once was her weariness penetrated.
> She passed by some unfinished statues of Michaelangelo's.
> "What are those?" she asked, instantly struck.
> "Michaelangelo."
> "Oh!" after a quick moment of comprehension. "Now I understand him."[27]

Adelaide Draper was fascinated by Crapsey, her apparent shifts of interest and conflicts of personality. She thought of the violent twistings of the subjects of Michelangelo—the passion, vigor, and violence—as syntonic with those of her diffident and gentle friend. On the one hand Draper considered Crapsey "as a very adventurous person, almost a rebel"; on the other, she thought her "a person of such diffidence as nearly to counteract the vigor of her personality."[28] Draper, who was returning to the United States to continue her studies in psychology, could only analyze her friend from external details, for Crapsey did not confide in her, but she found the subject sufficiently interesting to consider writing Crapsey's biography herself.

Even now that she seemed almost immobile, Crapsey exuded a restlessness and defiance. Her professed reasons for moving around were to control her expenses and to continue her studies, but even now she loved to travel—to experience exciting things, to meet people. The places she didn't manage to visit she hungered for. The longing is felt in cinquains like "Blue Hyacinths":

> In your
> Curled petals what ghosts
> Of blue headlands and seas,
> What perfumed immortal breath sighing
> Of Greece?
>
> (*CP*, p. 104)

As a pupil at Kemper she had written of the "valiant struggles of Greek Patriots"[29] and had expressed great admiration for Greece. She would never see that country. She read Lafcadio Hearn's books on Japan and Japanese verse, but remained herself in the West.[30]

Given the extent to which Crapsey's health was affected by weather, it is surprising that she didn't choose to spend her life chasing after the warmth of Roman springs. But a rebelliousness and stubbornness influenced her decision to go to England. "Yes I have thought about the English climate," she wrote her father, "—but I cant go on paying attention to climate forever. I don't believe either that staying in Rome another year would be of much use. If it didn't do the business in one winter I don't believe it would in two. Not that I don't think it was a very good place to have been last winter—because it was. But I don't think it will hurt to try England. I can always leave if it gets too bad. Of course what I hope to do is to settle down to about five months of study and then come back say in March and look for a job."[31] The explanation slips from an avoidance of the fact of the good influence of weather to the academic and financial drive that overrides all other considerations, as if to say: "What I want to do, father, is work, and if I martyr myself in the process, I hope to be even more appreciated by you."

It was easy to travel if she attached herself to the Drapers and followed their plans. "It is so much nicer than trying to do it myself—and so much cheaper."[32] This way she could see what she wanted and still avoid some of the terrible fatigue to which she was prone when travelling.

From San Girolamo at Fiesole the Drapers and Crapsey left for Genoa, where they stopped at the port to send Adelaide Draper back to the United States. The Hotel Smith was convenient because it was "right on the docks and I can look out on some dozen or so of ships. It almost seems as if I ought to take one of them and return to my native land."[33] But money had been sent to keep Crapsey in Europe, as long as she economized, and she wrote her mother, "I am very glad that I can stay over a little longer and you may be sure I'll keep expenses as near the vanishing point as possible."[34]

Adelaide Draper was gone, but the party had been joined by Louise Brigham, Mrs. Draper's niece, and her friend Helen Meeker, so that there were a good number of young women with whom to share the experiences of travel and sightseeing. And once out of Rome Crapsey began to feel a special freedom. "I took a bath," Crapsey rejoiced to her mother: it was the first one since her stay in the hospital in February. "I enjoyed it very much—and it was such an excitement that I forgot to be tired from the journey."[35]

Whatever sightseeing Crapsey did in Genoa, the city Henry James called "the queerest place in the world,"[36] could not have been extensive, for by that night they were on the midnight train for a fourteen-hour trip to Paris. "The night journey was what night journeys always are. The train was crowded, everybody packed on top of everyone else. We did not get a whole compartment—nor even all in one. We alternated between suffocating tunnels and icy alps. Sleep of course was out of the question. We kept up our spirits with Marsalla (a very special kind of Italian wine) and weakened coffee at four o'clock in the morning—and some more at six. So you see we lived through it—and even found it amusing in spots. But oh, such dirt and dust! I've really come through most awfully well. Poor Mary Draper caught cold on the alps and has been laid up almost ever since."[37]

How it must have reminded her of the infirmary at Kemper fourteen years ago, when, returning from Chicago, she was almost confined with Mary Draper for suspected chicken pox. With her studies and the protection of an older woman she must have felt like a child again, her physical weakness of today comparable to the restrictions on behavior of her adolescence.

The Hotel des Etats Unis where they stayed during the month of September was on the Boulevard Mont Parnasse in Montmartre, minutes from 27 Rue des Fleurus to which Gertrude Stein had repaired upon her return from Fiesole. The hotel was a newly reconditioned one, similar to others that were springing up in Montmartre to accommodate the growing tourist class. A few years ago it had been "authentic" but, Crapsey was sure, "like many another Latin Quarter hostelry rather uninhabitable."[38]

Crapsey was in need of amenities and was not in the mood for the hunger and filth to which the artists who were making such advances in Montmartre were accustomed. She probably didn't even meet Picasso, Juan Gris, and Utrillo and the others who imitated their style by dressing and living like them. The possibility that she might have run into Guillaume Apollinaire (then a Symbolist poet), Pierre Reverdy, André Salmon, and Max Jacob is also small, given her physical inability to travel around alone and her need to conserve her strength. She may have attended a reading performance at the cafe made famous by Picasso, the lapin agile, but her influences remained literary; she bought no books, but she spent much time with them.

This was not her first time in Paris. She had come in 1907 with her father to spread the word of peace and might have renewed some of the connections she had made then. She thought little of visiting tourist spots, even though she felt the obligation to make the effort. "As usual," she wrote her parents, "I'm not trying to do any sightseeing," and then belied this proclamation in the next sentence: "We are near the Luxembourg Gardens and I've been there—and to the Museum—also to the Pantheon. Next week I'm going to get over to the Louvre."[39] She managed Notre Dame as well, a couple of trips up and down the Seine in a small boat, and a few "nice little Latin Quarter Concerts,"[40] perhaps one of Erik Satie. Her denial of interest in the standard sights was partly real. She continued to be too ill to enjoy strenuous outings and was incapable of approaching art with anything but her entire attention. But this seeming indifference to the sights of Europe was also motivated by the old Puritan guilt she felt at the thought of her leisure, made possible by the labor of her family. Even the money for food was difficult to part with. Thanking her mother for a check for $100, she adds, "But alas! that it couldn't have gone for some sort of a grand nice time for you and Father or the children. It seems so sad to be spending money on doctors and nourishing food when it might be used for a good time."[41]

She was sure that her health and stiuation were not significant, particularly in light of the industrious charitable work her parents and brother were undertaking. Writing about her health, she would add: "How very futile and selfcentered this must seem to you in the middle of all your work. I'm waiting to hear if you really have started the diet kitchen. That would be the splendidest thing."[42] She then goes on to discuss her mother's impending summer vacation, suggesting that Cook's Point had deteriorated in recent years and another place might be better advised.

It was not a show for her mother. Work for others was good not because the others were more worthy than she was, but because the orientation toward others was an ennobling emotion. While Algernon and Paul were supervising the raising of enough cabbages to feed eighty families on their vacant lot project, Adelaide was spending her summer taking care of herself. It was that exclusive self-concern that she regretted. The regret made the necessity of working at something—even something small, within her physical power—ever greater. She planned to spend the entire next winter working in isolation in England, and quite likely collected material for her long sojourn at Herne Bay in the bookshops of Montmartre.

She felt at home in Paris, as only an American thoroughly versed in the French language and literature could feel at home among a people who do not recognize the existence of other languages. And she felt at home on the West Bank, as a person who was totally "bohemian" in the definition of Maurice Barrès, the quintessential Bohemian. Barrès, in an essay on "The Marvellous Secret" (1892), described the ultimate freedom of the person who masquerades as a respectable citizen, whose imagination can run wild, allowing him to do things undreamed of precisely because no one would dream it of him.[43]

Clearly the poem "Evil" could have only come from this mentality, perhaps from this very place.

> In place secluded from the skies
> A silent woman with strange eyes
> Hiddenly waiting sits alone
> Upon a royal-massive throne
> Of smoothly polished malachite;
> An emeraldine curious light
> Fills all the place and through its chill
> Sapphired pale glow, arrested still,
> Unpalpitant as heart of death,
> I watch her soft-drawn patient breath . . .
>
> I will go creeping softly in
> Her eyes are promises of sin.
> (*CP*, p. 124)

Although Adelaide Draper wrote in 1928 that Crapsey "had read French lyrics but had disliked them,"[44] she was not in Paris with them, and from Crapsey's poetry a clear, sudden, and temporary influence of Baudelaire, his followers, and the Latin Quarter in general bursts out. "La Morte" might have been standing on one of the side streets radiating out of squares like the place Pigalle or the boulevards.

LA MORTE

> Vision of vice grown old,
> Harlot with wisped grey hair

Streaked drab and green
Where once was false gold's sheen,
Slack chin, rough wrinkled cheeks, lips bloodless cold,
Going at mid-day through the city streets
In hideous slattern guise;
She whose whole business was to show her body's sweets
Alluringly, indifferent leaves her ugliness unobscured.

And yet look long and secretly . .
Doth there not emanate from where
She is a strange concentrate glow?
Doth not the air about her show
A dove-throat iridescence copper-blue? . . beauty mysteriously
Present in scum blurred thin on stagnant ill-odoured pond?
Corpse-light of lust . . desire's fixed death-filmed eyes.
Still ghost of touch once lived and eager-fond . .
Who kissed her pale stale lips would kiss ten thousand thousand kisses
    sepulchered.

(*CP,* p. 124)

The theme of the attraction of the artist to filth was an appropriate one for the Latin Quarter. When Crapsey was there the close association between criminals, prostitutes, lowlifes, and artists and writers was never more evident.[45] The internal conflict her surroundings were exhibiting strengthened the image.

"Before we women can write," declared Virginia Woolf, "we must 'kill' the 'angel in the house.' "[46] Crapsey's portraits of women in these two poems are attempts to do just this, to destroy the elevated image of woman in her own mind and in her concept of literature. For as long as she continued to be influenced by ideals of women in her self-conception as a woman and as a poet, there was no way she could develop the one step further, the necessary step toward an individual unique vision. Her poems began to explore characters that ran the gamut of women from the most innocent to the most fallen.

For Lucas Cranach's Eve

Oh me,
Was there a time

When Paradise knew Eve
In this sweet guise, so placid and
So young?
    (*CP,* p. 103)

More complex is "The Two Mothers," in which Eve, the night before the Fall, splits into two "Mothers" of mankind.

Snow-white, rose-red, a twi-forked [*sic*] flame,
The evening before the serpent came,
Kindled and burnt in the heart of Eve.
    (*CP,* p. 122)

The wise, fallen woman is both passionate red and pure white, both the sinner and the redeemer: "*Oh dew! Oh tears! in Eden's bowers / Fell sweet, fell bitter on Mary's flowers*" (*CP,* p. 123). The mutual nurturing of the divided self is a sophisticated twist suggesting that neither the angel nor the devil must be murdered, but both must be incorporated into two parts. The woman outside of society has no better existence than the "angel in the house."

CLOTILDA SINGS

What is the bitter song that young
 Clotilda sings and works all day
And will not go where lad and lass
 Are met in joyous village play?

Oh, young Clotilda sings, how clear
How high and sweet for all to hear,—

Blossoming plum and cherry,
Flowering apple and quince,
 In springtime I was merry,
I've learned weeping since,
 Bitter weeping since.

Her baby at her woeful breast,
Clotilda sings who has no rest.
    (*CP,* p. 126)

The fact that woman is created in man's imagination is an extreme hindrance to a would-be woman writer and may have been the basis for some of Crapsey's own college stories about men falling in love with mistakes. The literary extension of this idea is that the woman's role in poetry is simply to be the inspiration for male poets, and this idea in fact turns up in such poems as "The Proud Poet":

> Great Kings were dust and all their deeds forgot
>> Did my harp's taut and burnished strings stand mute;
> The fragrance of dead ladies' lovely names
>> Blew never down the wind but for my lute.
>
> (CP, p. 108)

The image of the artistic woman, the inspiration for Pre-Raphaelite artists as well as Impressionist and Cubist, and its impracticality in the real world was also a subject for examination in one of her earlier poems:

> THE CHANGED REQUEST
>> *O que m'importe que tu sois sage*
>>> *sois belle et sois triste*
>
> "Be sad, be beautiful, my love,"
>> He prayed, oh ardent lad;
> "Be never a lesser thing, sweet love;
>> Than beautiful and sad."
>
> But now what while the coffee steams,
>> And he grows wise the while,
> His ardour prays—"The coffee steams,
>> Good Lord, my dear—please smile!"
>
> (CP, p. 133)

Eve and Mary, victim and heroine, romantic and practical—Crapsey's women now became realistic people.

The awareness of the many aspects of female identity was not repressed in Crapsey but it was, for safety's sake, hidden from the world. It could comfort her, this acknowledgment of the secret self of women, and perhaps, as she continued her proper existence, she pondered this secret identity as an anarchist fingers the bomb in his pocket.

She exhibited little of her self to her mother. In writing of her months in Paris, Crapsey chose two adventures to describe—her visit to the YWCA for a bath and the story of the corsets she had fitted. They were both slightly naughty, but their naughtiness reaffirmed the essential values. At the "Y," "the tubs are nice and there's spendid hot water—but they are so oppressively christian,—the people not the tubs. However a bath is a bath and Helen and I are going again armed with books and a general appearance of deafness to avoid conversation."[47] This was a naughtiness her mother and father could associate and identify with. It reaffirmed her essential "good" values.

> But my own Parisian extravagance—was a pair of made to order corsets—or not really corsets—girdle things that really fit. We had the funniest time over them. We asked the woman if she could make them—she was doubtful—yet she *could* make them but corsets, real corsets, were the proper the only thing to wear, she was eloquent on the subject of corsets. I began to feel as if my past had been a mistake—because I had spent it without corsets—as if my future would be a disaster if I didn't get some at once. However I stood firm—I hadn't, didn't, couldn't, wouldn't wear corsets. Well then she would make me something—something that would please me forever. Well then we got to work—we got rid of steels, we got buttons instead of hooks—we had the lacing loose—in fact we did everything that would strike a Parisian corsetmaker as mere madness, —and the result is excellent. You see she got quite interested in what she called my "miniatures,"—and I wish you could have seen the final fitting, when she and her two assistants tried them on. They invented more enthusiastic descriptive terms for that one girdle in five minutes than I could think of in a lifetime for Alps or Cathedrals or Pictures or statues or heroic acts and great events. It really became a Parisian adventure and we were all much amused.[48]

Of course Crapsey had been outfitted by her mother from childhood and her continued belief in the essential health of the corsetless figure was an association with her mother as well as a mark of rebellion against the confining world. The Parisian adventure was a proof to her mother that she had not changed at all and that they were both a touch more sophisticated than these women of the world.

But the story was a true Parisian adventure in another sense. It was a confrontation of values—the European establishment and the independent practicality of the Crapseys. The frivolity and provinciality of this seemingly sophisticated fashion center is exposed in a brief "sketch," a sudden coming to life of Crapsey's businesslike and sentimental letters that proved she had not lost her touch at what she called "doing" people and places.

She "did" the owners and servant of the hotel she was staying at, where "room and breakfast and dinner" was to be had for the slightly elevated price of 5.50 francs because she wanted a room of her own. The ritual of social communication was her subject here.

> Monsieur and Madame Penant tell us how it was when they came and we exclaim over it and then we tell them how nice it is now. And so it is and how they work over it! Monsieur Penant does most of the cooking,—and when dinner is over comes up to ask us politely if everything has been right. Delicious we answer. He names the masterpiece of the evening, the steak, the rabbit, the sweet,—he puts his fingertips together, his eyebrows are lifted. . "Ah . . Ah yes that was good—and all the best materials—it costs— but!—if you wish things good. . and in his house—" then we finish up with the assurance that in his house it is always perfection.[49]

As they began to make arrangements for leaving Louise Brigham was hospitalized with typhoid. Mrs. Draper put off the trip and began spending her afternoons at Louise's bedside in Trinity Lodge, leaving Crapsey and Meeker to their own devices. "In the mornings we kept out of doors. Took small boats up and down the Seine once or twice."[50] They ate inexpensively at local restaurants and tried unsuccessfully to resist the many street beggars.

But all this was expensive and distracting, and Adelaide's guilt at parasitism increased. Crapsey looked forward to the winter she had arranged with another friend, Mrs. Thomas, at Herne Bay, where there would be few distractions and fewer expenses.

London

Adelaide and Mrs. Thomas settled in Herne Bay, six miles from Canterbury, together with Mrs. Thomas's little girl. Crapsey had never seen Herne Bay before and knew little about it, but the weather was supposed to be good and the sea air healthy. She had high hopes for the situation. "I go to Canterbury by train and drive the rest of the way. That sounds nice and out in the country doesnt it."[1]

The town was disappointing, "a fairly large town of the rather awful English sort and also a London summer resort. There is a Parade and bathing machines and all the rest of it."[2] But Crapsey was not looking for pleasant surroundings. She was planning a quiet and inexpensive existence, and excitement and expenses were indeed few here.

As usual, expenses might have been kept down further if Crapsey had taken care of the housekeeping herself, but it was a physical impossibility by now. The women paid a maid $6 a month. "My socialistic conscience doesn't approve but that, it seems, is a good wage in Herne Bay."[3] And the maid, the house, the weather—all combined to make ideal working and living conditions.

Because the house was so central to the felicity there and so much a part of the success of her arrangements, Crapsey described it in detail to her mother:

The house of course is tiny. The bedrooms small and the beds so large that you have to squeeze around them; the wallpaper, carpets [sic] woodwork and the rest by no means a dream of beauty—but $3.50 a week! That would reconcile you to almost anything and then its quite clean—and a whole house to live in instead of one room. Downstairs there is really only one room besides the kitchen—a combination living and dining room. Off the kitchen there is a fair sized scullery with a small place for coal—garret and cellar of course are not. And no bath—however as we hope to get sea baths that its [is] not so bad. . . . Mrs. Thomas has the largest south room for herself and the baby. The other south room is really too small for comfort so I have the next largest one, that faces north, but it has the sea view, a balcony and a fireplace. The other north room I use also—the furniture is shoved against the wall and I have the remaining space for a small writing table. My books are piled on the beaureau [sic]. We keep the tin tub in the other south room and go in there for morning baths,—that keeps our own rooms a little clearer. Beatrice (the $6 maid) arrives at about half past seven, gets breakfast and brings it up—we each have it in our own room. . . . Then she brings the hot water for my bath—and when we've finished empties the tub and brings up more for Mrs. Thomas and Marie. . . . We have luncheon or rather dinner about twelve or half past—tea at half past four—Beatrice goes home about half past five or six. She leaves the supper table all set and we use the kitchen so that we can have the other room free.[4]

Paul Wilmont, Mrs. Thomas's nephew, was also there for much of the winter. A Rhodes scholar at Oxford, he had failed his entrance examen twice and came to Herne Bay to study and relax. His aunt was certain that he had failed only because he was so nervous, and Crapsey took him in hand. She spent a great deal of time with him, building up his confidence "in his capacity to write examen papers." "He did pass and was a brilliant scholar," his aunt recalled.[5] Predictably, Crapsey neglected to mention him to her mother.

The time at Herne Bay was ideal. There were none of the seductions of clothes that Crapsey found almost irresistible in London and especially in Paris. There were no taxis, no extra expenses for laundry and food. The $3.50 per week at Hill Crest on Alma Road was all-inclusive. Crapsey could work uninterrupted for hours, with only Mrs. Thomas, Marie, and Paul for company.

But there were no books other than those she had brought, and after developing her own ideas it was necessary to discover what others had to say about the same subject. She had been gathering data which influenced and directed her theories but had no real notion of what the leading prosodists were saying. For this she would need the British Museum, and early in the spring she and Mrs. Thomas gave up their cottage and went to London. "The weather is horrid—grey and cold and bleak—it congeals me—. Its lucky I didn't try London in the winter if this is what it is like in the spring. And at Herne Bay it was so warm that I got all ready for the summer," Crapsey complained to her mother.[6] "Now I've gone back to winter things and have another chillblane [*sic*]."[6]

London made her realize how ideal her situation at Herne Bay had been. Not only was the city cold, it was expensive, inconvenient, and unhealthy. She found her expenses went up five shillings to the pound, despite her strenuous effort to maintain solvency.

The British Museum, a good distance from her room on Ebury Street in Chelsea, could be reached by bus (taxis were expensive), but the long ride made it more practical for Crapsey to visit the Chelsea library whenever possible. Yet it was not always possible; the books she needed for her research were too specialized. So Crapsey made the trip about once a week from April to July. On those days she would order her books, then, because the wait while the books were being retrieved was rather long, would write letters or do her own work. "At least I am looking at the outsides of books that I ought to have know[n] long ago," she wrote her mother, characteristically demeaning her efforts.

It might have been hard for her to do more than just look at book covers, since the environment of the BM was precisely the antithesis of Herne Bay. Where the house on Alma Road was silent, except for the sea, the BM was filled with scholars and the noisy undercurrent of reading and thinking people. More significantly, the physical situation was antithetical. A large, poorly ventilated hall seated the scholars in radiating circles as they waited for their books, and the cold and poor air could not have made concentration easier. After lunch at a nearby dairy, she would return to inspect the volumes she had ordered, rarely reading them through but browsing, searching for relevant data, for similar thoughts to hers, or even opposite approaches that dealt with the same topic.

Sometimes she went to the Drapers' for tea if she could stop work an hour or so before the closing of the BM. If not, she would return to her rooms and have her dinner there.[7] This was the most inexpensive way. That was why she was living in a room that Medora Addison, who came to visit her former teacher, considered inferior and dismal. Medora, who had known her teacher in comparatively better times, was shocked, both at her poverty and the degeneration of her health. Crapsey's equanimity and her humor, however, were as bright as ever.[8] "Expenses," written during this period, confirms Medora's evaluation of Adelaide's mood and attitude.

EXPENSES

Little my lacking fortunes show
   For this to eat and that to wear;
Yet laughing, Soul, and gaily go!
   An obol pays the Stygian fare.

Crapsey was happy: the more cheaply she lived, the less space she took in the universe, the less of a parasite she was. Medora left her with the little she could to alleviate the starkness of the situation—gifts, roses, and Frances Thompson's *Shelley.*

The presence of Mrs. Thomas and the Drapers gave Crapsey a form of social security, and the Drapers felt they were still taking care of little Adelaide. Later Adelaide Draper remembered that "their friendship for the young woman gave her a place in a literary set, where she met most congenial people."[9] But whether Crapsey was introduced to the Bloomsbury crowd, Robert Bridges, W. B. Yeats, and the Theosophy people with whom Adelaide Draper had just begun to become acquainted, or just some people with intellectual and artistic interests may never be known.

Crapsey tried to stay away from social diversions. Her work was not progressing as quickly as she had planned, and she had no money. In May she began looking for employment for the fall, either in the United States or in England. Her parents and Mr. Seward continued to provide her with funds, but her guilt and her desire to be independent made these gifts as much of a strain as a relief. "Maybe your daughter will manage to get on her own feet again sometime," she wrote her parents.[10]

The uncertainty of her work in isolation was understandably demoralizing. With no external assurances and no means of evaluating herself, it was almost impossible to know that the time she was spending and the exertions she was making were justifiable.

It was the pressure to know that made her overcome her shyness. Choosing the one prosodist whose approach most resembled hers, T. S. Omond, she gathered together her courage and wrote him a letter, asking him if she could send her work to him for evaluation. "Politely but not enthusiastically" he agreed,[11] and Crapsey sent him a version of an essay entitled "An Experiment on English Prosody." His reply, excited and encouraging, promised her that she was on the right track. "I feel that it is only on lines like yours that progress can be made," he wrote her.[12]

Her principles of operation were based not only on Omond's method but on her own and her father's. Dr. Crapsey had recently published in his *Rebirth of Religion* a description of Crapsey's system. His opinions on the scientific method are worth quoting not only for their descriptive accuracy but also because they hint at the theological basis.

> Ancient thinking assumed that the earth was the center of the universe, and it reasoned from that assumption, and as long as it so reasoned astronomy could never become an exact science. Likewise theology assumes that God is so and so; but the validity of that assumption is in question, and all of the reasoning that hangs upon it hangs upon a loose nail and is liable to fall.
>
> Modern thinking is based upon the inductive method. It looks first at the fact, and then it generalises after a long and patient investigation of all that relates to a given fact, and it does not generalise until it has sufficient knowledge upon which to base a generalisation.[13]

The method is not derived from the fashion—successful in science but denounced in art—but from the impossibility of relying on any divine order. If God did not do everything, then it is the responsibility of the individual to find out the rules, to take over for God.

The technique itself was learned at Vassar. Crapsey wrote about it in the *Vassarion*.

THE PROPERLY SCHOLARLY ATTITUDE

The poet pursues his beautiful theme;
The preacher his golden beatitude;
   And I run after a vanishing dream—
   The glittering, will-o'-the-wispish gleam
Of the properly scholarly attitude—
The highly desirable, the very advisable,
The hardly acquirable, properly scholarly attitude.

I envy the savage without any clothes,
Who lives in a tropical latitude;
   It's little of general culture he knows.
   But then he escapes the worrisome woes
Of the properly scholarly attitude—
The unceasingly sighed over, wept over, cried over,
The futilely died over, properly scholarly attitude.

I work and I work till I nearly am dead,
And could say what the watchman said—that I could!
   But still, with a sigh and a shake of the head,
   "You don't understand," it is ruthlessly said,
"The properly scholarly attitude—
The aye to be sought for, wrought for and fought for,
The ne'er to be caught for, properly scholarly attitude—"

I really am sometimes tempted to say
That it's merely a glittering platitude;
   That people have just fallen into the way,
   When lacking a subject, to tell of the sway
Of the properly scholarly attitude—
The easily preachable, spread-eagle speechable,
In practice unreachable, properly scholarly attitude.[14]

The fine points of this technique and the feminine emphasis given it by the women scholars are significant. Lucy Maynard Salmon, the history professor, pointed out not only the necessity for scholarship, but also the diminutive significance of the individual in the scholarly hierarchy:

> Investigation is the product of training, of education, of an eager and absorbing desire for knowledge, of minds open to conviction and ready to hold the judgement in suspense until it can be based on facts. The steps in the process of the evolution are equally clear. Given an investigating spirit, it follows that every investigator must work with singleness of purpose, in his search for facts, that is, for truth; and that this truth, when found, is to be held, not as a personal acquisition, but as a good to be shared with all. Thus progress is made, not through the individual efforts of isolated investigators, who are working along parallel lines, but it is made by geometrical progression, because each investigator is able to take, as a starting-point, the goal reached by his predecessor, and because he knows he is co-operating with all other investigators to secure the same end. Everywhere today scientists appreciate the fact that progress in science is conditioned on scientific investigation. They also appreciate the fact that this progress can be made only as each investigator shares in the results obtained by every other investigator.[15]

Crapsey's method was the same as it was when the good teachers of Vassar were trying to teach it to her, but the principle was now more desperate. For to discover rules, any rules, by which the systems operate, by which the senses apprehend, is to become part of the human substitute for divine order, is to become in a sense part of the immortal eternal universe.

There was one problem with her acceptance of this theory—the assumption that research was by nature collaborative and collective rather than competitive, that if the work is correct the researcher became a part of a huge system of inquisitors, the seekers after truth. The modest Crapsey, under this assumption, would only have to write to Omond to prove to him that her work was worthy, to be discovered as one of the fold. The fact that Omond, like those who gave away fellowships at Cornell, would not only be influenced by the academic value of her work but also by her academic and social connections, her sex, the quirky uniqueness of her work, and individual prejudices was not a consideration to her.

Scholarship was the subjection of the individual character to the scientific, and Crapsey was extremely careful to remove any traces of her self in her work. There was none of her humor, her poetry, her beauty; none of her rebelliousness and genius. All that was left was the humble scholar, diffident, unwilling to jump to conclusions, concerned only with the object under observation. As a result her language when she wrote about metrics became dry, almost boring. And the conclusions to which she was coming remained unsaid, awaiting more certain evidence.

It was not that she saw no correspondence between creativity and criticism. She wrote in her notebook about this time

> that every art is to be regarded as an organic whole passing through certain recognized stages from its most rudimentary to its most developed form. Two sorts of processes (analysis and synthesis) are involved in the development: the creative and the critical. Creative work in the strictest definition, is the actual handling of material by the artist with the intention of producing a new arrangement; this resultant new arrangement is the creative synthesis, the aesthetic whole of art itself. Critical work, in its strictest definition is the analysis by the critic of the aesthetic whole [written on top of "creative synthesis"] with the intention of discovering the principles of its existence. The result is the critical synthesis, the coherent verbal statement of the discovered aesthetic laws. Creation and criticism are to be regarded as supplementary architectonic processes and the development of any art and a whole is conditioned by their perpetual reaction on each other.[16]

There is enough crossing out in this paragraph to see that Crapsey was reconsidering its emphasis and significance, although the initial ideas may have stemmed from a lecture on Coleridge's *Bibliographia Literaria*.

"A certain type of mind [is] not content in a vague sense of unity and is impelled by the desire to find out what in fact is the structure that determines it," she wrote on the other side of the page, and added the address of the *Nation* in London, as if justifying her reasons for presenting this scholarship to the journal, explaining her concern with the basis and structure of poetry.

The basic principles guiding her research were simple: (1) Poetry has not progressed, primarily because of a lack of awareness of the tools of poetry and their uses. (2) There are technical reasons why things move us that we should be able to understand and then use. It is not simply a matter of "emotion." (3) In discovering the principles of form and putting them to use, the mystery of the creation is eliminated and is substituted by a logic that *permits* creation.

The basic methods of the research itself were equally simple: (1) an exploration of meter, its rules and relationship to syllable-length of words; (2) the study of the relationship between meter and stress and its effect on a line, because tension or congruence between meter and stress make for different emotions in a poem; (3) the examination of other possible factors involved in metrical patterns. What, for example, can be done with a polysyllabic word that is not midstressed in an iambic line?

Her certainty on the one hand that the work upon which she was engaging was significant, worthy, and ultimately valuable was balanced with the diffidence inculcated in her concerning the "method," and she called her work on metrics and phonetics "The Favorite Literature," impishly, impiously indicating the old "emotive," Arnoldian way of looking at the subject she had chosen.

For the summer she went to Cornwall—"two farm houses at long intervals in the middle of hills, fields, pastures, wood etc." As she rested, engaging "in my favorite occupation of ceiling-gazing," she longed for Medora's company—"I wish you could come in and beguile some of the time for me"—as well as Medora's youthful dreams—"You and Louise and I on a farm combining prosody and philanthropy (is that the way to spell it?) sounds very nice. I wish it could happen." Unwilling to destroy even the most remote of her pupil's fantasies, she added, "Perhaps it will—you never can tell."[17]

The idea of her trip to Cornwall was to give her a complete rest, to allow her to engage in "the gentle occupation of doing nothing." To this end she allowed herself not to take her books with her. "It was hard work but I did it." And rest helped. She felt the renewal of her strength and the desire to take over her own affairs again. Returning the money she had borrowed from her parents by borrowing it from a presumably wealthy friend, she relieved herself of some measure of guilt. "After this I am going to try to be a better businesswoman than I have been and perhaps sometime help to make things easier for you and father," she wrote her mother. "I ought to after everything you have done for me."[18]

Crapsey had applied for a travelling fellowship from Cornell, and, since she had never met with an academic failure before, was expecting it to come through. Perhaps she even counted on this money to repay her debt. But when she returned to London in the fall, the rejection was waiting. She also discovered that the rooms at Ebury Street had been rented to someone else and, despite her unwillingness to make changes, she had to move down to Bushey with Mrs. Thomas for a while until new rooms on Oakley Street were available. With the insecurity of her financial future, this contretemps was another uncertainty to add to her confusion. She would be taking new rooms, but now had no idea where her money would be coming from.

It came from William Seward in the form of Kodak stock. The stock would give Mrs. Crapsey the security to make some investments in the clothing company that was beginning to emerge from the baby clothes she continued to sew for underprivileged families. Crapsey wrote excitedly:

Dearest Mother

I read Father's letter with its beautiful good news in the Am. expres [*sic*] companys office and nearly wept then and there for joy. If any one ever deserved such a thing it is you and Mr. Seward is angelic—wise to have seen it and acted on it.

I'm having a celebration all by myself over here—

This is in a hurry. I'll write more later.

I am back in my room—feeling better and intending to stay so if prudence, caution and good intentions count for anything—

Yours with love & rejoicing—Adelaide

My love to Mr Seward—isn't he wonderful.[19]

Crapsey, still financially uncertain herself, began to make plans to come home, but once again William Seward stepped in. Two weeks later she was exclaiming, "Isn't Mr Seward per[f]ectly perfectly wonderful. Will you tell him so and thank him because it will be a day or two before I can manage a decent letter for myself."[20] The next day she moved to 86 Oakley Street.

For the next four months she continued to avail herself of the libraries and intellectual stimuli of London, planning to return for a spring semester at Cornell. She had the Drapers for company, and they ate frequently together in one of the many cafes and restaurants in her neighborhood, such as the Blue Cockatoo.[21]

To encourage herself she copied into the back page of her copy of Keats:

K. ON CRITICISM

My own domestic criticism is—said also where I feel I am right, no external praise can give me such a glow as my own solitary *re*perception and ratification of what is fine— . . I will write independently. I have written independently *without judgement*. I may write independently and *with* judgement hereafter. The genius of poetry must work out its own salvation with man. It cannot be matured by law and precept, but by sensation and *watchfulness in itself* M. E. sely etc.[22]

Suddenly, independently, for none of the reasons on which she had based her travels, she decided to return home.

Smith College

When Adelaide disembarked from the freighter in Philadelphia on February 22, 1911, after an absence of two and a half years, she sent a telegram home—ARRIVED SAFELY LOVE TO ALL—and went directly to her younger sister Rachel's house in nearby Plainfield, New Jersey.[1]

She may have been in an evaluative mood, wondering whether her indifferent health or unusual pursuits had changed the course of her life unalterably for the worse. Had she been like Rachel, her healthy and determined sister, her present might have been different, her prospects more rosy. Four years her junior, Rachel Morris Crapsey—called "the Duchess" by the family because she was like the "Duchess of Kent, who raised hell wherever she went"—had been married to a wealthy man, Arthur Clark, for seven years and was living in a large home with her two children, Anne, six, and Phillip, born soon after his uncle's death and named for him. These were happy years for Rachel, though traces of her husband's dissatisfaction with his passive position as heir-dependent to his domineering mother were beginning to show. Rachel seemed to have fulfilled even more of an ideal life than her mother. But if Crapsey felt a sense of failure at the domestic bliss she was now becoming too old to attain, she could be comforted by the academic prospects that suddenly materialized.

240

Crapsey had informed all of her friends searching for employment for her of Rachel's New Jersey address, and the long-distance lobbying now paid off. She no sooner arrived at Rachel's when a telegram came from Smith College inviting her to come to teach—immediately. This position had probably been arranged by Mary Delia Lewis, who had been impressed with Crapsey years before. Lewis, who had been chairperson of the Department of English at Kemper Hall when Crapsey taught there, had become a significant member on the staff at Smith, and, having kept in touch with Crapsey, knew that she would be available when a vacancy arose that semester. This was an important achievement for Crapsey. The teaching was a necessary evil, but the academic status, which would provide a respectable framework for her research, had long been anticipated.

Knowing her mother's expectations and feeling not only a longing to return home but a desire to make her own academic arrangements for the future, Crapsey telegraphed to Smith for a few days' leave to see her parents and wrote them of her anticipations. She hoped to discuss further studies in Milton with Professor Martin Sampson at Cornell, who had edited Milton's lyrics and published a handbook for composition; he was known to be a great encouragement to young poets and scholars. The free time a grant would sanction was becoming more and more important, and she thought a personal interview might help her where the letters and applications from England had failed.

The same day she received another telegram requesting her immediate arrival at Smith, and five hours after her previous wire home she wired again. TELEGRAM FROM SMITH TO GO AT ONCE TERRIBLY SORRY WILL COME HOME SOON SPLENDID POSITION CAN'T REFUSE. Since the second semester was already under way the request from Smith was neither surprising nor extreme, but Mrs. Crapsey was disappointed and wrote sadly in her journal, ignoring Crapsey's visit with her sister: "FEBRUARY 23, 1911 Adelaide returned to America. Went directly to Smith College. Not home."[2]

A letter from Mary Lewis came soon after the telegram, and her elaboration of the teaching responsibilities made the news even more exciting. "The work is *Poetics*—just what I want—only 13 hours a week—

and only *one* course to give—no two—salary $600 from now till the end of the year."[3]

She went to Smith breathlessly and began to teach immediately after two years of relative inactivity and only superficial responsibilities. The pressure and excitement must have been considerable, since Crapsey had never taught before on a college level and respected the status considerably. The course, "2a The Principles of Exposition," was manageable and predetermined although time consuming, but the course in "Poetics. A critical study of verse forms," which would give her the opportunity to examine and formulate her ideas about the scientific bases for poetry, brought her to a high pitch of excitement. Yet she made time to meet her father in New York City during one of his many speaking engagements or his meetings with the Socialist party, deferring the reunion with her mother, who, although no longer burdened with small children, was becoming involved in her own business and could not be expected to make the trip to her daughter.

The rush to get to Smith did not allow her to make proper provisions for a place to stay, and she spent that first semester at the Plymouth Inn. Yet Crapsey was not one to remain isolated. With every threat to her strength, with every recognition of the need for independence from her family, she realized more and more her dependence upon others. And at Smith it was upon women that she came to rely not only for her livelihood but also for the other necessities of life—friendship, encouragement, and succor.

The English chair at Smith was held by Mary Augusta Jordan, whose middle name was well deserved. She was a famous figure, with many connections and important friends and a majestic presence. "Small and wirey," Henry McCracken, her employee for two years, described her. "She was portentous in her wrath and cryptic with inspiration. A great talker, she often found her words running far ahead of her ideas, and ending in complete incoherence. It was an entertaining exercise to try to detect the exact point at which sound took command over sense. She was sharp, devastating, and even cruel at times; at other times she was kindness itself. She hated cant, banality, and all mechanical forms of speech; life with her must be always tense with and at strife with something."[4] Her attitude toward literature was well described by a friend: "Stirring about in the classics, she would dig out a choice morsel, and run off with that. Her style was dramatic and she was popular. She would not have chosen Crapsey, the scholar, as her colleague." Her friend continued: "The dry scientific approach could not have appealed to her, and its implications must have been unclear. And apparently Crapsey kept the literary side of her hidden." Jordan knew nothing of her employee's poetic efforts.[5]

Even if Jordan had known about Crapsey's creative side, she was not a person in whom Crapsey would have confided or with whom Crapsey could converse. Jealous of the position which she had attained, she was suspicious of the capacities of women and even wrote a pamphlet in 1901 for the Massachusetts Association Opposed to the Further Extension of Suffrage to Women entitled "Noblesse Oblige."[6]

Jordan's department, unlike the Crapsey home, was ruled with an iron hand. And although it was because of this iron hand that the English Department managed to obtain such professional plums as Professor Henry McCracken, who left two years later in 1915 to become president of Vassar, and Katherine Woodward, whose critical accreditations increased steadily with the years, it was also because of this iron hand that Crapsey stuck to her job and kept silent.

Teaching at Smith did not give her the professional camaraderie she had longed for, but Crapsey was not without the comfort of friends. There was the goodhearted and sensitive Mary Lewis, and Crapsey was also fortunate in finding Esther Lowenthal.

Since they both came from Rochester, Crapsey and Lowenthal probably began their relationship during the long train rides home and learned gradually that despite many differences they had much in common. Lowenthal was five years younger than Crapsey but had not paused in her academic determination and had consequently achieved much more. After graduating from Bryn Mawr in 1905 she went straight on to Columbia for a doctorate in economics. The subject of her thesis was one Crapsey respected, Ricardian socialists, and her research consisted in a delineation of the various theories of the Ricardian or "Scientific" socialists of the nineteenth century in the vein of Marx and

Engels. The thesis was solid, scientific, and not at all theoretical, with no room for criticism of her "proper scholarly attitude." Lowenthal's work emphasized the significance of women, their oppression under the present system, and the need to consider them as equal workers. Repeatedly she noted the attitude of the socialists she explored to the status and function of women. Crapsey must have admired the strict, clear organization and careful thought of Lowenthal's thesis and thought—these were features to emulate. She shared her plans and studies on phonetics with Lowenthal and came to confide in her about her own scholarly activities even more than she confided in the colleagues in her field.

Lowenthal's doctoral thesis might have been the kind of work Crapsey would have done had she gone on with her studies after Vassar. But Lowenthal could afford to research the poor man's subject of socialism in a manner Crapsey could not even dream of pursuing. Lowenthal's wealthy capitalistic family supported her studies completely and with a generosity that proved their respect for learning and the leisurely scholarly life.

Max Lowenthal, Esther's father, was a wealthy Jewish fur and clothing manufacturer who had arrived in Rochester less than a decade before the Crapseys and distinguished himself in that city during the years that Algernon Crapsey had shone. In 1873 Lowenthal obtained control of a Rochester invention, the Lamb machine, which made possible mass production of knit goods. By 1890 the family factory was producing an annual 75,000 dozen of skirts, scarves, mittens, and leggings,[7] and twenty-one years later, when Lowenthal and Crapsey were becoming friends, the Rochester Knitting Works employed over three-hundred workers, with an annual output of $500,000. Lowenthal was also the director of the National Bank of Commerce and vice-president of the Locke Manufacturing Company[8] and was on the committee for the promotion of trade and other local chamber of commerce committees.[9] For this reason Lowenthal could choose her schools and her employment within, of course, the limits granted to Jews.

Max Lowenthal's success was not only personal but social. Because of him, many other Jews succeeded in finances and therefore became socially involved in the community, bringing about the "arrival" of the

German-Jewish entrepreneur as a recognized leader of Rochester industry. Lowenthal was also an intellectual and addressed the annual turn-verein picnics in Rochester with literary and scholarly lectures.[10] Esther Lowenthal's family may have done as much or more for the city with their continuous successful capitalism as Algernon Crapsey with his socialism, but the two families were certainly on opposite sides of the fence.

Despite the differences in their fields, finances, and background, the two women became friends. Their relationship, as Lowenthal described it, was "brief but intense." They were both tiny and walked well together. Together they learned about local academic politics and discussed economic and social issues. And Lowenthal watched over her frail and comparatively impoverished friend, keeping her as close as she could.

As soon as she was able, Crapsey went to visit Webster in her Greenwich Village apartment in New York City and at her retreat in Tyringham, Massachusetts, Beulah Canon's Canon House, the wonderful resort hotel where she wrote so well. Webster, also overjoyed at the reunion, organized their mutual friends for reunions and parties given for Crapsey at the Cosmopolitan Club, they went together to watch her father "on the speaker's platform at left-wing meetings in New York City,"[11] and they relived old college days. It was so much excitement in so short a time—so many of her dreams were becoming fulfilled, all her wonderful memories reawakened. For Easter she returned home and the rush of joy at the six-weeks-delayed reunion should have made her feel almost complete.

Except for one thing. She had so little on paper to show for the hours of drudgery and contemplation she had endured, and there was still no fellowship, no academic encouragement in sight. Nevertheless, she remained determined. She returned to Smith by way of Boston, finished the last two months of the semester, and went back to Rochester for the summer, determined to make these three months count.

The summer of 1911 gave Crapsey the opportunity to do many of the things she had missed during the years in Europe and to see old friends and important scholars. She began her summer vacation riding a dark

gelding named Sweeney for relaxation with her brother Paul. Her choice
of horseback riding may have been influenced by Keats, who rode
through the streets of Rome in the vain hope that the activity stimulated
breathing. But it was more likely that her love of activity was also
related to her desire to renew her acquaintance with Paul, whose return
during or just before her departure after so many years forced an extended postponement in the development of their relationship.

Paul was to be her most frequent companion that summer. Together
they would go riding in the woods. Together they went to visit the
newly widowed Claude Bragdon. If they succeeded in comforting Bragdon, it was not with the thought that it had been his wife's time to die,
as their father had said at her funeral, nor with the theosophical advice
he may have wished to hear, that he would be reunited with her soon.
The encouragement of the two siblings was likely to be of a practical
nature, an affirmation that character alters destiny. Years later, Paul
wrote a poem entitled "Weavers."

> We're weavers, you and I,
> upon the ways laid down by life.
> The woof is ours to plan,
> to choose the colors and the strands,
> to throw the shuttle back and forth
> and tie the broken ends.[12]

On June 30, less than a week after Crapsey returned, she attended a
dinner party at Bragdon's. Dr. Hoyt, his wife, Miss Dale, Bragdon, Paul,
and Adelaide were treated to what Bragdon called in his diary an "ad-
mirable" dinner. "Everybody had a good time," Bragdon wrote. "The
talk after dinner was of Theosophy." Bragdon was not a good judge,
however, for Paul later recalled that Bragdon's vegetarianism made dinners a laugh and neither Paul nor Crapsey was serious about theosophy.
Crapsey later wrote Lowenthal a few mocking words about the triteness
of any strict set of his beliefs. "Did I tell you that [Mr. Bragdon] . . . and
Mr. Tucker wrote me letters that you could just have interchanged—
only one used Xian [Christian] Science terms + the other Indian Philosophy—Both awfully sweet nice letters—but it was a little funny wasnt'
it."[13]

Lonely and miserable over the sudden death of his wife in childbirth and bewildered with the status and duties of a new widower with two sons, Bragdon was excited about renewing his friendship with Crapsey and called on her two days later.[14] He noted her departure for summer school at Cornell three days after that in his "line-a-day" diary, as if tracking her steps. Her appeal to his children was also a significant point for him.

Summer school at Cornell was something Crapsey had been looking forward to for months. Ever since she returned from Europe she had been trying to arrange a visit with Professor Sampson. "My Prosody work and the Fellowship at Cornell is the main thing of course but the work at Smith will give me some money now." On July 5 she enrolled in summer school. She was sure that Professor Martin Sampson, the Milton scholar, would be willing to help her and that perhaps Professor Nathaniel Schmidt and other friends of her father would be helpful to her as well.[15]

Schmidt knew Sampson, a kindly man with an extraordinary reputation for personal attention. Forty-four years old, he had been at Cornell for five years. His versatility was an added attraction, for in addition to Milton scholarship he had done a considerable amount of original writing, including stories for children, plays, satires, and poetry.[16] He also encouraged creative writing and founded the Manuscript Club for aspiring student writers.

But although she had been anticipating her studies at Cornell with a hope of recognition and direction, she officially withdrew from summer school two days after she registered. She did not inform her family and returned home on July 22, when the course was supposed to be over.

She might have found the formal studies irrelevant and preferred to deal with Professor Sampson as a mentor rather than a formal teacher, but another reason is also possible. When she returned to Smith in the fall, Crapsey told Lowenthal that she had been diagnosed as having tubercular meningitis, a disease that was usually fatal within weeks. If the diagnosis was made while she was at Cornell or shortly before, then her erratic behavior is understandable.

Still, when she returned to Rochester on July 22, she was immersed in her studies. Paul was impressed by the hours she spent "in the study measuring verse." Paul had a great deal of freedom to observe her, for while he and his sister remained in Rochester, Mrs. Crapsey took the children to White House, probably on Greene Lake.

Paul remained in Rochester because he was helping his father with the vacant lot farming business. Algernon Crapsey had obtained use of numerous vacant lots scattered about the town for the purpose of communal farming and parcelled them out each summer to scores of needy families. The year before Paul had taken over the program and was now maintaining it, both by supervising the planting and by raising money for the project. He even visited Bragdon in his office to ask for money. His guilt over his sudden disappearance, abandoning his family, and his exhaustion after years of hard living in the army may have transformed him for the time into an obedient son and devoted brother. Adelaide remained home in order to work and avoided the distracting temptations of swimming and romance.

Bragdon's visits to the Crapseys that summer were frequent and became even more frequent when Mrs. Crapsey returned on August 24. Yet his attentions to Adelaide were significant enough to rejoice that his son seemed to like her. He noted in his diary that on her birthday Adelaide was thrown by her horse and sprained her arm, he visited her the day after to make sure she was all right, and went again to say goodbye as she made plans to leave for Tyringham on her way to Smith. But despite his solicitude his attentions were more due to his boredom and loneliness than any great closeness with Crapsey. "He really is so awfully nice," she wrote a friend later,[17] but her comment is an amelioration of the sarcasm with which she described him, and she exchanged Rochester and Bragdon for Tyringham and Webster with some joy.

That summer Webster was writing *Daddy Long-Legs*. The plot was to some extent Webster's fantasy of her affair with Glenn Ford McKinney, which was now being conducted through correspondence, group parties and outings, and occasional clandestine meetings. But the fictionalized romance took place in happier times—college days—and under more auspicious and psychologically acceptable circumstances. Webster's Daddy Long-Legs was a man who appeared as a father-surrogate in the heroine's story at the precise time in Webster's life when her own father took an overdose of drugs. Her Daddy Long-Legs invisibly supported the emotional and intellectual growth of the heroine, Judy Abbott. Like the father Webster had missed when Charles Webster died in her twelfth year, he provided Judy with independence and the freedom to make significant choices as a woman. Then, when Judy was mature, their relationship became a romantic one and their decisions were mutual. Since McKinney, worn out by the strain of his marriage, was an alcoholic who would disappear on drinking jags, his weakness gave Webster the same kind of leverage Judy had in *Daddy Long-Legs,* when her rejection of the man makes him ill and her acceptance makes him well. As a married man, albeit unhappily, McKinney had no control over the sophisticated and world-travelled Webster, and their relationship was one of laissez-faire at least on his part.

So the plot of *Daddy Long-Legs* was, for Webster, the ideal love story; a girl is brought by a distinguished man to absolute independence and is then in a position to have an equal relationship with him. In other circumstances, too, Judy Abbott followed her creator—her desire to be an author, her ardent socialism, her use of the summer farm in the Berkshires for writing. Jean, like Judy, changed her name. Even Judy's sketches that illustrate and enliven the epistolary novel came from Webster's letters to others, usually Glenn.

However, the character of Judy Abbott put those who knew both Webster and Crapsey in mind of the latter. As the child of a large impecunious family, Crapsey was in greater need of the education that would lead to a free existence. Webster had always been financially independent, was even taking care of her mother. It was Crapsey who had found an elder man to support her in her studies in Europe and Crapsey who had been alone during her boarding school days, even on vacations. Webster had attended the Lady Jane Grey School in nearby Binghamton, New York, a small and cozy place that emphasized individuality and the arts, and the opportunities it afforded her talents probably cushioned the terrible blow of her father's death.

But although Crapsey must have contributed not a little to the book and it was Webster who had been successful in writing the kind of fiction they had practiced together in college, Crapsey's only response to

Webster's completion of *Daddy Long-Legs* was her joyful participation in the celebration.[18] She went up to Canon House at Tyringham on her way to Northampton at the end of the summer and shared with her only good news. She did not tell Webster of her own prognosis. Webster was too optimistic and joyful a soul to disturb.

Instead, Crapsey went back to Smith and told Lowenthal, and Lowenthal brought her under her ministering auspices. The problem of rooms was soon solved by an available space in the house where Lowenthal lived, on 10 West Street, a strange white house built by a colleague, Katherine Woodward. It was set back from the street, around the corner of another house, and entered "through a gate and up a steep staircase."[19] Lowenthal had a bedroom and sitting room on the second floor there and was comfortably situated. For Crapsey, who could afford considerably less, there was "a 'measly' room on the ground floor, narrow, too narrow for the height of the ceiling." But the proximity was convenient. Crapsey would visit Lowenthal's room every afternoon and enjoy the mothering of her friend. There would be tea and a great deal of sympathy as well.[20]

The women also spent much time away from home together. When she wasn't teaching, "Adelaide spent many, many hours in the English Seminar Room, an airless room upstairs in the Smith College Library." Because she was often overcome by fatigue, she went to the Smith College doctor. Perhaps out of modesty he did not examine her, but concluded that Crapsey's problem must be the typical complaint of the scholarly woman—too much time with books, wasting away her vital organs. The doctor prescribed daily walks and Lowenthal would accompany her up "a rather steep hill in Northampton." Occasionally they stopped at Boyden's for refreshment and Crapsey would remind Lowenthal to eat milk, eggs, and steak for her own delicate health. Lowenthal became in this way another on a long list of maternal women who helped to solve the daily problems of existence for Crapsey.

The continuing problem of Adelaide's fading health made concentration on her work even more important. It was not a piecemeal kind of work that, if left behind, could be understood. If it was not all finished, it would be worth nothing. And if her weakness could not be overcome, it would not be finished. It was this awareness that gave her a distracted, mysterious air; "young, but very set apart," Louise Townsend Nicholls, who took both of her courses, noted.[21]

One day Nicholls, who was writing her freshman theme on the Brontës, talked about it to Crapsey, who invited her to visit in her rooms. Excited by the prospect, Nicholls discovered once there that Crapsey was distant and uninterested. "Suddenly, from the faraway place where she always seemed to be, she came back for a moment, her eyes looking up at me with an intense and searching interest. 'How did you happen to write about Charlotte Brontë?' she asked. And then her eyes forgot me and the paper in her hands and looked farther than the white wall of the small, square room—onto the gray moor, perhaps, where that other woman had walked alone. I think she also had a moor, 'with a name of its own,' some gray moor of the spirit where she also walked alone."[22]

Only after the whole picture of Crapsey's life and death would become clear could Nicholls come to understand her fully. Then she would define the cinquain as a metaphor for Crapsey's life. In her copy of *Verse*, Nicholls commented: "as with a little gasp of terror at the artistic unfulfillment caught back again to die," and referred to "the brief life being like her cinquain form caught back again to one."[23] But neither the structure of Crapsey's life nor the cinquain itself was available to Nicholls then and Crapsey remained a mysterious figure.

The color Crapsey cultivated was now exclusively gray. Her dresses, coats, and hats were all gray and her predilection for the color so extreme that even her pencils were bought to match. It was part economics and part a careful, unique attitude to her inner tragedy, an acknowledgment of the bleakness of her future and her attempts to work within its limitations:

> As it
> Were tissue of silver
> I'll wear, O Fate, thy grey,
> And go mistily radiant, clad
> Like the moon.
>
> (*CP*, p. 75)

Her passion for gray became a manner of coping with her tragedy as well. It was a way of neutralizing, of rising above the limitations of a confined terminal existence. It was also a practical and simultaneously mysterious way of dressing. Her mother had long adopted the habit of wearing only black and would later switch to white. Narrowing one's color scheme was like narrowing one's horizons—ensuring perfection in a single sphere.

Crapsey's passion for poetry did not diminish now. It was becoming even more intense, and the intensity was contagious. Her students, like those at Miss Low's and Kemper, were amazed by her devotion to her subject and full of admiration for her style. "She never let poetry be only feeling. It had form; it had technique. It, like music, from its very form achieved beauty. A rondel had meaning because of its very form, a ballad became alive like a person—it had its own body." Even those who barely knew her personally described her with an amazing warmth. The testimonies from students like Dora Goldberg, gathered years after her departure, mark the strength of her personality: "She never knew how much I loved her, how even today her courage, her passionate desire to be correct, accurate, truthful, influence my intellectual attitude. Her scholarly approach was a rare thing, and that she gave us if she gave her pupils nothing else."[24] Medora Addison had also been impressed in just this way at Miss Low's. But at Smith, Crapsey's presence seemed to remain years after her departure. Lola Ridge, who did not study with her but was influenced by her at Smith, published the poem "Adelaide Crapsey" in her third book, *Red Flag,* which came out in 1927. The poem shows the intensity of her personality and the impression she left with her students:

Light as the bare hold
of a birdfoot,
less weight
than resting moonlight and as luminous,
the thought of you
hovers at my heart.

Few heard your feet,
soft as the webfeet of snow,

as wrapped in a thin cloak,
looking about and wondering,
you flitted between larches in the lean twilights.
It is, almost, as though you had not spoke,
but existed merely
as some certain
function of the spring,
and shall return with the primroses.

Is there not on this campus slope,
in the snow-encompassed
evening closing like an indefinite death
worn down at the edges,
some lasting tenure of your loneliness—
some hollow that your little heel has left
in the soft-shell snow,
or any delicate report of you,
who moved as a wind
slight enough
to pass between two violets
and not put them apart?[25]

But though her life was becoming more and more pure, more refined from any activity other than poetics, Crapsey remained true to her old friends and family.

Her father, who had applied for the job of parole officer for the State of New York, was lecturing on socialism, women's suffrage, and church and prison reform in the New York City area, and Crapsey tried to attend. On December 3, 1911, Algernon gave a speech in the Free Synagogue at Carnegie Hall about the anarchist confession of the bombing in Los Angeles, which, he claimed, was the "greatest blow to organized labor that was ever struck." "The struggle between capital and labor means the destruction of the commonwealth. It is not alone capital that will suffer, but the innocent bystander, who will be made to take part in the struggle."[26]

To these kinds of lectures Crapsey was faithful in her attendance. The trip to New York City was a relief from the confinement of the small town: in February that winter she went to visit Webster in her Greenwich Village apartment for four days in preparation for the final marathon of examination paper grading.[27] Webster, who knew New York City well and was always happy to be with her friends, probably took her to her favorite haunts, such as the Women's University Club on 17 Madison Square and the Cosmopolitan Club.

Crapsey returned to the city in the spring to visit Adelaide Draper, carrying a sheaf of poems. For the past two years she had continued to write poems, affected by her increased sensitivity to rhythms afforded by her research, and she was anxious to share it with her old friend. It was clear to Draper that Crapsey was not in good health, that she had deteriorated even since their meetings in Fiesole, but then, Crapsey assured her friend, sloughing off the threat, "She was never very well." Then Crapsey lay back on the hotel bed and read Draper one of her poems.

I make my shroud but no one knows,
So shimmering fine it is and fair,
With stitches set in even rows.
I make my shroud but no one knows.

In door-way where the lilac blows,
Humming a little wandering air,
I make my shroud and no one knows.
So shimmering fine it is and fair.

(*CP*, p. 87)

It was an amazing poem to read to someone who was studying psychology. Adelaide's knowledge of the inevitability and imminence of her death was straightforwardly communicated. But as strong as the need to share her fate with someone was the desire to prevent or at least postpone the suffering of others. So she pretended the subject matter was not an issue and concentrated on the form, reading the poem again with "the vowel sounds alone to show the sequence of rising and falling tones." "She felt that certain combinations of sound were particularly effective, and she had tried for these combinations," she explained to Draper.[28] She also read a few cinquains, enthusiastic about the form she had created and emphasizing its formal "inevitability." It must be a "working up to and falling away from a climax," she explained.[29] Nothing was said about the emphasis on impending and isolated death.

Her ambivalence could not have been demonstrated in a more clear-cut manner. On the one hand the terrible knowledge with which she was burdened had to be shared, on the other hand the guilt of inflicting pain on others, of not being independent and stalwart, of needing other people, must have been as painful as the knowledge of her death. Better to behave, whenever possible, as if nothing were wrong. She parted from Draper with no mention of her terrors.

In April, Algernon Crapsey came from Rochester to New York City to join the Women's Suffrage May Day parade. Webster and some of her friends were also marching, each with the group with which she identified.[30] Crapsey's presence was not recorded, but her professional duties, as well as her weakness, in all likelihood kept her away.

The positive attitude Algernon projected toward the situation of women was an enviable one. Jean Webster's liberal lover, Glenn, was not as supportive, and when Webster marched by his office building with her group of writers she saw the back of his bald head in the window as he and his colleagues joked about the demonstration. His attitude toward her politics was horrifying. She returned his ring, and, although she asked for it back the next day, her request came in the form of a letter wrapped with a yellow "VOTES FOR WOMEN!" banner.[31]

Crapsey could not have had the free time that Webster had for dalliance and politics now that she was a working woman. She certainly didn't have the time or money to take off that summer for Ireland as Webster did with Glenn, his sister, and their friend Lena Weinstein. Instead, she spent her vacation helping her parents in their latest venture.

Her disease had not fulfilled the doctors' expectation. Not only was she still alive, she appeared that summer to be in even better health than before. Her mother recorded her appearance on June 18, 1912, when Crapsey arrived home, as "looking splendidly well." She was active and enthusiastic in helping to set up the company that her family diminutively called "maternity work" and seemed "deeply interested" and optimistic.[32]

Her awareness of her family's need for moral support and a financial focus necessitated this optimistic front. Mrs. Crapsey was still somewhat unsure about her future and that of her family and felt the need for a more practical and secure source of income. Casting about for an idea, she listened when her daughter Adelaide suggested a clothing factory. It would mean taking up something that Mrs. Crapsey knew well and had long been praised for, the sewing of children's clothes and layettes. It would also mean the involvement of all the family, something else they knew well.

As in everything else the Crapsey family did, there was a philosophy to the making of the clothing and to the form of the garments. When Mrs. Crapsey took on three women to help her with the sewing, she was careful to allow them "free scope to invent models and new embroidery stitches and to work their own personality into the little garments."[33] The idea of individuality and creativity in work was thereby preserved even in an employer-employee situation, and socialist principles were maintained even in a structurally capitalistic framework. In every way Mrs. Crapsey restructured the factory concept to enable the workers to maintain their dignity and their private lives, with pleasant, lighted surroundings, personal involvement, celebrations, frequent breaks, and even day care for children.

Mrs. Crapsey also preserved her basic principles of the function of clothing—freedom of movement—with large armholes, fullness from the smocking, large hems to grow into, and easy maintenance to enable the child to fulfill the ideal of self-expression.

The idea of a factory was a good one, but many looked at it dubiously, and Mrs. Crapsey was in need of the courage her daughter was willing to give her. Crapsey was more than encouraging that summer, and despite her intellectual inclination and her desperation to fulfill the promise of her research was willing to lend a hand. "She turned from the theological part of the tragedy to helping me organize my work giving the little garments stock numbers, sitting up nights to make out bills. In every way she filled me with courage," her mother wrote.[34] "She liked the completeness of the little garments as they were turned out,"[35] despite her well-known lack of needlework dexterity. Crapsey may also have enjoyed the irony of it: as a result of her father's being "defrocked," they began frocking children.

While she and her mother were busy with their sewing, Algernon Crapsey was busy with his lectures and was constantly stirring up interest. On July 12 of that summer he was taken for a tramp and jailed in Dunkirk, New York. The insult was too much for a man recently and wrongfully prosecuted, and Dr. Crapsey, incensed, thought prosecution of the arresting officers unavoidable. Once again the family was involved in uncomfortable legal entanglements.

Even after Crapsey had left for Smith in September, Dr. Crapsey remained in the headlines when a month later he was arrested in Little Falls for speaking in a public place about women's rights.[36] Two months later, denying rumors that he would seek the bishop's pardon and endeavor to return to the church, he claimed he would preach nothing but socialism.[37]

Her father was moving in many new directions, but Adelaide Crapsey was satisfied to tread water, writing the class secretary for the first time in many years and registering her address as 10 West Street, adding: "As you see there are no changes." The secretary was petulant and commented, "This seemingly brief response was only extracted with the greatest difficulty." But this "seemingly brief response" was a significant message to herself. "No change" was an achievement. In the face of an unsympathetic chairman, she had managed to hang on to what was essentially offered as a temporary job, she had managed to continue her research, and she had succeeded in remaining alive and functional. It seemed as if the completion and publication of her work was yet possible. She was elated with her narrowed expectations, optimistic, and immersed in work.

That summer, Crapsey went directly to Webster's in Tyringham from Smith. She passed over the honor of presenting her old college president James Monroe Taylor, who was retiring, with an honorary Smith degree and went to help Webster with the script for *Daddy Long-Legs*. "She will be here several weeks—until it's time to go down to N.Y. with a tentative play under my arm,"[38] Webster reported to Glenn, indicating Crapsey's involvement with the actual writing.

The weeks that followed seemed joyous ones to Webster, who noted with her typical colorfulness the activities of the two friends. Glenn was out of the picture for propriety's sake, and Webster wrote him, "If you ever did come up you'd have to stay the night in Lee. Even with Adelaide for a chaperone I don't think it would be quite seemly to put you up in Canon House."[39]

Daddy Long-Legs was undergoing amazing alterations in the process of its revision for the stage. Judy was now exclusively concerned with romantic relationships and her individual development was ignored. Although at least part of this change was due to the impossibility of revealing intellectual development on stage, it was also connected to Webster's individual concerns at the time, and Judy's dramatic personality consequently took on much more of Webster than Crapsey. Crapsey too was busy with her own project. She had finally completed an article on her subject of metrics and sent if off to Paul Elmer More of the *Nation* with a tentative and officious note.

My dear Mr. More,

It is not, I know, usual for The Nation to publish a paper of the sort I am forwarding to you yet I send it on the bare chance that you may perhaps consider it. It is, as you will see, a study in English verse-technique and after a good deal of rather rueful wondering I am still able to think only of you and perhaps Mr Irving Babbitt as at all likely to be interested in the sort of work it represents. And, indeed, whether you find it available for the Nation or not, it would be to me the greatest pleasure if you would read it. There are only forty-two pages—and the conclusions, if they will hold, are I think important enough to be interesting.

If I am not other than frankly and anxiously concerned over the matter of publication it is because I can see no other way in which to bring the matter under discussion—working alone is always dangerous—and because it may be a first step toward gaining the free time that detailed investigation of this kind really demands.

I am sorry to send the paper just on the edge of the summer but I work subject to such constant interruption that I have not been able to finish it earlier as I had hoped to do.[40]

The paper completed and sent off, she could afford to relax with Jean, admiring and empathizing with nature to such an extent that she was inspired to write "Laurel in the Berkshires":

Sea-foam
And coral! Oh, I'll
Climb the great pasture rocks
And dream me mermaid in the sun's
Gold flood.

The joy of beauty seemed so great that poetry was inevitable, uncontrollable. The need to communicate the wonder of the world was almost religious in its intensity.

The situation was just like college with Crapsey and Webster involving themselves in creative activities, with their intellects and their grand hopes for the future keeping them at just a bit of ironic distance from the social experiences they simultaneously enjoyed. Jean wrote, "We froze 10 gallons of ice cream yesterday for a church social. The ladies furnished the cream + things + worked all day + then bought it in the evening. They made $21. It looks as though they were going to be able to pay the minister."[41]

Webster was in good humor. One day she found "13 4 leaf clovers (all but 3 in different places). What loads of luck you and I must be tottering on the brink of!" she wrote to Glenn McKinney.[42] But she did not notice that Crapsey's luck was going in a totally different direction. Crapsey described it with her customary humor and emphasis on self-reliance:

Oh dear me, a maid unlucky,
Though I've searched the green fields over,
Peering, peeping, I have never
Found a single four-leaf clover.
Oh dear me, it's *most* unlucky.

(*CP*, p. 119)

Webster continued to write to McKinney: "Your knife—mine—has been sharpened and cleaned + oiled. It works like a charm. I can open it with one finger; no ten cents necessary. I cut down a tree with it yesterday and made a staff for Adelaide."[43] The fact that Crapsey was in need of a staff went unnoticed, and her continued ill health must have gone unreported by Crapsey, for the two women engaged in what would most certainly have been considered reckless behavior had a hint of Crapsey's situation been an issue. On July 4 they went out to see the fireworks: "Adelaide and I nearly slept out-of-doors the night of the 4th. Lightly clad for the night, we took a steam rug and two pillows out under a tree in the orchard to watch Mr. Clarkson's fireworks—which were not exciting enough to keep us awake. If some bad boys hadn't broken into the church at midnight, + waked all Tyringham with their ringing, I think the morning would have found us still under the trees. . . . this has been a particularly lovely week."[44] The next night Webster complained of the cold: "This is just a post script to ask you if you are freezing? We are! Its colder than it was a year ago today when we landed in Londonderry. I had to hold on to the bed post all night to keep me + the mattress from blowing away. . . . I'm starting 1st draft of Act II—with luck maybe I'll finish it also before my descent."[45] The day after, Crapsey collapsed.

Stepping out of her bath, she was caught by a pain in her side so violent she dropped naked to the floor and was forced to wait a few moments before she regained sufficient control to pull on her nightgown. Returning soon after to her room, she summoned help. The pain was so alarming that her friends drove her to the local doctor, who in turn sent her immediately to a hospital in Pittsfield.

But even this alarming incident could not dampen Crapsey's spirits. "As a matter of fact I think its been rather a lucky chance," she wrote Esther. "I'm rather tireder than I thought I was and I'm positively thankful to be here."

Crapsey's optimism was nothing compared to Webster's:

I have just returned two hours ago from putting Adelaide in a hospital in Pittsfield! Nothing so serious as appendicitis—but the doctor thinks that three weeks flat on her back in a hospital will improve her—and I think so too. We put her in, at about six hours notice while she was too dazed to object. I discovered a very nice private hospital in Pittsfield on very high ground (1500 feet up) and a splendid surgeon at the head. She has a very pleasant room with three windows and a very pretty smiling nurse. I am sorry Pittsfield is so ungettatable at from here—the only way now, since the evening stage is off, is to motor. But I dare say her rest cure will work quite as well without too many callers—and I left her in a very contented frame of mind.[46]

The strange collapse was seen not as a terrible turning point but as an illuminating breakdown that would reveal at last the source of her symptoms as some rare but insignificant disease. Now she would be as she was years ago, Webster wrote McKinney in exuberant terms. "I think at last—after 4 years of silly tonics and rest & fresh air & everything else that didn't work—we are going to cure her up!"

But Webster was gradually disappointed as it became clear that the tonics wold not "cure her up." Three weeks later it was decided that at least one more week was necessary to do the trick. After that the plan was to spend a few more days in the Berkshires with Webster.

Webster was the most proximate and therefore the most frequent visitor and her optimism, therefore, was tried almost daily, so that it became increasingly difficult for her to hope for improvement. One day, when the Gilders, a neighboring family, drove her over to the hospital, she was forced to see the truth. "I didn't find her nearly so well as I had hoped—in fact I am sort of worried about her. She has a dreadful cough and hadn't slept for five nights." Yet she quickly caught herself on the brink of truth and turned, "I am hoping that when I get her out in the sunshine she will get over it. Unfortunately she can only stay here 4 days. Her family want her in Rochester as soon as she can travel."[47]

As it became apparent that Crapsey was in need of serious medical attention and that her parents were actually incapable of arranging it, Webster took over more responsibility for her treatment. She brought Crapsey back to Canon House on August 6 and was shocked by her deterioration. "She has been awfully ill since she came back—simply coughed all night long; couldn't lie down a minute. And of course she got terribly tired from being awake."

No diagnosis had yet been made, although the local doctors ruled out pulmonary tuberculosis; and when Webster sent her off to Rochester to a throat specialist she was hoping he would "spot the trouble." "It seems an awful pity—after working over her all summer to have to return her worse than I got her," she mused. "I promised her father on my word of honor that I'd send her back well."[48]

But Webster was not capable of returning Crapsey well. When Crapsey finally did come home, she was "hardly able to speak a loud word"[49] and continued to suffer from the other alarming symptoms Webster had described. It was beginning to become clear that Crapsey might not even recover in time for the next semester, and on August 19 Webster wrote "Adelaide is still in bed being ill, I hear from Rochester. She hasn't a lot of time before college opens."[50]

The dream of youth and impermeability was shattered. Webster's sudden knowledge of Crapsey's vulnerability was a painful blow, one from which she had been sheltered for years, and it was all the more shocking when it arrived. Their lives were so deeply interrelated; when Webster was asked for information for the alumnae bulletin she would write of Crapsey, ignoring her own activities to such an extent that in 1912 the bulletin published Webster's notice: "I have just returned from the station after seeing Adelaide Crapsey off on a train for Northampton. She goes back to Smith and examination papers after a four-day excursion to the city. Not particularly cheerful news, but it is all I can think of at the moment." The editor added drily, "Next time will somebody kindly tell us something about Jean?"[51]

The shock of Adelaide's condition put Webster back a decade, and she became wistful and a bit nostalgic about the danger for her friend, lapsing into pleasant memories. Glenn went to visit Poughkeepsie and Webster asked him, "Did you by chance notice the office of the Poughkeepsie Sun Courier one door below Smith Bros with a fat little man with a red moustache standing on the step? That is where my literary career started. The fat tubby man Mr. Toby by name shoved out $3. thro his little brass window and we all (Marion + Adelaide + I) had dinner at Smith's with broiled live lobster 35 cents to start with."[52]

If Crapsey had hoped to keep at least one area of her life inviolate from the sickness that invaded and destroyed so much of her dreams, she was now proven entirely unsuccessful.

Saranac Lake

Another week went by before two local throat and lung specialists were arranged to examine Adelaide. One was Dr. Hoyt, with whom she had shared dinners at the Bragdons'. The other, Dr. Jewett, was the more famous and authoritative.

The examination was more complete and the symptoms more pronounced. With no need of X-rays, the doctors diagnosed tuberculosis "in rather an aggravated form."[1] The white death, which had taken away so many young people in the nineteenth century, should have been diagnosed years ago, but the earlier absence of pulmonary symptoms had been misleading, and even the doctor who had diagnosed her two years before had been proven wrong by the patient's survival. Now the specialists told her that she had been suffering from the disease for three or four years; the signs were clear.

Perhaps the doctors were wrong once again. Crapsey distrusted their diagnoses almost as much as she doubted their cure. "If illness' end be health regained," she wrote, "then / I will pay you Asculapeus, when I die."[2] Nevertheless she knew that the extremity of her symptoms demanded extreme measures, and the only possible prescription could be a rest cure.

In recent years the renowned Edward Livingston Trudeau had been having a great deal of success in his clinic at Saranac Lake, a mountain

263

town only a few hours from where Adelaide's grandmother had lived, and it was recommended that Crapsey go there for diagnosis, prognosis, and cure—at least a two-year rest. There was no choice, and Crapsey did not bother to consult with her family. She called them into her room and made the announcement.

Earlier that morning, August 26, she had written to Esther Lowenthal a characteristically straightforward cheerful letter, which did not avoid the truth but still anticipated a positive direction. "I'm still playing semi-invilade [*sic*] having added unto myself a fearsome cough and a still more fearsome throat—and no voice to speak of—or rather to speak with—I tried to telephone your family one day—on the theory that my voice was better—it was an untenable theory. Its coming back now though—the voice I mean."³ That afternoon all optimism vanished.

Upon hearing the news five days later Webster began to make plans, as if only with her organizational efforts and her new-found importance was there a chance for her friend's recovery.

There is a very good Sanitarium about a mile & a half out of the village where it isn't so depressing nor abnormally expensive. I am hoping to be able to get her in there but there's a big waiting list & it requires some pull. I have written to every one I know of who has any interest with the head doctors. I may have to take her up to Saranak myself & make sure that she is comfortably installed with all the queer things she needs for a winter in the open.

Her family are not awfully efficient about putting things like that through and of course they are most dreadfully upset. She was just about their last hope. All the rest of them more or less have had accidents or illnesses or operations & they are nervously worn-out with 12 years of that strain. Nine children are too many in a nervous family! There is always something awful just going to happen.

I am sort of hanging on the end of a telegraph wire—hoping to hear more definitely just how far the thing has gone & what plans we will have to make. I may come down to N.Y., Wednesday evening & back up here on Friday—and I may go straight on to Rochester & take her up to Saranak immediately before this silly Western trip of mine. . . .

I positively haven't the slightest idea whether I'll be here, or in Saranak, or in N.Y. this next weekend. . . .

It seems to me simply criminal for this to have happened after all the doctors we have had. No one ever suggested tuberculosis & I had her examined twice in Pittsfield by 2 different men.[4]

Webster's hysteria about the arrangements were unnecessary: Paul took his sister to Saranac Lake and within two weeks of the diagnosis Crapsey was installed in a "cure cottage." The arrangements were not, after all, so very complicated. What was complicated and cause for hysteria was the dreaded disease itself; tuberculosis to Webster and to Crapsey as well was not the kind of illness suitable to their self-image.

In literature tuberculosis is a romantic disease, one long ago associated by Dumas with sexual and romantic attractiveness. *La Dame aux camélias,* delicately turning to cough blood into her handkerchief, Mimi of *La Bohème,* fading away selflessly in her sweet soprano, Marie Bashkirseff, raging at the very disease that seemed to have been caused by her literary rage—all these women were familiar to Crapsey. There was also the ideal woman of recent adult literature, the saintly, frail, pale, specterlike image, the perfect wife for Poe and Emerson and Mencken, one who posed no threat to men. The tubercular woman, in fact, could in many ways be the ultimate perfection in womankind: utterly dependent, virtuous by necessity, pale, delicate, slim. Furthermore, the economist Thorsten Veblen had recently described just such a woman as the ideal creation of the "leisure class." A man who could afford to keep such a useless wife or daughter was proving to the world just how wealthy he was; the helpless woman was his perfect symbol of conspicuous consumption.

But these images of the ideal woman—of the helpless saint—had been supplanted by that of the practical modern woman, the one Webster had tried to flesh out in Judy Abbott, who despised physical weakness and made every effort to maintain fitness through exercise, practical food, and the proper attitude. "I am going to pretend that all life is just a game which I must play as skillfully and fairly as I can. If I lose, I am going to shrug my shoulders and laugh—also if I win," Judy joyfully asserted,[5] and this optimism allowed her to overcome all the limitations with which she began and the confinements of her unique dependency in college: not to give in to self-pity, not to allow the self to fade away, but to proclaim one's own fate. "Character is destiny," the philosophies of Nietzsche, Schopenhauer, and the others were proclaiming, and Darwin's theories, applied to society, affirmed it as well. The modern woman, as visualized by Crapsey and Webster, was Nietzschean, pulling herself out of the quagmire of Victorian womanhood.

How could Crapsey have consoled herself with that image of the consumptive?

Others might have been comforted by the popular philosophy of the artist and by the theory that it was the burning creative spirit that destroyed the body. Thus were Aubrey Beardsley, Ernest Dowson, Lionel Johnson, and many others of their generation described by Yeats as having been burned away in their artistic fervor. There was even a reminder of the consumptive writer at Saranac Lake. Robert Louis Stevenson, one of Webster's early favorites, had preceded Crapsey to Saranac Lake by a few years and had become a personal friend of the director of the institution, Dr. Trudeau. He had stayed there during the winter of 1887 and had improved, using the time well to write a series of essays for *Scribner's Magazine* and his novel *Master of Ballantrae.*[6] Stevenson's house was one of the sights regularly visited by tourists to Saranac Lake, and his cure was one of the many successes attributed to the Trudeau Institute. But to Crapsey the link between illness and creativity was not a comfort. Even though she might have noticed in her own body that the slight fever that tuberculosis gave sometimes increased her creative intensity, and she might have heard some of the stories, such as those about Balzac, who claimed his productivity was increased greatly by the fever, she vastly preferred living to writing.

Even if she had taken into consideration the number of admired authors with tuberculosis who preceded her she could not have accepted the myth of the relationship between tuberculosis and art. The disease disgusted her. This fact was immediately apparent to Dr. Edward Baldwin, who examined her upon her arrival at Saranac Lake. She shrank from the ugliness of the physical signs, the weakness, the sleeplessness, "night sweats," the need to be cared for by others, the sputum cup and the other "paraphenalia" (as Crapsey spelled it) she needed to prevent contagion. Most of all the inability of her body to function disgusted her, and the disgust was doubled by the knowledge that the infernal weakness she had been fighting for years would now be coupled by enforced idleness and isolation.

Paul brought her up to Saranac Lake on September 9. The fact that it was her thirty-fifth birthday added to their gloom as they took the long train ride up the Adirondacks, and the gloom was only partially alleviated by the sandwiches, slippers, and newspapers provided by Esther Lowenthal. Had Webster been free to accompany her friend her wit might have penetrated the gloom. But Paul was closer, and the family felt more secure with one of their members in charge. Despite Webster's fears, Paul was practical and managerial enough to be capable of dealing with the situation effectively.

Paul could not have done much to cheer up Adelaide, no matter how great his love and admiration, no matter how profound his intentions. He had already seen two of his elder siblings die, and now the third one was on her way, leaving him next in line. Any attempt he must have made to brighten the voyage could not have been successful, could not dispel the mirrored fear in his face.

The fame of Saranac Lake was a reason for hope. Dr. Trudeau had gone up to this small town in the Adirondacks when he was ill with tuberculosis, so weak he had to be carried into his hotel, and he began there to experiment with various treatments. His discovery was that the cold air killed germs and that a germ-free environment contributed to recovery. After he instituted simple sanitary techniques which prevented infection and made quarantine less necessary[7] he was joined by other doctors who furthered his research and continued his practices. Among those doctors was Edward Baldwin, a young man who had also suffered from tuberculosis when he first came to Saranac Lake. By the time Crapsey arrived, Baldwin was cured and had taken over for Dr. Trudeau, who, though still living, was busier with his autobiography than the institution.

At the railroad station the Crapseys were met by people from Trudeau's and taken, as were all prospective patients, to the Riverside Inn. The next day brought an examination by Doctor Baldwin to determine the severity of the disease and to evaluate the appropriate environment for cure.

Usually patients were placed with other patients in similar circumstances, with similar interests, age, and background, so they could boost each other's spirits and contribute to each other's cure. Those placed in the large sanatorium were usually only mildly ill, and their chances of recovery and departure were great. The groups that would form in the smaller "cure cottages" were often close-knit and socially, sometimes even romantically, active.[8] For the most seriously ill, there were also "accommodations for private treatment at home" with private nurses.[9] These cottages and private homes taking in patients were scattered about the town and the patients were more dependent on their nurses.

Once Dr. Jewett's diagnosis that Crapsey's case was "well established"[10] was confirmed by Dr. Baldwin, Crapsey was sent to a private cottage. With some misgivings about the personality of the nurse, Baldwin recommended Miss Lucy's cottage at 39 Clinton Avenue. Despite the obvious implications in Crapsey's banishment to a totally isolated cottage, Baldwin was "hopeful" when he spoke to Paul the next day, suggesting that a few months of bed rest in the cold air might well be all that was needed to "turn the disease around."

Although the medical records of Trudeau's institution were destroyed in a fire, it is possible to reconstruct the slight misdiagnosis. Because the overt symptoms stemmed from pulmonary tuberculosis, other manifestations of the disease might have been overlooked. Had tuberculous meningitis been diagnosed, the outlook could not have been so optimistic. "The outcome of tuberculous meningitis is usually fatal," Baldwin noted, although qualifying this death sentence with twenty-three cases of exceptions to the rule.[11] But whether Baldwin knew more and failed to inform the family or was uncertain or misled by the symptoms, he recommended the only possible hope—total isolation and total rest.

The cottage, situated on Helen Hill, cynically referred to by the patients as "hemorrhage hill,"[12] was on an out-of-the-way street which bordered the town and the cemetery. Miss R. Helen and Miss Julia Lucy had been keeping the three-story cottage as a nursing home for three years. There was room for many patients; on the first floor were living room, reception hall, nurse's room, and kitchen; the second floor had three bedrooms; the third floor one bedroom. But because Baldwin did not get along well with the Lucys he did not refer many patients to them (except for a short interval during Adelaide's stay no other patient was housed there), and he knew that Crapsey would receive the total attentions of the nurse.

Crapsey was in the third-floor room, which had two windows and a closet and cost $30 weekly, including board and nursing care. The Lucy cottage was considered a very high-class and fairly expensive place, and it is probable that this ideal treatment was funded by Seward or the now aware and helpful Webster, or both of them.[13] Crapsey, who had limited her expenses in Europe to far less money per month than she was now paying per week and would have destroyed the effects of the treatment with worry over expenses, must have been kept in at least initial ignorance of this phenomenal fee.

Saranac Lake had not been intended for single, lonely patients. Many people came with their families, and some families, such as the family of the writer T. B. Aldrich, bought houses to be near their ailing relatives. Even those without relatives benefited from the company of other patients. Trudeau himself felt he had been helped immeasurably in this way and thought of the fellowship of tubercular patients as one of the benefits of his institution: "A beautiful feature of Saranac Lake and its problems is that in the meeting of these, which the world turns from with dread and discouragement, the visitors who have taken up their residence in Saranac Lake find life here satisfying, filled with interests, and surrounded by an atmosphere of friendliness, good feeling and cheerfulness which is not found to the same degree anywhere else."[14] But company and hobbies were not for Adelaide Crapsey. Baldwin noted that she was not a social being. "Her spirit was so shrinking and sensitive that she was unsuited for association with other patients." She was depressed by seeing in others what she preferred to avoid in herself and wished only to hang on to the world outside—the world of friends, scholarship, and academia.

The avoidance was not a negation of reality. She was also trying to overcome her disease through positive thinking. At Kemper Hall she had written praise for those soldiers who went into battle singing,[15] lauding the valor of warriors who "face the enemy with songs on their lips."[16] Now she too would have that opportunity. Her songs would be poems, prosody, and cheerful letters. She knew she was in battle and that battle was more likely to succeed when morale was high. She became, then, isolated from her friends and family, not only from their company, but also from their potential uplift, and could not replace this loss with new friends at Saranac Lake.

Crapsey's sense of gratitude would have made her nurse a devoted companion, a Severn to her Keats, a Horatio to her Hamlet. Wherever she had gone before she had attached herself to a caring woman. But, although Miss Lucy was a competent nurse, she was not suited to the task of companion. "She has two manners—her natural one—and the veneer—Normally she discourses about 'society drunks' 'dope fiends' and such like—In the other manifestation she affects a careful elegence [sic] and distinguishes languidly between people who are some one and the unfortunates who are nobodies . . . all the things you see in burlesque and don't expect to meet in real life—and she blissfully unconscious the while."[17] Provincial yet pretentious, Miss Lucy had remote knowledge of a world that Crapsey had intimately known. When Miss Lucy "alluded learnedly to the 'Lookout,' " Crapsey could only laugh. Her father and friends had published in the *Outlook*. Miss Lucy's distant knowledge of the significant world increased Crapsey's feeling of alienation, both from her nurse and from the world. She was now out of the center of existence, an outsider.

Perhaps (adopting Crapsey's own philosophy of life) it was just as well. Crapsey had other plans for herself in any case. She needed privacy and all her energies for the purpose of continuing her work, and Baldwin, seeing how desperate she was, broke his general habit of demanding total bedrest and consented to it.

At first, however, her only link to the world outside was the daily letter she was allowed to write ("+ that frowned on")—one letter a day that was sometimes impossible to write when pains in her side would suddenly debilitate her.

The single letters had to be artfully managed in order to maintain maximum contact with as many friends as possible with minimum writing. Letters to her parents were supplemented by occasional telegrams to let them know she was all right. A letter and gift from Maud Temple—a younger admirer whose delicate nerves required stroking—could be acknowledged through Esther Lowenthal or Mary Lewis. News of the death of a mutual acquaintance and the nervous breakdown of Elizabeth Kemper Adams—Crapsey's Kemper schoolmate and Vassar instructor—reached her through Esther, who also took over the instructions for Miss Hyde, the typist working on the manuscript on metrics.

These letters were rigorously self-censored. If she told the truth about the pain of her situation, her loneliness, her discomfort, she would cause her family and friends unnecessary grief, and yet if there were situations that might be correctable she had no recourse but to make requests. Books, creams, sickroom wear—she was accustomed to things that were not available in Saranac Lake and her friends were happy to alleviate their own pain at her condition by sending everything to her. But she was always afraid that they would tire of her endless requests and tried to keep them minimal.

So there were no outlets for her honesty. The poems that began to emerge at this point were the result of this emotional confinement. By turning the pain she could not discuss with anyone into a cinquain, she could render the situation somehow manageable. To Esther she could only veil her complaints: "I'm an Idiot—would have written before to give you news but for the beast of a pain right side—nothing serious—I'll write next week."[18] To the white paper she wrote:

RELEASE

With swift
Great sweep of her
Magnificent arm my pain
Clanged back the doors that shut my soul
From life.

(*CP*, p. 90)

In this way the pain had an end as well as a beginning and an excruciating middle.

The pain is of course the center. Envisioned in the first two lines as an omnipotent, graceful diety, Pain in her munificent charity permits the peeking appearance of the poet. It is as if Crapsey has taken Swinburne's romantic personification of pain as a goddess and inspiration and reversed its significance. Only to a comfortable theoretician is pain truly a pleasure and inspiration. To one truly in agony the blessings and the creativity are in the respites and not the attacks.

She was not entirely desperate about the physical situation in which she found herself. There was a breathtaking view from afar of Mount Baker, an imperious and beckoning peak reminiscent of the Alps in their grandeur. But below her window was the village graveyard, "Trudeau's Garden," Crapsey called it, with characteristic clearsighted humor, even though most of the patients who expired were shipped home on the same train that had brought Crapsey there. The graveyard was in use, but because of the size of the town's population there were only a few burials a year, and only two or three within view of her window.

Between the cemetery and the mountains were huge pine trees divided by a sand road which began at the graveyard, and it was upon this scene that Crapsey looked for hours each day when reading became tiring and writing was restricted. Even an occasional visitor could not divert her for a long time: rest hours were rigidly enforced by the nurse anxious for her reputation, and Miss Lucy proudly proclaimed, "I never let her do anything."[19]

It was hoped that the enforced rest would have a positive effect. Crapsey wrote Lowenthal: "A month of this ought to start me on the right road—Dr. Baldwin says that the next three months will show what can or can't be done."[20] Because of this hope, her mind and her interest remained with the college, and her attention was fixed on the unfinished tasks she had left. She worried about having her books packed and out of the way so that her room could be rented, about the developing gossip in the department, even about corrected papers.

I left some papers (students papers) lying around in Seely—Will you gather them up + tear them up? They will be all the bad ones[—]The others were taken by their owners[—]and I dont care to have the whole English department going over them—An unworthy spirit but why not be unworthy! You will find them[—]They are marked with my name I think—but you will

recognize them anyhow—they have bibliographies—lists of technical terms
etc—on the table opposite Seelye 11 or 12—or else in the drawer marked
with Miss Woodwards or my name—we used the same drawer at the end of
the year . . .
Love to Mary—and the Lady of the House—and C.B. and proper messages
to everyone else—
I do hope the household won't be too uneasy + uncomfortable—I'm glad
theres at any rate Mary to fall back on—Perhaps there will be some nice
new people—My line is getting to[o] long! Probably I won't write for 10
days or two weeks—They tell me I must keep perfectly still—and so I
suppose I must—[21]

"Send me the news and all the scandal," she wrote Esther, and rejoiced
both in the gossip and her distance from the involvement. Henry Mc-
Cracken from Harvard had recently been lured to Smith, and his sex and
stature were upsetting the genteel balance Mary Jordan had imposed.
This gave the perspective of Saranac Lake a little humor: "Isn't the simple
joy of Smith over a faculty *gent* too touching! Of course the Drama drew
the crowds—That was a foregone conclusion. Poor C.B. and the others
with their seminar wrested from them! Don't stop your small bulletins
until you grow weary—they beguile empty moments. . . . The days,
truth to tell, are rather long."[22]

She had requested a leave of absence for a year, but knew almost
immediately that even a year would not be sufficient and considered
resigning altogether. The thought was painful, but not because of her
affection for instruction. "Of course I'm not mad about teaching—and if
I were giving it up because I had enough money to live without it and
spend all my time on metrics that would be one thing—but after all its
my profession—and I've put a fair amount of time and energy into it—
and its not wholly a festal business to have to chuck it all."[23] It was the
need for a connection with reality that made her cling with such desperation to her job, and in October she relievedly wrote Esther, who suggested that she wait before making any rash decisions: "If you and Mary
think it perfectly fair to let my application for leave stand of course I'll
do it and feel rather relieved—less swing off into space without any
connection anywhere. Of course no one knows what the Trustees will

say—but we can leave that to them as you say."[24] She needed the reminder of the college, the only link now to the world of the living, as she
continued in the silent house with her address at the edge of life. This
way her identity would be connected with the world—she would be a
sick instructor and not merely a tubercular patient. Until she would be
able to work again, gossip was her only tie. Soon the decision of the
Smith trustees to grant her a paid leave of absence at $20 a month in-
creased the feeling of connection and lifted her spirits considerably.

Not being able to work on her "FL," her "favorite literature," was a
great frustration. The immediate response to the article she had sent
More in June had been encouraging, and when she wrote Lowenthal
about it, just after her collapse, the possibility of publication was so
important that news of her hospitalization became buried in the letter.
The structure of the letter is the key to her enthusiasm and academic
expectation as well as the content. I quote the letter in full to illustrate
the manner in which the intimate details of her collapse are buried in
more public and prestigious scholarly expectations.

17 July 1913
Hillcrest Hospital, Pittsfield, Massachusetts

Dear E—What do you think of that? But as you see I can still hold a pen!
How are you and where are you and what have you been doing? I do hope
it has been and is being awfully nice and restful—

Here's a telegraphic report of my news. I finished the favorite literature and
sent it off on Saturday the 21st of June. I reckoned that it would take P.E.M.
[Paul Elmer More, editor of the *Nation*] about three weeks to get around to
reading his surprise and settled back to rest during that time. It came back
on Tuesday the 23rd of June—but with (not to employ the method of
suspense) a really very nice (if in spots funny) letter. The thing was too long
for the Nation but I seem to have "hit on a very interesting point"—but the
argument was hard to follow (E! that masterpiece of lucidity!) and "it
would be a satisfaction to me personally if I could see your argument shorn
of all secondary issues and presented in its barest skeleton." Being willing to
oblige I sat me down—(after a day or two to get my breath) and ripped the
favorite literature up the back and did a condensed version—sending it off

to be typed on the 7th of July—l stayed in Tyringham to avoid the interrupt-
ing packing + unpacking. Of course in the meanwhile I had written Mr
More saying that I would like very much to send the shorter paper—and
getting in reply a nice note with his vacation address—to send the thing to.
On the 8th of July as I got out of my bath I leaned over quickly felt a
remarkable pain and after a second found it more discrete [*sic*] to drop full
length on the bathroom floor than to stand up. After a while I got up
grabbed a nightdress—and retired again to the floor. No not really faint-
ing—just staving it off by lying flat you know. It was awfully funny. After
one moment or two I got back to my room and went to bed and we got—or
rather the others got hot water bags + such and it really was a[w]fully
funny—and nothing at all serious—Just one of those things you can do by a
queer little twist—the filament of a muscel [*sic*] or something broke. But of
course we didn't know that + decided not to take chances so in we motored
to a doctor—He has turned out to be a very nice sensible person—poked
about settled the back as nothing—it was better by that time anyhow—but
told me the best thing I could do would be to cut to a hospital for three or
four weeks—have some mild treatment, absolute rest etc.—and here I am.
As a matter of fact I think its been rather a lucky chance. I'm rather tireder
than I thought I was and I'm positively thankful to be here.

Forgive this scribble—I'll be here four weeks anyhow—Isnt it funny—

I'm hoping to hear from you and I'll be furious with fate if you havent had a
truly nice time—How has the weather been—

No more at peril! Your—A.C.[25]

Who could possibly care about health when success was so close?

The very mention of the interest of Paul Elmer More in her research
was enough to bring her to a high peak of embarrassment. Mary Lewis
had lunch with Mary Willard, an "allumna [*sic*] trustee,"[26] and let slip
the fact that More and Omond had been encouraging to her. "Needless
to say my hair is grey with horror—You couldnt possible [possibly] on
the basis of the letter or two he wrote say that Mr. More is any such
general thing as 'interested in my work'—He's undoubtedly entirely forgotten it by this time. And just because he has been so nice I would
make a special point of *never* mentioning it Mr Omond—this is without

his very special + explicit permission. . . . Anyhow you know my met-rical work isn't yet finished enough to talk about—in public I mean."[27] There could be no indicator more clear of the extreme significance to her of this work than this pained embarrassment.

But even with her network of typists and correspondents she could not get back to the article now; it would have to wait until she im-proved. And now that she knew her condition there was the danger that all the waiting would lead nowhere but to the cemetery outside.

She ran out of paper soon after her arrival and began to use index cards. "I write on these wretched little cards because my paper is giving out and my nurse hasn't got down town to get me more."[28] How strange that her nurse and her family did not respond immediately to this obvious separation from the world! The lack of basic equipment and the inability to secure it could not have added to her sense of connec-tion. Her mention of it in a letter to Lowenthal brought a package in the return mail.

Webster sent her many gifts, " 'peppering' her with small offerings so that she will always have an abundance of mail to open." One day she sent soap, the next day a "tokimento." This was for morale as well as Webster's conscience and it must have had a wonderful effect. Esther sent more practical gifts—books, newspapers, and magazines like *Punch*, a subscription to the *Times* and the *Nation*, gifts that would allow Adelaide to "beguile a lonely hour."[29]

She read when she had the strength—all of her gifts, the monthly *Poetry*, the *Atlantic*, Meynell's biography of Francis Thomson, "$3.75 worth of Willy Yeats,"[30] Henry James, her own "little chunky brown bible," *Blast!*. Lowenthal sent her a book of Japanese prints, a perfect alternative for someone who had nothing to do but look when her eyes tired of reading, and the prints may have influenced her as much as the books. "Your Times," she wrote Lowenthal, "saves my life once a day. It comes usually at about 4 o'clock just when I'm ready to cut the throat of the universe from shere [*sic*] boredom and I read it from end to end. I hope there will be a great many murders and scandals this winter. It will be much nicer for me."[31]

Miss Lucy would select books from the local library—"trash,"

Crapsey called it—and, hungering for an emotional and intellectual challenge, she requested *"The Idiot*—Dostoyef [ends in a scrawl] I can't spell it but you'll recognize it just the same. . . . I really think The Idiot would be nice—or is is The Idiots—the more the merrier."[32] Later she commented that it had been a lifesaver. "Its such a relief to have something worth reading."[33]

The first months in total suspension brought an apparent improvement. Even after a few weeks she was feeling better: "pulse down, temperature down, cough better and at least a little sleep o'nights," she reported to Esther, and then added, "I always feel an idiot when I talk about symptoms."[34] But the desperation of the inactivity and the terrible fear of its uselessness terrified her. She watched the dirt road between the pine trees at the base of the cemetery, the woodland beyond, and Mount Baker rising abruptly, and her longing for that "open road" flared:

How can you lie so still? All day I watch
And never a blade of all the green sod moves
To show where restlessly you toss and turn,
And fling a desperate arm or draw up knees
Stiffened and aching from their long disuse;
I watch all night and not one ghost comes forth
To take its freedom of the midnight hour.
Oh, have you no rebellion in your bones?
The very worms must scorn you where you lie,
A pallid mouldering acquiescent folk,
Meek inhabitants of unresented graves.
Why are you there in your straight row on row
Where I must ever see you from my bed
That in your mere dumb presence iterate
The text so weary in my ears: "Lie still
And rest; be patient and lie still and rest."
I'll not be patient! I will not lie still!
There is a brown road runs between the pines,
And further on the purple woodlands lie,
And still beyond blue mountains lift and loom;
And I would walk the road and I would be

Deep in the wooded shade and I would reach
The windy mountain tops that touch the clouds.
My eyes follow but my feet are held.
Recumbent as you others must I too
Submit? Be mimic of your movelessness
With pillow and counterpane for stone and sod?
And if the many sayings of the wise
Teach of submission I will not submit
But with a spirit all unreconciled
Flash an unquenched defiance to the stars.
Better it is to walk, to run, to dance,
Better it is to laugh and leap and sing,
To know the open skies of dawn and night,
To move untrammel'd down the flaming noon,
And I will clamour it through weary days
Keeping the edge of deprivation sharp,
Nor with the pliant speaking on my lips
Of resignation, sister to defeat.
I'll not be patient. I will not lie still.

And in ironic quietude who is
The despot of our days and lord of dust
Needs but, scarce heeding, wait to drop
Grim casual comment on rebellion's end:
"Yes; yes . . . Wilful and petulant but now
As dead and quiet as the others are."
And this each body and ghost of you hath heard
That in your graves do therefore lie so still.

(CP, p. 101–2)

The starkness of "To the Dead in the Graveyard Under My Window:—
Written in a Moment of Exasperation" was a direct attempt to confront
her situation. While Crapsey was writing these lines, Trudeau, writing
his autobiography, was discussing his experiences with the few patients
whom he was unable to help. "From these I have learned that the con-
quest of Fate is not by struggling against it, not by trying to escape from
it, but by acquiescence; that it is often through men that we come to
know God; that spiritual courage is of a higher type than physical cour-

age; and that it takes a higher type of courage to fight bravely a losing than a winning fight especially if the struggle from the first is evidently a hopeless one, and is protracted for years."[35]

Crapsey was unaware that she was not the only one to struggle this way with her disease. She only knew that she could rely on no one. She had just her Dr. Baldwin, with whom she strained to identify herself because her life was in his hands. She could even mock these obvious attempts at identification. "Its a great relief to me to find that he is as careful about his greys as I am. Grey overcoat, grey other things, grey tie and a scarf pin of some cloudy grey crystal—All of this I am sure will be a great help (These frivolous comments for your ear alone)."[36] Even their birthdays were only one day apart.

However, Baldwin, upon whom so much depended, was a busy man, distracted, and although he seemed to approve her work and her progress, could visit rarely and understood little of the desperation of her physical situation and its effect on her psychological state. " 'Trudeau's Garden' was not all a fanciful imagery," he pointed out later, "for in one direction she could see in the distance glimpses of the village cemetery."[37] The cemetery met him across the narrow street as he stepped out the door. If he looked out the window, Baldwin could not have failed to see it—not in the distance, but in the immediate, all-encompassing foreground—and could not have ignored the negative effect such a view must have on a mortally ill patient.

Baldwin believed that Crapsey was improving. By November she was pronounced well enough to leave her room, although she complained of "fresh and inexplicable weights of fatigue," and her first move was an attempt to find more congenial lodgings.[38] For two nights she tried to live in a larger "cure cottage," but found the room dark, damp, and "there was only one nurse for the whole collection of invalids."[39] More important, unable to even brush her own hair, she could not function without personal care. "There were two reasons for the contemplated change," she confessed to Esther Lowenthal, "the expense here wh[ich] is scandalous for me I mean and the more amusing psychological fact that my doctor doesn't like my nurse."[40] The weariness, boredom, and depression she omitted.

She returned to Miss Lucy, resigned to a tedious and irritating winter. The snow was already deep enough on those peaks to support sleighs and the cold air and motion was thought to stimulate the lungs. Dr. Baldwin prescribed sleigh rides, and Crapsey wrote home for her hat and overshoes. Toward the end of the month she went out almost every other day with the horses for an hour or so, braving the Adirondack cold.

Webster visited during the last week of November and accompanied Crapsey on one or two of these rides when they visited some of the local attractions, perhaps even the cottage of Robert Louis Stevenson, whose writings had inspired the young Webster. Jean selected three postcards, souvenirs of their ride, to send to Glenn, showing Caribou Bill's wolf dogs (with sleds), and wrote Glenn on the back:

> How do you like these dogs for household pets? Their mother is a collie and their father is a wolf. They snap.

> We visited Caribou Bill yesterday and admired his dogs' teeth. It is snowing hard and is *cold.* I am going for a walk over the hills and through the woods while Adelaide rests. . . .

> I wish you could come! I like the climate and am thinking of spending the winter.[41]

"Its awfully nice to have some one around," Crapsey confided,[42] and hoped Webster would be able to help her decide what to do with her depressing surroundings.

Webster was unable to help in this area. She could only try to bolster her friend's spirits. Her general attitude can be gleaned from an undated notebook, in which she wrote: "There is nothing tragic in death. It is a natural and fitting completion of life. Death is only tragic when it means the death of the spirit—and that occurs during life, and then the tragedy is heightened by the fact that the body lives on instead of dying too. The man who still lives after his spirit is dead is the greatest tragedy life can present."[43] Webster encouraged Crapsey to write creatively, asking her for ideas, suggestions, and help with her own work, and Crapsey rallied. Her mind filled with ideas and she began to think of plays, poems, and her own "FL." She returned to her work on metrics and in her poetry experimented with the theories she was determining. Her time in bed had led to more complex thoughts on metrics and she was trying to put them into words.

Explaining the theories was not easy. On the one hand, she was too deferential to state outright the ideas that so disagreed with the revered professors she had been reading. On the other hand, she had thought so long and deeply that many things struck her as self-evident and almost self-explanatory, so it was difficult to phrase, to decide what was obvious and what not, to write sentences, to make statements. Her isolation and the dizziness of her disease made exposition difficult. Her style, as a result, was utterly unlike the clear prose pieces she had written in college, unlike even the pieces she had sent to Omond and More: "That I give the merest first sketch of such inclusive formulation has already been stated and is surely too obvious to need repetition, but I should like to add that, acutely aware at once of the difficulties involved and my own but slender competence, I mean to go no further in the unavoidable generalizations than is necessary in order to indicate the connections which I think it may be possible to establish."[44] A similar point concluding less basic evidence only months before was stated with more force: "It is, of course, obvious that the amount of evidence so far obtained does not make possible any final conclusion. The coherence of result up to this point, however, seems interesting enough to justify further experiment with the same scheme, and it is as a part of continued experiment that I am giving this first test statement."[45]

But she had so much more to say now. The problems of stress and their interrelationship with meter were more clearly a matter of prosody, of the length of the words used and the "secondary stress," the slighter accent on syllables in polysyllabic words. And it was more clear to her now that only through scientific investigation could these factors be studied and employed more effectively in poetry. Metrical facility in poetry, her studies proved, had not progressed from the time of Milton but had, in some ways, regressed, because if poets like Swinburne were using primarily a monosyllabic vocabulary their jobs as poets were easier, their poetry less complex. Progress at this point could only be instituted by an understanding of the rules of the music of poetry and a conscious effort to employ them.

The work was exhausting and the technical difficulties of research and writing overwhelming. Crapsey wrote Lowenthal: "I'm at present sitting up because I'm tired of lying down—bye and bye I'll be lying down because I'm tired of sitting up and either way I write on a portfolio balanced on my knee and I wonder how much torture it is to read it."[46] But there were few distractions.

On New Year's Day, Mrs. Crapsey came to visit. It was the first time she had been there, and she was shocked. Her daughter was as weak as before, and so alone. Her first look out the window revealed a man digging a black grave in the snowy ground.

> "Mother's looking out of the window," she said, "and I don't think she likes the view!"
>
> "But it doesn't disturb me, dear," said Mrs. Crapsey, "except for you."
>
> "Oh, I don't mind, mother, —except for you." And the incident was closed, Adelaide adding only, "They don't dig graves here very often. It's an abandoned cemetery, really."[47]

Adelaide was able to rise from her bed for only one of the three or four days her mother was there. Fortunately for Mrs. Crapsey, her husband arrived at Saranac Lake at the same time and she did not have to face the sad sight by herself. "It was very gay to have both parents at once," Crapsey said.[48] When they left she returned to her work.

By February, Crapsey mailed Esther Lowenthal a draft of "A Study in English Metrics," and Lowenthal read it over before she sent it to the typist. With no one else had Crapsey shared this more advanced research. She was afraid to send it to More, Omond, or some of the others who had previously turned her down for fear it would stop her impetus, but she needed feedback and was gratified at Lowenthal's response. "Does it really pass muster—the poor old fav. lit. It's cheering to hear you anyhow say so."[49] Lowenthal paid a "flying visit" in February, when the temperature went down to twenty below, "although you didn't feel the cold as much as you might think because it was so dry."[50] The visit helped, not only because it relieved the loneliness but also because the business of scholarship that was transacted gave her a purpose, a sense of significance, a reason to live. It also gave her an opportunity to play with great irony the role of Important Career Woman to her nurse, mentioning as if in passing that a stenographer was awaiting her instructions and she should not be disturbed while she completed her work.

At the same time Webster was trying to cheer her friend up by surprising her with a bathrobe—blue flowered broadcloth with red French linen collar and cuffs.[51] Her pain at her friend's illness and isolation was somewhat alleviated by the twin robes she had made for Crapsey and herself, and the running around to the dressmakers and Wanamakers Department Store gave her a chance to burn off some of that energy stemming from her desire to help. For the fashion-conscious Adelaide it would be a joy to vary her limited wardrobe.

Webster was bringing Crapsey other joys as well. *Daddy Long-Legs* opened in Atlantic City on February 20, was sold out by the 22nd in Washington, and was a sure hit by the time it reached Rochester on March 7. At the request of Adelaide, the Crapsey family arranged a theater party for Mrs. Crapsey's birthday and invited Webster to dinner before.

Now that the period of enforced rest was coming to a conclusion, diagnoses and attempts at treatments were being made. As soon as Crapsey sent her bundle to Lowenthal for Miss Hyde to type, Dr. Baldwin began more active treatment. An X-ray, which Baldwin called "by far the most important advance in diagnosis,"[52] suggested the possibility of success of the novel pneumothorax treatment. "The lung is collapsed—therefore gets an absolute rest—therefore heals more rapidly. It succeeds in 60% of the cases where it is used," Crapsey wrote Lowenthal in the crisp style that would have benefited her expositions of "Favorite Literature."[53]

The low percentage of success, the need for such treatment, and even the obvious failure of the "rest cure" which had worked reasonably well in the past must have indicated to Crapsey the mortal danger in which she found herself. Privately, she was writing poems that revealed her thoughts during those sleepless nights of fever:

ANGUISH

Keep thou
Thy tearless watch
All night but when blue dawn
Breathes on the silver moon, then weep!
Then weep!

But the direct expression of feeling was controlled, not only in the tight cinquain form, but in the syncopation of the syntactic "pull" with the stress and meter. The rhythm of the poem breaks midway, and with "but when," two intellectually unaccented syllables, shifts both rhythm and direction. With a single anapest and strong end stopping the fourth and fifth lines are full of motion compared to the static run-on first two lines. The second person imperative accents the importance of self-control involved. The parallel and rhyme of the first and last words of the poem also reveal the breakdown in the poem of the enforced control, as from "keep" the poem moves to "weep." The technical virtuosity with which Crapsey here delineates the actual anguish of the night realization of the mortal danger and the growing terror in the situation in which she found herself shows her incredible ability to structure her open-eyed agony into art.

Another way to turn her fears into art was comedy. The pneumothorax treatment was sketched for Lowenthal as if it were a droll anecdote:

It was rather funny. 1st Much beating of rugs + general clearing of room. 2d—Me fresh from the tub and all scrubbed + clean—Miss Lucy in spick + span uniform—all this in honor of the "surgical" character of the event. 3d—Arrival of Dr. Baldwin and Dr. Price with gas + things. Most businesslike 4th Jamming of hollow . . . needle through which the gas goes (or is supposed to go) into me—then ought to come 5th entrance of gas and collapse of lung but what as a matter of fact happened was—nothing! Dr. Baldwin tried 3 places and struck each time in [an] adhesion (inner and outer lining or something stuck together) so that the gas wouldn't go in. They worked a little over an hour and by that time we were all tired so we gave it up and now we'll try again. It isn't awfully bad you know though not what one would choose for a diversion. I had a hypodermic injection of morphine and atropine and Dr Baldwin used cocaine for each of the places. The only (slightly) trying thing was doing it all over again 3 times + still getting no where—and I admit that no one cares less for this sort of thing than I do. Somehow when a competent finger goes tapping along my side and a placid meditative voice says—"Now, Price, do you think we can get in here?"—and "in here" is between my own most precious ribs I do feel a bit of a qualm. However everyone was gay—my "pnemo thorax party" it got called—and chatted most sociably—the patient occassionally lapsing into silence (after her usual fashion)—I report one nice retort—It was getting to be pretty clear that the 3d try was not going to be successful—and I heard Dr Price say gaily—"Well, you know, with one man we tried 57 times" and placidly Dr. Baldwin's voice remarking—"Oh, Price is thinking of pickles."[54]

In the same spirit she advised her friends not "to pneumothorax— These new dances are a menace to society!" and enclosed "Lines Addressed to My Left Lung Inconveniently Enamoured of Plant-Life" in a letter to Lowenthal.

It was, my lung, most strange of you,
   A freak I cannot pardon,
Thus to transform yourself into
   A vegetable-garden.

Though laking William set erewhile
   His seal on rural fashions,
I must deplore, bewail, revile
   Your horticultural passions.

And as your ways I thus lament
   (Which, plainly, I call crazy)
For all I know, serene, content,
   You think yourself a daisy!
          (*CP*, p. 119)

Underneath this little piece of flippant humor is the basic lack of belief in any kind of order. No God, no romantic nature, nothing is watching out for her. Only an arbitrary accidental growth has determined her fate. But it is perfectly easy to overlook this kind of heresy: Crapsey certainly wasn't going to point it out to friends. Her overt purpose in writing the poem was to relieve the strain and to control in verse the uncontrollable growth in her lungs. Both methods of coping with the increasingly certain fate were basically similar—the use of structure and form to encompass a not-to-be-avoided truth.

The "P-T" (pneumothorax treatments) were abandoned in favor of tuberculin, an experimental treatment in which the live germ was injected into the patient. The doctors of the clinic at Saranac Lake had had previous success with this treatment. "By its intelligent use some of the latent defensive resources of the living organism may be successfully stimulated in chronic cases, when the disease tends to localize and the infected individual is still capable of responding to the stimulation, and an arrest of the onward progress brought about," wrote Trudeau.[55] The catch, however, was clear: the patient must have sufficient defenses to be activated by the vaccine.

When the treatment was successful, the first sign would be a high fever and an initial intensification of the symptoms, followed by a gradual improvement. Crapsey was busy with the color-contrasting notes on her study of metrics when the serum was injected and was fearful that the treatment would slow down her research, so she was somewhat relieved when there was no difference. She concentrated on her work and ignored the implications, discovering the next day that "red ink and tuberculin are not incompati a? ble."[56] "As the doses increase I may feel them a little more—It sticks vaguely in my mind that Dr. Baldwin said something about not using much 'when there is a pulse like yours'—but I'm not sure. My attention was all on the matter of working next year wh. [which] was also being discussed."[57] Baldwin was not really surprised when the tuberculin did not cause a reaction. He was administering tuberculin as much for research as for immediate cure. "The special studies on tuberculin and hypersensitiveness made in the period between 1910 and 1920 . . . were the means of explaining many obscure problems. A fuller understanding of the symptoms of tuberculosis was for the first time made possible by these experiments."[58]

It was far more pleasant to concentrate on research and future plans. The intrigues of the politics at Smith were exciting to her, especially when they concerned her only vaguely and punctuated her suspicion that the people in positions of power were all motivated by the silliest and most banal considerations. Throughout the winter Crapsey encouraged Lowenthal to send as much news of faculty meetings and backstabbings as she could provide, while she waited impatiently to be given permission by her doctors to rejoin the fray.

She had asked for more time to decide about next year and was mildly surprised by the silence of her "chief" at Smith, Mary Jordan, in reply. "I've heard nothing at all from the Trustee Meeting," she wrote at the end of February, "so its probable, as you say, that nothing was done. Well that gives me a little more time in wh. [which] to make a complete recovery."[59] The hope was strong, and every sign made her feel closer to her goal to return to her employment and her research. In the last week of March she reported improvement: "I *am* getting stronger; theres that much on the credit side. I went out yesterday—sleighing—for the first time in 2 months. And lately (for a few days) I've dressed in the morning—and gone out for a little while (on the porch) then as well as in the afternoon. The cough is ever with me—If only I could get rid of that. But I'll be back at work next year—see if I'm not."[60] The decision, however, had already been made for her.

The evidence came all at once—in a letter from her mother in the beginning of April. Enclosed were two letters from the president of Smith to her father, dated January 13 and 23, that had determined her future.

In January, when Miss Jordan had begun to inquire about the possibility of Crapsey's return to Smith, Crapsey herself had written for more time, but her father, responding to an official letter from M. L. Burton, the president of Smith, informed the college that his daughter would not be returning next year. Uncomfortable with his decision, Dr. Crapsey neglected to inform his daughter that he had in effect resigned her from her future and allowed her to continue to hope. While she was connecting the gradual improvement of her symptoms with her return to work, her career and life had been determined for her as if she were already a corpse.

When Crapsey discovered her death-in-life, she reacted immediately with shock and anguish. She realized suddenly that life was continuing on in absolute oblivion of her existence, that her chairperson had not written her because she knew of Crapsey's ingorance, that her family was treating her as if her future was not a factor for consideration. When the letter from Smith arrived, Crapsey explained to Lowenthal, her father was out of town and so her mother, "instead of doing automatically the only thing to do—namely send the letter on to me—called in Dr Jewett asked him to consult Dr Baldwin and then write Dr Burton. In the meanwhile Father returned, was taken into consultation—and Dr Jewett first and then Father wrote Dr Burton definitely giving up my position for next year. After this Father, as far as I can make out, forgot all about the transaction and Mother put the letters away (forgetting about them too probably!)—and by no breath or sign of any description was it intimated to me that anything had been done."[61]

Perhaps there really was no alternative, but Crapsey felt betrayed. And she was not at all sure that the decision was inevitable. The doctors, she reasoned, did not know much about college teaching and probably didn't even realize the flexibility of the schedule, the limited teaching hours, and the possibilities for recovery in the positive attitude a productive life could give.

Both her protective figures had failed her, and Crapsey, shattered, unable even to recount the event with her customary humor, wrote Esther Lowenthal on April 7: "And, oh, do you really think it was quite necessary to have all this happen? It gives me the most insecure, exposed feeling. From what unexpected corner will the next bolt be shot!"[62]

It was a bit of a relief to discover that at least Dr. Baldwin had not been involved in the "keep it from her policy."[63] With an uncharacteristic persistence, Crapsey pursued the busy Baldwin in the matter until he looked up his records and determined absolutely that he had not been consulted in this decision.

The relief was mitigated by his agreement with the decision: "As for the other part of it—whether I can work—why no. The conclusion is the same but I would have chosen a different manner of arriving at it."[64] But honesty allowed for clear-sighted future plans: "I put in my main declaration wh. [which] is just this—that if its chronic tuberculosis why thats what it is and I'm just going to go ahead, find a way of living thats as little invalidish as possible get what I can out of things and let it go at that. You know Dr Baldwin is awfully nice—Instead of the usual professional psuedo-optomism [*sic*] etc he just said—'Yes, that would be my philosophy.' "[65]

She was proud of her superiority to her doctor, her ability to accept a situation despite its bleakness: "Well—its somehow all a little disconcerting. 'Invalid' isnt a word I'm attached to. It was amusing, and nice, to see Dr. Baldwin chose the very farthest mountain top to look it [at] when he said it."[66]

The treatment at Saranac Lake had failed. In his publications Baldwin mentioned many scientific causes of tuberculosis but made no note of the emotional one he attributed to this patient: "Adelaide Crapsey was too frail, too sensitive for a physical body to bear, and her body too frail to carry such intense emotion in a soul too delicate for suffering mortal disease."[67] That the frailty may have been the result of her disease, the years of suffering and struggle, did not occur to him. Instead he adopted the attitude of the bourgeois to the artist, the society to the "new" educated woman, and reverted to the popular superstitions of tuberculosis. Whatever the reason, Baldwin gave up. He rushed a letter to Dr. Crapsey, who came immediately to Saranac Lake to discuss with the doctor Adelaide's return home.

The world went on without her. The Vassar bulletin of 1901 came out in June, for the first time omitting Crapsey's name as class poet. The poetry manuscript Webster sent out to publishers came back once, and then again. Yet the last two months at Saranac Lake brought scattered attempts at creativity. A halting letter to Professor Grandgent, who had been recommended by a colleague, Maud Temple, as one potentially interested in Crapsey's research, was finally sent off with the manuscript, after many failed attempts. The manuscript of poems was organized in a satisfactory and meaningful arrangement. The paper on metrics was sent to the Modern Language Association. At Webster's request, Crapsey wrote a song to be used in the troublesome third act of *Daddy Long-Legs*. The song, "Infamy" was to have provided a poignant interlude, a contrast with the shallowness of the rejected suitor. Jimmie, the young man who proves himself too young and incapable of comprehending the depths of the New Woman, repeats one line of the song, " 'There is no joy but sleep.' You know that makes an awful hit with me."[68]

There were also other creative bursts, as if this was her last chance to write things down, that anything was better than nothing, and if she left behind clues at least there was a chance that somehow the entire thought could be reconstructed. There was, for example, a list of characters for a play, "Doctor, Priest, Interne, Hospital Superintendent, Nurse, 2nd Nurse," and snatches of dialogue for another play.

James
Oh yes—we'll eat plenty of dinners still between this and the grave—just the same—the things gone bang.

C.
What's gone bang?

J.
Oh this—the whole so comfortable arrangement

C. (laughing)—
My dear—my dear—*comfortable!* For whom besides you has it ever been that—Oh!

Oh Kenneth's half way between poetry and philanthropy—where he wants to be a poet he turns into a philanthropist and when he wants to be a phil. he turns into a poet—and he doesnt know the technique of either job

Stephan
Clarissa—if you dont mind . . I think I'll go too—I'm I'm tired—I'll come tomorrow—Don't think I'm going to hold or . . make a row or anything—I'll

come tomorrow—see here dont look so . . so . . unhappy about it all. It wasn't particularly new—
—Exhalation—the *things out*

J.T.
Well, what are you going to do

Clarissa
Jimmy—how can I tell—Inside of five minutes what I'm going to do Anyhow I won't slam the door and go out into the night—I'll have dinner first.

C.
I'm not you know a fussy woman . . Oh its done as a make-shift—But then
what isn't a make—shift . .

No wonder I love you you're a hopeless baby—

J.
Clarissa—has it been so bad—Youve seem'd happy.

In spite of being her father I don't *get* Rosy—
Rosy's as suave as cream—you don't know she's there she's so quiet

The other papers that might have made this dialogue into a play are
missing. What remains is only the hint that Crapsey spent her time in
recapturing a genre she had unfortunately abandoned, perhaps to help
out Webster but certainly to help herself out of the gloom of Saranac
Lake. The romantic dialogue, sophisticated if disjointed, indicates her
continuing concern with the old issues of sexual relationships and
identity.

When she wrote prose, she wrote with the poetic fluidity missing
from her efforts at research.

> Never did love light up a purer flame, never did Fate conjoin two hearts
> more congenial— . . .
> The evening of their meeting was also that of their nuptials. The same
> night that brought them together as lovers, also witnessed the ceremony
> which perpetuated their union, and the morning sun beheld the completion
> of their felicity and the joy of the whole island of Medinay.[69]

The passion and simplicity of the Italian countryside is captured in this
little glimpse of her longing.

Concentration was difficult, not only because of the distraction of her
disease and her bleak future. The world's future was bleak as well, its
delicate infrastructure decaying as surely as her body. The war, developing like the vegetable garden in her lungs, filled the newspapers she read

from cover to cover. The end of July brought the Austrian declaration of war and the Russian mobilization, and Crapsey must have feared for her friends in Europe as she mourned the failure of the peace processes in which she had participated. To what extent the political situation contributed to the decline of her condition cannot be measured. Since, however, the leaders of the peace movement found the shock of war physically traumatic and some fell seriously ill,[70] one may assume that Crapsey was not encouraged by the chain of events.

Webster, exhausted from her participation in the Chicago production of her play, was in Tyringham from July to September and could do little to buoy her friend's spirits. Lowenthal, with her pragmatic maternality, was the one designated to aid Crapsey with her arrangements to return home. Then Lowenthal's father died and once again Paul stepped in.

On August 29, Crapsey took the train for Utica, leaving the hated cold behind. Paul met her there and accompanied her home. The purpose of this visit during the month of September was to consult with her family about a more congenial and less drastic institution, since her infectiousness made institutionalization necessary. Paul and Rachel would scout around potential places, perhaps southern New Jersey, where she could be near Rachel, and Adelaide, with her parents at her side, would decide what to do with the remains of her life.

Part Five

Forever and forever my soul speaks
Saying: I am thy self: Look on me—
And weep. Never and never shalt thou be
As I. Weep; for weeping and hard pain
Of loss measure joy of last visioned gain.
                    "Tears," *CP*, p. 110

Home

As she turned from Saranac Lake, Adelaide began to plan for her future as an invalid. A future as an invalid was better than no future at all, and she was hoping to find a place in pleasant surroundings that would give her more aesthetic and social stimulation than she had found during the past year. Knowing the physical effects psychological influences had upon her, she thought that being home would make her better, and for this reason was willing to bear the long, hot, complicated train ride from Saranac Lake to New York City, even though Esther, who was supposed to accompany her home, was called away by her father's death. It was a hot Saturday on August 29 and Paul met her at Utica to return together to Rochester.

Her spirits were good, and it was optimism as much as fear of another Adirondack winter that caused her to leave Saranac Lake before any specific plans had been made. Jean seemed more worried than Adelaide and had written Glenn weeks before, weighing the kinds of facilities available to a woman who could no longer be independent: "The more I think of a house for Adelaide the more dubious I become. Pipes might freeze—roof might leak—walks need shovelling—butcher forget meat—all very trying to a sick person. Adelaide leaves Saranac Saturday for a week or so in Rochester before moving on to a new place. I've just written to Dr. J. Alexander Miller in New York to see if he won't be able to suggest a place where he could take charge of the case. He has a wide variety of non-charity patients and he must know some nice places for them to live."[1]

But to Adelaide there were encouraging signs of life, the possibility of a new beginning that made the arrangements for an invalid life less crucial, less central. She passed her thirty-sixth birthday at home with her family and wrote Dr. Baldwin, "It's ever so nice to be at home for a little while, and to see my family and various other people."[2] More encouraging, Jean's intervention with *Century* magazine had succeeded and a poem was to be published—the first sign in years that she actually had some significance in the world.

The poem was not a compromise, not written in imitation of the spirit of the age. It typified her unique attitude, based on her complex hatred for hypocrisy and awareness of the history of social blindness. "The Witch" is about the eternal woman, eternally ignored and misunderstood and most dangerous when she is most creative.

When I was girl by Nilus stream
  I watched the desert stars arise;
My lover, he who dreamed the Sphinx,
  Learned all his dreaming from my eyes.

I bore in Greece a burning name,
  And I have been in Italy
Madonna to a painter-lad,
  And mistress to a Medici.

And have you heard (and I have heard)
  Of puzzled men with decorous mien,
Who judged—The wench knows far too much—
  And burnt her on the Salem green?
                    (*CP*, pp. 93–94)

The poem's antipatriarchy may have been influenced by her recent dealings with editors as well as the incredible lessons she had learned from her father's trial. The superciliousness to which a female, unconnected to an academic institution, working independently, was subjected to by More and other editors certainly influenced her attitude in the poem.

And now the poem would see light, and the title, "Adelaide Crapsey, Class Poet," which had defined her in the alumnae bulletins for the past sixteen years, since she was a sophomore, would finally be justified. It wasn't much, but as she explained to Jean, "the thinnest blade of an opening wedge is the thing that counts now, and the times are all against us."

Her optimism manifested itself in arrangements for clothes. Her wardrobe, out of fashion after her year-long isolation, had to be updated—a new hat, travelling clothes, and dresses gave almost as much pleasure as seeing Marie-Louise and Arthur.

The week that Adelaide was planning to be home stretched into a month as the correspondence concerning her future residence became more intricate. Jean wrote to Dr. Miller in New York City. Dr. Jewett, the local lung specialist, wrote to a few places. Paul inspected a place in Brown's Mills that looked promising, Dr. Baldwin wrote Dr. Hance, and Adelaide wrote Dr. Baldwin for advice.[3] "Isnt Dr. Baldwin ever so nice about it all," she wrote Jean. But Dr. Baldwin didn't respond with his suggestions or opinions about Brown's Mills, Jean became involved in the opening night of her play on Broadway (scheduled for September 28 at the Gaiety Theatre),[4] and Esther was diverted from her usual fidelity by the tragedy in her family.[5]

The need was apparent. "Cough raging and temperature moving up to a persistent 101—I must get me to a solitary life as rapidly as may be—I've not yet heard from Dr. Baldwin about Brown's Mills—I'm fairly sure he didn't know about it and would have to do some asking wh. [which] always takes time. I'm *praying* that it will be all right."[6] Her health deteriorated as she stayed in Rochester. "Of course there is nothing new," she wrote Baldwin. "It's just the old things, especially my cough, which seems to get more horrid every day."[7] The humid summer weather—the antithesis of the cold healthy climate of Saranac Lake—made breathing difficult, and Baldwin could not have been surprised at this, since even Edward Trudeau could not leave Saranac Lake without a recurrence of his tubercular symptoms. "Present breakdown worst of lot," she wrote to Jean on September 19. "I'm back in bed with a trained nurse and every bit of strength I ever had vanished—Isn't it sort of tiresome."[8] And it began to be clear that this was not a reversible situation. "I wonder whether I'll ever see the play!" she wrote Jean, hoping perhaps for reassurance.[9]

Despite all this, Adelaide was happy. The joy of Jean's success was infectious, and Adelaide too had a song on Broadway. She wrote Jean with enthusiasm: "I'm just most awfully glad about the play. The press is certanly 'good'—and Ziegfield who came here on Tuesday told Mr. Corris the play was 'a complete success' 'a perfect knockout'—and if that isn't the voice of the box office I dont know what is. So now your [sic] off!"[10] She worried over Jean, over the time Jean was spending on Adelaide's career, over Jean's headaches, over her play. It was comforting that others too had troubles and managed to accomplish something. She still had a chance.

This hope must have kept her going. All that was missing was word about her academic ventures, and the three-month-long interval since her submission of the metrics paper to the publication of the Modern Language Association might indicate their serious consideration. Then, at the beginning of October, a letter arrived from the MLA.

My dear Miss Crapsey:

If you feel that the Modern Language Association has been very neglectful of your interests, I do not wonder, and I must confess to a certain sense of humility, though our delay in sending you word with reference to your article has come about thru no fault of mine. The scattering of academicians at the end of the academic year sadly interferes with the orderly conduct of our business—and this year we hav [sic] had to contend with the European war to boot.

Your MS. has been since last June in the hands—or at least at the address—of a member of the Editorial Committee from whom I receivd [sic] a report only yesterday.

I regret to say that this report and my own opinion do not warrant me in accepting your work in its present stage for appearance in our *Publications*. We recognize with admiration the extent and the scrupulus [sic] accuracy of your labors; but we do not see that you hav [sic] arrived at results which may be cald [sic] commensurate with the labors, and which your method

may hav [*sic*] in store for the future. This negativ [*sic*] answer is perhaps due
to our own blindness, and you may be assured that we ar [*sic*] open to
conviction and that personally I am at the servis [*sic*] of any further proposition that you may care to make.[11]

Even though the tone was supercilious and self-righteous, W. H. Howard,
the secretary of the MLA who signed the letter, had justified, accurate,
and well-considered reasons for rejection. In her weakened state, however, Adelaide could probably not comprehend that what was wrong
with her work was her deference, her hesitation to draw conclusions in
the face of greater, recognized, licensed scholars. Who was she to call
attention to a serious gap in the scholarly approach to poetry? A tubercular female with almost no scholarly credentials and little academic
support, a woman who had spent much of her life physically isolated
from the mainstream of intellectual life and the last year of her life isolated from everyone.

And if she did recognize that her deference was the defect of her paper, what good would that recognition do? She had no strength and
would not live long enough to alter it, to add the few key lines which
would make the whole work understandable, to actuate the potential of
the paper. "I am thy self," she had written in a poem. "Look on me—
/ And weep. Never and never shalt thou be / As I."[12]

On October 4 her situation worsened suddenly. Two nurses were put
on duty. Her coughing increased and breathing became so difficult she
was unable to lie down. She asked that her beloved books be removed.
The flowers in the room choked her and had to be taken away. Fresh air
offered some relief, so she was set out to sleep on the porch, a back
porch that was not enclosed but otherwise resembled the porch adjoin-
ing her room at Saranac Lake. There was no relief from coughing, no
relief from consciousness. Sleep evaded her as coughs wracked her
body, and she could only breathe in an upright position. But no longer
strong enough to hold herself up, she was forced to lean forward over
the shoulder of Ferne Hincher, her night nurse, and Ferne would sit,
immobile, cradling Adelaide while she slept. "Severn . . . lift me up,"

Keats had said in his last days, and surely Adelaide recalled the end of which she had written.[13]

  . . . "Child,
Even thy careful nurse,
I lift thee in my arms
For greater ease."

With so little respite in sleep, she faced her death for days with open eyes. Dr. Ruggles, who attended her, noted this and was impressed. He wrote the Crapsey family afterward of "her noble courage in facing her illness," and emphasized that it was "not sustained by the hopeful illusions of most tuberculosis patients."[14] It was this clear-sightedness that impressed all those about her, that would be most remembered.

She had hoped for unconsciousness, as with Keats—a dignified and noble death.

  . . . and while
Thy heart still beats, place my
Cool fingers of oblivion on
Thine eyes and close them for
Eternity. Thou shalt
Pass sleeping, nor know
When sleeping ceases. Yet still
A little while thy breathing lasts,
Gradual is faint and fainter.
                (*CP*, p. 68)

But her last days would not be characteristic of Keats. "There isn't anything to do to help," Jean wrote Glenn. "If they gave her enough morphine to relieve the pain, it would kill her."[15] Her consciousness was accompanied by the enormous frustration of not having completed anything, with not having anything final to show for all her endeavors. "It's too much," she wept, "just as I have my work, I can't do it."[16]

All those she loved surrounded her in those last days. Esther, still in Rochester before the fall semester, came twice, and Adelaide whispered, "Nice E."[17] Mary Lewis too came to wait in Rochester. Jean received a summoning telegram and, leaving her Broadway opening, took the midnight train. Rachel, Paul, and Algernon joined Arthur and Marie-Louise. "And here they sit," Jean wrote Glenn, "listening to her moaning and waiting for her to die." Even Claude Bragdon left his new wife, Eugenie, to see Adelaide.[18] And this was good, for she could recognize them all and give them a feeling that they were needed and useful. "She recognized me and talked a little in whispers," Jean wrote. "I staid all day at the house and went in and sat with her three times when she asked for me."[19]

But it was bad. Never desiring the spotlight, never seeking to be singled out even for her talents, she was doubly embarrassed now to be the center of attention for so repugnant a reason. Her attitude was apologetic, deferential, polite, and concerned with others even on her deathbed, and even her nurses were impressed with her unconditional love and concern for others. Ferne Hincher remembered Adelaide as having had great consideration for the feelings of others, despite the gravity of her illness. Even with the greatest deference and consideration for others she knew she was the cause of pain to all those she loved. "Poor Mrs. Crapsey is worn out with the nervous strain. It is the most ghastly thing I have ever seen!" Jean, who had never had much sympathy for Adelaide's mother, wrote.[20]

Adelaide had imagined death as an isolated confrontation and written of it in these terms in "The Lonely Death":

> In the cold I will rise, I will bathe
> In waters of ice; myself
> Will shiver, and shrive myself,
> Alone in the dawn, and anoint
> Forehead and feet and hands;
> I will shutter the windows from light,
> I will place in their sockets the four
> Tall candles and set them a-flame
> In the grey of the dawn; and myself
> Will lay myself straight in my bed,
> And draw the sheet under my chin.
>   (*CP*, p. 96)

She had wanted to take control, had never conceived of death—or life for that matter—as a gentle suitor taking her to eternity but as another one of those inevitable aspects of existence that struggled against the individual to negate his significance. Now, "wasted away till she is just like a little child,"[21] she could do nothing but await the inevitable end. There was no personal confrontation—everyone else was doing the work for her. She could just lie in bed and suffer.

On Tuesday Jean looked at her best friend, huddled in the arms of the nurse, saw that the situation was "horrible," and wished that she would die. That night Adelaide was placed on the porch. With Ferne, Adelaide looked at the moon and remembered the Italian moon-charm about which she had written a love poem. "You must say it nine times, curtseying, and then wish," she had explained in parentheses in the poem. She had written it in an obvious state of infatuation:

In rose-pale, fading blue of twilight sky,
   See, the new moon's thin crescent shining clear;
Nine times I'll curtsey murmuring mystic words,—
   And wish good fortune to our love, my dear.

(*CP*, p. 111)

Now she looked up at the moon and tried the charm: "O mia Luna! Porta mi Fortuna!"[22]

If she thought of days of love and hope at all, it must have added to the poignancy of loss. For Adelaide, like Jean, now knew that a quick death would be the happiest wish come true. Keats had made the distinction: "there is a great difference between going off in warm blood like Romeo, and making one's exit like a frog in a frost."[23]

She lingered. "She suffered terribly all night and began to sink this morning," Jean wrote. "I talked to her a little at eleven; then she became partially unconscious, so that her suffering at the end was not so terrible. We could not wish for anything else. Both lungs had collapsed and every breath hurt her. We had been hoping and praying for the end ever since yesterday morning."[24]

Adelaide died at three o'clock. By four Jean and Esther had presented to her parents the typewritten copy of *Verse*. The two friends explained to the Crapseys that Adelaide had not shown them the poems so that they might be spared the impotent knowledge of the suffering she was enduring. "Yes, it was like the child to try to spare us," they replied.[25]

Her ashes were placed in a receptacle presented by Adelaide's classmates of Vassar and buried in the family plot at Mount Hope Cemetery. It was a small plot for so large a family, and the graves were modest and simple. Algernon Crapsey set the tone his daughter would have wanted as he spoke over her grave:

> And death does not startle us, because death is a part of the plan. Our Father causes us to be born and to die, and one event is just as natural as the other. Goethe says, "Death cannot be an evil, because death is universal." To die is to change one's state; to go, "either to the country of the blessed God, or else to enter into that great unconsciousness which is the source of all unconsciousness, to enter into that sleep out of which comes all awakening." What is to come to pass after our death does not disturb us any more than what came to pass before our birth. Before we were born we existed in the thought of God, and after we die we shall still have our place in that Infinite Intelligence.[26]

For someone seeking symbolism and connection, her grave bordering the street was strikingly congruent with her room in Saranac Lake overlooking the cemetery. But for Adelaide, this would have had no significance. She had arranged her poems for that purpose.

THE IMMORTAL RESIDUE

Inscription for my verse

Wouldst thou find my ashes? Look
In the pages of my book;
And as these thy hand doth turn,
Know here is my funeral urn.

(*CP*, p. 97)

Afterword: The Urn

> They are the work of a lady
> who was obsessed with the
> necessity of writing well; we
> should not let them
> disappear.[1]

The poems selected for publication and their arrangement were vital to Crapsey. Like dots on a chart, the poems illustrate the progress of a comprehension about death and poetry, one that did not occur chronologically but retrospectively, and a close sequential reading of the choice of poems selected in the order she determined suggests a growing awareness that may have helped the dying poet cope with and accept her fate, one which proposes an unusual theory of poetry and death.

In concentrating on the order of these poems she felt compelled to leave out those poems that did not fit in with the manuscript. Ignoring quality, beauty, and profundity, she put in only those poems that illustrated the precise progress she wanted. "To the Dead in the Graveyard by My Window," one of her best-known poems, is missing from this book, as are many others quoted here in preceding pages. And yet many of

304

these excluded poems were copied over and accented with as much painstaking attention as those selected to give to Jean Webster as a "Presentation Piece," a complete manuscript to present for publication.

Given Crapsey's meticulous care, it seems only fitting that a study of her life should be concluded with the significance of the poems in their order. And even a superficial overview of the poems reveals patterns, patterns that often alter the initial significance, the biographical context of the poem. A poem written during a period of anticipation, of expectation for novelty and development in life, may reflect accurately the mood of the time. Ten years later, if it is placed alongside a poem of utter disappointment, the emphasis is altered by the experiential contrast, the "meaning" may be inverted. The following analysis should be read in this light—as a reworking of life experiences in the context of the anticipated closure of death.

It is important to reiterate this point: although the poems are the same ones previously quoted to illustrate biographical phenomena, they are to be understood in a completely different way in a poetic context. The raw material of biographical events, reworked into art, are in this "Presentation Piece" an artistic and philosophical inquiry with a significance of its own.

There are three parts to the manuscript, three divisions which cannot be explained chronologically, since the dates of composition are uncertain and there are other poems written between these poems that Crapsey did not select for inclusion. An initial reading suggests that the poet attempted a formal and thematic arrangement: (1) Part I—free verse "portraits of life," (2) cinquains on various subjects, and (3) Part II—assorted forms and topics connected with fairy tales and death. However, her organization of the poems into three parts also indicates a division of types of poems and of forms which describe and illustrate a spiritual progress. The first part consists primarily of free verse and seemingly free but poetically conventional answers to general questions of life. These answers prove unsatisfying once outside conventional frameworks, however, and lead to the need for a consciously different approach—to poetry and to existence—in the next section. The second part is a series of cinquains. The alteration of subject providing the contrast to the rigidly single form, the cinquains are breathless observations seeking, through observation, the accumulation of phenomena and poetic organization, answers to the theological questions of existence. The third section includes poems of varying lengths, form, and subject matter, held together by the subject suggested in the beginning and concluding poems, the search for a meaning to life and death through poetic inquiries, although not through poetry. The writing of poetry, then, becomes in the course of the sequence a means of understanding some aspects of happiness, existence, and immortality and ceases to be the media of fulfillment and immortality itself.

I

Part I is composed of three long poems: "Birth Moment," "The Mother Exultant," and "John Keats (February 1820–February 1821)."[2] The poems cover the major plateaus of life; their order and their formlessness are the most salient aspects. They do not seem to be superior in any way to many of the poems Crapsey rejected for this piece but are selected for the relatively conventional "coverage" of life and death and the concept of time as a series of relatively static stages the individual must pass through, so that the first word of this section is "birth" and the last "died."

The birth described in this poem is that of Aphrodite, identifying the awakening of life with that of love. Desire and love are equated with life, freedom, and union with nature.

> And she who runs shall be
> Married to blue of summer skies at noon,
> Companion to green fields,
> Held bride to subtle fragrance and of all sweet sound,
> Belovèd of the stars,
> And wanton mistress to the veering winds.

The birth of life/love, moreover, is paralleled with the awakening of individual desire, the "keenest personal moment" before an anticipated sensual kiss.

When mouth unkissed turns eager-slow and tremulous
Towards lover's mouth,
That tremulous and eager-slow
Droops down to it:
But breathless space of breath or two
Lies in between
Before the mouth upturned and mouth down-drooped
Shall meet and make the kiss.

Anticipatory desire here is described in a kind of slow motion, as if it were the most fulfilling moment of all, and it is appropriate that Crapsey's introductory poem emphasizes this hunger for life yet unknown, the innocent anticipation of a world that too soon in the poems becomes unattainable to her and yet for which she does not cease to hunger.

The "clichaic images,"[3] the archaic language, the unself-conscious passion, all may have been written in innocence or naiveté, but Crapsey's later choice to include this poem in her *Verse* as an introduction indicates her intention to utilize precisely these poetic naivetés to illustrate poetic naissance and to contrast with the emotional and technical sophistication that follows. Here, and elsewhere in what Susan Smith had titled Crapsey's "Presentation Piece," positioning of a poem forces reinterpretation. In the last verse, for example, the speaker addresses Aphrodite directly, associating herself with the passionate solitary birth of the goddess and attempting to identify with this eternity in the moment of life granted to her—to unite the personal with the mythic.

O Aphrodite!
O Aphrodite, hear!
Hear my wrung cry flame upward poignant-glad . . .
This is my time for me.
I too am young;
I too am all of love!

But the second poem continues the poetic journey through life to describe fruition, the time of motherhood, of vintage, "the wine of the dream of life," contrasting with and giving perspective to the poem it follows.

"The Mother Exultant," the second poem, uses echoes of Isaiah, the Song of Songs, and the story of Mary in an attempt to eternalize and mythicize the moment of fruition. The poem begins and ends with the same verse, an image that could, as Butscher has pointed out, "be a verbal mirror for one of Delacroix's lush paintings."[4]

> Joy! Joy! Joy!
> The hills are glad,
> The valleys re-echo with merriment,
> In my heart is the sound of laughter,
> And my feet dance to the time of it;
> Oh, little son, carried light on my shoulder,
> Let us go laughing and dancing through the live days,
> For this is the hour of the vintage,
> When man gathereth for himself the fruits of the vineyard.

Butscher's painterly parallel is appropriate for more than a comparison of images. We are presented with a tableau in which time is in harmony and everything fits together. There is no contrast, as there will be in later poems, between the natural, religious, spiritual, physical, and emotional world. Furthermore, this momentary unity is one of fruition, and fruition, creation, is here eternal:

> Shall we not rejoice
> Who have made eternal
> The days of our living.

Poetry is also the underlying subject of this poem—the fulfillment of eternity from the materials of the temporal:

> Now is the wonder accomplished;
> Out of the heart of the living grape
> Hath the hand of my belovèd
> Wrung the wine of the dream of life.

The thematic echoes are of Keats, and Crapsey couples this early poem with a later one dedicated to Keats. This final poem, addressed to the poet not at his death but in the final year of his life, when he was confronting the end of his productivity and potency and wrote to Charles Brown of feeling himself "leading a posthumous existence" (November 30, 1820), concludes the progress of the mind's awakening. Immediate knowledge of death changes and reinterprets the significance of the images of the previous poems as well as the concept of time as a series of frozen tableaus or stages of life.

The loose, unrhymed, exclamatory lines of the first two poems are replaced by a stark, four-stress line form that drums in a truth as much by contrast with the rhythms of the previous poems as by the beat of the four-stress line and the driving force of the repetition:

> With dumb, wide look
> Thou, impotent, dost feel
> Impotence creeping on
> Thy potent soul.

The speaker addressing Keats follows him to his death when destiny and nature, eternal, rise above the temporal identity of the poet and his poetry.

The great pyramid grave of Caius Cestius, inscribed with its list of inheritors, was one which Crapsey, as a student of architecture in Rome, certainly studied, perhaps on one of her weekly walks with Professor Carter's course on Roman inscriptions.[5] Unlike the inscription of, for example, Ozymandias, this inscription points forward to a new generation, one that will continue to carry on and to modify the qualities of the dead.

> Rest. And you others . . All.
> Grave-fellows in
> Green place. Here grows
> Memorial every spring's
> Fresh grass and here
> Your marking monument
> Was built for you long, long
> Ago when Caius Cestius died.

Out of biographical context, the emphasis in this poem is upon the dead poet and the power to renew life granted by the poems.

The starkness, sadness, and sense of responsibility in this poem qualify the exuberance of the two previous celebrations, and this poem to Keats seems to prepare the reader, both by its form and by its thematic revelation, for Part II. The cinquains of Part II are characterized by a terseness and a refusal to look through any softening lenses at reality, including the lenses of poetic convention, that are introduced in this address to Keats on the reality of death and personal oblivion. The poetic, romantic approach to life and poetry may have shown the eternality of Keats's significance, but it does so by avoiding the human pain of dying and poetic impotence with which the poem began. Keats the poet is immortalized while Keats the man suffered great agonies and then disappeared. In this context the concept of the immortality of verse has one major drawback—the human being and all he experienced vanish. Because of this unwillingness to deny the reality of existence, a phenomenal approach is attempted in the second part, one which concentrates upon actual data and actual existence.

II

It is no accident that Crapsey created the verse form of the cinquain nor that she used this new form here. When the old poetic answers do not satisfy the hunger for a relationship between poetry and life, a new approach is needed, and the cinquain provides this approach. The 1,2,3,4,1 stress of the cinquain frames and forms the poem, allowing no space for poetic images, poetic language, and the looseness or sentimentality of the poems of Part I, but only descriptions, contrast, and a spareness which leave room for the reader. The contrast is intentional, and the lack of commentary encourages the reader's innovation, the biographer's suppositions, the relating of parallel events. The single stress of the introductory and concluding lines, for example, suggests a surrounding void, a quiet out of which the observation is made, as in the first cinquain, "November Night." Here the first word emerges from an observation made in the previous silence, and the last line is a death, a conclusion after which no action can follow and no sound be added:

> Listen . .
> With faint dry sound,
> Like steps of passing ghosts,
> The leaves, frost-crisp'd, break from the trees
> And fall.

The first poem of the cinquain sequence begins with the word "Listen," and, indeed, these poems demand an active reader who will heed both the voice of the speaker and the objects and scenes described. In this first poem, "November Night," the speaker asks for the reader's attention to the sounds of the leaves.

We hear both poem and leaves, both the beautiful artifice and the object which it describes. They are interdependent: a part of the appreciation of the poem is the accuracy of the imitation. But poem and object are interchangeable in more than one way: we are asked to listen to the poems as leaves, the individual perfect five-line verses like maple leaves, breaking off one by one as the individual observation is supplanted by another. Each poem is a separate, different observation, obsolete when it is over, superseded by the next poem, the next mood, the next answer.

Not only are the cinquains different from the previous poems in their openness to interpretation, but also the shift from long verse to cinquains and/or from progressive poems to individual ones indicates a different approach to the entire concept of time. Time in the cinquains consists of a series of frozen isolated moments, each moment an opportunity for deciphering a small secret of life, although the deciphering may not necessarily be significant or eternal. In some ways, the "data" presented in some of the cinquains might be likened to the syllabic charts Crapsey so laboriously constructed in her study of metrics. She was certain there was significance to the syllable counting on which she spent long years, but until she could chart the results in some objective order, the precise nature of the significance could not be read.[6] The cinquain series, then, appears as the charting of a series of data points in the expectation of an eventually revealed significance.

With swift
Great sweep of her
Magnificent arm my pain
Clanged back the doors that shut my soul
From life.

"Release," the almost concrete poem that joins with "November Night" in introducing the cinquain sequence, presents the grand gesture of Pain, nobly granting temporary release of the Soul from imprisonment in agony. The awakening of senses that occurs in the first few cinquains must surely be linked to this release. That this reaction to the release from pain is not the only one possible can easily be seen in a comparison between "Release" and a later cinquain describing the same event, "Languor After Pain," in which a very different reaction occurs. Release here is an emotional awareness of the physical and temporal limitations to observation, of the temporary stay allotted the speaker, and the necessity of racing through those doors of life while they remain open.

"Triad," which follows, describes "Three silent things," objects which do not "communicate," do not give forth their meaning:

These be
Three silent things:
The falling snow . . the hour
Before the dawn . . the mouth of one
Just dead.

Despite the gnomic quality of this poem, its significance is amplified and altered by the three cinquains placed just after it which describe, one by one, the sounds of these "three silent things." "Snow" is an exhultation of nature that might have been written by William Carlos Williams—the direct address, the exhortation to the reader, the sensual joy of the aroma of nature.

Look up . . .
From bleakening hills
Blows down the light, first breath
Of wintry wind . . . look up, and scent
The snow!

Reminiscent of Psalm 121, "I will lift up mine eyes unto the hills / From whence cometh my help," this poem attests to an important affirmation, visual, olfactory, and theological, in the apparently silent snow. There is, of course, an important difference between this poem and its source: "My help cometh from the Lord, which made heaven and earth." Illumination in this cinquain comes not from the invisible, abstract creator, but the world apprehensible through the five senses.

The hour before dawn is also not silent. The ruthless, "tearless" observer of "Anguish" is enjoined to weep precisely at that moment after the long watch of night. Perhaps the perception is of the contrast between the day's cycle and the chronological progress of the individual life. In any event, the silence of dawn is broken by the human anguish, just as the silence of snow has been broken by the breathless affirmation of the poet.

Although the third cinquain to follow "Triad," "Trapped," does not mention death, it portrays the "deadened" reaction, the inability to perceive significance in universal cyclicity.

> Well and
> If day on day
> Follows, and weary year
> On year . . and ever days and years . .
> Well?

These three poems, then, do more than negate the "truth" of "Triad." Silence inspires human speech, and it inspires three entirely different reactions: joy melts into despair and then into apathy.

"Moon Shadows," as if in answer to the "Well?" which, concluding "Trapped," asks for the ultimate direction of a directionless existence, deals with the natural quiet of death. Here there is no reaction to phenomena, no noise, and the "triad" of reactions follows a direction that leads to this silence—joy, despair, apathy, nothing.

> Still as
> On windless nights
> The moon-cast shadows are,
> So still will be my heart when I
> Am dead.

The first mention of the death of the self, "Moon Shadows" seems to lead directly into the next cinquain. The question "Susanna and the Elders" answers is that of Job, "Why does suffering touch the good, the beautiful?" The tragedy is that it is precisely those praised virtues which are the cause of the fall, "For that / She is beautiful, delicate: / Therefore."

> But me
> They cannot touch,
> Old age and death . . the strange
> And ignominious end of old
> Dead folk!

This next poem, "Youth," is an answer to the elders, a vain, naive denial of their vindictive power. The elders become Old Age, and the story of Susanna an allegory for the temporal destruction of nature and youth.

The following poem, "Languor After Pain," recalling the delicacy and beauty of Susanna, emphasizes vulnerability and transience.

> Pain ebbs,
> And like cool balm,
> An opiate weariness
> Settles on eye-lids, on relaxed
> Pale wrists.

The "me," the youthful Susanna, the pale wrists, all have been touched, and, although the moment of pain is so great it itself cannot be described, the initial reaction to this overwhelming force is a new passivity, an "opiate weariness" forced by the reality of pain.

As if in anticipation of "biographical" readings of the cinquains, the next poem, "The Guarded Wound," universalizes the significance of this knowledge.

> If it
> Were lighter touch
> Than petal of flower resting
> On grass oh still too heavy it were,
> Too heavy!

The specific agonies of the poet are negated, and the recognition of universal doom neither lightens nor rationalizes the burden.

"Winter" is a confrontation with this recognition, the actual fact of future death.

> The cold
> With steely clutch
> Grips all the land . . alack
> The little people in the hills
> Will die!

This exclamation of death leads into "Night Winds," which follows.

> The old
> Old winds that blew
> When chaos was, what do
> They tell the clattered trees that I
> Should weep?

"Night Winds," with its echoes of pregenesis, suggests a lack of meaning, a reason for mourning, a contrast to the ordered significant life of the God-created world. The tree in the poem which follows, however, is not one of the clattered trees that have absorbed the chaotic message of the old wind. The arbutus is "cool," "virginal," unconcerned with the terrifying message of insignificance. The arbutus has its own significance. It exists for its own sake, and through this aestheticism escapes the weeping of other trees. The nadir of cosmic order and control here leads to the perfection of self-control.

> Not spring's
> Thou art, but hers,
> Most cool, most virginal,
> Winter's, with thy faint breath, thy snows
> Rose-tinged.

"Arbutus" is the first poem that suggests the creation of the self as an artifact: the next seven cinquains deal with the distancing process between self and body as the self attempts association with the elevated, mysterious, indifferent moon.

It is the classical motivation of "Arbutus" that brings "Roma Aeterna" into a group of poems that seem otherwise concerned almost myopically with the immediate environment. The recollection of the warm sun of Rome and the awareness of the historical and mythic continuity of this warm, "creative" atmosphere contrast sharply with the ancient chaos of "Night Winds." The classical seems infinitely more attractive than the Christian, the aloofness and unconcern of the Greek deities superior to the agonies of Christianity.

The next poem seems to be a *nonsequitur,* but the choice of roses in the cinquain, entitled "He's killed the may and he's laid her by / To bear the red rose company," is directly related to the direction of the previous poem.

> Not thou,
> White rose, but thy
> Ensanguined sister is
> The dear companion of my heart's
> Shed blood.

In the face of suffering, the white rose, Christian resignation, is rejected in favor of the "ensanguined sister." This allegorical interpretation of the poem also makes the title comprehensible.

The next cinquain, perhaps the most exquisite in conversational tone and compression, is usually considered in a biographical context.

> AMAZE
>
> I know
> Not these my hands
> And yet I think there was
> A woman like me once had hands
> Like these.

The hands here remain the same; it is the concept of self which has changed. Within the context of the cinquains, the change has been a drastic one. From the conventional attitude toward birth and death the poet has turned to embrace the facts of reality and the knowledge that actuality has a significance which alters with perception.

In this contrast, "Shadow" describes the photographic technique the poet uses on reality:

A-sway,
On red rose,
A golden butterfly . .
And on my heart a butterfly
Night-wing'd.

Photographing the reality, the golden butterfly, the poet also perceives the negative, the shadow, the equal and antithetical truth of the night-wing, and the knowledge of fickle transience. This is not a cause for depression but defiance. The image of "night-wing'd" butterfly is transformed into Fate's "grey" in the next poem, "Fate Defied," and is worn "As it / Were tissue of silver."

Like a series of time-exposed snapshots, the poems from "Shadow" to "Fate Defied," "Madness," "The Warning," and "The Saying of Il Haboul" shift the reaction slightly each time to the same phenomenon. The pride of controlling fate by accepting it in "Fate Defied" becomes an Ophelialike masochism in "Madness":

Burdock,
Blue aconite,
And thistle and thorn . . of these
Singing I wreathe my pretty wreath
O'death.

The wreath of thorns implicates Christ in the mad embrace of suffering, as if the "control" sought over fate in the previous poems has become an insane attempt to approach divinity, to take over not only one's fate but all fate. "The Warning" which follows seems to be this recognition.

Just now,
Out of the strange
Still dusk . . as strange, as still . .
A white moth flew. Why am I grown
So cold?

Identifying with the smallness and insignificance of the moth, the poet has understood the folly and extremity of the previous direction. The pathetic fallacy is a form of heresy as well as a poetic mistake.

The warning of the moth is also a reminder of the unknown, uncontrollable elements of the universe. And since this is an incomprehensible world, the attitude toward it cannot be one of comprehension and control. For this reason the themes now become oriental, philosophical. "The Saying of Il Haboul" is a lesson:

> My tent
> A vapour that
> The wind dispels and but
> As dust before the wind am I
> Myself.

This quietly resigned poem, "The Saying of Il Haboul," leads to a triumph against all odds, the mythification of the self. If I am nothing, I can be made into anything, even a myth. From an identification with the victorious Judith (in "The Death of Holofernes"), she progresses to willing herself a mythic being in "Laurel in the Berkshires":

> Sea-foam
> And coral! Oh, I'll
> Climb the great pasture rocks
> And dream me mermaid in the sun's
> Gold flood.

She finally completes an identification she had previously made in "Fate Defied" by joining her frail self with the moon:

> NIAGARA
>   Seen on a night in November
>
> How frail
> Above the bulk
> Of crashing water hangs,
> Autumnal, evanescent, wan,
> The moon.

The irony is that the moon, which seems so frail above the torrent of

Niagara, is at least as eternal as the torrent. The evanescent speaker, too, like "dust before the wind," is also enormous in stature.

"The Grand Canyon," so much less successful than Niagara, is necessary in the progress of mythification. One step beyond and the beautiful becomes grotesque, the elevation of self becomes braggadocio, and mythification becomes caricature.

> By Zeus!
> Shout word of this
> To the eldest dead! Titans,
> Gods, Heroes, come who have once more
> A home!

It is an exaggeration that reveals in "Now Barabbas Was a Robber" the guile that has been used by the poet in self-comfort. Recalling the choice of the people of Israel to save the thief from the cross instead of Jesus, Crapsey illustrates the error of her own way. The wrong hero, the wrong ideal, has been preserved. The aggrandizement of the self has proven a dead end. A greater solution must be found. And the cinquains end with a plaintive honest description of a weary human being.

REFUGE IN DARKNESS

> With night's
> Dim veil and blue
> I will cover my eyes,
> I will bind close my eyes that are
> So weary.

If vision had been so significant in the cinquains as a means for comprehension and acceptance, it is now rejected. With the same image of night, used before to emphasize her unique perspective of shadow, Crapsey blacks out the experience. Reminiscent of "Languor After Pain," this poem is a reminder of the tremendous effort to comprehend made in the cinquains and the great disappointment at their lack of success.

From an attempt to perceive and chart reality and the self as it progresses, the cinquain sequence moves to a negation of the significance of the self as perceiver as well as the self as subject. The attempt to create a lasting monument to the poet and the poet's vision has ended in failure.

III

The similarities in style and theme of the poems in Part I indicate immediately the possibility of a single sequential reading for all the poems; the identity of form and the general thematic conformity in the cinquains enable the poems to be read as a unit; the third section, entitled Part II, is more complex and, while certain themes are developed in this section, a single, linear development is more difficult to trace. This lack of a linear development is directly related to the conclusion of the cinquain section, the failure of the logical and progressive vision of the poet.

The entire sequence explores the concept of self-identity, before and after death, and does not come to traditional Christian or standard poetic conclusions. The poet as self (so apparent in the cinquains) disappears early in this sequence and emerges only at the end of the book as ashes. The poet is what she is, a simple human being who wrote, died, and was cremated. The daughter of the author of *The Last of the Heretics*, who denied the divinity of the Son and emphasized his humanity, brings her final vision to conclusions not unlike those of her father. The actual reality of existence, with all its limitations, is far more worthy of consideration than all the comforting mythification of truth. Myths are explored and discarded methodically but almost in random order in this section.

The first poem, addressed to Walter Savage Landor and dated "Fiesole, 1909," sets a key note:

Ah, Walter, where you lived I rue
　These days come all too late for me;
What matter if her eyes are blue
　Whose rival is Persephone?

In the framework of Landor's vision, the blue of his love's eyes are no contest to the force of death, as emotions and experience cannot be said to be given eternal significance by their transformation into art. As the opening poem to the third and final section of poems, it sets the tone, the refusal to be comforted with notions of immortalizing the spirit in verse and, later, in religion. That the two contexts are interchangeable becomes evident in the progress of the poems.

In this context, the title of the second poem, "The Pledge," seems perverse.

> White doves of Cytherea, by your quest
>   Across the blue Heaven's bluest highest air,
> And by your certain homing to Love's breast,
>   Still to be true and ever true—I swear.

To vow "Still to be true and ever true—I swear" in the same form of poem and following such an ironic quatrain is either to be entirely insensitive to context or purposely defiant. The pledge is not to immortalize love, however, but simply to love, despite the uselessness of poetry in fixing love forever. "Still" is not only "yet" but also "despite all." This defiant affirmation is followed by a poem describing the generous forgetfulness sown by "Hypnos, God of Sleep," and the twenty succeeding poems endeavor to ignore the need for immortality, to concentrate on the life framed by parentheses, life with no significance outside itself.

If death is the only end, then needs and responsibilities are diminished. The fourth poem extolls the freedom inherent in this realization in the image of the gay, impoverished traveller.

EXPENSES

> Little my lacking fortunes show
>   For this to eat and that to wear;
> Yet laughing, Soul, and gaily go!
>   An obol pays the Stygian fare.

By placing the happy traveller in a mythic context not only does Crapsey increase the contrast between the insignificant self and the vast human condition but she also manages a classic removal from immediate situations and from the personal speaker.

The next poem, "Adventure," removes the same thought from the mythic and makes it so individual and personal that the effect is childish, naive.

Sun and wind and beat of sea,
Great lands stretching endlessly . . .
Where be bonds to bind the free?
All the world was made for me!

As Edward Butscher notes, "Adventure" "denies the existence of . . . bitterness with a kind of hymn to free will, to the broad horizons offered by 'Sun and wind and beat of sea,' "[7] and the hymnlike quality is reinforced by the strict *a-a-a-a* rhyme scheme. Its conclusion, however, marks a return to an adolescent optimism that achieves ironic depth only in biographic retrospect: "All the world was made for me!"

In this context, the epigram that follows seems a stern reminder. "On Seeing Weather Beaten Trees" suggests that consequences exist and are visible, that the freedom of the previous poem is not without consequences: "Is it as plainly in our living shown, / By slant and twist, which way the wind hath blown?" Wind, that in itself is invisible and whose existence may be denied, nevertheless can be seen in its effects on the tree.

If consequences exist, responsibility exists, and the greatness of freedom is diminished. Predictably, "Warning to the Mighty" carries the old message of "Ozymandias": "When the pomp is passed away, / 'Here's a King,' the worms shall say," for this is another limitation on the freedom and greatness of the individual.

The wind, the sorrow, and the world are diminished in power and color in the next poem, directly as a result of the previous illuminations. The colors in "Oh Lady, Let the Sad Tears Fall" are silver, the wind like a "soft sigh," death, not violent or grand, as in "Warning to the Mighty," but the pale death of roses, and the emotions gentle, passive, unlike the exuberant previous poems. Coming after this poem, "Dirge" develops the same spirit. The ebullience brought on by awareness of a world of no afterlife, no consequences, and no responsibilities is replaced by the recollection of such an emptiness. The repeated "Never" is the underlying reason for the dirge.

Never the nightingale,
    Oh, my dear,
Never again the lark

Thou wilt hear;
Though dusk and the morning still
Tap at thy window-sill,
Though ever love call and call
Thou wilt not hear at all,
My dear, my dear.

Time, in this context, takes on an ominous significance. Leading no-where, time becomes cyclical, meaningless.

Every day,
Every day,
Tell the hours
By their shadows,
By their shadows.

"The Sun-Dial" is a straight description of this theological state, but, as Butscher notes, "the simple repetitions achieve a persuasive Gothic atmosphere, implying futile, dreaded, unseen Poe-like depths."[8] The depths are those of meaninglessness, the theological and poetic void to which the poems have been leading, and it is not surprising that the poem to follow is a denial of the Resurrection.

In a cave born
(Mary said)
In a cave is
My Son burièd.

The singular lack of comfort she could take in her religion (unique for a young woman of her time), particularly at a period when Crapsey carried the secret of her uncurable tuberculosis, may well have intensified this examination of "myths" in her poems and increased the pain of their failures.

The next poem, "Autumn," describes "Autumn, the maiden" wistfully turning back as she prepares to leave. A relatively standard image, the maiden whose refusal is "lovelier / . . than / Yielding" nevertheless takes on greater significances in context. A backward gesture of regret coupled with the previous giant step away from a belief in divine birth and resurrection is both touching and appropriate.

The next two poems, "Ah me . . . Alas" and "Perfume of Youth," make little sense out of context. "Ah me . . . Alas" consists of two speeches, the first by "(He)," the second by "(She)." This is neither a love nor a seduction poem, however. "He" describes "my love's heart" as a "frail flower," growing "on the cliff's edge," "aloof, apart." "She" turns his description, presumably of her heart, into one of his own. It is his heart that he has discovered by turning "dreaming into faith." The poems which follow develop the concept of the self-seeing self, the creation of a deceptive image of the idealized lover, and indeed all the world from the limited vision of the self.

In "Perfume of Youth" the speaker is the quintessential young woman, perhaps the feminine inspiration or muse for poety, whose gift of youth is to be given to all; although in "Vendor's Song," three poems later, no one wants to purchase the vendor's wares of knowledge. The speaker of "Perfume of Youth" generously pours a rare ointment that gives "look of youth . . . Oh, golden hair." The vendor in the later poem begs to be allowed to share these benefits, to dispense them to others, but is ignored.

> My songs to sell, sweet maid!
>   I pray you buy.
> This one will teach you Lilith's lore,
>   And this what Helen knew,
> And this will keep your gold hair gold,
>   And this your blue eyes blue;
> Sweet maid, I pray you buy!
>
> *Oh, no, she will not buy.*

The poem concludes with the petulant lines:

> *If I'd as much money as I could tell,*
> *I never would cry my songs to sell.*
> *I never would cry my songs to sell.*

Between these two radically different attitudes to the same story and theme are two poems which depict well-known characters in moments of reflection. Out of the limitations of the tale these snapshots of Rapunzel and Narcissus allow reinterpretations of classical situations.

"Rapunzel" is the one who was given in youth, possessing the golden hair of "Perfume of Youth" and "Vendor's Song," but the result of her beauty is emptiness and isolation. Hidden from all eyes, alone, she is forced to look out in the night, waiting for whoever comes, lover or witch.

All day, all day I brush
   My golden strands of hair;
All day I wait and wait . .
   Ah, who is there?

Who calls? Who calls? The gold
   Ladder of my long hair
I loose and wait . . and wait . .
Ah, who is there?

She left at dawn . . I am blind
   In the tangle of my long hair . .
Is it she? the witch? the witch?
   Ah, who is there?

Her similarity to Narcissus in the next poem is clear.

"Boy, lying
Where the long grass
Edges the pool's brim,
What do you watch
There in the water? the blue
Colour of Heaven
Mirrored, repeated? the brown
Tree-trunks and branches
Waveringly imaged? These,
Boy, do you watch?"
"Nay but mine eyes;
Nay but the trouble
Deep in mine eyes."

Both are closed in the self, although the situation of Narcissus is far more internal; Rapunzel cannot see and Narcissus chooses not to look at anything but his own pain.

The group of mythic figures concludes with "Avis." With "Avis" there is the creation of a stereotype, the perfect medieval innocent, and the shattering of it. The first part creates the image, the second, different in tone and subject, destroys the value of this image. The last two lines, "Go thou from thence of thy pity! / Thou lov'st not me," suggest the lack of value in perfection when it is self-enclosed.

The self-centeredness of the previous six poems, brought on by the awareness of the lack of significance outside the self, is stopped, as it were, at the gates of paradise in "Doom," as the angels Peter and Michael remind "Whose spirit prayed never at the gate / In life nor at the throne / In death he may not pass the gate / To come before the throne." Self-absorption limits the significance of the world as well as the self. "Grain Field" consequently seeks symbolism, signification, a reason to pray— the gold of the hair and the blue of the eyes become figurative:

Scarlet the poppies
Blue the corn-flowers,
Golden the wheat.
Gold for The Eternal:
Blue for Our Lady:
Red for the five
Wounds of her Son.

These interrelations between beauty, self-sacrifice, and death are picked up in "Song," making the secret shroud the inclusive image.

I make my shroud but no one knows,
So shimmering fine it is and fair,
With stitches set in even rows.
I make my shroud but no one knows.

In door-way where the lilac blows,
Humming a little wandering air,
I make my shroud and no one knows,
So shimmering fine it is and fair.

This celebration of martyrdom is most certainly related to the "wounds of her Son" but is rejected here as a "solution." The careful attention to the shroud or the poem itself is an escape from the realities of existence.

The "Pierrot" poem which follows depicts Beardsley's clown dying, despite his visitors, alone, the secret of his death and his feelings removed from the scene. Beardsley's drawing of a doll clown dying is itself a removal, a distancing from death, and the poem even more a removal from the scene to emphasize the isolation of death to the dying, the mystery of death to the observer. This decadence of "Pierrot"—a pretending acceptance of the harsh reality of existence with the removal of art—contrasts sharply with the joy of life emphasized in "The Monk in the Garden / He comes from Mass early in the morning":

> The sky's the very blue Madonna wears;
>   The air's alive with gold! Mark you the way
> The birds sing and the dusted shimmer of dew
>   On leaf and fruit? . . Per Bacco, what a day!

Like a snippet of Browning, religion, reality, and universal order are here manifested in the observation of the Creation. "I am afraid," Crapsey's father was to write, "lest the instruction of the schools should usurp that instruction which is unlettered and cannot be printed on the pages of a book; that divine instruction which must be read directly from the pages of the earth and the sky; the letters of which are the flowers and the stars."[9] The monk turns all the world into a sign of the divine creation. Death in this context becomes a part of the natural world.

> I have no heart for noon-tide and the sun,
> But I will take me where more tender night
> Shakes, fold on fold, her dewy darkness down.
> And shelters me that I may weep in peace.

With the opening lines, "The Mourner" turns from what is here, with an acknowledgment of its existence, and seeks what is missing. The emphasis in this poem is on the observer and the message of the last line: "for the forgotten dead are dead indeed." The necessity is for awareness—and not ignorance, artistic distance, or romanticization—of both the value of life and the reality of death. "Night" deals with consciousness, awareness that doesn't allow "sleep," and "Harvester's Song" is concerned with the lack of harvest in mourning. There is noth-

ing to reap from the dead, "nor bread nor wine." Even the song that
follows, "Rose-Mary of the Angels," appears to be one of the deceptive
songs of Blake's *Songs of Innocence*, which resign the individual to inevitable tragedy by making it into a delight: "How God will be glad of
thee / Little Sister Rose-Marie!"

"Angelique" and "Chimes" increasingly make the realities of death
conscious. "Chimes," in particular, combines both the joy of nature and
the essence of death: one foretells the other and death is, therefore, not
the opposite of life but merely the other side.

> The rose new-opening saith,
> And the dew of the morning saith,
> (Fallen leaves and vanished dew)
> Remember death.

It is apparent from the way in which dew has been repeated in the
previous poems (as has the gold hair and blue eyes of the various female
characters and speakers) that it is used as a symbol of the nectar of life,
the transience of which must be acknowledged, accepted, and finally
welcomed. But in "Mad-Song," though the speaker understands and
welcomes death, her behavior is "socially unacceptable" and she is labeled mad.

> Grey gaolers are my griefs
>   That will not let me free;
> The bitterness of tears
>   Is warder unto me.

These lines begin and end "Mad Song." Initially, the reader tends to
accept the madness of the speaker, seemingly overwhelmed and inca-
pacitated by grief. As the poem progresses, however, it becomes clear
that the madwoman's knowledge and anticipation of her death orient
her behavior in a manner that is not understandable to others.

> My griefs, my tears must watch,
>   And cold the watch they keep;

They whisper, whisper there—
  I hear them in my sleep.

. . . .

But in the dark of a night,
  Too dark for them to see,
The refuge of black gates
  Will open unto me.

Imprisoned in a limited life, the speaker anticipates the liberation of death. If one compares these gates with those in "Release," one can see how far the speaker has travelled. The gates that then kept her back from life now keep her back from death. Placed in a biographical context, not of Crapsey's death but of the heresy trial of her father that proved society unworthy of the superior man,[10] this poem and the one that follows, "Witch," take on a social significance only partly relevant here. It is the society throughout history that deemed the speaker of "Witch" wrong because she transcended the limited concepts of humanity.

And have you heard (and I have heard)
  Of puzzled men with decorous mien,
Who judged—The wench knew far too much—
  And burnt her on the Salem green?

Perhaps even more relevant is the eternalization of the individual who steps outside of life, who views all of history because she participates as a concept rather than an involved person, limited by the parentheses of life.

It is the attachment to the ideals of the eternal that permits this transcendence, as the two parallel poems to follow illustrate. "The Cry of the Nymph to Eros" and "Cradle-Song" must be seen together, for their images of the mother-child relationships of Aphrodite and Eros and Mary and Jesus are two frameworks, the pagan and the Christian. The pagan relies entirely on the natural and erotic world and can provide no comfort in the face of death:

. . . Oh, violets,
Ye are dead and your whiteness, your sweetness, availed not. Thy
   mother
Is cruel.

The Holy Mother and child, however, do indeed provide comfort:

The blesséd Queen of Heaven
Her own dear Son hath given
For my son's sake; his sleep
Is safe and sweet and deep.

The fruit of "Cradle Song" is the fruit tree God provides for the hungry Mary and contrasts sharply with the living sacrifices offered to Aphrodite and found dead at her feet. The search for "Life" which began the sequence of poems with "Birth Moment" has been shifted from the pagan, the erotic, and the physical to the spiritual. The physical, the actual, is never rejected, but its emphasis shifts until it is finally only the "residue" of life.

"Immortality" turns back from spiritual answers, from the miracles of Christianity, to the actual facts of existence. Without rejecting the comforts of religion outright, it emphasizes the responsibility of the self in the determination of fate.

Butscher points out the connection to Landor's concept of memory as opposed to immortality.[11] "Crapsey's poem itself achieves a certain lyrical poignancy that concludes with a strong image of Memory as another self, a ghostly alter ego holding out its hands (as a Madonna statue might) to offer the only immortality possible: the personal past." Paul Crapsey, the poet's brother, wrote in apparent imitation of his sister a poem called "Legacy." "Immortality lies in the / memories we bequeath."[12] This is indeed the only immortality of which the individual has control.

As a result of the previous poem, "Immortality," the speaker in "The Lonely Death" is able to prepare herself for death, even to take her own death into her own hands and, with no emotion, no regret (unlike "Song"), accept her fate. Her description of death in "Lo, All the Way," the break in bad weather for the funeral procession, ending in "Grey road, grey fields, wind and a bitter rain," runs into the next poem, "The Crucifixion," which begins "And the centurion who stood by said; / 'Truly this was a son of God.' " The landscape of the previous poem is here a consequence of the Crucifixion.

> Not long ago but everywhere I go
>   There is a hill and a black windy sky.
> Portent of hill, sky, day's eclipse I know;
>   Hill, sky, the shuddering darkness, these am I.

"The Crucifixion" incorporates all the witnesses, all the possible reactions to the death of Jesus, into the person of the speaker. The catalog of characters reads like a catalog of the personae in the poems of the "Presentation Piece," "I am—the thief redeemed and the lost thief; . . . the careless folk . . those bereft . . the Well-Belov'd, the women bowed in grief. / The gathering Presence that in terror cried, / In earth's shock . . . / a watcher, ignorant, curious-eyed, / . . . the centurion who heard and knew." The spiritualization process in these poems has not been one of the shedding of identities, of reactions, of beliefs and loves, but the shaping of all of them into the final verse, the urn that contains the "residue" of what once was a living, vital person:

THE IMMORTAL RESIDUE

Inscription for my verse

Wouldst thou find my ashes? Look
In the pages of my book;
And as these thy hand doth turn,
Know here is my funeral urn.

There can be no way of reading this poem as a conclusion without acknowledging the imperative to the reader to see the poems as one urn, containing poetic ashes of life. This is not an immortalization of the self. Most significantly, the poet does not perceive the purpose of her verse as providing her immortality. She reminds the reader carefully of the fact of her death: the poems are only here because she's dead. If she were not ashes one would not have to peruse what's left in an urn. The poems may be immortal, but they are only the residue of a life, shaped into an artistic unit in preparation for departure.

"Artists," Crapsey copied into her commonplace book, "give us not conclusions but evidence."[13] The evidence of these poems is that life is preferable to verse, but the writing and ordering of poems may ease this painful truth.

Notes

Introduction: The Return

1. The typescript for Lola Ridge's "Adelaide Crapsey" is among the papers at the University of Rochester, apparently sent to Mrs. Crapsey by the poet. The text, with some variations, is in Lola Ridge, *Red Flag* (New York: Viking, 1927), 82.

2. *Oracle*, arranged, edited, and introduced by Claude Bragdon (Rochester: Manas, 1921), 2.

3. Ibid., 8.

4. Ibid., 8–9.

5. Claude Bragdon, *More Lives than One* (New York: Knopf, 1938), 31, 259.

6. Ibid., 60.

7. Susan Sutton Smith, *The Complete Poems and Collected Letters of Adelaide Crapsey* (Albany: State University of New York Press, 1977), 222.

8. Eugenie Bragdon's automatic writing can be found in the Claude Bragdon Collection, Special Collections, University of Rochester.

9. Bragdon, *More Lives*, "Take me to see . . ." This story clashes with Bragdon's earlier version in *Merely Players* (New York: Knopf, 1929), 208, in which he claims to have initiated the visit.

10. Bragdon Collection, University of Rochester.

11. Ibid.

12. Ibid. The "SSS" are found in the automatic writing text and appear to be some form of extended punctuation.

13. Bragdon, *More Lives*, 67.

14. Bragdon Collection, University of Rochester.

15. Ibid.

333

16. Bragdon, *Merely Players*, 209.
17. Bragdon, *More Lives*, 68.
18. Ibid., 259.
19. Bragdon Collection, University of Rochester.
20. Adelaide Crapsey Collection, University of Rochester.
21. Conversation between Esther Lowenthal and Susan Smith, in Smith, *Complete Poems*, 22.
22. I have retained throughout the two-dot ellipses used by Crapsey in all of her poems and some of her prose. Her intention was apparently to create further compression.
23. Louise Townsend Nicholls, *New Republic*, January 31, 1923, 258.
24. Bragdon Collection, University of Rochester.
25. Ibid.
26. Claude Bragdon, *Verse* (Rochester: Manas Press, 1915), 10.
27. Ibid., 11.
28. Adelaide Crapsey Collection, University of Rochester.
29. Bragdon Collection, University of Rochester.
30. Bragdon, *Merely Players*, 212.
31. Harriet Monroe, *Poets and Their Art* (New York: Macmillan, 1926), 137–38.
32. Alice Corbin Henderson, "The Great Adventure," *Poetry: A Magazine of Verse* 10 (1917):317.
33. Carl Sandburg, "Cornhuskers," 1918, in *Collected Poems* (New York: Harcourt, Brace and Jovanovich, 1970), 101–2.
34. Carl Sandburg, *The Letters of Carl Sandburg*, ed. Herbert Mitgang (New York: Harcourt, Brace and World, 1968), 124.
35. Ibid., 115.
36. Smith, *Complete Poems*, 101. Hereafter cited in text as *CP*.

The Choice to Serve

1. Mary Osborn, *Adelaide Crapsey* (Boston: Bruce Humphries, 1933), 9.
2. Ibid., 8.
3. Adelaide T. Crapsey Journal, Arthur H. Crapsey Collection, Rochester, New York.
4. Osborn, *Crapsey*, 10.
5. Crapsey Journal, Arthur H. Crapsey Collection.
6. Adelaide Crapsey Collection, University of Rochester.
7. Algernon Crapsey, *The Last of the Heretics* (New York: Knopf, 1924), 3.
8. Ibid., 3.
9. B. F. Morris, *The Life of Thomas Morris* (Cincinnati: Wilstach, Keys and Overend, 1856), xii.
10. Ibid., 13.
11. Ibid., 23.
12. Crapsey, *Heretics*, 2.
13. Ibid., 2.
14. Ibid., 20.

15. Ibid., 21.
16. Ibid., 122.
17. Ibid., 122.
18. Ibid., 123.

19. *Catskill Examiner*, August 11, 1878.
20. Crapsey, *Heretics*, 125.
21. Ibid., 126.

Rochester

1. *Catskill Examiner*, January 31, 1891.
2. Ibid., April 26, 1879.
3. Ibid., June 14, 1879.
4. Ibid., January 31, 1891.
5. Ibid., January 31, 1891.
6. Ibid., May 24, 1879.
7. Scrapbooks, Arthur H. Crapsey Collection.
8. Crapsey, *Heretics*, 126.
9. Susan Smith, "Adelaide Crapsey: Materials for a Biographical and Textual Study," *University of Rochester Library Bulletin* 25, nos. 1, 2 (1969–1970):5.
10. Crapsey, *Heretics*, 126.
11. Ibid., 126.
12. Ibid., 128.
13. Ibid., 154. His wife also gives a version of this in her journal.
14. Ibid., 129.
15. Ibid., 130.

16. Ibid., 129.
17. Crapsey Journal, Arthur H. Crapsey Collection.
18. Osborn, *Crapsey*, 8.
19. Mary Delia Lewis, "Adelaide Crapsey," *Smith College Monthly* 23, no. 8 (December 1915):114.
20. Crapsey, *Heretics*, 7.
21. Sister Mary Edwardine O'Connor, "Adelaide Crapsey: A Biographical Study" (master's thesis, University of Notre Dame, 1931), 5.
22. Osborn, *Crapsey*, 10.
23. Edwardine, "Crapsey," 5.
24. Crapsey, *Heretics*, 131.
25. Edwardine, "Crapsey," 5.
26. Crapsey, *Heretics*, 191.
27. Ibid., 193.
28. Osborn, *Crapsey*, 12.
29. Smith, *Complete Poems*, 164.

Kemper Hall

1. Crapsey, *Heretics*, 18.
2. Algernon Crapsey, *The Rise of the Working Class* (New York: Century, 1914), 94.
3. Crapsey, *Heretics*, 151.
4. Ibid., 151.

5. Smith, *Complete Poems*, 159.
6. Ibid., 159.
7. Algernon Crapsey, *The Rebirth of Religion* (New York and London: John Lane, 1907), 56.
8. Crapsey, *Rise*, 98.

9. Arthur H. Crapsey Collection.

10. James Holley Hanford, letter to Thomas Mabbott, April 21, 1963, Mabbott Collection, University of Iowa. Phillip Henry Savage was admired by Wallace Stevens for extraliterary reasons. See Holly Stevens, *Souvenirs and Prophecies: The Young Wallace Stevens* (New York: 1977), 82–83.

11. Smith, *Complete Poems*, 167.

12. Ibid., 161.

13. Ibid., 191.

14. Osborn, *Crapsey*, 13.

15. Ibid., 14. Mrs. Crapsey's diary also describes this event.

16. Edward Foreman, ed., *Centennial History of Rochester, New York*, vol. 3 expansion (Rochester: Historical Society, 1933), 321.

17. *Kemper Hall Alumnae Journal* (Kenosha, Wisconsin), 4.

18. Smith, *Complete Poems*, 158.

19. Ibid., 169.

20. Ibid., 160.

21. Ibid., 166.

22. Ibid., 165.

23. Ibid., 169.

24. Ibid., 163.

25. Ibid., 159.

26. Ibid., 161.

27. Blake McKelvey, *Rochester: The Quest for Quality, 1890–1925* (Cambridge, Mass.: Harvard University Press, 1956), 129.

28. Crapsey, *Heretics*, 171, 174.

29. Smith, *Complete Poems*, 167.

30. *Kemper Hall Kodak* 28 (1945):29.

31. Smith, *Complete Poems*, 167.

32. Sister Mary Hilary, C.S.M., *10 Decades of Praise: The Story of the Community of Saint Mary During Its First Century, 1865–1965* (Racine, Wis.: De Koven Foundation, 1965), 153.

33. Elaine Edwards, "Room to Be Themselves," *Kenosha News*, May 21, 1970.

34. Smith, *Complete Poems*, 162.

35. Ibid., 164.

36. Morris, *Thomas Morris*, 22–23.

37. Smith, *Complete Poems*, 167.

38. Letter of consolation by Mary Braislin to Mrs. Crapsey, Adelaide Crapsey Collection, University of Rochester.

39. "Guiding Young Minds," interview with Mother Mary Ambrose by Elaine Edwards, *Kenosha News*, December 21, 1974, 5.

40. Smith, *Complete Poems*, 159.

41. *Kemper Hall Kodak* 2, no. 1 (May 1895):13–14.

42. Ibid.

43. *Kemper Hall Kodak* 3, no. 2 (November 1895):3–5.

44. Jean Webster, *Daddy Long-Legs* (New York: Bantam, 1982), 13. The original edition was copyright in 1912 by the Century Publishing Company.

45. *Kemper Hall Kodak* 4, no. 2 (September 1896):13, and *Kemper Hall Kodak* 4, no. 4 (January 1897):9.

46. Smith, *Complete Poems*, 163.

47. *Kemper Hall Kodak* 3, no. 3 (October 1895):3.
48. Ibid., 5.
49. Smith, *Complete Poems,* 170.
50. *Kemper Hall Kodak* 3, nos. 4, 5 (January–February 1896):10.
51. *Kemper Hall Kodak* 3, no. 6 (March 1896):65–66.
52. *Kemper Hall Kodak* 4, no. 6 (March 1897):2.
53. Smith, *Complete Poems,* 170.
54. Mrs. Stuart Fuller, letter to Helen Birkett, Adelaide Crapsey Collection, Smith College Archives.
55. Osborn, *Crapsey,* 18.
56. Of Crapsey's work with the Cherokee Indian charms (found in Smith, *Complete Poems,* 143–48) little is known, except the fact of their existence. They seem to be exercises in sounds and oral patterns that may originally have been made at Kemper.
57. Smith, *Complete Poems,* 161.
58. Sister Flora Theresa C.S.M., in Walter C. Loescher, "The Personality and Poetry of Adelaide Crapsey" (master's thesis, University of Rochester, 1947), 7. Adelaide's "youthful plumpness" was a family legend.
59. Mrs. Stuart Fuller, letter to Mrs. Birkett in 1960, Smith College Archives, and Osborn, *Crapsey,* 16.
60. Mary Osborn's letter to Thomas Mabbott, February 27, 1933, Mabbott Collection, University of Iowa.
61. *Kemper Hall Kodak* 3, no. 2 (November 1895):13.
62. *Kemper Hall Kodak* 3, no. 9 (June 1896):20.
63. *Annual Catalogue of Kemper Hall 1902–3* (Kenosha, Wis.: Kemper Union Printing House, 1902), 15.
64. *Kemper Hall Kodak* 4, no. 9 (June 1897):5.

The Decision for Education

1. "Women in Politics," *North American Review* 137 (August 1883):142, reprinted in Barbara Kuhn Campbell, *The "Liberated" Woman of 1914: Prominent Women in the Progressive Era* (UMI Research Press, 1979), 29.
2. Edward H. Clarke, *Sex in Education* (Boston: J. R. Osgood and Company, 1873); Lowry, *Herself,* 24, reprinted in Campbell, *"Liberated" Woman,* 29.
3. M. Carey Thomas, "Present Tendencies in Women's College and University Education," quoted in *Up from the Pedestal,* ed. Aileen S. Kraditor (Chicago: Quadrangle Books, 1968), 93–94; Hall, *Adolescence,* 2:612, reprinted in Campbell, *"Liberated" Woman,* 28–30.
4. Morris, *Thomas Morris,* 43.

5. Crapsey, *Rise*, 85.
6. Smith, *Complete Poems*, 169.
7. Crapsey, *Rise*, 83.
8. Ibid., 75.
9. Ibid., 77.
10. Ibid., 77, 78.
11. Ibid., 94.
12. *Kemper Hall Kodak* 3 (June 1896):3–7.
13. *Kemper Hall Kodak* 4 (June 1897):1–4.
14. Foreman, *Centennial*, 249.
15. William Peck, "A Historical Sketch of Monroe County and the City of Rochester," in *Landmarks of Monroe County* (Boston: E. Boston History, 1895), 168.

Vassar

1. Osborn, *Crapsey*, 26.
2. Webster, *Daddy Long-Legs*, 61.
3. Henry MacCracken, *The Hickory Limb* (New York: Scribners, 1950), 21.
4. Crapsey, *Rise*, 74.
5. Crapsey, *Heretics*, 195.
6. Alan and Mary Simpson with Ralph Connor, *Jean Webster, Storyteller* (Tymor Associates, 1984), 55.
7. Crapsey, *Heretics*, 195.
8. Scrapbooks, Arthur H. Crapsey Collection.
9. *Vassar Miscellany* 27 (February 1898):71.
10. Edwardine, "Crapsey," 14.
11. Webster, *Daddy Long-Legs*, 55.
12. Simpson, *Jean Webster*, 11.
13. Philalethetis Collection, Vassar College.
14. Simpson, *Jean Webster*, 52–53.
15. Ibid., 175.
16. February 12, 1899, Jean Webster McKinney Collection, Vassar College.
17. That Vassar basketball was kept from prying eyes is confirmed in alumnae anthologies and photographs. See, for example, Dorothy Plum and George B. Dowell, *The Magnificent Enterprise: A Chronicle of Vassar* (Poughkeepsie: Vassar, 1961) and *The Great Experiment* (Poughkeepsie: Vassar, 1961).
18. January 22, 1899, McKinney Collection, Vassar College.
19. Edwardine, "Crapsey," 10.
20. *Vassar Miscellany* 27 (February 1898):94.
21. *Vassar Miscellany* 27 (December 1898):137, reprinted in Smith, *Complete Poems*, 138.
22. *Vassar Miscellany* 28 (February 1899):229, reprinted in Smith, *Complete Poems*, 138–39.
23. Crapsey, *Heretics*, 218, 220.
24. *Poughkeepsie Chronicle*, May 21, 1899. Webster's column can be found in a bound volume among her papers in the McKinney Col-

lection at Vassar College. As a reporter Webster showed a disproportionate interest in events that concerned her roommate and covered the Reverend Mr. Crapsey's brief visit.

25. Loescher, *Personality,* 49.
26. Webster, *Daddy Long-Legs,* 38–39.
27. "I am informed that the verses actually appeared on the blackboard of the English class at Vassar and that the students were asked to explain and comment on the text." Unidentified article in Jean Webster Papers III, nos. 7, 9. Clippings, *Daddy Long-Legs,* McKinney Collection, Vassar College.
28. *Vassar Miscellany* 28 (June 1899):457–58. Edward Butscher points out that the review, which praises a rather second-rate poet, nevertheless has prophetic aspects, because the characteristics she singles out are those she herself aspired to. *Adelaide Crapsey* (Boston: Twayne, 1979), 41.
29. See, for example, Algernon Crapsey's famous cure for a cold in *Heretics,* in which he recommends taking a bottle of whiskey and a hat to bed and, while staring at the hat on the bedpost, drinking until there are two hats.
30. *Chronicle,* January 21, 1900; Plum and Dowell, *Magnificent Enterprise,* 37.
31. *Chronicle,* March 11, 1900.

32. *Socialist Spirit* 1, no. 2 (October 1901):8.
33. MacCracken, *Hickory Limb,* 33.
34. Louise Fargo Brown, *Apostle of Democracy: The Life of Lucy Maynard Salmon* (New York: Harper, 1943), 134–35.
35. Ibid., 165.
36. Ibid., 171.
37. Plum and Dowell, *Magnificent Enterprise,* 86.
38. Edwardine, "Crapsey," 9.
39. Agnes Rogers, *Vassar Women* (Poughkeepsie: Vassar, 1940), 91.
40. *Vassar Miscellany* 28 (December 1899):148. See also letters of Jane Addams, Charlotte Perkins, and other contemporary women.
41. *Vassar Miscellany* (January 1900):229.
42. *Chronicle,* November 19, 1899.
43. *Vassarion* (1900):169 has two photos.
44. *Vassar Miscellany* 29 (May 1900):446–47.
45. Osborn, *Crapsey,* 35.
46. *Chronicle,* October 21, 1900.
47. Sam Webster, *Mark Twain, Businessman* (Boston: Little, Brown, 1946), 226.
48. *Chronicle,* November 11, 1900.
49. Inez Millholland in 1909 turned the whole campus socialist. See, for example, the *New York Times,* May 9, 1909, 8:1. A 1916 sketch dramatically displays this in *The Fiftieth Anniversary of the Opening of Vassar College, October 10 to 13,*

1915, a Record (Poughkeepsie: Vassar College, 1916), 255.

50. Adelaide Crapsey, "Report on the Social Democratic Party of America" (1901), 38–40, Adelaide Crapsey File, Vassar College Library.

51. McKelvey, *Rochester,* 123.

52. Letter, Miss Florence V. Keyes, March 21, 1929, in Loescher, *Personality,* 10.

53. Mrs. Stuart Fuller to Mrs. Birkett, Smith College Archives.

54. Edwardine, "Crapsey," 13.

Emily and Patty

1. *Chronicle,* February 14, 1901.
2. Ibid., and April 9, 1899.
3. Simpson, *Jean Webster,* 70.
4. Edwardine, "Crapsey," 17.
5. *Chronicle,* April 9, 1899. The annual outing to Lake Mohonk was considered the highlight of the year.
6. Clara Barrus, *Our Friend, John Burroughs* (New York: Houghton Mifflin, 1914), 26.
7. *Chronicle,* October 22, 1899.
8. Adelaide Crapsey, *Vassar College Exhibition, #1901,* Vassar College Archives.
9. *New York Times,* Septemter 27, 1902, 642.
10. Algernon Crapsey, *The Greater Love* (New York: John Lane, 1902).
11. Letter to Dr. John A. Lowe, October 8, 1948, Adelaide Crapsey Papers, Rochester Public Library.
12. McKelvey, *Rochester,* 189.
13. "A Constitutional Defense of the Negro," delivered at a Mass Meeting of Citizens in the Metropolitan AME Church, Washington, D.C., December 15, 1901, copyright A. S. Crapsey. 10 in Swarthmore College Peace Library.
14. *Vassar Class Bulletin* 31, no. 1 (October 1901):34.
15. April 14, 1900.
16. Simpson, *Jean Webster,* 123.
17. *Vassarion* (1900).
18. *Kemper Hall Kodak* (January 1902):1–2.
19. "Review of Martha Gilbert Dickinson, *Within the Hedge,*" *Vassar Miscellany* 6 (June 1899):457.
20. *Kemper Hall Kodak* 8 (December 1901):4.
21. Announced in the *Socialist Spirit* 1, no. 1 (September 1901):13.
22. A Vassar alumna, not close to Jean but close enough to share some of the sources of her inspiration, wrote a rave letter to D. Z. Doty, the staff member of the Century Company who would handle Jean's stories for the rest of her life: "I read 'Patty' through

the night I got it and wanted more! . . . I rather imagine that 'Patty' is a certain roommate Jean Webster had in her sophomore year, with a few added traits and some idealization." The memorial tribute, as it appears in *The Book of Enduring Names* (Town Hall, New York) also suggests that Adelaide Crapsey was the original of Patty. But surely the funny, high-spirited, lovable Patty drew something from Jean Webster and Jennie Hyde—Webster's teacher in boarding school—as well as from Adelaide. Simpson, *Jean Webster*, 65.

23. *When Patty Went to College* (New York: Century, 1902), 20.
24. Simpson, *Jean Webster*, 65.
25. Ibid., 63.
26. Ibid., 61.
27. Ibid., 67.

The Escape to Kemper

1. *Kemper Hall Kodak* 7, no. 9 (June 1900):24.
2. *Kemper Hall Kodak* 4, no. 9 (June 1897):4.
3. *Kemper Hall Kodak* 9, no. 9 (June 1902):15. She is listed as teaching history and rhetoric in a later *Kodak* 10, no. 1 (November 1902):10.
4. "Adelaide Crapsey," *Smith College Monthly*, 114.
5. *Catalogue of Kemper Hall*, 11.
6. Ibid., 12.
7. Osborn, *Crapsey*, 37.
8. *Catalogue of Kemper Hall*, 15–16. Mary Braislin of Crosswick, N.J., the librarian, wrote Mrs. Crapsey a sympathy card.
9. Ibid., 12.
10. Osborn, *Crapsey*, 37.
11. Lewis, "Crapsey," 114.
12. *Catalogue of Kemper Hall*, 10.
13. Sister Superior C.S.M., April 21, 1928, in Loescher, *Personality*, 7.
14. Lewis, "Crapsey," 114.
15. Osborn, *Crapsey*, 38.
16. Simpson, *Jean Webster*, 73.
17. Ibid., 74.
18. Ibid., 77.
19. Alan Cook, "The History of Elm Lodge and Cook's Point," unpublished paper (1983), 5. Canandaigua Historical Society, Canandaigua, N.Y.
20. Ibid., 5–6.
21. James Holley Hanford, letter to Thomas Mabbott, April 21, 1963, Mabbott Collection, University of Iowa.
22. Algernon Crapsey, *The Rebirth of Religion* (New York: John Lane, 1907), 151.
23. Mabbott Collection, University of Iowa.
24. Schmidt, Adelaide Crapsey Collection, University of Rochester.

Roma Aeterna

1. Lucia Valentine and Alan Valentine, *The American Academy in Rome 1894–1969* (Charlottesville: University Press of Virginia, 1973), 50.
2. "Tenth Annual Report of the Managing Committee of the American School of Classical Studies in Rome," *American Jour-* Abington Press, 1966), 191. *nal of Archeology,* 2nd ser. 9, 19.
3. Ibid., 19.
4. Valentine and Valentine, *American Academy,* 6.
5. Edwardine, "Crapsey," 20.
6. Osborn, *Crapsey,* 41.
7. *Vassar Class Bulletin* (May 1905):26.

The Heresy

1. Crapsey, *Heretics,* 189. Jane Addams describes a similar experience in London in 1883 in *Twenty Years at Hull-House* (New York: Macmillan, 1910). "One of the most poignant of these experiences, which occurred during the first few months after our landing upon the other side of the Atlantic, was on a Saturday night, when I received an ineradicable impression of the wretchedness of East London, and also saw for the first time the overcrowded quarters of a great city at midnight." Quoted in *The Oven Birds,* ed. Gail Parker (New York: Doubleday, 1972), 294.
2. *Inventory of the Church Archives of New York,* 18, quoted in Hugh M. Jansen, Jr., "Algernon Sidney Crapsey: Heresy at Rochester," in *American Religious Heretics,* ed. George H. Shriver (Nashville:
3. Ibid., 190.
4. *Argument of Edward M. Shepard as Counsel for the Rev. Algernon S. Crapsey, S.T.D. Before the Court of Review of the Protestant Episcopal Church upon his appeal from the judgement of the Court of the Diocese of Western New York,* October 19, 1906, 1.
5. Jansen, "Heresy," 196.
6. *Argument,* 107.
7. Morris, *Thomas Morris,* 34.
8. Algernon Crapsey, *Religion and Politics* (New York: Thomas Whittaker, 1905), 291.
9. *Churchman,* July 8, 1905, editorial page.
10. *Churchman,* August 19, 1905, editorial page.
11. *Churchman,* September 9, 1905, 24.
12. Ibid., 25.
13. *Outlook,* September 2, 1905, 26.
14. Ibid., 28.

15. Ibid., 28.

16. Ibid., 15.

17. Jansen, "Heresy," 202.

18. *Churchman*, October 14, 1905, editorial page.

19. Osborn, *Crapsey*, 42.

20. *Living Church*, November 4, 1905, quoted in Jansen, "Heresy," 198.

21. *Proceedings on the Trial and Appeal of the Reverend Algernon Sidney Crapsey S.T.D. Rector of St. Andrews Church, Rochester, New York, Upon His Presentment for Heresy* (New York: T. Whittaker, 1906), 202.

22. "Report of the Committee," *Church Standard*, November 18, 1905, 77, quoted in Jansen, "Heresy," 198.

23. "Report of the Committee," *Church Standard*, November 25, 1905, 114–15, quoted in ibid., 198. The *Living Church*, November 18, 1905, 78–79 entitled its article "Is There No Evidence Against Dr. Crapsey?"

24. *Churchman*, November 25, 1905, 849.

25. *Churchman*, January 6, 1906, 13.

26. *Argument*, 108.

27. *Churchman*, December 16, 1905, editorial page.

28. *Church Standard*, January 20, 1906, 389–90.

29. *Churchman*, January 13, 1906, 46.

30. "A Reported Second Trial of Dr. Crapsey," *Church Standard*, February 3, 1906, 496.

31. *Living Church*, February 3, 1906, 486, quoted in Jansen, "Heresy," 200.

32. *Proceedings*, 4–8.

33. Crapsey, *Religion*, 288–89.

34. Diocese of Western New York, *Journal of the Seventieth Annual Council of the Protestant Episcopal Church in the Diocese of Western New York* (1907), 96–97; *Proceedings*, 8.

35. *Churchman*, April 21, 1906, 604–5.

36. Crapsey, *Heretics*, 260.

37. Ibid., 262.

38. *Proceedings*, 225.

39. *Churchman*, May 5, 1906, 677.

40. Crapsey, *Heretics*, 263.

41. Ibid., 261.

42. Bragdon, *More Lives*, 258.

43. *Proceedings*, 54–55.

44. Ibid., 60.

45. Ibid., 62–63, 65.

46. *New York Times*, April 27, 1906, 10.

47. *Proceedings*, 144.

48. *Churchman*, May 5, 1905, 677.

49. *Proceedings*, 99–100.

50. Ibid., 95.

51. Ibid., 161, 166; Jansen, "Heresy," 210.

52. *Proceedings*, 185–86.

53. Osborn, *Crapsey*, 43.

54. *Proceedings*, 196.

55. Alexander Viets Griswold Allen,

Freedom in the Church (New York: Macmillan, 1907).

56. Charles Lewis Slattery, *Alexander Viets Griswold Allen, 1841–1908*

(New York: Longmans, Green and Company, 1911), 235.

57. *Proceedings*, 226–27.

58. Ibid., 241.

The Verdict

1. *New York Times*, April 30, 1906, 7.

2. *Kemper Hall Kodak* 3, no. 9 (June 1896):10.

3. *Churchman*, May 5, 1906, 673.

4. *Churchman*, May 16, 1906, 817.

5. *New York Times*, May 9, 1906, 1:2.

6. Jansen, "Heresy," 215.

7. *Proceedings*, 262.

8. *Argument*, 84–85.

9. Allen, *Freedom*, 236.

10. Ibid., 236–37.

11. *Churchman*, October 6, 1906.

12. *Argument*, 21.

13. *New York Times*, October 20, 1906, 7.

14. Ibid.

15. On October 20, 1906, Jean Webster wrote to Louise Platt, "I met Lucy Bartlett on the street the day before and am expecting Adelaide Crapsey today." McKinney Collection, Vassar College.

16. *New York Times*, October 21, 1906, 6:4.

17. *Churchman*, November 24, 1906, 786.

18. This sermon, quoted in the *New York Times*, November 26, 1906,

2:2, was revised for Crapsey, *Rebirth*, chap. 23, 227.

19. *New York Times*, November 26, 1906, 2:3. Spencer Trask was the founder of the artists' community of Yaddo.

20. Crapsey, *Heretics*, 275.

21. *New York Times*, November 28, 1906, 6:5.

22. Ibid., 2.

23. *New York Times*, November 27, 1906, 1:1.

24. "If the judgement stands," Shepard had said when the Batavia court had condemned Crapsey, "I suppose the Bishop of the Diocese of Western New York would have the right practically to exclude St. Andrews Church from the diocese, in case the church should refuse to give up Dr. Crapsey and Dr. Crapsey should prefer to remain in his present rectorship without accepting the conditions presented by the judgement" (*New York Times*, May 16, 1906, 6). Despite Shepard's continued dissatisfaction with the judgment and his constant urging to continue the

struggle, Algernon Crapsey was looking forward to his greater work. To Shepard's avowal that the case should be tried in civil court, where a conviction could not hold up, "that upon two points at least which Mr. Perkins and I had argued, the judgement would be held void by a civil court . . . Dr. Crapsey peremptorily rejected the idea of appeal to a civil court. Even though the highest existing court of the Church had found itself powerless to deal with the only questions of real moment, nevertheless the action of his clerical brethren in the lower court had, for the world at large, been unstained, and his personal fortunes should, he said, abide by the decision, right or wrong. The cause of intellectual honesty and free study had been opened to the Church; and he would not hinder it by further personal controversy."

25. *Argument*, 217.
26. *New York Times*, November 29, 1906, 6.
27. *New York Times*, November 29, 1906, 1.

Miss Low's School

1. Tercentenary Edition, *Stamford Advocate* (1941), 82.
2. May 1907 and 1908. A photograph of the Ferguson place with a note dated 12/22/06 indicates that Adelaide Crapsey must have taught when it was in this stage of expansion.
3. *Alumnae Bulletin*, 1907.
4. Charlotte Brontë, *Jane Eyre* (Boston: Houghton Mifflin, 1959), 101. The case of Clemenceau, who had been very happy at Miss Low's but left in the wake of some romantic scandal, helps to underline this attitude.
5. Loescher, *Personality*, 16.
6. Louise Merritt, letter to Sister Edwardine, April 5, 1929, Adelaide Crapsey Collection, University of Rochester.
7. Ibid.
8. Ibid.
9. Ibid.
10. Louise Merritt, letter to Mrs. Adelaide T. Crapsey, University of Rochester.
11. Ibid.
12. Ibid.
13. Simpson, *Jean Webster*, 85.
14. Crapsey, *Heretics*, 287.
15. Osborn, *Crapsey*, 43–44.
16. Crapsey, *Heretics*, 236–37.
17. Ibid., 238.
18. Osborn, *Crapsey*, 44.

The Hague

1. *New York Times*, April 17, 1907, 2.
2. Jean Webster to her mother, May 31, 1907, McKinney Collection, Vassar College.
3. *Boston Evening Transcript* (1911) in Crapsey scrapbook, Arthur H. Crapsey Collection.
4. *Life*, December 6, 1906, 779.
5. David S. Patterson, "An Interpretation of the American Peace Movement: 1898–1914," in *The Peace Movement in America*, ed. Charles Chatfield (New York: Schocken, 1973), 30.
6. Calvin DeArmond Davis, *The United States and the Second Hague Peace Conference* (Durham: Duke University Press, 1975), 187.
7. *New York Times*, May 1, 1907, 4:1.
8. *New York Times*, July 5, 1907, 4:5.
9. Davis, *United States*, 194.
10. Andrew Hull, letter from The Hague, *Friends' Intelligencer*, June 27, 1907, 561.
11. Davis, *United States*, 188–89.
12. Suzanne Wilcox, "The Hague Conference from a Woman's Point of View," *Independent* 64, no. 1 (1908):567.
13. Davis, *United States*, 192.
14. Ibid., 195.
15. Ibid., 195.
16. Wilcox, "Hague Conference," 567.
17. According to Article 12, French was the official language of the conference, and speeches in other languages were summarized in French.
18. William Stead, "Impressions," *Contemporary Review* 92 (1907):724.
19. George Dillon in ibid., 727.
20. Wilcox, "Hague Conference," 570.
21. Dillon, *Contemporary Review*, 727.
22. Davis, *United States*, 219.
23. Arthur Crapsey Jr. Collection.
24. McKelvey, *Rochester*, 138; Dores Robinson Sharpe, *Walter Rauschenbusch* (New York: Macmillan, 1942), 128–29.
25. Foreman, *Centennial*, 350.
26. February 8, 1909, according to scrapbooks of Arthur Crapsey.
27. Crapsey, *Heretics*, 288.
28. Jean Webster, letter to Lena Weinstein, McKinney Collection, Vassar College, 1907.
29. Louise Merritt, letter to Mrs. Crapsey, Adelaide Crapsey Collection, University of Rochester.
30. Louise Merritt, letter to Sister Edwardine, Adelaide Crapsey Collection, University of Rochester.
31. Osborn, *Crapsey*, 47.
32. Crapsey, *Heretics*, 297.
33. Ibid., 289.
34. McKelvey, *Rochester*, 141.
35. Mary Osborn, letter to Thomas

Mabbott, Mabbott Collection, University of Iowa.

36. Osborn, *Crapsey,* 48.

37. *Kemper Hall Kodak* 15 (December 1908), 23.

The Return to Rome

1. Smith, *Complete Poems,* 175.
2. *Vassar Class Bulletin* (May 1909):39.
3. Elbert Hubbard, *Selected Writings,* vol. 8 (Batavia: Elbert Hubbard Roycrofters, 1922), 335–36.
4. Smith, *Complete Poems,* 180.
5. Ibid., 177.
6. Ibid., 178.
7. Osborn, *Crapsey,* 50.
8. Smith, *Complete Poems,* 177.
9. Ibid., 176. Smith punctuates Fräu and Fräulein with both an umlaut and an accent. The accent was used in handwriting to differentiate between a *u* and an *n*.
10. Ibid., 179.
11. Louise Merritt, letter to Mrs. Crapsey, Adelaide Crapsey Collection, University of Rochester.
12. *Keats, Shelley & Rome: An Illustrated Miscellany,* Neville Rogers, comp. (New York: Frederick Ungar, 1949), 66.
13. Ibid., 15.
14. Smith, *Complete Poems,* 179.
15. See Walter Jackson Bate, *John Keats* (Cambridge: Harvard, 1963), 606.
16. Henry James, *Portraits of Places* (New York: Lear, 1948), 112.

17. Smith, *Complete Poems,* 176.
18. Ibid., 180.
19. August 9, Adelaide Crapsey Collection, University of Rochester.
20. *Vassarion* (1907):35.
21. Loescher, *Personality,* 28.
22. T. S. Omond, *A Study of Metre* (London: Folcroft, 1920; original version, 1903), ix.
23. Butscher points out the significance of "Memory" to Landor in this context, *Crapsey,* 64.
24. Osborn, *Crapsey,* 55. Another version of this appears in a manuscript by Mary Osborn in the collection of Edith Martin, Hightstown, New Jersey. Crapsey's mother, incidentally, was known for a similar personality characteristic. She would frequently sew layettes for unwed mothers and help them in many ways but would not dicuss the issue.
25. Meryle Secrest, *Being Bernard Berenson* (New York: Holt, 1979), 186.
26. Van Wyck Brooks, *The Dream of Arcadia: American Writers and Artists in Italy, 1760–1915* (New York: Dutton, 1958), 256.

27. Osborn, *Crapsey,* 57.
28. Letter, September 24, 1928, in Loescher, 18. Draper later wrote a number of books on theosophy, yoga, and psychology but did not publish anything concerning her friend.
29. Edwardine, "Crapsey," 7, quoting *Kemper Hall Kodak* 4, no. 6 (March 1897):2.
30. Lafcadio Hearn's *Letters from the Raven* remained in her library, a book her family was told she valued. It would be interesting to discover what else she read of Hearn and whether Japanese influences in her poetry have anything to do with his reading, but this has proved impossible.
31. Smith, *Complete Poems,* 182.
32. Ibid., 183.
33. Ibid., 182.
34. Ibid., 183.
35. Ibid., 284.
36. James, *Portraits,* 86.
37. Smith, *Complete Poems,* 184–85.
38. Ibid., 187.
39. Ibid., 185.
40. Ibid., 187.
41. Ibid., 177.
42. Ibid., 177.
43. Maurice Barrès, "Le Secret merveilleux," in *Du sang, de la volupté et de la morte* (1894), quoted and discussed in Jerrold Siegel, *Bohemian Paris* (New York: Viking, 1986), 284–86.
44. Adelaide Draper, letter, Mrs. Adelaide Gardner, September 24, 1928, in Loescher, *Personality,* 59.
45. Siegel, *Bohemian Paris,* 344–45.
46. Virginia Woolf, "Professions for Women," *The Death of the Moth and Other Essays* (New York: Harcourt, Brace, 1942), pp. 235–38.
47. Smith, *Complete Poems,* 187–88.
48. Ibid., 191.
49. Ibid., 187.
50. Ibid., 190.

London

1. Smith, *Complete Poems,* 188.
2. Ibid.
3. Ibid., 189.
4. Ibid., 189.
5. Adelaide Crapsey Collection, University of Rochester.
6. Smith, *Complete Poems,* 192.
7. Osborn, *Crapsey,* 72.
8. Medora Addison Nutter, Smith College Archives.
9. Edwardine, "Crapsey," 29.
10. Smith, *Complete Poems,* 194.
11. Ibid., 194.
12. Ibid., 194.
13. Crapsey, *Rebirth,* 66, 65.
14. *Vassarion* (1901):189.
15. Brown, *Apostle,* 134–35.
16. Adelaide Crapsey Collection, University of Rochester.
17. Adelaide Crapsey, letter to

Medora Addison Nutter, August 31, 1910, Adelaide Crapsey Collection, University of Rochester.

18. Smith, *Complete Poems*, 197.
19. "London," added Mrs. Crapsey, and pasted the letter in her Brown photograph albùm. Arthur H. Crapsey Collection.

20. Smith, *Complete Poems*, 198.
21. Osborn, *Crapsey*, 82.
22. Keats, October 29, 1795, Adelaide Crapsey Collection. The mysterious "M. E. sely," etc., I assume to connote agreement, perhaps "Amen, Selah."

Smith College

1. Arthur H. Crapsey Collection.
2. Ibid.
3. Smith, *Complete Poems*, 200.
4. MacCracken, *Hickory Limb*, 8.
5. Esther Lowenthal, interview with Susan Smith, October 8, 1969.
6. Adelaide Crapsey Collection, University of Rochester. After her death, Mary Jordan sent a copy of the manuscript of Crapsey's poems to a friend, G. H. Palmer, the professor of philosophy at Harvard who had edited his late wife's poems. He was as amazed as Jordan herself must have been by their perfection and his compliments were profuse. "She is ever weaving a spell, an unescapable one. And her magic is as easy as breathing." Palmer's later wife had also written poetry, love poetry to him, which he published after her death in *A Marriage Cycle* (Boston, 1915). See *The Life of Alice Freeman Palmer* (Boston, 1910) for a contrasting portrait of Crapsey.

7. *Jewish Tidings*, September 24, 1887, December 20, 1889, in Stuart Rosenberg, *The Jewish Community in Rochester, 1843–1925* (New York: Columbia, 1954), 122.
8. Isaac Wile, *The Jews of Rochester* (Rochester, N.Y.: 1912), 64.
9. *Jewish Tidings*, February 7, 1890; Rosenberg, *Jewish Community*, 292.
10. Rosenberg, *Jewish Community*, 132.
11. Simpson, *Jean Webster*, 166.
12. Manuscript of Paul Crapsey, possession of Arthur H. Crapsey.
13. Smith, *Complete Poems*, 222–23.
14. Claude Bragdon Collection, University of Rochester.
15. Selected relevant publications by Sampson: with E. O. Holland, "Written and Oral Composition," editor of *Milton's Lyric and Dramatic Poems, Milton's Minor Poems, Selections from Milton.*
16. *Ithaca Journal News*, August 23, 1930.

17. Smith, *Complete Poems,* 222.
18. Simpson, *Jean Webster,* 115.
19. Nicholls, *New Republic,* 258. See also Esther Lowenthal, "Personalities of a Bygone Era," Adelaide Crapsey Collection, Smith College Archives.
20. Esther Lowenthal, interview with Susan Smith, October 8, 1969.
21. Louïse Townsend Nicholls, in copy of Adelaide Crapsey's *Verse,* Adelaide Crapsey Collection, University of Rochester.
22. Nicholls, *New Republic,* 258.
23. Adelaide Crapsey Collection, University of Rochester, 28.
24. Edwardine, "Crapsey," 31. Dora Goldberg had become Dora Schatz by the time Edwardine corresponded with her.
25. Ridge, *Red Flag,* 85–86.
26. *New York Times,* December 4, 1911, 3.
27. *Vassar Alumnae Bulletin* (February 1912).
28. Osborn, *Crapsey,* 90.
29. Ibid.
30. Simpson, *Jean Webster,* 116.
31. Ibid.
32. Osborn, *Crapsey,* 90. See also the excerpts from Mrs. Crapsey's diary at the University of Rochester.
33. A five-page typed sheet concerning Mrs. Crapsey's factory may be found in the Vassar College Archives.
34. Mrs. Crapsey is quoted in Edwardine, "Crapsey," 21.

35. Osborn, *Crapsey,* 91.
36. October 19, 1912, Arthur H. Crapsey Collection.
37. November 11, 1912, Arthur H. Crapsey Collections.
38. Simpson, *Jean Webster,* 166; Webster letter, June 19, 1913, McKinney Collection, Vassar College.
39. Adelaide Crapsey Files, McKinney Collection, Vassar College.
40. Adelaide Crapsey Collection, University of Rochester.
41. Jean Webster to Glenn Ford McKinney, June 21, 1913, McKinney Collection, Vassar College.
42. Jean Webster to Glenn Ford McKinney, June 27, 1913, McKinney Collection, Vassar College.
43. Jean Webster to Glenn Ford McKinney, June 21, 1913, McKinney Collection, Vassar College.
44. Ibid.
45. Ibid.
46. July 9, Simpson, *Jean Webster,* 167–68.
47. August 5, ibid., 167.
48. Ibid., 168.
49. Mrs. Crapsey's diary, Adelaide Crapsey Collection, University of Rochester.
50. Simpson, *Jean Webster,* 168.
51. McKinney Collection, Vassar College.
52. Ibid.

Saranac Lake

1. Simpson, *Jean Webster,* 169.
2. Smith, *Complete Poems,* 107.
3. Ibid., 208.
4. Simpson, *Jean Webster,* 169.
5. Webster, *Daddy Long-Legs,* 40.
6. Lloyd Osbourne, "Preface to *The Wrong Boy*" by Robert Louis Stevenson, collaboration with Lloyd Osbourne (New York: Charles Scribner's Sons, 1925), xi.
7. Edward Livingston Trudeau, *An Autobiography* (New York: Doubleday, 1916), 316.
8. Phillip Gallos, *Cure Cottages of Saranac Lake* (Saranac Lake: Historic Saranac Lake, 1985), 17.
9. Edward R. Baldwin, M.D., director of the Edward L. Trudeau Foundation, "Saranac Lake and the Saranac Laboratory for the Study of Tuberculosis," *Quarterly Bulletin of the Millbank Memorial Fund* 10, no. 1 (January 1932):2.
10. Esther Lowenthal, interview with Susan Smith, October 8, 1969.
11. Edward R. Baldwin with S. A. Petroff, Ph.d. and Leroy S. Gardner, M.D., *Tuberculosis, Bacteriology, Pathology and Laboratory Diagnosis* (Philadelphia: Lea and Febiger, 1927), 200.
12. Gallos, *Cure Cottages,* 47.
13. Saranac Lake record cards of 39 Clinton, Historic Saranac Lake Collection.
14. Trudeau, *Autobiography,* 316–17.
15. *Kemper Hall Kodak* 3 (January 1896).
16. Edwardine, "Crapsey," 7.
17. Smith, *Complete Poems,* 217.
18. Ibid., 216.
19. Adelaide Crapsey Collection, University of Rochester.
20. Smith, *Complete Poems,* 209.
21. Ibid., 209–10.
22. Ibid., 211.
23. Ibid.
24. Ibid., 212.
25. Ibid., 207–8.
26. Ibid., 215.
27. Ibid.
28. September 25, ibid., 211.
29. Simpson, *Jean Webster,* 170; Smith, *Complete Poems,* 211. "Tokimento" was Webster's term for a token memento.
30. Smith, *Complete Poems,* 239.
31. Ibid., 214.
32. Ibid., 213.
33. Ibid., 218.
34. September 25, ibid., 211.
35. Trudeau, *Autobiography,* 319; Edward Livingston Trudeau, *T.B., Bacteriology, Pathology, and Laboratory Diagnosis,* with sections on immunology, epidemiology (Philadelphia: Lea and Febiger, 1927).
36. Smith, *Complete Poems,* 212.
37. Baldwin, Adelaide Crapsey Collection, University of Rochester.
38. Smith, *Complete Poems,* 216.
39. Ibid., 217.

40. November 6, 1913, ibid., 216–17.

41. McKinney Collection, Vassar College.

42. Smith, 222.

43. Vassar College.

44. Adelaide Crapsey, *A Study of English Metrics* (New York: Alfred A. Knopf, 1918), 29.

45. "An Experiment in Prosodic Analysis," Adelaide Crapsey Collection, University of Rochester, 12–13.

46. Smith, *Complete Poems*, 221.

47. Osborn, *Crapsey*, 97–98.

48. Smith, *Complete Poems*, 225.

49. Ibid., 229.

50. Lowenthal interview in ibid., 229.

51. January 12, 1914, McKinney Collection, Vassar College.

52. Edward Baldwin, "History of Tuberculosis Research in America," *Yale Journal of Biology and Medicine* 15, no. 301 (1943):304.

53. Smith, *Complete Poems*, 230.

54. Ibid.

55. Trudeau, *Autobiography*, 214.

56. Smith, *Complete Poems*, 234.

57. Ibid., 235.

58. Baldwin, "Saranac Lake," 10.

59. Smith, *Complete Poems*, 236.

60. Ibid., 238.

61. Ibid., 241.

62. Ibid.

63. Ibid., 242.

64. Ibid., 244.

65. Ibid.

66. Ibid., 245.

67. Baldwin, Adelaide Crapsey Collection, University of Rochester.

68. The song itself is missing from the text of the play, although it is indicated in the play and the notes. See Jean Webster's letter to Glenn Ford McKinney, June 3, 1914, McKinney Collection, Vassar College.

69. Ibid.

70. "The aftermath of Sarajevo seriously tested the superficiality unity of the entire movement. For some of those most emotionally committed to the cause, the shock of war was traumatic. Carnegie, Trueblood and Edwin Mead fell seriously ill in 1915 and there is evidence that their illnesses were as much psychosomatic as physical in origin. Not all the peace workers suffered so unhappily, although the World War undermined their most optimistic assumptions about world politics and forced a painful reassessment of their approaches to peace questions" (Patterson, *Peace Movement*, 32).

Home

1. Thursday, August 20, Simpson, *Jean Webster*, 170–71.
2. Osborn, *Crapsey*, 102. The original letter seems to have disappeared.
3. September 15, Osborn, *Crapsey*, 102.
4. Simpson, *Jean Webster*, 171.
5. Lowenthal interview.
6. Smith, *Complete Poems*, 202.
7. Osborn, *Crapsey*, 103.
8. Smith, *Complete Poems*, 202.
9. Ibid., 203.
10. Ibid.
11. Adelaide Crapsey Collection, University of Rochester.
12. Smith, *Complete Poems*, 110.
13. Bate, *John Keats*, 623.
14. Adelaide Crapsey Collection, University of Rochester.
15. Simpson, *Jean Webster*, 173.
16. Osborn, *Crapsey*, 104.
17. Lowenthal interview.
18. Smith, *Complete Poems*, 17.
19. Simpson, *Jean Webster*, 173.
20. Smith, *Complete Poems*, 17. This nurse, Ferne Hincher, who met Adelaide's youngest sibling, Arthur, on this assignment and later married him, became the mother of the descendant whose generous sharing of his family's papers made great portions of this biography possible. As if at that last dying moment, unfulfilled, Adelaide passed on the torch to her nurse and said, "Let the story I was not able to tell be told."
21. Simpson, *Jean Webster*, 173.
22. Osborn, *Crapsey*, 105. "Oh, my moon! Bring me good fortune!"
23. Bate, *John Keats*, 640.
24. Simpson, *Jean Webster*, 173.
25. Osborn, *Crapsey*, 105.
26. Edwardine, "Crapsey," 37.

Afterword: The Urn

1. Ivor Winters, *Forms of Discovery: Critical and Historical Essays on the Forms of the Short Poem in English* (Chicago: Alan Swallow, 1967), 331.
2. The poems of the "Presentation Copy" can be found in the order in which they are discussed in this chapter in Smith, *Complete Poems*, 62–97.
3. Butscher, *Crapsey*, 57.
4. Butscher, *Crapsey*, 58.
5. *American Journal of Archeology*, 2nd ser. 9, 20.
6. "To deal with a definite, if still limited, range of fact before approaching the wider theoretical issues has seemed to me the better method, at least for the present. One offers thus as first

evidence the results of systematic analysis and in so far as these possess, or seem to possess, a certain solidity and coherence within themselves, they are in some sort a guarantee that the underlying theory is worthy of attention." Crapsey, *Metrics*, 13.

7. Butscher, *Crapsey*, 63.

8. Ibid., 95.

9. Crapsey, *Heretics*, 20.

10. The Reverend Dr. Crapsey, in one of the lectures which helped to damn him in the church, discussed the hanging of witches in Salem and the responsibility of religion for this act, *Heretics*, 245.

11. Butscher, *Crapsey*, 64.

12. Arthur H. Crapsey Collection.

13. Smith, *Complete Poems*, 45.

Index